SUBSIDIA BIBLICA

16/I

subsidia biblica - 16/I

JAMES SWETNAM, S.J.

An Introduction to the Study of New Testament Greek

Part One: Morphology

Volume I: Lessons

Second, Revised Edition

EDITRICE PONTIFICIO ISTITUTO BIBLICO — ROMA 1998

This is the second printed edition, in revised form, of a series of type-written notes by the same author and bearing the same title, "ad uso degli studenti" of the Pontifical Biblical Institute of Rome, first published in mimeographed form in 1981, and subsequently reproduced unchanged several times.

ISBN 88-7653-600-0

© E.P.I.B. – Roma – 1998

EDITRICE PONTIFICIO ISTITUTO BIBLICO
Piazza della Pilotta 35 - 00187 Roma, Italia

For my students—past, present, future.

Preface to the First Edition

This, the first printed edition of my mimeographed notes on Greek grammar which initially appeared in 1981, has been long delayed by a variety of causes, some of which where not under my control. But the delay has probably made possible a more thorough and more imaginative reworking of the original version. The latter had a success which I had not foreseen.

For this edition as well as the antecedent notes I am grateful above all to my past and present students, especially those of the Pontifical Biblical Institute beginning in 1963, for their help in indicating what might be useful for learning Greek. In particular I am grateful for advice and encouragement to six fellow teachers of Greek: Rev. Leo Arnold, S.J.; Rev. Anthony J. Forte, S.J.; Rev. William J. David Holly, O.S.B.Cam.; Don Carlo Rusconi of the Diocese of Rimini; Rev. Silvano Votto, S.J.; Rev. John Welch, S.J. For the finished product, however, I take full responsibility.

I would be grateful for any suggestions or corrections which users may think advisable.

Rome   James Swetnam, S.J.
Feast of the Epiphany
January 6, 1992

Preface to the Second Edition

For this second edition I am particularly indebted to the patient advice and assistance of my colleague, the Rev. Silvano Votto, S.J. To him, and to all who contributed suggestions or corrections for the first edition, I am grateful.

Rome   James Swetnam, S.J.
Feast of St. Mark Evangelist
April 25, 1998

Table of Contents

Volume I: *Lessons*

Volume II: *Key, Lists of Words by Categories, Verb Paradigms, Indices*

Key

Lists of Words by Categories

Verb Paradigms

Abbreviations

I. New Testament

Mt	Matthew
Mk	Mark
Lk	Luke
Jn	John
Acts	Acts of the Apostles
Rom	Romans
1 Cor	1 Corinthians
2 Cor	2 Corinthians
Gal	Galatia.s
Eph	Ephesians
Phil	Philippians
Col	Colossians
1 Th	1 Thessalonians
2 Th	2 Thessalonians
1 Tim	1 Timothy
2 Tim	2 Timothy
Tit	Titus
Ph	Philemon
Heb	Hebrews
Jas	James
1 Pt	1 Peter
2 Pt	2 Peter
1 Jn	1 John
2 Jn	2 John
3 Jn	3 John
Jude	Jude
Apoc	Apocalypse (Revelation)

II. General

a	accusative
Adj	Adjectives
Adv	Adverbs
ap	accusative plural
as	accusative singular
Conj	Conjunctions
cont.	continued
d	dative
dp	dative plural
ds	dative singular
DV	[List of] Difficult Verbs
e.g.	exempli gratia [*for example*]
f	feminine
fem.	feminine
g	genitive
gp	genitive plural
gs	genitive singular
hapax	hapax legomenon [*once said*, i.e., a single occurrence]
i.e.	id est [*that is*]
Inter	Interjections
N	Nouns
N.B.	Nota Bene [*Note Well*]
Neg	Negatives
neut.	neuter
n	nominative
np	nominative plural
ns	nominative singular
p	plural
Part	Participles
Prep	Prepositions
Pro	Pronouns
s	singular
v	vocative
V	Verbs
v	vocative
vp	vocative plural
vs	vocative singular

VP   Verbs, Paradigms
x   symbol for "times"
         [i.e., "2x" indicates
         that a word occurs
         twice on the page
         indicated]

Lessons

Introduction

No textbook is ever entirely satisfactory except, possibly, to its
author. The present author is under no illusions in the matter. He
simply offers this grammar as a result of a number of years of
teaching students from a wide variety of backgrounds (over fifteen
hundred, from eighty-five countries). His hope is that this
grammar will prove helpful for other teachers by way of direct use
or as an incentive for writing their own. <u>But this book is especially
written for students who are constrained by circumstances to
attempt to study New Testament Greek without the aid of a teacher,
even though its use as a class text is not precluded</u>.
        This textbook is based on a number of the author's views
which in turn are based on his experience:
        1) Learning New Testament Greek is not easy; except
for persons who are abnormally gifted it requires considerable,
persevering effort. On the other hand, any person of normal
intelligence can learn much of the language, provided that he or she
is willing to do a sufficient amount of work.
        2) Learning New Testament Greek demands a sense of
achievement if the student is to persevere to a point where mastery
of the language is rewarding in terms of the ability to read the New
Testament text.
        3) Learning New Testament Greek is ordinarily best
achieved by an approach which is both deductive (involving the
memorization of vocabulary, paradigms, and rules) and inductive
(involving contact with the New Testament text).
        4) Learning New Testament Greek can be made less
difficult by the careful presentation of new material in such a way
that essentials are set forth clearly and non-essentials are assigned
a subordinate place or relegated to a subsequent treatment.
        In line with the above opinions this textbook is characterized
by the following features:
        1) There are no short-cuts offered. Everywhere it is
presumed that the student is interested in learning the language
well and will pay the price to achieve this learning.
        2) The lessons are structured in such a way that a

continuing progress in understanding the text of the New
Testament is verified.

3) The deductive approach is honored by giving
vocabulary, paradigms, rules, and exercises from English to Greek.
The inductive approach is honored by presenting exercises from
Greek to English and by placing the student in contact with the
Greek text of the New Testament starting with Lesson 1, beginning
with the first verses of the Gospel of Mark.

4) Clarity of presentation is aimed at by a format of one
hundred lessons, each with its own carefully defined material.
Each lesson can be considered sufficient for at least one class period,
if the book is used in connection with class presentation. No attempt
has been made to give each lesson exactly the same amount of new
material. The normal beginner will require at least three or four
additional hours to master the material in each lesson, sometimes
more. Periods of repetition are advisable if for no other reason than
to let the student catch his breath.

The general structure of the book is as follows:

a) Paradigms of the verb: The verb εἰμί is presented
first, followed by the thematic verb λύω. Only when λύω is fully
presented are major "variations" given (e.g., "contract" verbs,
irregular verbs, deponent verbs, and non-thematic verbs).

b) Paradigms of nouns, pronouns, and adjectives:
These are presented as soon as possible: first the second declension,
then the first, and finally, the third.

c) Prepositions: The most important prepositions are
presented gradually, but steadily, so that by Lesson 30 the student
has seen all those which are essential for facility in reading the New
Testament.

d) Adverbs: These are presented gradually as a feature
of almost every lesson's vocabulary.

e) Vocabulary: All New Testament words, excluding
proper nouns, occurring more than twelve times are presented,
where possible, in conjunction with the presentation of the
appropriate paradigms.

f) New Testament readings: The Gospel of Mark is
presented in the first sixty-seven lessons in conjunction with the
presentation of the paradigms and a basic vocabulary; then the
same Gospel is presented again in Lessons 68 to 81. The Gospel of
John is presented in Lessons 82-100.

g) Syntax: Sufficient syntax is given to enable the
student to read the New Testament text on the level of a basic
comprehension. A second part for this *Introduction to the Study of*

New Testament Greek is envisaged which will give a more comprehensive treatment of syntax.

h) Lists and paradigms: An elaborate system of vocabulary lists has been devised which ties in various types of words with their initial presentation in the text of Volume I and with the paradigms in the text and at the end of Volume II. The lists are intended to aid the student in seeing how individual words fit into the categories of the language. They can also be used as a device to help memorization.

The mode of presentation in this grammar will undoubtedly be accused of explanatory over-kill. The author pleads guilty in advance, having read one computer instruction manual too many without the benefit of a teacher. If there is one thing that stands out in his experience of thirty-four years as a teacher of Greek it is this: *Repetitio mater scientiae* —"Repetition is the mother of learning". This mode of proceeding is particularly necessary with regard to such basics as voice, mood, and tense. But simple repetition is not sufficient: a beginner's textbook in grammar should provide the possibilities for an interplay of perspectives, perspectives which can generate a repetition leading to ever-growing understanding.

The detail with which the forms and vocabulary are categorized also constitutes an attempt to counter the lack of a knowledge of grammar, a lack which has manifested itself more and more in recent years among students who speak an Indo-European language. It is also an attempt to aid students from language families other than Indo-European who will study Greek from this grammar, or from a translation based on it.

Throughout the book, references to the New Testament are used wherever feasible in order to give the student maximum exposure to the sacred text, a knowledge of which is the ultimate goal of the present work.

The "key" to this textbook should enable the student to work through the grammar and exercises intelligently. A teacher, of course, is recommended: a good textbook is an excellent teacher, but an excellent teacher is something more than a good textbook.

An unwise use of the key could prove to be counterproductive.

The English language is particularly blessed with grammars of New Testament Greek of all shapes and sizes. If the present grammar does not appeal to the prospective user, he or she is advised to keep looking: they will eventually find something more to their taste. The important thing is to learn Greek!

**The Alphabet. Pronunciation. Breathings.
Accents. The Iota Subscript.**

Lesson 1

The Alphabet.

Capital Letters	Small Letters	Name	English Sound
A	α	alpha	*a* (as in *father*)
B	β	beta	*b*
Γ	γ	gamma	*g* (as in *gun*)
Δ	δ	delta	*d*
E	ε	epsilon	*e* (as in *let*)
Z	ζ	zeta	*dz*
H	η	eta	*a* (as in *late*)

Θ	ϑ	θ	theta	*th*
I	Ɩ	ι	iota	*i* (as in *lit*)
Κ	Κ	κ	kappa	*k*
Λ	λ	λ	lambda	*l*
Μ	μ	μ	mu	*m*
Ν	Υ	ν	nu	*n*
Ξ	ξ	ξ	xi	*x*
Ο	ο	ο	omikron	*o* (as in *all*)
Π	π	π	pi	*p*
Ρ	ρ	ρ	rho	*r*
Σ	σς	σ, ς	sigma	*s*

T	Τ	Τ	τ	tau	*t*
Υ	Υ	U	υ	upsilon	*ü* (see below)
Φ	Φ	φ	φ	phi	*ph*
X	X	X	χ	chi	*ch*
Ψ	Ψ	ψ	ψ	psi	*ps*
Ω	Ω	ω	ω	omega	*o* (as in *old*)

Pronunciation.

Gamma (γ) is pronounced as nu (ν) when it immediately precedes kappa (κ), chi (χ), or another gamma (γ). For example: ἄγγελος is pronounced a<u>n</u>gelos, (with the accent on the first syllable); ἄγκυρα is pronounced a<u>n</u>kyra, (with the accent on the first syllable). (The accent and its placement are not related to the sound of the gamma.)

    Sigma is written as σ at the beginning of a word or within a word, and as ς at the end of a word. But the pronunciation is the same in all instances.

    Upsilon has no real equivalent sound in English. It is akin to the French *u* or the German *ü*. An approximate description of how it is formed is as follows: with the lips rounded, tongue high, and the sound focussed in the middle of the mouth, the *u* of *tune* is pronounced with the introduction of the *ee* sound of *sheen*.

    Chi is pronounced like the *ch* of *loch*.

The letters α, ε, η, ι, ο, υ, and ω are vowels. The rest are consonants. η and ω are always long; ε and ο are always short; α, ι, and υ can be long or short, but the length is not indicated by the orthography and can be inferred, if at all, only by the accent of the word in which the vowel is present. (In specialized linguistic treatments the length of the ambiguous vowels α, ι, and υ is sometimes specified by the following signs. A macron (⁻) over one of these vowels indicates that it is long [e.g., ᾱ], a sign for a short vowel (˘) over one of these vowels indicates that the vowel is short [e.g., ᾰ].) But ordinarily in Greek texts these signs are not given.

There are eight diphthongs, i.e., combinations of two vowels pronounced as one sound:

αι   Pronounced like *ai* in *aisle*.

ει   Pronounced like *ei* in *eight*.

οι   Pronounced like *oi* in *toil*.

υι   Pronounced like *uee* in *queen*.

αυ   Pronounced like *ow* in *owl*.

ευ   Pronounced like *e* in *end* and shading into the *w* of *win*.

ηυ   ηυ   Pronounced like *a* in *ale* and shading into
                         the *w* of *win*.

ου   ου   Pronounced like *oo* in *moon*.

The above system of pronunciation is to some extent arbitrary, and is designed to facilitate communication among contemporary students of New Testament Greek in the United States of America and in countries where English is spoken. Students working in a different tradition should not hesitate to adopt the standards of New Testament Greek pronunciation in their area.

Breathings.

A vowel or diphthong at the beginning of a word always has a "breathing", which is either "smooth" (᾿) or "rough" (῾). A smooth breathing is not pronounced; a rough breathing is prounounced like the English *h*. When a single vowel begins a word, the breathing is written directly over this vowel if it is a small letter (ἀ, ἁ), or immediately in front of it if it is a capital letter (᾿Α, ῾Α). When a diphthong begins a word, the breathing is placed over the second vowel regardless if the first vowel is a small letter or a capital letter (αὐ, αὑ, Αὐ, Αὑ).

The consonant ρ, when found at the beginning of a word, always has a rough breathing: ῥ.

Accents.

Accents in Greek were originally devised to indicate the musical pitch of the voice used in pronouncing a word. Eventually (possibly even by New Testament times), accents came to indicate stress on a syllable in the pronunciation of a word. The rules for placing accents in Greek are complicated and will therefore be introduced only gradually in the lessons which follow. Accents are important principally for pronunciation (by indicating the syllable of a word which is to be stressed) and, occasionally, for providing a means of distinguishing between different words with the same spelling (e.g., τίς, *who?*, and τις, *someone*).

There are three types of accent in Greek: the acute (´), the circumflex (ˆ), and the grave (`). Accents are written over single vowels or diphthongs. Accents over diphthongs are always written over the second vowel. When a breathing occurs over the same letter as an accent, the breathing is always written first, except in the case of a circumflex, in which instance it is written under the accent (ἄ, ἅ, αἲ, αἵ, ἆ, ἇ).

The Iota Subscript.

For certain words an iota is written under the long vowels α, η, and ω. This iota is called the "iota subscript" and does not affect the pronunciation (i.e., ᾳ, ῃ, ῳ are pronounced as α, η, ω). It is a scribal convention to indicate a letter that had been pronounced at one time.

Exercises for Lesson 1.

I. Memorize the alphabet and the diphthongs both actively and passively.

II. Practice writing the letters until you can reproduce them from memory.

III. Work through the first five verses of Chapter 1 of the Gospel of Mark (Mk 1:1-5), checking the text against the information given above. Pronounce the words of all five verses until there is no need to check the information given in the lesson to see if the pronunciation is correct.

[Any critical edition of the Greek New Testament may be used to do the exercises for this grammar. The text followed in the composition of this grammar was that of *The Greek New Testament*, Fourth Edition, The United Bible Societies, 1993.]

εἰμί, **Present Indicative. The Present
Tense. The Indicative Mood. Person.
Number for Verbs. The Movable –ν. The
Article. Gender. Number for the Article,
Nouns, Pronouns, Adjectives. Case.
Declension of the Article. The Nominative
Case. The Sentence. The Clause. The
Predicative Use of the Adjective. The
Attributive Use of the Adjective. Adjectives
as Substantives. Agreement. The Noun
λόγος.**

Lesson 2

εἰμί, Present Indicative.

The verb *to be* in Greek is used much as it is in English, either to
indicate existence (*God is*), or to link a subject with an adjective as
predicate (*God is good*). In the present tense of the indicative mood
it is conjugated as follows (cf. V 16, DV 78, VP 9 [for an explanation
of these abbreviations see below in this lesson]):

	Singular	Plural
1st Person	εἰμί	ἐσμέν
2nd Person	εἶ	ἐστέ
3rd Person	ἐστί(ν)	εἰσί(ν)

I am	*We are*
You (sg.) *are*	*You* (pl.) *are*
He (She, It) is	*They are*

The Present Tense. The Indicative Mood.

"Tense" and "mood" are difficult to define. The precise function of
"tense" in the Greek verbal system is particularly complex and
much discussed For the time being, the student need only think of
the "present tense" as referring to present time in contrast to the

past and future. For the "indicative mood" the student need only know that it is used to express simple statements (e.g., *It is raining.*) and to ask ordinary questions (e.g., *How tall are you?*).

Person.

"1st person" is used to refer to the person speaking: *I, we;* "2nd person" is used to refer to the person spoken to: *you,* whether one or more than one; "3rd person" is used to refer to the person or thing spoken of: *he, she, it, they.*

Number for Verbs.

"Singular" refers to "one"; "plural", to "more than one".

The Movable –ν.

In the third person singular and plural the ν in parentheses indicates that the complete form can be either ἐστί / ἐστίν or εἰσί / εἰσίν. The forms <u>without</u> the ν are normally used if the word which follows begins with a consonant; forms <u>with</u> the ν are normally used if the word which follows begins with a vowel, or if the verb form ends the sentence. But the usage is not rigid: there are many exceptions, especially in favor of use of the –ν.

The Article.

In English there is a definite article, *the,* and an indefinite article, *a* or *an.* In Greek only the definite article exists. Hence a simple Greek word like λόγος may be translated either as *word* or as *a word,* depending on the context. But the use of the Greek article parallels the use of the definite article in English to a large extent. The differences are often too subtle to be treated in an introduction. Attention should be paid to the way the article is used in the Greek and English exercises which follow and in the New Testament.

The Greek article usually acts like an adjective, agreeing with the word it modifies in gender, number, and case.

but there is an indefinite pronoun

Gender.

Greek divides nouns into three groups which are distinguished according to the articles they are consistently found associated with. Thus λόγος is associated with ὁ and is called "masculine" Nouns which are associated with ἡ are called "feminine", and those with τό are called "neuter". "Gender" is thus primarily grammatical. But where appropriate it often, although not always, follows sexual divisions. For example, a man is masculine gender, a woman is feminine gender. But a child can be referred to by a word which is associated with a neuter article.

Number for the Article, Nouns, Pronouns, Adjectives.

New Testament Greek divides the article, nouns, pronouns, and adjectives into two groups—those referring to one person or thing, and those referring to more than one person or thing. In other words, it has the same force as the use of number for the verb.

Case.

"Cases" (nominative [n], vocative [v], genitive [g], dative [d], accusative [a]) are expressions of the ways in which a noun, pronoun, or adjective may be used in a sentence. The meaning of the cases will be introduced gradually in the course of the following lessons.

Declension of the Article.

The Greek article is declined as follows (cf. Adj 1Pro and Art [for the explanation of these abbreviations see below in this lesson]).

	Singular		
	Masculine	Feminine	Neuter
n	ὁ	ἡ	τό
g	τοῦ	τῆς	τοῦ
d	τῷ	τῇ	τῷ
a	τόν	τήν	τό

	Masculine	Plural Feminine	Neuter
n	οἱ	αἱ	τά
g	τῶν	τῶν	τῶν
d	τοῖς	ταῖς	τοῖς
a	τούς	τάς	τά

There is no vocative case of the article.

In this and in the other paradigms which follow and in the exercises for translation, the accents will be written to familiarize the student with the way the words in question actually appear in the New Testament text. But active command of the accents is not advisable in memorizing paradigms and vocabulary, at least in the early stages of studying Greek. Exceptions are to be made where the accent is necessary or useful for distinguishing between two words otherwise alike (e.g., ὁ, masculine nominative singular of the article, should be carefully distinguished from ὅ, the neuter nominative singular of the relative pronoun, as will be explained in Lesson 3). The rules for accents will begin in Lesson 9.

The Nominative Case. The Sentence. The Clause.

The nominative case is used principally to indicate the "subject "of a sentence or clause. It expresses the main topic being considered, the "subject" of discourse, that which is being talked about.

A "sentence" is a word or words stating or implying a complete judgment with regard to some aspect of existence, and usually is expressed as an assertion, a question, a command, a wish, or an exclamation. Ordinarily a sentence contains a subject and a predicate, i.e., a substantive and a verbal form, which are either expressed or implied. Examples of sentences: *God is good.* [Assertion]. *Is God good?* [Question]. *Come!* [Command—the nominative case "You", singular or plural, is understood]. *May God come.* [Wish]. *Oh God!* [Exclamation—some verb is to be understood, depending on the context].

A "clause" is a word or words which do not state or imply a complete judgment with regard to some aspect of existence. Examples of clauses: ... *when he comes* ...; ... *in which he lives* ...; ... *although she is still alive* .... Sometimes sentences are referred to as "main clauses". In the context of such usage, what are here termed simply as "clauses", are accordingly called "subordinate clauses".

Inasmuch as clauses cannot stand grammatically by themselves, they must be found as part of a sentence. Such sentences are called "complex sentences". The part stating or implying a complete judgment is called a "main clause". The "clause" is specified as a "subordinate clause". Examples of complex sentences: *When he comes* [subordinate clause], *we shall be happy* [main clause]. *Although she is still alive* [subordinate clause], *she is unwell* [main clause].

Sentences containing two or more main clauses are called "compound sentences": *God is always good, but humans are sometimes evil.* Compound sentences containing one or more subordinate clauses are called "compound-complex sentences": *God, who is creator, is always good, but humans, who are creatures, are sometimes evil.*

The Predicative Use of the Adjective.

The verb εἰμί is peculiar in that it can be used not only to indicate existence (ὁ θεός ἐστιν—*God is*), but also to link the subject with an adjective as a "predicate" (ὁ θεός ἐστιν ἀγαθός—*God is good*). In the latter example, "goodness" is being "predicated" of God, i.e., affirmed.

The verb εἰμί in the present tense of the indicative mood can be omitted, if its meaning is clear from the context. This omission is usually indicated by the position of the article, which is normally not found with a predicate. Thus the sentence ὁ λόγος ἐστὶν ἅγιος (*The word is holy*) can also be expressed as ὁ λόγος ἅγιος or ἅγιος ὁ λόγος (the difference in word order implies no difference in the basic meaning).

Such a use of an adjective is called "predicative" because the adjective functions as the predicate of a sentence, with the verb εἰμί understood. That is to say, the adjective is used to affirm or "predicate" something about the subject. "Holiness" is being affirmed, i.e., predicated, about "the word" in both expressions: it is the point being made. When an adjective is thus used predicatively, the mind can rest in what has been stated because what has been stated is implicitly a sentence.

This use of adjectival predication extends beyond simple sentences such as the ones given above and is relevant to the use of the adjective in many other situations.

The Attributive Use of the Adjective.

In each of the three examples of the "predicative" use of an adjective (1. ὁ ἄγγελός ἐστιν ἅγιος, 2. ὁ ἄγγελος ἅγιος, 3. ἅγιος ὁ ἄγγελος) the adjective stands outside the combination ὁ ἄγγελος. If the adjective stands inside the combination ὁ ἄγγελος so that the words run ὁ ἅγιος ἄγγελος or if the adjective is given its own article so that the words run ὁ ἄγγελος ὁ ἅγιος, the usage is called "attributive".

When an adjective is used attributively the word εἰμί is not implied. Thus no complete judgment is made; the mind cannot rest in what has been stated because what has been stated is not a sentence, not even implicitly. "Holiness" is not being predicated. It is not the point being made; something else is.

This usage of the article to distinguish between predicative and attributive use of an adjective is not uniform. Adjectives which do not use the article in this way will be noted as they occur (for example, the adjective ὅλος in this lesson). These adjectives are few in number.

Distinction between predicative and attributive use of an adjective can also occur independently of the use of the article.

Finally, use or non-use of the article need not always have relevance to the distinction between predicative and attributive use of an adjective.

The distinction between the predicative and attributive use of the adjective is also found in other cases, but it is particularly used in regard to the nominative.

The examples given above have been in the singular; but the distinction between attributive and predicative is equally applicable to the plural.

Adjectives as Substantives.

Not only do many adjectives have the same ending as nouns, (i.e., they are declined in the same way as nouns), but also many adjectives (normally of the first and second declensions) can be used as a noun. Thus ἅγιος, *holy*, is normally an adjective: ὁ ἅγιος λόγος, *the holy word*. But the adjective can be used by itself, in which instance it can be translated as a noun: ὁ ἅγιος, *the holy man*, or ἅγιος, *a holy man*.

Agreement.

Implicit in the above discussion about the use of adjectives with
nouns is the basic rule that adjectives can "modify" nouns or
pronouns, that is, they can be used to qualify nouns or pronouns. In
these instances the adjective "agrees" with the noun or pronoun in
gender, number, and case. This rule is seen in the examples of
adjectives given above.

  A noun or pronoun can be explicitly mentioned when used as
the subject of a verb or it can be implied. For example, in the
sentence ὁ ἄγγελος ἀγαθός ἐστιν the noun ἄγγελος is explicitly
mentioned when used as the subject of ἐστιν. But in the sentence
ἀγαθός ἐστιν, the adjective ἀγαθός agrees with the subject *he*
which is implicit in the third person singular form ἐστιν, as is clear
from the fact that ἀγαθός is in the nominative case. Hence it must
refer to a nominative—in this instance, the implied subject of ἐστιν.
ἀγαθός is also masculine in gender and singular in number (see
below for the declension, in Lesson 3), indicating that the implicit
subject of ἐστιν is also masculine and singular. Hence the
translation *He is good* for the sentence ἀγαθός ἐστιν.

The Noun λόγος.

  The noun λόγος, *word*, is a masculine noun of the second
declension, i.e., the second of the three main categories of nouns in
Greek. It is presented before nouns in the first declension because it
is similar in its forms to the masculine of the article and because it
is found frequently. Further, many masculine adjectives are
declined in the same way as λόγος.

	Singular	Plural
n	λόγος	λόγοι
v	λόγε	λόγοι
g	λόγου	λόγων
d	λόγῳ	λόγοις
a	λόγον	λόγους

Vocabulary for Lesson 2.

In the vocabulary listings of this and subsequent lessons, only the
most fundamental distinctions among the various meanings of a

word are given. These listings may be called "introductory meanings" because they are regarded as giving the student an introduction to the possible meanings of the words in question. For the various shades of meaning a detailed dictionary is indispensable. Ultimately, of course, it is the context of the biblical text which gives the meaning of a word in any given case.

In the vocabulary each word is followed by one or more abbreviations, usually with numbers. The abbreviations and numbers refer to the lists and/or paradigms in Volume Two of this grammar. There are two types of lists: "Lists of Words by Categories" and "List of Difficult Verbs". In addition there are twelve sets of "Verbs, Paradigms". (There are also paradigms for all the categories of adjectives and nouns, but these paradigms are included in the "Lists of Words by Categories". Thus a reference to a category for an adjective or noun will automatically include access to the appropriate paradigm.) The paradigms in Volume Two are repetitions of the paradigms which are presented in the lessons. (Only the paradigms of the irregular nouns and adjectives provide an exception to this rule of a two-fold presentation.)

As illustrations for the explanation given in the preceding paragraph the following may serve: The entry "οὐ, οὐκ, οὐχ" is followed by the entry "[Neg]", which means that the words οὐ, οὐκ, οὐχ are to be found in the category "Negatives", along with a number of other words. The word "λόγος" is followed by the entry "[N 6m]", which means that the word λόγος is to be found in the category "Nouns" under the number "6m" (the "m" indicates words of masculine gender to distinguish this category from nouns with the exact same forms which are of feminine gender—cf. Lesson 8, Vocabulary) together with a number of other words and the paradigm for its declension. Some words are found in more than one list. Thus, the entry "[Adj 1Pro]" and "[Art]" after "ὁ, ἡ, τό" indicates that the article is to be found listed both as an adjective, under the heading "Adjective 1Pronoun", and under the heading "Article".

All verbs are found in the appropriate category of "Lists of Words by Categories" (some verbs are found in more than one category—the norms for defining the categories are not rigorously scientific [which would demand a carefully-elaborated but possibly confusing system of sub-categories], but fundamentally pedagogical). In addition, most verbs are illustrated by one of the paradigms found in the separate "Verbs, Paradigms", as mentioned above.

Finally, a large number of verbs (350) are to be found in the
"List of Difficult Verbs" (as mentioned above). For example, the
entry "εἰμί" is followed by the entry "V 16, DV 78, VP 9", which
indicates that εἰμί is found in the "Lists of Words by Categories"
under "Verbs 16", in the "List of Difficult Verbs" under Number 78,
and in the "Verbs, Paradigms" in Section 9.

A certain degree of redundancy will be honored in giving
vocabulary listings for nouns and adjectives. Even though the
references to vocabulary lists are enough to place a given word in a
category, an abbreviated form of the genitive of nouns will be given
with the nominative case, together with the appropriate article.
Adjectives will be given with the nominative in all three genders.
This redundancy will aid in memorization.

Verbs are indicated in the vocabulary normally by a citation of
the first person singular of the present tense, active voice, indicative
mood. Thus "εἰμί, *I am*". (εἰμί, strictly speaking, has no "voice".)
But until the conjugation of other verbs can be presented, some verb
forms will be given in the third person, as "εἶπε(ν), *He (She, It)
spoke; He (She, It) said*", and "ἔρχεται, *He (She, It) is coming*". (If
there is no expressed subject for a verb in Greek, *he, she,* or *it* is to
be understood from the context, as was stated above.) Other forms of
such verbs given in the third person should not be used by the
student until they have been adequately presented later on in the
course of the lessons. These third persons forms are given to help in
creating variety in the exercises of translation at the end of the early
lessons.

εἰμί [V 16, DV 78, VP 9] *I am; I exist.*

εἶπε(ν) [from the verb λέγω: cf. Lesson 50] *he (she, it) spoke; he (she,
     it) said.* The plural form is εἶπον, *they spoke, they said.*

ἔρχεται [from the verb ἔρχομαι: cf. Lesson 45] *he (she, it) comes or
     arrives; he (she, it) is coming or is arriving.* The plural form
     is ἔρχονται, *they arrive, they are coming, they are arriving.*

ὁ, ἡ, τό [Adj 1Pro, Art] *the.*

ἄγγελος, –ου, ὁ [N 6m] *angel, messenger.*

ἀδελφός, –οῦ, ὁ [N 6m] *brother, [blood] relative.*

ἄνθρωπος, −ου, ὁ [N 6m] usually *man* in the sense of *human being*;
but occasionally *man* in the sense of *male*.

θεός, −οῦ, ὁ [N 6m] *God; god.*

κόσμος, −ου, ὁ [N 6m] *world, universe.*

κύριος, −ου, ὁ [N 6m] *Lord; lord; sir* [in forms of address]. By
convention this word is not capitalized in some editions of the
Greek text when it refers to God or to Christ.

λόγος, −ου, ὁ [N 6m] *word, discourse.*

οὐρανός, −οῦ, ὁ [N 6m] *heaven; heavens, sky.*

υἱός, οῦ, ὁ [N 6m] *son; descendant.*

___

ἀγαθός [Adj 1] [Masculine form of the adjective, declined like λόγος.]
good.

ἅγιος [Adj 2] [Masculine form of the adjective, declined like λόγος.]
holy, consecrated.

καλός [Adj 1] [Masculine form of the adjective, declined like λόγος.]
beautiful; good.

ὅλος [Adj 1] [Masculine form of the adjective, declined like λόγος.]
whole, entire, complete. When used with the article in the
New Testament this adjective is always in the predicative
position even though the meaning is attributive. For example,
ὅλος ὁ λόγος means "The entire word" and not "The word
(is) entire".

___

οὐ, οὐκ, οὐχ [Neg] *not; no* . This negative is ordinarily used with
the indicative mood. οὐ is used before words beginning with a
consonant; οὐκ is used before words beginning with a vowel
having a smooth breathing; and οὐχ is used before words
beginning with a vowel having a rough breathing.

Exercises for Lesson 2.

In the exercises which follow, the reference to the New Testament indicates a text useful in some way for understanding the sentence in question (and vice versa). At first, this usefulness will be minimal and the references will have only a tenuous relation to the particular exercise in question. But as the exercises become more complex, the references will become more meaningful, until they eventually become a handy tool for becoming acquainted with the New Testament text. Preference will be given to the gospels, wherever possible, in giving references.

I. Translate into English:
1. ὁ υἱὸς εἶπεν, εἰμί. (Mk 14:62)
2. ὁ υἱὸς τοῦ ἀνθρώπου κύριός ἐστιν. (Mk 2:28)
3. ἔρχεται ὁ ἀδελφὸς ὁ καλός. (Mk 3:31)
4. ὁ ἄνθρωπος ἔρχεται. (Mk 6:1)
5. οἱ ἄνθρωποι οὐχ ἅγιοί εἰσιν. (Mk 1:24)
6. ὁ θεὸς εἶπεν. (Mk 2:19)
7. ὁ ἄγγελος ὁ ἅγιος οὐκ ἔρχεται. (Mk 8:38)
8. ὅλος ὁ κόσμος καλός ἐστιν. (Mk 14:9)
9. ὁ οὐρανός οὐ καλός ἐστιν. (Mk 13:31)
10. ὁ υἱὸς τοῦ θεοῦ ἐστιν ἀγαθός. (Mk 3:11)

N.B. The absence of accents on certain words, and the presence of more than one accent on some words, will be explained beginning in the "Rules for Accents" in Lesson 9.

II. Translate into Greek:
1. The sons are not holy. (Mk 2:19)
2. The heavens of God are beautiful. (Mk 1:10)
3. The good brother is coming. (Mk 10:18)

III. Work through the first five verses of Chapter 1 of the Gospel according to Mark (Mk 1:1-5), checking the text against the information given in Lesson 2. Do not be discouraged by the many aspects of the text which remain unclear. As the lessons progress, the texts will become clearer and clearer.

The Imperfect Indicative. εἰμί, Imperfect
Indicative. The Relative Pronoun. The
Accusative Case. The Noun ἔργον. Neuter
Plural Subject and Singular Verb.

Lesson 3

The Imperfect Indicative.

The imperfect tense of most verbs in New Testament Greek is used
to express past action which is not viewed as terminated (cf. Lesson
10). Inasmuch as the imperfect tense of the verb εἰμί is the only past
tense which the verb has, the imperfect serves to indicate any type of
past action, even if it is being viewed as terminated. The imperfect
tense is found only in the indicative mood.

εἰμί, Imperfect Indicative.

The imperfect indicative of the verb εἰμί is conjugated as follows (cf.
V 16, DV 78, VP 9):

	Singular	Plural
1st Person	ἤμην	ἦμεν / ἤμεθα
2nd Person	ἦς / ἦσθα	ἦτε
3rd Person	ἦν	ἦσαν

I was	We were
You (sg.) were	You (pl.) were
He (She, It) was	They were

ἦσθα is an alternative form for ἦς; ἤμεθα is an alternative
form for ἦμεν.

The Relative Pronoun.

The relative pronoun is declined as follows (cf. Pro):

	Masculine	Singular Feminine	Neuter
n	ὅς	ἥ	ὅ
g	οὗ	ἧς	οὗ
d	ᾧ	ᾗ	ᾧ
a	ὅν	ἥν	ὅ

	Masculine	Plural Feminine	Neuter
n	οἵ	αἵ	ἅ
g	ὧν	ὧν	ὧν
d	οἷς	αἷς	οἷς
a	οὕς	ἅς	ἅ

these accents messed

Care should be taken to distinguish the following forms of article and relative pronoun:

οἱ – οἵ   ἡ – ἥ   αἰ – αἵ   ὁ – ὅ

In Greek the relative pronoun follows much the same grammatical rules as in English. The pronoun agrees with its antecedent (i.e., the word it refers to) in gender and number, but takes its case from its use in its own clause:

ὁ λόγος ὅς ἐστιν ἀγαθός ἐστι καλός.
The word which is good is beautiful.

ὁ λόγος ὃν εἶπεν ὁ θεὸς ἅγιός ἐστιν.
The word which God spoke is holy.

The Accusative Case.

A noun or pronoun can be used in the accusative case in Greek as the object of a verb:

ὁ θεὸς εἶπε τὸν λόγον.
God spoke the word.

A noun or pronoun can be put in the accusative case as the object of a preposition:

ὁ Κύριος ἔρχεται εἰς τὸν κόσμον.
The Lord comes into the world.

The Noun ἔργον.

The word ἔργον, *work*, a neuter noun of the second declension, is declined as follows (cf. N 7):

	Singular	Plural
n	ἔργον	ἔργα
v	ἔργον	ἔργα
g	ἔργου	ἔργων
d	ἔργῳ	ἔργοις
a	ἔργον	ἔργα

The neuter forms of adjectives like ἀγαθός (which is declined like λόγος in the masculine forms) are declined like ἔργον. It should be noted that the neuter nominative and accusative forms of ἔργον, in both the singular and the plural, are alike. This is true of all neuter nouns and adjectives in Greek.

Neuter Plural Subject and Singular Verb.

A noteworthy aspect of the neuter gender in Greek is that a neuter plural subject usually governs a singular verb:

τὰ ἔργα τοῦ θεοῦ ἀγαθά ἐστιν.
The works of God are good.

But the plural form of the verb is also found on occasion with a neuter plural subject:

τὰ ἔργα τοῦ θεοῦ ἀγαθά εἰσιν.
The works of God are good.

Vocabulary for Lesson 3.

εἰς [Prep 1] Always governs tne accusative case: *into; towards; for*
(purpose).

___

ὅς, ἥ, ὅ [Pro] *who, which.*

___

δαιμόνιον, –ου, τό [N 7] *demon; evil spirit.*

ἔργον, –ου, τό [N 7] *work; deed; thing made.*

εὐαγγέλιον, –ου, τό [N 7] *Gospel, Good News.*

ἱερόν, –οῦ, τό [N 7] *temple, sanctuary.*

ἱμάτιον, –ου, τό [N 7] *garment; outer garment.*

σημεῖον, –ου, τό [N 7] *sign.*

___

The adjectives ἀγαθός, ἅγιος, καλός, and ὅλος of Lesson 2 are
declined in the neuter like ἔργον.

The following adjectives—ἕτερος, ἴδιος, νεκρός, and πρῶτος—are
declined like λόγος in the masculine and like ἔργον in the
neuter.

ἕτερος [Adj 2] *other; another.*

ἴδιος [Adj 2] *one's own; proper to one.*

νεκρός [Adj 2] *dead.* This word is often used as a noun with the
meaning "[*the*] *dead*" [N 6m].

πρῶτος [Adj 1] *first.*

___

ἀκούεις [from ἀκούω: cf. Lesson 10] *you* (sg.) *hear, listen to; you*
(sg.) *are hearing, are listening to.* This verb governs the
genitive or the accusative with no easily distinguishable
difference.

ἔχω [cf. Lessons 9 and 49] *I have, I am having; I possess, I am possessing.*

λέγει [from λέγω: cf. Lessons 9 and 50] *he (she, it) speaks, says; he (she, it) is speaking, is saying.*

———

πρῶτον [Adv 2] *first; first of all.*

Exercises for Lesson 3.

I. Translate into English:
1. ὁ κύριος εἶπε τὸ εὐαγγέλιον. (Mk 1:14)
2. ἔχω τὰ ἱμάτια. (Mk 2:10)
3. τὸ σημεῖον καλὸν ἦν. (Mk 8:11)
4. ὁ ἕτερος ἄγγελος ἔρχεται εἰς τὸ καλὸν ἱερόν. (Mk 16:12)
5. τὰ ἱμάτια ἦν καλά. (Mk 9:3)
6. οὐκ ἀκούεις τῶν ἀνθρώπων. (Mk 9:7)
7. ὁ κύριος οὐκ ἔστι νεκρός. (Mk 9:26)
8. τὰ δαιμόνια οὐκ εἰσὶν ἀγαθά. (Mk 1:34)
9. ὁ κύριος ἔρχεται εἰς τὸ ἱερόν. (Mk 11:11)
10. εἰ ὁ πρῶτος ὃς λέγει τοὺς λόγους. (Mk 9:35)
11. τὰ ἔργα ἦν καλά. (Mk 14:6)
12. τὸ ἱερὸν καλὸν ἦν. (Mk 11:15)
13. τὰ ἴδια ἱμάτια καλά ἐστιν. (Mt 22:5)
14. οἱ λόγοι οὓς εἶπεν ὁ κύριος ἀγαθοί εἰσιν. (Mk 3:14)

II. Translate into Greek:
1. The work was holy. (Mk 14:6)
2. The person who is coming into the temple is good. (Mk 10:18)
3. You are not holy. (Mk 1:24)

III. Work through Mk 1:6-10, checking the text against the information given above and in Lesson 2. Read the verses aloud at least three times.

The Infinitive. The Complementary
Infinitive. εἰμί, Present Infinitive.
The Imperative. εἰμί, Imperative. The
Nouns ζωή, ἁμαρτία, δόξα. The
Adjectives ἅγιος and ἀγαθός. The Stem.
The Genitive Case. The Five Principal
Punctuation Marks.

Lesson 4

The Infinitive. The Complementary Infinitive.

The infinitive in Greek corresponds approximately to the English
infinitive, e.g., *to see,* or to the English gerund, e.g., *Seeing is
believing.* The Greek infinitive is considered to be a verbal noun.
Like a verb, it has voice, mood, and tense. These are the categories
under which it is normally treated. On occasion, its category as
noun also needs to be analyzed.

The infinitive has a variety of uses which will be explained in
subsequent lessons. One common use is the "complementary"
infinitive in which the infinitive "complements" or "completes" the
meaning of a verb, just as in English:

Θέλω ["I wish"—cf. Lesson 15, Vocabulary] εἶναι ἀγαθός.
I wish to be good.

εἰμί, Present Infinitive.

The present infinitive of the verb εἰμί is εἶναι.

The Imperative.

The imperative mood is used to express a command. It is found
only in the second and third persons.

εἰμί, Imperative.

The imperative of the verb εἰμί is as follows (cf. V 16, DV 78, VP 9):

	Singular	Plural
2nd Person	ἴσθι	ἔστε
3rd Person	ἔστω / ἤτω	ἔστωσαν / ἤτωσαν
	You (sg.) *be!*	*You* (pl.) *be!*
	Let him (or *her* or *it*) *be!*	*Let them be!*

ἴσθι ἀγαθός.	ἴσθι ἀγαθή.	ἔστε ἀγαθοί.	ἔστε ἀγαθαί.
Be good!	*Be good!*	*Be good!*	*Be good!*

ἔστω ἀγαθός.	ἔστω ἀγαθή.	ἔστωσαν ἀγαθοί.
Let him be good!	*Let her be good!*	*Let them be good!*

The Nouns ζωή, ἁμαρτία, δόξα.

The nouns of the first declension are either feminine or masculine. The feminine nouns are divided into three categories:

1) Nouns ending in −η in the nominative singular (cf. N 1):

	Singular	Plural
n	ζωή	ζωαί
v	ζωή	ζωαί
g	ζωῆς	ζωῶν
d	ζωῇ	ζωαῖς
a	ζωήν	ζωάς

2) Nouns ending in −α preceded by ε, ι, or ρ (cf. N 2):

	Singular	Plural
n	ἁμαρτία	ἁμαρτίαι
v	ἁμαρτία	ἁμαρτίαι
g	ἁμαρτίας	ἁμαρτιῶν
d	ἁμαρτίᾳ	ἁμαρτίαις
a	ἁμαρτίαν	ἁμαρτίας

3) Nouns ending in –α not preceded by ε, ι, or ρ (cf. N 3):

	Singular	Plural
n	δόξα	δόξαι
v	δόξα	δόξαι
g	δόξης	δοξῶν
d	δόξῃ	δόξαις
a	δόξαν	δόξας

The Adjectives ἅγιος and ἀγαθός. The Stem.

In adjectives of the first and second declensions, the presence of an α preceded by ε, ι, or ρ in the feminine nominative singular indicates that all singular endings of the feminine have α, like ἁμαρτία (cf. Adj 2):

	Masculine	Singular Feminine	Neuter
n	ἅγιος	ἁγία	ἅγιον
v	ἅγιε	ἁγία	ἅγιον
g	ἁγίου	ἁγίας	ἁγίου
d	ἁγίῳ	ἁγίᾳ	ἁγίῳ
a	ἅγιον	ἁγίαν	ἅγιον

	Masculine	Plural Feminine	Neuter
n	ἅγιοι	ἅγιαι	ἅγια
v	ἅγιοι	ἅγιαι	ἅγια
g	ἁγίων	ἁγίων	ἁγίων
d	ἁγίοις	ἁγίαις	ἁγίοις
a	ἁγίους	ἁγίας	ἅγια

In the same way as ἅγιος, ἁγία, ἅγιον are declined ἕτερος, ἑτέρα, ἕτερον — ἴδιος, ἰδία, ἴδιον — νεκρός, νεκρά, νεκρόν.

Adjectives which do not have an ε, ι, or ρ before the ending of the feminine nominative singular, have the feminine nominative singular ending in –η. All adjectives of the first and second declensions which are not contracted (see below, Lessons 31 and 32) and which are not limited to two endings (cf. below, Lesson 24), are divided into two categories: 1) those whose feminine nominative singular ends in an –α because the stem of the adjective ends in an ε–, ι–, or ρ– ; 2) those whose stem ends in a letter different from these, in which instance the ending is –η. The "stem" of a word (the concept is applicable to all verbs, nouns, and pronouns as well as adjectives) is that part of a word which is constant in relation to its variable part or "ending". Thus, the adjective ἀγία has a stem ἀγι–, and the ending α, in the feminine nominative singular. Because the stem ends in ι–, the ending is in –α. Stems ending in ε– or ρ– also have –α as an ending. All other stems have η as the ending. The adjective ἀγαθός is in the latter category (cf. Adj 1):

	Masculine	Singular Feminine	Neuter
n	ἀγαθός	ἀγαθή	ἀγαθόν
v	ἀγαθέ	ἀγαθή	ἀγαθόν
g	ἀγαθοῦ	ἀγαθῆς	ἀγαθοῦ
d	ἀγαθῷ	ἀγαθῇ	ἀγαθῷ
a	ἀγαθόν	ἀγαθήν	ἀγαθόν

	Masculine	Plural Feminine	Neuter
n	ἀγαθοί	ἀγαθαί	ἀγαθά
v	ἀγαθοί	ἀγαθαί	ἀγαθά
g	ἀγαθῶν	ἀγαθῶν	ἀγαθῶν
d	ἀγαθοῖς	ἀγαθαῖς	ἀγαθοῖς
a	ἀγαθούς	ἀγαθάς	ἀγαθά

Thus also: καλός, καλή, καλόν — ὅλος, ὅ λη, ὅλον — πρῶτος, πρώτη, πρῶτον.

The Genitive Case.

The genitive case is used to signify possession.

> ὁ λόγος τοῦ θεοῦ
> *the word of God*

The genitive case can also be used as the object of certain prepositions:

> ἐκ τοῦ ἱεροῦ
> *from the temple*

These are only two of the most fundamental uses of the genitive case.

The Five Principal Punctuation Marks.

The five principal punctuation marks are as follows:

English	Greek	Comment and Example
.	.	The same as in English: λόγος.
,	,	The same as in English: λόγος,
;	·	Dot above line: λόγος·
:	·	Dot above line: λόγος·
?	;	Like English semi-colon: λόγος;

Greek distinguishes the period from the comma as does English, and uses the same marks to indicate them. Greek does not distinguish a colon and semi-colon, but uses a dot above the line to indicate a stop which is less than that indicated by a period but more than that indicated by a comma. Greek uses what looks like an English semi-colon to indicate a question mark at the end of a sentence. There are no quotation marks or exclamation point in Greek.

Vocabulary for Lesson 4.

ἀπό [Prep 1] Always governs the genitive case: *from*; *away from*.

ἐκ [Prep 1] Always governs the genitive case: *from*; *out of*. Before vowels the ἐκ becomes ἐξ.

___

ἀγάπη, -ης, ἡ [N 1] *love*.

γῆ, -ῆς, ἡ [N 1; because of accent is also irregular (N 33)] *earth, land*.

ζωή, -ῆς, ἡ [N 1] *life*.

φωνή, -ῆς, ἡ [N 1] *voice; sound*.

___

ἀλήθεια, -ας, ἡ [N 2] *truth*.

ἁμαρτία, -ας, ἡ [N 2] *sin; mistake, error*.

βασιλεία, –ας, ἡ [N 2] *kingdom*.

ἐκκλησία, –ας, ἡ [N 2] *assembly; church*.

ἐξουσία, –ας, ἡ [N 2] *authority; power*.

ἡμέρα, –ας, ἡ [N 2] *day*.

καρδία, –ας, ἡ [N 2] *heart*.
―――

γλῶσσα, –ης, ἡ [N 3] *tongue; language*.

δόξα, –ης, ἡ [N 3] *glory; splendor*.

τράπεζα, –ης, ἡ [N 3] *table*.
―――

ἀγαπητός, –ή, –όν [Adj 1] *beloved, dear*.

ἕκαστος, –η, –ον [Adj 1] *each, each one* [as a noun]. This word is not
   used with the article.

πιστός, –ή, –όν [Adj 1] *faithful; believing*.
―――

δίκαιος, –α, –ον [Adj 2] *just, righteous*.

πονηρός, –ά, –όν [Adj 2] *evil*.
―――

μή [Neg, Conj] *not*. This negative is parallel to the negative οὐ. οὐ
   is normally used with the indicative mood, whereas μή is
   normally used with all other moods. Exceptions to this
   general rule do occur.

Exercises for Lesson 4.

I. Translate into English:
   1. ὁ υἱὸς ἔρχεται ἀπὸ τοῦ ἀγαθοῦ ἀνθρώπου. (Mk 5:35)
   2. ἔχω τὴν ἐξουσίαν ἣ ἐκ τοῦ θεοῦ ἐστιν. (Mk 2:10)
   3. ἡ φωνὴ τοῦ υἱοῦ καλὴ ἦν. (Mk 9:7)
   4. τὸ δαιμόνιον ἔρχεται ἐκ τοῦ ἀνθρώπου. (Mk 5:8)
   5. ὁ ἀδελφὸς οὐκ ἦν δίκαιος. (Lk 2:25)

6. τὸ δαιμόνιον πονηρὸν ἦν· ὁ ἄγγελος ἀγαθὸς ἦν. (Mk 7:22)
7. ὁ ἀδελφὸς ἔρχεται εἰς τὴν ζωήν. (Mk 9:43)
8. ἡ δόξα τοῦ θεοῦ οὐκ ἔστιν ἡ δόξα τῶν ἀνθρώπων. (Lk 2:9)
9. ὁ ἀδελφὸς εἶπεν τὴν ἀλήθειαν. (Mk 5:33)
10. ἡ τράπεζα τοῦ κυρίου ἁγία ἐστιν. (Lk 1:9)
11. μὴ ἔστε πονηροί. (Acts 1:20)
12. οὐκ ἐστὲ πονηροί. (Mk 13:11)
13. ἕκαστος υἱὸς ἀγαπητὸς ἦν. (Lk 6:44)
14. εἶ πιστός; (Mk 14:61)
15. ἡ ἀγάπη τοῦ θεοῦ καλή ἐστιν. (Jn 5:42)
16. ἡ ἐξουσία ἐκ τοῦ θεοῦ ἐστιν. (Lk 22:53)
17. ἐκ τῶν καρδιῶν τῶν ἀνθρώπων ἔρχεται ἡ ἁμαρτία. (Mk 7:21)
18. ἡ βασιλεία τοῦ θεοῦ ἐξ οὐρανοῦ ἦν. (Mk 4:26)
19. ἡ ἐκκλησία τοῦ κυρίου ἁγία ἐστιν. (Acts 9:31)
20. ἡ γῆ οὐκ ἔστιν οὐρανός. (Mk 13:31)
21. ἡ γλῶσσα τοῦ ἀνθρώπου καλή ἐστιν. (Lk 1:64)
22. ἔρχεται ἡ ἡμέρα τοῦ κυρίου. (Lk 22:7)
23. ὁ υἱὸς ἀγαπητός ἐστιν. (Mk 1:11)
24. αἱ ἁμαρτίαι τοῦ κόσμου οὐ καλαὶ ἦσαν. (Mk 2:5)
25. ἐκείνη θέλει εἶναι ἀγαθή. (Mk 9:35) ["That woman wishes"—cf. Lesson 5 for the explanation of the pronoun ἐκείνη.]

II. Translate into Greek:
   1. That man wishes to be good. (Mk 9:35) [Cf. Lesson 5 for the explanation of "That man".]
   2. The authority of the assembly is from God. (Lk 22:53)
   3. We are not holy. (Lk 17:10)

III. Work through Mk 1:11-15, checking the text against the information given above and in the previous lessons. Read the verses aloud at least three times.

The Subjunctive. εἰμί, Subjunctive. ἵνα
Purpose Clause. The Demonstrative
Pronouns οὗτος and ἐκεῖνος. The Dative
Case. The Apostrophe. Crasis. Diaeresis.

Lesson 5

The Subjunctive.

The subjunctive mood in Greek, being found in both main clauses
and subordinate clauses, is used much more extensively than the
subjunctive mood in contemporary English. Some of these uses will
be explained in the following lessons of this volume. These uses
have a common element in that they tend to put in relief the mental
attitude of the agent of an action, or, of the attitude of an agent to a
reality, even when that reality is not under the control of the agent.
(For example, in certain types of conditions.)

Perhaps the most widespread use of the subjunctive mood in
New Testament Greek is to express "purpose", that is, the intended
effect of some action. (Cf. below, in this lesson.)

εἰμί, Subjunctive.

The present tense of the subjunctive mood of εἰμί is conjugated as
follows (cf. V 16, DV 78, VP 9):

	Singular	Plural
1st Person	ὦ	ὦμεν
2nd Person	ᾖς	ἦτε
3rd Person	ᾖ	ὦσι(ν)

The iota subscript is written under the η of the second and
third person singular. This iota subscript, as the iota subscript

elsewhere when used under letters, does not affect the
pronunciation. It is useful in identifying forms visually.

ἵνα Purpose Clause.

A purpose clause is a clause which expresses the intended result of
an action. The subjunctive mood introduced by ἵνα or ὅπως (no
difference in meaning; ἵνα is more common) is a frequently used
way of expressing purpose in New Testament Greek. This is only
one way in which purpose is expressed in New Testament Greek.

> ἔρχεται εἰς τὸ ἱερὸν ἵνα ἅγιος ᾖ.
> *He is coming into the temple in order to be holy.*

> ὁ θεὸς λέγει ὅπως ἄνθρωποι ἅγιοι ὦσιν.
> *God speaks in order that men may be holy.*

The particle μή is used to negate the verb in a purpose clause.
This particle may be used with ἵνα or ὅπως, or it may be used by
itself, to introduce a negative purpose clause:

> ὁ θεὸς λέγει ἵνα ἄνθρωποι μὴ ὦσι πονηροί.
> ὁ θεὸς λέγει ὅπως ἄνθρωποι μὴ ὦσι πονηροί.
> ὁ θεὸς λέγει μὴ ἄνθρωποι ὦσι πονηροί.
> *God speaks in order that men may not be evil.*

The Demonstrative Pronouns οὗτος and ἐκεῖνος.

Greek has two principal demonstrative pronouns, i.e., pronouns
which "point out" or "indicate" some reality. They can be used as
adjectives, agreeing with a noun in gender, number, and case, or
they can be used as substantives. οὗτος means *this* and is used to
indicate someone or something near at hand; ἐκεῖνος means *that*
and is used to indicate someone or something at a distance.

	Masculine	Singular Feminine	Neuter
n	οὗτος	αὕτη	τοῦτο
g	τούτου	ταύτης	τούτου
d	τούτῳ	ταύτῃ	τούτῳ
a	τοῦτον	ταύτην	τοῦτο

	Masculine	Plural Feminine	Neuter
n	οὗτοι	αὗται	ταῦτα
g	τούτων	τούτων	τούτων
d	τούτοις	ταύταις	τούτοις
a	τούτους	ταύτας	ταῦτα

The absence of final –v in the nominative and accusative neuter singular should be noted.

	Masculine	Singular Feminine	Neuter
n	ἐκεῖνος	ἐκείνη	ἐκεῖνο
g	ἐκείνου	ἐκείνης	ἐκείνου
d	ἐκείνῳ	ἐκείνῃ	ἐκείνῳ
a	ἐκεῖνον	ἐκείνην	ἐκεῖνο

	Masculine	Plural Feminine	Neuter
n	ἐκεῖνοι	ἐκεῖναι	ἐκεῖνα
g	ἐκείνων	ἐκείνων	ἐκείνων
d	ἐκείνοις	ἐκείναις	ἐκείνοις
a	ἐκείνους	ἐκείνας	ἐκεῖνα

It should be noted that pronouns have no vocative case.

When used as adjectives, οὗτος and ἐκεῖνος do not come between the article and the noun they modify even though they are used attributively. In other words, by position they are predicative, but in meaning they are attributive.

ἔρχεται ἐκ τούτου τοῦ ἱεροῦ.
He (she, it) is coming out of this temple.

As was stated above, οὗτος and ἐκεῖνος can also be used as substantives, and when so used, normally do not have an accompanying article.

ἐκείνη ἔρχεται.
That woman is coming.

The Dative Case.

The dative case is used to express the "indirect" object of a verb, i.e., the person to or for whom something is done:

ὁ Κύριος λέγει τῷ ἀγγέλῳ.
The Lord speaks to the angel.

ἔχω σημεῖον τῷ υἱῷ.
I have a sign for the son.

The dative case also can be governed by a preposition:

ἔρχεται σὺν τῷ υἱῷ.
He (she, it) is coming with the son.

The Apostrophe. ῾Crasis. Diaeresis.

In addition to the punctuation marks explained in Lesson 4, several signs—the apostrophe indicating elision, the smooth breathing indicating crasis, the two dots indicating diaeresis—are important for understanding the Greek text of the New Testament.

Apostrophe is the sign used to indicate the elision (dropping) of a vowel. It is either similar to or identical with the sign used to indicate a smooth breathing ('). Such elision takes place when a word ending in a vowel drops the vowel before a word beginning with a vowel. Thus, the phrase ἀπ᾿ οὐράνου, *from heaven,* results when the final ο of the word ἀπό is dropped before the vowel, ο, of the word οὐρανοῦ. The apostrophe (') indicates the omission of the ο. This omission of the ο does not affect the meaning in any way.

Crasis (from the Greek κρᾶσις, meaning *mingling*) is the "fusing" of two words into one and is marked by a coronis (from the Greek κορωνίς, meaning *hook*). Again, the coronis is either similar to or identical with a smooth breathing. Thus, the words καὶ ἐγώ become, through crasis, κἀγώ. This is a phenomenon involving only sound. The meaning is not affected in any way.

Diaeresis (from the Greek διαίρεσις, meaning *separation*) is the phenomenon in which two vowels which might otherwise be read as a diphthong are distinguished so that they are pronounced separately. The sign to indicate the diaeresis consists of two dots placed over the second of the two vowels. Thus the word ῾Ησαΐας, *Isaiah,* is pronounced as four syllables and not as three. The word

Μωϋσῆς, *Moses*, is pronounced as three syllables and not as two. (In the early stages of the development of the Greek language the combination ωυ had the force of a diphthong.) Note that the sign for diaeresis is written only over ι or υ.

Vocabulary for Lesson 5.

ἐν [Prep 1] Preposition governing the dative case: *in; within,* on .

σύν [Prep 1] Preposition governing the dative case: *with, together with*.

―――

ἵνα [Conj] *in order that; that*. (This word can also be used with different meanings which correspond to other functions. Cf., for example, Lesson 75.)

ὅπως [Conj] *in order that, that*.

―――

ἄλλος, ἄλλη, ἄλλο [Adj lPro, Pro] *other; another*. This word is used with regard to two, or more than two things.

ἐκεῖνος, ἐκείνη, ἐκεῖνο [Adj 1Pro, Pro] *that*.

οὗτος, αὕτη, τοῦτο [Adj 1Pro, Pro] *this*.

τοιοῦτος, τοιαύτη, τοιοῦτο [Adj 1Pro, Pro] *such, of such a type*. Such a one
This word is declined by prefixing τοι– to οὗτος, αὕτη, τοῦτο with the initial τ of the latter omitted wherever it occurs.

Exercises for Lesson 5.

I. Translate into English:
1. ἐν ἐκείναις ταῖς ἡμέραις οὗτος ὁ ἀδελφὸς ἦν πιστός. (Mk 1:9)
2. αἱ ἐκκλησίαι τοιαῦται οὐκ ἀγαθαί εἰσιν. (Mk 6:2)
3. ὁ ἄγγελος ἔρχεται σὺν τοῖς ἀνθρώποις. (Mk 8:34)
4. τῶν τοιούτων ἦν ἡ βασιλεία τῶν οὐρανῶν. (Mk 10:14)
5. ὁ κύριος ἔρχεται ἵνα οἱ ἄνθρωποι ὦσιν ἅγιοι. (Mk 3:14)
6. ἄλλοι οὐκ ἦσαν ἐν τῷ ἱερῷ. (Mk 4:36)

7. ἐν ἐκείνῃ τῇ ἡμέρᾳ ἦν σημεῖον ἐκ τῶν οὐρανῶν. (Mk 8:1)
8. ὁ θεὸς εἶπεν τὸν λόγον ὅπως μὴ ἡ ἁμαρτία ᾖ ἐν τῇ ἐκκλησίᾳ. (Mk 5:33)
9. ἄλλοι ἀδελφοί εἰσιν ἐν τῇ ἐκκλησίᾳ. (Mk 4:36)
10. οὗτοί εἰσιν οἱ υἱοὶ οἱ ἀγαπητοί. (Mk 9:7)
11. ἐκείνη ἣ ἐν τῇ βασιλείᾳ ἐστὶν ἁγία ἐστίν. (Mk 15:41)
12. οὗτος ὁ ἀδελφὸς ἔρχεται ἐκ τοῦ ἱεροῦ. (Mk 7:6)
13. ἔχω ταύτην τὴν γῆν. (Mk 4:5)

II. Translate into Greek:
   1. That brother is coming in order that the assembly may not be evil. (Mk 3:9)
   2. This is the brother who is coming. (Mk 12:7)
   3. Other garments were with that son. (Mk 2:26)

III. Mk 1:16-20.

The Optative. εἰμί, Optative. The Nouns
μαθητής and νεανίας. The Personal
Pronoun ἐγώ. Emphasis and the Explicit
Use of the Personal Pronoun. The Vocative
Case.

Lesson 6

The Optative.

The optative mood is used principally in New Testament Greek to
express a wish in a main clause. *least used mood in Gk*

εἰμί, Optative.

The Present Optative of εἰμί is conjugated as follows (cf. V 16, DV 78,
VP 9):

	Singular	Plural
1st Person	εἴην	εἴημεν / εἶμεν
2nd Person	εἴης	εἴητε / εἶτε
3rd Person	εἴη	εἴησαν / εἶεν

The optative is used in the main clause of a sentence to
express a wish:

εἴη ἀγαθή.   εἴησαν δίκαιοι.
May she be good!   *May they be just!*

The Nouns μαθητής and νεανίας.

The majority of nouns in the first declension are feminine. But
some masculine nouns occur which have the following forms (cf. N
4 and N 5):

	Singular	Plural
n	μαθητής	μαθηταί
v	μαθητά	μαθηταί
g	μαθητοῦ	μαθητῶν
d	μαθητῇ	μαθηταῖς
a	μαθητήν	μαθητάς
n	νεανίας	νεανίαι
v	νεανία	νεανίαι
g	νεανίου	νεανιῶν
d	νεανίᾳ	νεανίαις
a	νεανίαν	νεανίας

It should be noted that the genitive singulars of both nouns have the same ending as the genitive singular of the second declension, where many of the nouns are of masculine gender (e.g., λόγος). It should be noted also that nouns like νεανίας have only ε, ι, or ρ as the final letter of the stem, whereas nouns like μαθητής can have any other letter as the final letter of the stem.

The Personal Pronoun ἐγώ.

A "personal pronoun" is a pronoun which refers to a person or persons without specifying a name. In Greek there are personal pronouns for the singular and plural of all three persons. The personal pronoun of the first person singular and plural, that is, for "I" and "we", has the following forms:

	Singular	Plural
n	ἐγώ	ἡμεῖς
g	ἐμοῦ / μου	ἡμῶν
d	ἐμοί / μοι	ἡμῖν
a	ἐμέ / με	ἡμᾶς

The forms μου, μοι, and με differ from the parallel forms in the singular in that they are less emphatic and in that they are "enclitic", i.e., tend to lose their accent to the preceding word. Enclitics will be explained below in the Rules for Accents. For the difference in meaning the following examples should be noted.

a) ὁ θεὸς λέγει μοι.   a) *God speaks to me.*
b) ὁ θεὸς λέγει ἐμοί.   b) *It is to me that God speaks.*

(Of course the same wording could be used as in translation [a], with the emphasis being conveyed by the tone of voice.)

Emphasis and the Explicit Use of the Personal Pronoun.

Inasmuch as the indicative, imperative, subjunctive, and optative moods have forms which by themselves indicate the person and number of the subject, the use of the nominative of the personal pronoun with these moods often indicates emphasis. But often no particular emphasis seems to be intended. Here, as always, the context should be the guide.

> ἐγὼ ἔχω τὴν δόξαν.
> *I have the glory.*

The Vocative Case.

The vocative case is used to indicate a person (or a personified thing) who is being addressed. At times, the interjection ὦ (*O, Oh*) is used before a word in the vocative case. Occasionally the nominative case (possibly with the article) is used in place of the vocative to address a person.

> Κύριε.
> ὦ Κύριε.
> *O Lord!*

> ὁ θεός μου.
> *My God!*

The vocative, like the nominative, is never governed by a preposition.

Vocabulary for Lesson 6.

διά [Prep 2] Governs the genitive or the accusative case. With the genitive: *through* [time, space, agency]; with the accusative: *on account of.* ~~more common~~

βαπτιστής, –οῦ, ὁ [N 4] *baptizer*.

δεσπότης, –ου, ὁ [N 4] *master*.

ἐργάτης, –ου, ὁ [N 4] *workman, worker*.

'Ιορδάνης, –ου, ὁ [N 4] *Jordan [River]*.

κριτής, –οῦ, ὁ [N 4] *judge*.

λῃστής, –οῦ, ὁ [N 4] *robber*.

μαθητής, –οῦ, ὁ [N 4] *disciple*.

προφήτης, –ου, ὁ [N 4] *prophet*

στρατιώτης, –ου, ὁ [N 4] *soldier*.

ὑποκριτής, –οῦ, ὁ [N 4] *hypocrite; actor*.

ψεύστης, –ου, ὁ [N 4] *liar; deceiver*.
___
'Ανδρέας, –ου, ὁ [N 5] *Andrew*.

Μεσσίας, –ου, ὁ [N 5] *Messiah*.

νεανίας, –ου, ὁ [N 5] *youth, young man*.
___
ἐγώ [Pro] *I*.

ἡμεῖς [Pro] *we*.
___
ὦ [Inter] *O, oh*. [To be distingished from the first person singular of the subjunctive of εἰμί by the context.]
___
καί [Conj] *and; also; even*.

Exercises for Lesson 6.

I. Translate into English:
    1. διὰ τῆς ἡμέρας οἱ ἐργάται ἦσαν ἐν τῷ 'Ιορδάνῃ. (Acts 1:3)

2. διὰ τούτους τοὺς λόγους ὁ κριτὴς ἦν ἀγαθός. (Mk 7:29)
3. εἴημεν ἀγαθοί.
4. ὁ βαπτιστὴς λέγει τοῖς ἀνθρώποις τοὺς τῆς ἀληθείας
   λόγους. (Mk 1:38)
5. ὁ Μεσσίας ἔρχεται ἐκ τοῦ ἱεροῦ. (Jn 4:25)
6. σὺν τῷ κυρίῳ ἦσαν κριταὶ ἡμῶν. (Mk 15:27)
7. ὁ κύριος εἶπεν τοῖς μαθηταῖς. (Mk 2:16)
8. ὁ στρατιώτης ἐστὶ λῃστὴς καὶ ψεύστης. (Jn 8:44)
9. ὁ λῃστὴς ἦν σὺν τῷ στρατιώτῃ. (Jn 18:40)
10. ἐκεῖνος ὁ νεανίας ἦν υἱὸς νεανίου. (Jn 8:44)
11. οἱ ἐργάται πιστοί εἰσιν. (Mt 9:37)
12. ψεύστης ἐστὶν καὶ ὁ υἱὸς ἐκείνου τοῦ ἀνθρώπου. (Jn
    8:44)   φευστου.
13. ὁ βαπτιστὴς ἔρχεται ἐκ τοῦ ἱεροῦ. (Mt 3:1)
14. οἱ ἄνθρωποι ἦσαν ἐν τῷ Ἰορδάνῃ. (Mk 1:5)
15. ὦ ἄνθρωπε, ἴσθι ἀγαθός. (Rom 2:1)
16. ἐγὼ οὐκ εἰμὶ ἅγιος· ἡμεῖς οὐκ ἐσμὲν ἅγιοι. (Mk 1:7)
17. οἱ ἄνθρωποι ἦσαν ἐν τῷ οἴκῳ τοῦ Ἀνδρέου. (Mk 1:29)
18. μὴ ἴσθι ὑποκριτής. (Mk 5:34)
19. οὐκ ἔστιν προφήτης πιστὸς ἐν τῇ βασιλείᾳ. (Mk 6:4)
    [When a third person singular or plural of the verb "to
    be" (εἰμί) occurs at the beginning of a sentence, it can
    often be translated advantageously by the English
    expletive construction *there is* or *there were* or
    there will be, depending on the number, tense, and
    mood of the form of εἰμί being used. Such a
    construction can, of course, contain a negative, as
    here.]
20. ἴσθι ὑγιής. [For the meaning of ὑγιής, cf. Lesson 25.].
    (Mk 5:34)
21. εἴης ὑγιής.

II. Translate into Greek:
    1. The disciples of the Lord were in the temple and the
       disciples of the baptizer were in the Jordan. (Mk 2:18)
    2. Are you the master of the workmen? (Mt 20:2)
    3. Andrew was with the Messiah. (Mk 13:3)

III. Mk 1:21-25.

The Participle. εἰμί, Present Participle.
The Personal Pronoun σύ.

Lesson 7

The Participle.
PARTICIPLE IS A MOOD.
A participle is a verbal adjective. Like a verb, it has voice, mood,
and tense, and can take a direct object. Like an adjective, it has
gender, number, and case, and agrees with the noun or pronoun it
modifies. It can occasionally be found as a noun, usually in the
masculine or neuter gender. It can be used with respect to the first,
second, or third persons.

ὁ υἱός, σὺν τῷ θεῷ ὤν, ἅγιός ἐστιν.
The Son, being with God, is holy.

The Greek language is unusually rich in participles. English
is not as rich in participles, and frequently expresses in other ways
(for example, a relative clause) what Greek expresses with a
participle. Thus the above sentence can also be translated:

ὁ υἱός, σὺν τῷ θεῷ ὤν, ἅγιός ἐστιν.
The Son, who is with God, is holy.

This idea can also be expressed in Greek, of course, by a
relative clause, just as in English:

ὁ υἱός, ὅς ἐστι σὺν τῷ θεῷ, ἅγιός ἐστιν.
The Son, who is with God, is holy.

The precise function of the "tense" of a participle in relation to
the tense of the verb (usually in the indicative mood), with which it
is associated in a sentence or clause is a disputed point among
grammarians. The matter will be discussed more fully beginning
in Lesson 9, when the "aspect" of verbs will be introduced. For the
moment it is sufficient to know that the present participle usually

indicates that the action signified by the participle is contemporary with the time of the main verb of the sentence, whether that time is past, present, or future.

εἰμί, Present Participle.

The present participle of εἰμί is as follows (cf. V 16, DV 53, VP 9, Adj 7):

	Masculine	Singular Feminine	Neuter
n	ὤν	οὖσα	ὄν
v	ὤν	οὖσα	ὄν
g	ὄντος	οὔσης	ὄντος
d	ὄντι	οὔσῃ	ὄντι
a	ὄντα	οὖσαν	ὄν

	Masculine	Plural Feminine	Neuter
n	ὄντες	οὖσαι	ὄντα
v	ὄντες	οὖσαι	ὄντα
g	ὄντων	οὐσῶν	ὄντων
d	οὖσι(ν)	οὔσαις	οὖσι(ν)
a	ὄντας	οὔσας	ὄντα

The dative masculine and neuter plural result from the following sound changes:

1) The original form is οντ–σι (cf. the other plural forms: οντ–ες, οντ–ων, οντ–ας, οντ–α). The letter τ drops out before the letter σ so that the form ονσι results.

2) The form ονσι becomes ουσι because the consonant cluster νσ loses the ν, and the preceding vowel is lengthened from ο to the diphthong ου.

The movable ν at the end of the dative masculine and neuter plural functions in exactly the same way as the movable ν when it is found in the third person of verbal forms.

The masculine and neuter forms of ὤν, οὖσα, ὄν belong to the third declension. This declension has a number of substantives and adjectives in a variety of categories. These categories will be taken up in subsequent lessons. The feminine form of ὤν, οὖσα, ὄν is declined like δόξα.

The Personal Pronoun σύ.

The personal pronoun of the second person singular and plural has
the following forms (cf. Pro):

	Singular	Plural
n	σύ	ὑμεῖς
g	σοῦ / σου	ὑμῶν
d	σοί / σοι	ὑμῖν
a	σέ / σε	ὑμᾶς

The forms σου, σοι, and σε differ from the parallel forms in
the singular in that they are less emphatic, and in that they are
"enclitic", i.e., tend to lose their accent to the preceding word.
Enclitics will be explained below in the Rules for Accents. For the
difference in meaning, the following examples should be noted.

ὁ θεὸς λέγει σοί.
God speaks to you.

ὁ θεὸς λέγει σοι.
God speaks to you.

Inasmuch as the indicative, imperative, subjunctive, and
optative moods have forms which of themselves indicate the person
and number of the subject, use of the nominative of the personal
pronoun with these moods often indicates emphasis. But often no
emphasis seems intended. Context must be the guide.

ὑμεῖς ἔχετε [τὴν] δόξαν.
You [plural] have [the] glory.

Vocabulary for Lesson 7.

κατά [Prep 2] Governs genitive or accusative case. With the
        genitive: *down from*; *against*. With the accusative: *towards*;
        near; *according to*.

___

ἄρτος, –ου, ὁ [N 6m] *bread*; *food*.

δοῦλος, –ου, ὁ [N 6m] *slave*; *servant*.

θάνατος, –ου, ὁ [N 6m] *death*.

λαός, –οῦ, ὁ [N 6m] *people; nation*.

νόμος, –ου, ὁ [N 6m] *law*.

οἶκος, –ου, ὁ [N 6m] *house; family; dynasty*.

ὀφθαλμός, –οῦ, ὁ [N 6m] *eye*.

ὄχλος, –ου, ὁ [N 6m] *crowd*.

τόπος, –ου, ὁ [N 6m] *place*.

———
'Ιησοῦς, ὁ [N 33] *Jesus*. See N 33 for irregular declension.

———
σύ [Pro] *you* [sg.].

ὑμεῖς [Pro] *you* [pl.].

———
γάρ [Conj] *for, because*. This word is never found as the first word of a sentence or clause. The technical term for this restriction is "postpositive".

Exercises for Lesson 7.

I. Translate into English:
1. οὐκ ἦν σημεῖον κατὰ τοῦ Μεσσίου. (Mk 3:6)
2. ἦσαν γὰρ δοῦλοι. (Mk 1:16)
3. ὁ θάνατός ἐστι διὰ τὰς ἁμαρτίας. (Mk 7:29)
4. ἔρχεται ὁ κύριος ἵνα ὁ ἄρτος ᾖ ἅγιος. (Lk 4:3)
5. ὁ ὀφθαλμός σου οὐκ ἦν ἀγαθός. (Mk 9:47)
6. οὗτοι γάρ εἰσιν οἱ νόμοι καὶ οἱ προφῆται. (Mt 7:12)
7. οὐκ ἔστιν εὐαγγέλιον κατ' 'Ανδρέαν. (Mk 1:27) [When a preposition ends in a vowel and the following word begins with a vowel, the final vowel of the preposition is usually dropped and an apostrophe is written in its place to show that it is missing.]
8. ἔρχεται ὁ 'Ιησοῦς εἰς ἐκεῖνον τὸν τόπον. (Mk 1:35)
9. ἐκεῖνος ὁ λαὸς οὐκ ἦν πιστός. (Mk 7:6)
10. σὺ εἶ ὁ υἱὸς ὁ ἀγαπητός; (Mk 3:11)
11. ὁ 'Ιησοῦς ἔρχεται εἰς τὸν οἶκον 'Ανδρέου. (Mk 3:20)

12. οὐ γάρ ἐστε ὑμεῖς οἱ ὄντες ἀγαθοί. (Mk 13:11)
13. ἐκεῖνος ὁ ὄχλος ἔρχεται εἰς τὸν οἶκον τοῦ θεοῦ. (Mk 7:6)
14. δοῦλος Ἰησοῦ ἐστι δοῦλος ἀνθρώπων. (Mk 10:44)

II. Translate into Greek:
　1. This crowd is coming into the shrine. (Mk 2:13)
　2. The house of God is holy and the prophets who are in this house of God are holy. (Mk 11:17)
　3. Jesus spoke to us in those days. (Mk 2:19; Mk 1:9)

III. Mk 1:26-31.

εἰμί, Future Indicative, Future Participle,
Future Infinitive. The Future Indicative.
The Future Participle. The Future
Infinitive. The Accusative with the
Infinitive. The Adjective and Personal
Pronoun αὐτός. The Reflexive and Non-
Reflexive Use of αὐτός. The Noun σάρξ.

Lesson 8

εἰμί, Future Indicative, Future Participle, Future Infinitive.

In the future tense the verb εἰμί is conjugated as follows (cf. V 16,
DV 78; the future participle is declined like Adj 1; the future system
of εἰμί as such is not given in the paradigms of the verb at the back of
Volume Two of this grammar):

Indicative

	Singular	Plural
1st Person	ἔσομαι	ἐσόμεθα
2nd Person	ἔσῃ	ἔσεσθε
3rd Person	ἔσται	ἔσονται

I shall be	*We shall be*
You (sg.) *will be*	*You* (pl.) *will be*
He (*She, It*) *will be*	*They will be*

Participle
Singular

	Masculine	Feminine	Neuter
n	ἐσόμενος	ἐσομένη	ἐσόμενον
v	ἐσόμενε	ἐσομένη	ἐσόμενον
g	ἐσομένου	ἐσομένης	ἐσομένου
d	ἐσομένῳ	ἐσομένῃ	ἐσομένῳ
a	ἐσόμενον	ἐσομένην	ἐσόμενον

	Masculine	Plural Feminine	Neuter
n	ἐσόμενοι	ἐσόμεναι	ἐσόμενα
v	ἐσόμενοι	ἐσόμεναι	ἐσόμενα
g	ἐσομένων	ἐσομένων	ἐσομένων
d	ἐσομένοις	ἐσομέναις	ἐσομένοις
a	ἐσομένους	ἐσομένας	ἐσόμενα

The future infinitive of εἰμί is ἔσεσθαι.

The Future Indicative.

The future tense of the indicative mood in Greek corresponds to the future tense in English. It expresses a single action or repeated or continuous action in the future in an independent or dependent clause. (Cf. below, Lesson 11, for a more detailed presentation.)

ἔσομαι δίκαιος.   οὐκ ἔσονται ἐν τῷ οἴκῳ.
I shall be just.   *They will not be in the house.*

The Future Participle.

The future participle can express a single action or repeated or continuous action. Context shows that it indicates action subsequent to the main verb of the clause in which it stands, whether that action be past, present, or future:

> τὸ ἔργον τὸ ἐσόμενον ἀγαθὸν ἔσται.
> *The future work* [literally, *the work which will be*] *will be good.*

The future participle of εἰμί is rare in the New Testament. Its conjugation has an accidental importance in that it serves as a paradigm for participles, future and otherwise, of other verbs which are more common.

The Future Infinitive.

The future infinitive can express a single action or continuous or repeated action. Context shows that it indicates action subsequent to

the main verb of the clause in which it is found, whether that action
be past, present, or future.

The use of the future infinitive can perhaps best be seen in a
construction called the "accusative with the infinitive", although the
accusative with the infinitive is not limited to future infinitives (see
the following explanatory item).

The Accusative with the Infinitive. *used after verbs of saying & perceiving*

In the construction called "the accusative with the infinitive" a
noun or pronoun in the accusative case is construed as the subject of
an infinitive. The accusative with the infinitive is used in a variety
of ways in Greek, but one principal way is after a verb of saying:

> ὁ Ἰησοῦς λέγει τὸν βαπτιστὴν ἔσεσθαι δίκαιον.
> *Jesus says that the baptizer will be just.*

Here the word βαπτιστήν, *baptizer*, is placed in the accusative case
because it is the subject of the infinitive ἔσεσθαι. The word δίκαιον
is in the accusative case because it agrees with βαπτιστήν. (The
verb εἰμί "takes the same case after as before". Since the verb is
usually in the indicative mood, the word coming "before" it, i.e., the
subject, is usually in the nominative case, and the word "after" it,
i.e., the predicate, is in the nominative case as well. But if the word
"before" it, i.e., the subject, is in the accusative case, as it is if the
mood of εἰμί is infinitive, then the word "after", i.e., the predicate, is
in the accusative case as well. [It should be noted that occasionally
the subject of the infinitive is found after the infinitive, just as the
subject of a verb in the indicative mood can occasionally be found
following its verb.]) The future tense of the infinitive is used because
the future indicative was used in the direct discourse, i.e., *Jesus
says, "The baptizer will be just"*.

The same principles apply to infinitives in other tenses. Thus
the direct statement *Jesus says, "The baptizer is just"*, becomes the
indirect statement *Jesus says that the baptizer is just*. In Greek this
would be ὁ Ἰησοῦς λέγει τὸν βαπτιστὴν εἶναι δίκαιον, i.e., the
present infinitive of εἰμί is used because the time of the verb in the
subordinate clause is seen to be contemporaneous with the time of
the verb of the main clause.

εἰμί has no aorist infinitive, but if it had, the aorist would be
used to express the indirect statement *Jesus says that the baptizer
was just*, which in turn can be expressed as a direct statement as

follows: *Jesus says, "The baptizer was just"*. There is also another
form of the infinitive which most verbs have but which εἰμί does not
have: the perfect. The force of the aorist and perfect will be
discussed when these verbs are presented in connection with the
verb λύω. The lack of an aorist and perfect infinitive in εἰμί means
that another mood beside the infinitive, or another verb beside εἰμί
must be used for an accusative with the infinitive idea in these tense
areas.

With this lesson the presentation of all the forms of the verb
εἰμί is concluded. There is no future subjunctive or optative of any
verb in the New Testament.

The Adjective and Personal Pronoun αὐτός.

The adjective αὐτός, which also serves as the third person of the
personal pronoun, is declined as follows (cf. Adj 1Pro, Pro):

		Singular	
	Masculine	Feminine	Neuter
n	αὐτός	αὐτή	αὐτό
g	αὐτοῦ	αὐτῆς	αὐτοῦ
d	αὐτῷ	αὐτῇ	αὐτῷ
a	αὐτόν	αὐτήν	αὐτό

		Plural	
	Masculine	Feminine	Neuter
n	αὐτοί	αὐταί	αὐτά
g	αὐτῶν	αὐτῶν	αὐτῶν
d	αὐτοῖς	αὐταῖς	αὐτοῖς
a	αὐτούς	αὐτάς	αὐτά

As an adjective αὐτός has the meaning *same* when it is
preceded by the article, or *self* when there is no preceding article:

> εἶπε τὸν αὐτὸν λόγον.
> *He said the same word.*

> Ἰησοῦς αὐτὸς ἔρχεται.
> *Jesus himself is coming.*

When used as a pronoun, αὐτός indicates the third person:

ἔβλεπον αὐτόν.
I was seeing him.

ἔβλεπον αὐτούς.
I was seeing them.

The Reflexive and Non-Reflexive Use of αὐτός.

In classical Greek the genitive case of αὐτός was used only in a non-reflexive sense. That is to say, it did not refer back to the subject of the sentence or clause in which it is found.

ἔβλεπε τὸν οἶκον αὐτοῦ.
He was seeing his [i.e., another person's] *house.*

But in New Testament Greek the genitive case is often found in a reflexive sense. That is to say, it refers back to the subject of the sentence or clause in which it is found:

ἔβλεπε τὸν οἶκον αὐτοῦ.
He was seeing his [i.e., his own] *house.*

Whether αὐτός is being used in a reflexive sense or not is usually clear from the context.

The Noun σάρξ.

The importance of the stem of a noun or adjective is especially marked in the third declension. (The masculine and neuter genders of the present participle of the verb εἰμί belong to this declension. Cf. above, in Lesson 7.)

Third declension nouns are divided into categories according to the final sound of the stem.
Palatal stems (sometimes referred to as guttural stems) end in κ, γ, or χ and are so called because κ, γ, and χ are called "palatal" consonants, i.e., they involve the palate in their pronunciation. They are declined as follows (σάρξ, *flesh*, N 8f):

	Singular	Plural
n	σάρξ	σάρκες
v	σάρξ	σάρκες
g	σαρκός	σαρκῶν
d	σαρκί	σαρξί(ν)
a	σάρκα	σάρκας

The stem of a noun may be found by eliminating the ending of the genitive singular. In the third declension the ending for nouns is usually –ος. Thus, the stem of σαρξ is σαρκ–.

In the dative plural the ending is –σι(ν), but the form is not written σαρκσί but σαρξί. The letter ξ is called a "double consonant" because it is simply a way of writing the two consonants κσ. The letter ξ also results from the combinations γσ and χσ.

Vocabulary for Lesson 8.

μετά [Prep 2] Governs genitive or accusative case. With the genitive: *with, together with*. With the accusative: *after*.

A number of nouns in the New Testament are declined exactly like λόγος but are feminine, not masculine. The more frequently used are the following:

ἄβυσσος, –ου, ἡ [N 6f] *abyss*.

ἄμπελος, –ου, ἡ [N 6f] *vine*.

βίβλος, –ου, ἡ [N 6f] *book*.

ἔρημος, –ου, ἡ [N 6f] *desert*. [Also found as adjective. Cf. Lesson 24.]

νῆσος, –ου, ἡ [N 6f] *island*.

νόσος, –ου, ἡ [N 6f] *disease*.

ὁδός, –οῦ, ἡ [N 6f] *road; way, journey*.

ῥάβδος, –ου, ἡ [N 6f] *staff; wand, scepter*.

αὐτός, αὐτή, αὐτό [Adj 1Pro, Pro] *he, she, it; same; self*.

σάρξ, σαρκός, ἡ [N 8f] *flesh; human nature.*

——

δέ [Conj] This is a frequently-used conjunction with a variety of
subtle meanings. It is used either by itself or with other
conjunctions or particles. By itself it can have a mildly
adversative sense: *but, rather, on the contrary.* It can have a
linking sense: *and.* It can be used to continue a discourse or
narration: *now, then, so.* It is never the first word in its
sentence or clause, i.e., it is postpositive.

Exercises for Lesson 8.

I. Translate into English:
1. ὁ μαθητὴς ἦν μετὰ τῶν βίβλων αὐτοῦ. (Mk 1:13)
2. τὸ δαιμόνιον ἔρχεται ἐκ τῆς ἀβύσσου. (Apoc 11:7)
3. ὁ Ἰησοῦς λέγει· ἐγώ εἰμι ἡ ἄμπελος. (Jn 15:1)
4. ἡ ἀλήθειά ἐστιν ἐν ταύτῃ τῇ βίβλῳ. (Mk 12:26)
5. ὁ βαπτιστὴς ἦν ἐν τῇ ἐρήμῳ. (Mk 1:4)
6. ὁ στρατιώτης ἔρχεται εἰς τὴν νῆσον. (Acts 27:26)
7. νόσοι ἦσαν ἐν τῷ λαῷ. (Mt 4:23)
8. οἱ μαθηταὶ τοῦ Ἰησοῦ ἦσαν ἐν τῇ ὁδῷ. (Mk 8:27)
9. ὁ μαθητὴς ἔχει τὴν ῥάβδον. (Mk 6:8)
10. αὐτὸς γὰρ ὁ θεὸς εἶπεν τούτους τοὺς λόγους. (Mk 6:17)
11. τὸ δαιμόνιον ἔρχεται ἐξ αὐτοῦ. (Mk 1:26)
12. ὁ δὲ Ἰησοῦς λέγει αὐτοῖς περὶ αὐτῆς. (Mk 1:30) [Cf.
    Lesson 9, Vocabulary, for meaning of περί.]
13. ἔρχεται δὲ ἡ ἡμέρα τοῦ κυρίου. (Mk 2:20)

II. Translate into Greek:
1. After this day we shall be with the Lord in his kingdom.
   (Mk 8:31)
2. The baptizer comes into the desert with his disciples. (Mt
   11:7)
3. The disciples were with Jesus on that road. (Mk 9:33)

III. Mk 1:32-37.

The Inflection of Verbs and of Nouns,
Pronouns, and Adjectives. The Verbal
Systems in –ω and in –μι. The Active and
Passive Voices. The Meaning of "Aspect"
in the Greek Verbal System. λύω, Present
Active Indicative. Rules for Accents 1.

Lesson 9

The Inflection of Verbs and of Nouns, Pronouns, and Adjectives.

All verbs and almost all of the nouns, pronouns, and adjectives in
Greek can be "inflected", i.e., modified in some way or other to
indicate the function of the word in a sentence. The part of the word
which remains invariable is called the "stem"; the variable part is
called the "ending". The inflection of a verb is usually referred to as
a "conjugation"; the inflection of a noun, pronoun, or adjective is
referred to as a "declension". Terminology varies at times, and the
student should be alert to note the way in which the terms are being
used. See above, Lesson 4, for a preliminary discussion of the stem.
    The invariable part of a word is called the "stem" in relation to
its ending. This invariable part is often called the "root" in relation
to other words. But it should be kept in mind that the root and a
stem based in it do not always correspond exactly, even though a
"stem" is based on the "root". For example, the noun ἄγγελος and
the verb ἀγγέλλω in its present system share the root ἀγγελ–. Their
meanings—*messenger* and *I announce*—convey this sharing. But
the verb has ἀγγελλ– as a stem only in the present system. In the
future system the stem is ἀγγελ–, with only one λ. Such variations of
a root to form stems are usually not so great as to be unrecognizable.

The Verbal Systems in –ω and in –μι.

Greek verbs are divided into two main classes, those ending in –ω
and those ending in –μι. The verb εἰμί belongs to the latter category.
It was presented at the very beginning of this grammar because of

its frequent use and because of its importance for understanding the predicative and attributive use of adjectives.. But the verbs ending in –ω are far more numerous than the verbs ending in –μι, and their conjugation will be presented beginning with this lesson before the other verbs in –μι begin to be presented in Lesson 55. The technical difference between verbs in –ω and verbs in –μι will be discussed in Lesson 55.

The Active and Passive Voices.

"Voice" is the grammatical term used to express the relation of the subject of a verb to the action which the verb expresses. If the grammatical subject of a verb is identical with the real subject of the action which the verb expresses, the verb is said to be in the "active" voice. For example, *I see the book* is a sentence in which the grammatical subject of the verb, *I*, is the real subject or "doer" of the action of "seeing". The verb *see* is thus said to be in the "active" voice. If the grammatical subject of a verb is not identical with the real subject of the action which the verb expresses, the verb is said to be in the "passive" voice. For example, *The book is seen by me* is a sentence in which the grammatical subject of the verb, *the book*, is not the real subject of the action which the verb expresses. The real subject of the action, i.e., the "doer", is expressed by the phrase *by me*. The grammatical subject, *the book*, is entirely "passive" with regard to the action of seeing.

In Greek there is a set of forms for the active voice, and another set of forms for the passive voice. There is also a set of forms for a third voice called the "middle voice". This voice will be explained in Lesson 26.

The verb εἰμί is unique in that it has no voice.

The Meaning of "Aspect" in the Greek Verbal System.

The primary meaning of time in the Greek text of the New Testament is that conveyed by the division of time into past, present, and future. <u>This primary time in the New Testament is conveyed directly only by the indicative mood</u>. (See the explanations of the present ~~past~~ tense of εἰμί given on p. 10, of the imperfect tense on p. 21, and of the future tense on p. 50.) Expressions of this primary meaning of time are given in the indicative mood in various ways, but basically by the use of the verbal stem. (For a generic meaning of "stem" cf.

above, in this lesson.) Most verbs have four stems: present, aorist, future, and perfect. These four stems correspond to four verbal "aspects". <u>A verbal "aspect" in New Testament Greek is that grammatical category which expresses the viewpoint of the speaker about the action which the verb describes</u>. The present aspect (conveyed by the present stem) expresses the view of an <u>action as not terminated</u>; it regards an action from within, so to speak, with no reference to the beginning or end of the action; the action is viewed as open-ended. The aorist aspect (conveyed by the aorist stem) expresses the view of an <u>action as terminated</u>; it regards an action from without, so to speak, with reference to the ending of the action; the action is viewed as closed. The present and aorist aspects are paired in the sense that they are the main aspects used in discourse, often in subtle counterpoint with each other. They are the most important aspects in New Testament Greek and are used much more frequently than the other two "aspects", which are "aspects only in a weakened, analogical sense in comparison with the aspects of the present and of the aorist. The future aspect (conveyed by the future stem) expresses the view of an <u>action as in some way subsequent</u>. The perfect aspect (conveyed by the perfect stem) *following* expresses the view of an <u>action as in some way prior</u>. These two aspects are not played off against each other as the present and aorist often implicitly are. Use of the verbal stems implying aspects are the basic way of conveying primary time in Greek <u>when employed in the indicative mood</u>. Many other means are used to convey primary time in Greek. These include the meaning of the verb itself and the use of other words in the context.

The aspects exist in the non-indicative moods as well: subjunctive, optative, imperative, participle, and infinitive. In these moods the aspects do not indicate primary time, but retain their meaning of aspects as given above. Just how these non-indicative uses of the aspects are to be interpreted will be discussed as each new mood is presented.

The above interpretation of aspect is only one of many advanced in the study of New Testament Greek today and is presented here simply as a pedagogical device. The beginning student should be alert to see if the interpretation adequately serves to explain the text. Even if the student eventually does not agree with this interpretation it will have served as an introductory presentation.

A final word of caution. New Testament Greek has a lengthy linguistic pedigree. That is to say, it is the result of hundreds of years of linguistic evolution. Not every verb fits neatly into the theoretical outline given above. Certain verbs use stems in peculiar, often stereotyped ways. The authors of the New Testament were not professional linguists. They used the language as they felt it to be appropriate for their thoughts. The student should be aware of too facilely forcing the text into an overly logical mode.

See below, Appendix: "Aspect in the Greek Verbal System", p. 454.

λύω, Present Active Indicative.

For the meaning of the indicative mood cf. Lesson 2. The present tense in New Testament Greek is known by the fact that the stem of the verb is the present stem. This present stem conveys the idea of the aspect which views the action of the verb as not terminated. (Cf. above, in this lesson.) A verbal action which is viewed as not terminated, when presented in the indicative mood, indicates present time, if there is no augment. The augment is used with the present stem to show that the non-terminated action is in past time. (This is the imperfect tense, which will be presented in Lesson 12.)

The present tense of the indicative mood of the verb λύω, *I loose, I loosen, I untie, I dissolve* (root λυ–, present stem λυ–) is as follows (cf. V 1, VP 1):

	Active Voice, Indicative Mood, Present Tense	
	Singular	Plural
1st Person	λύ–ω	λύ–ομεν
2nd Person	λύ–εις	λύ–ετε
3rd Person	λύ–ει	λύ–ουσι(ν)

I loose, am loosing	*We loose, are loosing*
You (sg.) *loose, are loosing*	*You* (pl.) *loose, are loosing*
He (She, It) looses, is loosing	*They loose, are loosing*

Rules for Accents 1.

In Greek the acute accent (cf. Lesson 1) may stand over any one of the final three syllables of a word. The circumflex may stand over either of the final two syllables of a word. The grave may stand only over the final syllable of a word:

λύετε	λύω	σαρκός
	οὖσι	σαρκῶν
		μαθητής

"Rules for Accents" will be continued in subsequent lessons.

Vocabulary for Lesson 9.

περί [Prep 2] Governs the genitive and the accusative case. With the genitive: *concerning*; *about*. With the accusative: *around* [spatial or temporal meaning].

βλέπω [V 4, DV 43, VP 1] [The designation "VP 1" refers to the paradigm of the active voice of the verb in question. A verb will normally have a middle voice and a passive voice, but for the sake of simplicity, references to these voices will be omitted until they have been presented in the grammar in Lessons 26 and 36.] *I see, I am seeing.* [In all subsequent vocabulary listings the progressive tense in English—*I am seeing*—will be presupposed.]

γράφω [V 4, DV 53, VP 1] *I write.*

διώκω [V 2, DV 64, VP 1] *I pursue; I persecute.*

ἔχω [V 2, DV 109, VP 1] *I have, I possess.* Cf. above, Lesson 3. This verb is irregular in the future, aorist, and perfect systems.

κωλύω [V 1, VP 1] *I forbid; I prevent; I hinder.*

λέγω [V 2 (I); DV 179; VP 1, 4] *I say.* This verb is irregular in all other tense systems. In Lesson 2 the third person of the singular and plural of the aorist tense was given. In Lesson 3 the third person singular of the present tense was given.

λύω [V 1, VP 1] *I loose; I untie; I dissolve.*

πέμπω [V 4, DV 238, VP 1] *I send.*

σάλπιγξ, σάλπιγγος, ἡ [N 9f] *trumpet.*

Two other palatal stems frequently found in the New Testament are irregular in the nominative singular:

γυνή, γυναικός, ἡ [N 8f, N 33] *woman; wife.*

θρίξ, τριχός, ἡ [N 10f, N 33] *hair.*

———
νύξ, νυκτός, ἡ [N 8f, N 33] *night.* A τ is present in all forms except
in the nominative and vocative singulars and the dative
plural, but the root is palatal.

———
οὖν [Adv 3] *therefore.* This word is postpositive.

Exercises for Lesson 9.

I. Translate into English:
1. ἦν ὄχλος περὶ τὸν ᾿Ιησοῦν. (Mk 9:14)
2. ὁ οὖν κύριος ᾿Ιησοῦς ἔχει ἐξουσίαν ἐπὶ τῆς γῆς. (Mk
16:19; 2:10) [For the meaning of ἐπί cf. Lesson 12,
Vocabulary.]
3. λέγει ὁ κριτὴς αὐτοῖς περὶ αὐτῆς. (Mk 1:30)
4. κύριε, ὁ θεὸς γράφει τοῖς ἀνθρώποις. (Mk 12:19)
5. ἡ γυνὴ ἔχει τρίχας καλάς.
6. βλέπομεν τοὺς ἀνθρώπους. (Mk 8:24)
7. διὰ τῆς νυκτὸς ἦν ἐν τῇ ἐρήμῳ. (Mk 5:5)
8. ὁ ἀγαθὸς στρατιώτης ἔρχεται καὶ λύει αὐτόν. (Mk 11:4)
9. πέμπουσιν τοὺς ἀγγέλους μετὰ σαλπίγγων. (Mt 25:31)
10. οὐκ ἔχομεν ἐξουσίαν ἐν ἐκείνῳ τῷ τόπῳ. (Mk 1:22)
11. διώκετε τοὺς προφήτας. (Mt 23:34)
12. οἱ δεσπόται κωλύουσι τοὺς ἐργάτας. (Mk 9:38)
13. πέμπεις αὐτοὺς εἰς τὴν ἔρημον; (Mk 5:12)
14. ὁ ὄχλος λέγει περὶ τοῦ ᾿Ιησοῦ. (Mk 1:30)
15. περὶ ταύτην τὴν ἡμέραν ἔρχεται ὁ ᾿Ιησοῦς. (Mk 6:48)
16. ὁ λῃστὴς λέγει κατὰ τὴν σάρκα. (Jn 8:15)

II. Translate into Greek:
1. We are writing for our own disciples these books
concerning the truth of the Lord. (Mk 4:34)
2. We therefore send the trumpets which we have.
3. After those days our hearts were not good. Therefore we
were not holy. (Lk 1:24)

III. Mk 1:38-42.

The Imperfect Active Indicative. λύω,
Imperfect Active Indicative. The Augment.
Compound Verbs, I. The Noun Ἄραψ.
Rules for Accents 2.

Lesson 10

The Imperfect Active Indicative.

The imperfect indicative is formed from the present stem and thus
shows that the action expressed is viewed as not being terminated
(cf. Lesson 9). The indicative mood shows that primary time is
being expressed. The imperfect tense has an augment, which
shows that the action is in past time. (Cf. below for the formation of
the augment.) <u>When interpreted according to other elements in the
context the imperfect usually indicates a past action which is viewed
as repeated or continuing</u>. (Cf. below for the formation of the
augment.) For the meaning of the active voice cf. Lesson 9.

<u>The student should note well that the imperfect tense is based on the
present stem</u>. This indicates that the action is not considered as
terminated. The character of being "past" comes primarily from
the augment.

λύω, Imperfect Active Indicative.

The imperfect active indicative of λύω is as follows (cf. V 1, VP 1):

Imperfect Tense, Active Voice, Indicative Mood

	Singular	Plural
1st Person	ἔ–λυ–ον	ἐ–λύ–ομεν
2nd Person	ἔ–λυ–ες	ἐ–λύ–ετε
3rd Person	ἔ–λυ–ε(ν)	ἔ–λυ–ον

I was loosing	*We were loosing*
You (sg.) *were loosing*	*You* (pl.) *were loosing*
He (She, It) was loosing	*They were loosing*

The first person singular and the third person plural have the same form. They are distinguished by the context.

It should be stressed that the imperfect is formed from the same stem of the verb λύω (λυ–) as was used to form the present.

The Augment.

For verbs whose root begins with a consonant, the imperfect tense is normally formed by prefixing an ἐ to the present stem and adding the endings of the proper voice, either active or middle/ passive. The prefixed ἐ is called an "augment", and indicates that the action in question is in past time. It is found only in the indicative mood. The augment in ἐ always has the smooth breathing.

When the present stem of the verb begins with a vowel or a diphthong, the augment is formed not by prefixing the letter ἐ but by lengthening the vowel or diphthong according to the following rules:

α becomes η: ἀκούω > ἤκουον
ε becomes η: ἐσθίω > ἤσθιον
ι becomes ῑ: ἰσχύω > ἴσχυον (The macron [ˉ] over the iota is not written.)
ο becomes ω: ὀνομάζω > ὠνόμαζον
υ becomes ῡ: ὑβρίζω > ὕβριζον (The macron [ˉ] over the upsilon is not written.)
αι becomes η: αἴρω > ἦρον (The iota in the diphthong αι becomes a iota subscript in the augmented form.)
αυ becomes ηυ: αὐξάνω > ηὔξανον
ευ becomes ηυ or remains the same: εὑρίσκω > ηὕρισκον or εὕρισκον
οι becomes ῳ: οἰκτίρω > ᾤκτιρον (The iota in the diphthong οι becomes a iota subscript in the augmented form.)

The written forms of long ι and υ are not distinguished from the short ι and υ. In the pronunciation the distinction could be made by a slight lengthening of the sound.

The breathing for the augment formed by the prefixing of an ε is always smooth. But the breathing for an augment formed by the lengthening of a vowel or diphthong retains the same breathing as in the unaugmented form of the present root. Thus ἀκούω becomes ἤκουον and αὐξάνω becomes ηὔξανον, while ὑβρίζω becomes ὕβριζον and εὑρίσκω becomes ηὕρισκον / εὕρισκον.

The augment of ἔχω is irregular: εἶχον.

Compound Verbs, I.

In Greek, many verbs are called "compound" verbs because they are compounded of a prefix (usually a preposition) and a simple (i.e., non-compound) verb. Thus, the verb ἀπολύω, *I release*, is composed of the prefix ἀπό and the simple verb λύω. <u>In such verbs the augment is normally placed immediately before the simple verb or root</u>. Thus, ἀπέλυον is the form for the first person singular or the third person plural, i.e., the final vowel of ἀπο drops before the augment, and ἀπο–ἐλυον becomes ἀπέλυον. The final vowel of most prefixes drops before an augment. The most common exceptions to this rule are the prepositions περί and πρό: περιῆγον, προέβαινον. (It should be noted that these two prefixes retain their final vowel elsewhere before the verbal form, when the latter begins with a vowel. For example, περιάγω is the present tense of the verb from which the imperfect περιῆγον is formed. There is also a verb προάγω, the imperfect of which is προῆγον.) [Cf. also Compound Verbs, II, in the following lesson.]

The Noun Ἄραψ.

Labial roots of third declension nouns end in π, β, or φ, consonants which are called "labials" because their pronunciation involves the lips. They are declined as follows (Ἄραψ, *Arab*) (cf. N 12):

	Singular	Plural
n	Ἄραψ	Ἄραβες
v	Ἄραψ	Ἄραβες
g	Ἄραβος	Ἀράβων
d	Ἄραβι	Ἄραψι(ν)
a	Ἄραβα	Ἄραβας

The root of the labials may be determined by eliminating the ending –ος from the genitive singular. Thus the root of Ἄραψ is Ἄραβ–.

In the dative plural a root ending in π is not written πσ but ψ. The letter ψ is called a "double consonant" because it is simply a way of writing the two consonants πσ. The letter ψ also results from the meeting in the dative plural of β with σ (as in Ἄραψ) and of φ with σ. But the process by which this occurs is more complicated.

There are few nouns in this category in the New Testament.

Rules for Accents 2.

A syllable is short if it contains a short vowel or a diphthong which, for purposes of accent, is considered short. A syllable is long if it contains a long vowel or a diphthong which is considered long. (Diphthongs are normally considered long unless explicitly noted as being otherwise.)

An acute accent and a grave accent may stand over a syllable which is long or a syllable which is short. A circumflex accent may stand only over a syllable which is long. As was stated above in Lesson 1, the letters η and ω are always long. Thus, words accented in the following ways are found: βοῶντος, τῇ, ἁμαρτιῶν, τῷ, ἦν, ποταμῷ, ἦλθεν, τῶν, οὐρανῶν.

The letters η and ω need not always have a circumflex accent. Acute and grave accents over them are possible. Thus words accented in the following ways are found: Ἀρχὴ, καθὼς, προφήτῃ, προσώπου, τὴν, φωνή, ἐρήμῳ, χώρα.

The letters ε and o are always short. Thus words accented in the following ways are <u>impossible</u>: ἀποστέλλω, τόν, πρό, ὅς, πρός, ἐνδεδυμένος, μέλι, λέγων.

When the letters ε or o have accents they are either acute or grave: γέγραπται, ἀποστέλλω, τὸν, πρὸ, δὲ, ὁδόν, ἐγένετο, πρός.

The letters α, ι, and υ may be long or short. Thus they may have all three types of accent: εὐαγγελίου, κατασκευάσει, κηρύσσων, πᾶσα, Ἱεροσολυμῖται, λῦσαι, εἰμὶ, περὶ, ὀσφὺν, εὐθὺς, περιστερὰν, μετὰ.

The fact that πᾶσα, Ἱεροσολυμῖται, and λῦσαι have circumflex accents indicates that the vowels α, ι, and υ are long. But the fact that an α, a ι, or an υ has an acute accent does not necessarily mean that it is short, because other rules for accents may make the acute necessary.

Diphthongs are considered long except for final −αι and −οι (but even final −αι and −οι are considered long in the optative mood and in contracted adjectives). Thus the circumflex accent is often found over a diphthong: Ἰησοῦ, Χριστοῦ, ποιεῖτε, καταβαῖνον, πνεῦμα, τοῖς, καῦσις, ἐληλυθυῖαν. But even diphthongs which are considered long can, of course, have acute and grave accents: ἰδοὺ, εὐθείας, μετανοίας, ἐξεπορεύετο, Ἰουδαία, ηὔξησεν.

Final −οι and −αι never have circumflex accents: μαθηταὶ, μαθηταί, υἱοὶ, υἱοί. An exception to this rule is found in the case of syllables formed through contraction.

In the optative mood the fact that a final −αι or −οι is long shows itself only indirectly, by influencing the accentuation of the previous syllables in the word. This phenomenon will be pointed out when the optative mood is presented in the paradigms.

Vocabulary for Lesson 10.

ὑπό [Prep 2] Governs genitive or accusative case. With the genitive: *by* [This is the normal way in which the personal agent of an action is expressed with a verb in the passive voice.] With the accusative: *under*.

Ἄραψ, Ἄραβος, ὁ [N 12] *Arab.*

λαῖλαψ, λαίλαπος, ἡ [N 11f] *storm.*

αἴρω [V 6, DV 8, VP 1] *I take up; I remove.*

ἀκούω [V 1, DV 11, VP 1] Cf. Lesson 3, where the second person singular of the present indicative active was given. *I hear; I listen (to).* This verb is followed by the accusative or the genitive; various interpretations are given to explain the reason why one or the other case is used.

αὐξάνω [V 7, DV 30, VP 1]. When used transitively, i.e., with a direct object: *I make grow*; intransitively: *I grow* (this form, of course, can be transitive as well as intransitive in English).

ἐσθίω or ἔσθω [V 1, DV 101, VP 1] *I eat.*

εὑρίσκω [V 2, DV 106, VP 1] *I find, I discover.*

ἰσχύω [V 1, VP 1] *I am strong; I am able.*

οἰκτίρω [V 6, DV 214, VP 1] *I have mercy on.* This verb governs the accusative case and does not require a preposition as in English.

ὀνομάζω [V 5, VP 1] *I call by name; I name.*

ὑβρίζω [V 5, VP 1] *I insult.*

ἀλλά [Conj] *but*.

Exercises for Lesson 10.

I. Translate into English:
1. οἱ στρατιῶται οὐκ ἴσχυον εἶναι ἀγαθοί. (Lk 16:3)
2. ὁ Κύριος ᾤκτιρε τοὺς Ἄραβας.
3. ἀλλὰ ὁ Κύριος ὠνόμαζεν τοὺς μαθητὰς ἀποστόλους.
   (Mk 3:14)
4. οἱ δοῦλοι αἴρουσι τὰ ἱμάτια αὐτῶν εἰς ὁδόν. (Mk 6:8)
5. ὁ στρατιώτης ἠκούσθη ὑπὸ τοῦ Ἰησοῦ. (Mk 1:5)
   [ἠκούσθη is the third person singular of the aorist
   indicative passive and means "(he) was heard".]
6. ἐκεῖνοι οἱ πονηροὶ ὕβριζον τοὺς δούλους αὐτοῦ. (Mt
   22:6) [πονηροὶ is an adjective used here as a noun.]
7. ἄνθρωπός εἰμι ὑπὸ ἐξουσίαν ὤν. (Lk 7:8)
8. ὁ Ἰησοῦς ἔρχεται καὶ εὑρίσκει αὐτούς. (Mk 14:37)
9. ἀλλὰ ἡ λαῖλαψ ηὔξανεν ἐν ἐκείνῃ τῇ νυκτί. (Lk 2:40)
10. ὑμεῖς οὐκ ἠκούετε, ἀλλ' ἐλέγετε.
11. ὁ Ἰησοῦς ἤσθιε μετὰ τῶν πονηρῶν ἀνθρώπων. (Mk
    2:16)
12. καὶ ἐκεῖνοί εἰσιν οἳ ἀκούουσιν τὸν λόγον. (Mk 4:20)

II. Translate into Greek:
1. This crowd was listening to him, but that crowd was not
   listening to him. (Mk 12:37)
2. Jesus names Andrew a disciple. (Lk 6:14)
3. The word of God was growing in that kingdom. (Acts 6:7)

III. Mk 1:43-45.

The Future Active Indicative. λύω, Future
Active Indicative. Various Types of Stems
and the Formation of the Future. Verbs
Having Present Stems Ending in –ζ. The
Noun ἐλπίς. Compound Verbs, II. Rules for
Accents 3.

Lesson 11

The Future Active Indicative.

The future tense is based on the future stem, which conveys the
aspect of an action as being subsequent. In the indicative mood this
subsequent action indicates the future of primary time. (Cf. Lesson
9.) In the future system in the New Testament there are also the
infinitive and participial moods, but no subjunctive, optative, or
imperative. The precise force of these moods in the future tense will
be explained below, in Lesson 17. Only the indicative mood of the
future tense presents an action as taking place in a future viewed
independently of another verb. The infinitive and participial moods
in the future, as elsewhere, are dependent on other verbs and hence
can express the future only relatively, i.e., of themselves they cannot
express the future of primary time.
     For the meaning of the active voice cf. Lesson 9.

λύω, Future Active Indicative.

The future stem of the active voice in the indicative mood of λύω is
formed by adding a σ to the present stem: λυσ–. The endings are of
the present indicative active (cf. V 1, VP 1). (The present stem of a
verb is found by dropping the ending of the present infinitive.)

Future Tense, Active Voice, Indicative Mood

	Singular	Plural
1st Person	λύσ–ω	λύσ–ομεν
2nd Person	λύσ–εις	λύσ–ετε
3rd Person	λύσ–ει	λύσ–ουσι(ν)

I shall loose   *We shall loose*
You (sg.) *will loose*   *You* (pl.) *will loose*
He (She, It) will loose   *They will loose*

Various Types of Stems and the Formation of the Future.

Verbs whose present stem ends in a palatal (κ, γ, χ) form the future stem by having a ξ in place of the palatal and the σ. (Cf. the formation of the dative masculine and neuter plural of σάρξ, above, Lesson 9).   Verbs whose present stem ends in a labial (π, β, φ) form the future stem by having a ψ in place of the labial and the σ. (Cf. the formation of the dative masculine and neuter plural of Ἄραψ, above, Lesson 10.) Verbs whose present stem ends in a dental (τ, δ, θ) form the future stem by having one σ, i.e., the dental drops. (Cf. the formation of the dative masculine and neuter plural of ἐλπίς, below, in this lesson.)

$$ἀγ-ω > ἄξ-ω \qquad βλέπ-ω > βλέψ-ω \qquad πείθ-ω > πείσ-ω$$

A number of verbs have irregular forms in the future. This phenomenon will be explained in future lessons.
The future of ἔχω is irregular: ἕξω [note the rough breathing].

Verbs Having Present Stems Ending in –ζ.

Many verbs which have a dental root have a present tense in which a ζ appears before the endings, e.g., βαπτίζω. In the future the underlying dental root asserts itself normally so that the form has only a σ, the dental dropping, e.g., βαπτίσω. (The reason for the ζ need not be learned.) There are many verbs in this category.
There are also a few verbs having a present tense in which a ζ appears before the endings but which have a palatal stem, e.g., κράζω. These latter verbs have a future in which the palatal stem asserts itself normally so that the form has a ξ, e.g., κράξω.
There is no rule for distinguishing the two categories according to the appearances of the present tense. (Only a knowledge of the etymology of each verb in question makes categorization possible.) Hence in the vocabulary entries in this grammar any verb ending in ζ in the present tense will be accompanied by its future form so that the category in which the verb belongs, dental or palatal, will be clear.

In case of doubt, the student is advised to presuppose that the category is that of a dental, inasmuch as there are many more verbs in this category.

The Noun ἐλπίς.

Dental roots of third declension nouns end in τ, δ, or θ. They are declined as follows (ἐλπίς, *hope*) (cf. N. 14f):

	Singular	Plural
n	ἐλπίς	ἐλπίδες
v	ἐλπίς	ἐλπίδες
g	ἐλπίδος	ἐλπίδων
d	ἐλπίδι	ἐλπίσι(ν)
a	ἐλπίδα	ἐλπίδας

The root of the dentals may be determined by eliminating the ending –ος from the form of the genitive singular. (The root of any third-declension noun may be learned in this way.) Thus the root of ἐλπίς is ἐλπιδ–.

In the dative plural a root ending in δ is not written δσ but simply σ, i.e., the δ drops. The same is true for roots ending in τ or θ. (Cf. the formation of the future tense of verbs whose root ends in a dental, as explained above in this lesson.)

There are other types of nouns having dental roots, but they are not numerous. They will be presented in subsequent lessons.

Compound Verbs, II.

Some prefixes of compound verbs modify their final consonant. For example, the verb ἐκβαίνω becomes ἐξέβαινον in the imperfect, according to the normal rule: ἐκ before consonants, ἐξ before vowels. Still other final consonants of prefixes are modified when they are prefixed to a root, regardless of the tense. For example, the preposition ἐν becomes ἐμ before a verb beginning with a β. Thus ἐμβαίνω. In the imperfect, when the augment is interposed between the prefix and the root, the prefix regains its normal form: ἐνέβαινον. If the root begins with a rough breathing, the prefix may also be modified. For example, the final consonant π of the prefix ἀπο becomes φ before the root: αἰρέω becomes ἀφαιρέω (ἀπο–αἰρέω > ἀπ–αἰρέω > ἀφαιρέω). In the imperfect the form is ἀφήρουν, the ending being modified according to the rules for contract verbs in ε given below, in Lesson 46.

In the vocabulary entries dealing with compound verbs the prefix or prefixes will be given in their full form together with the form of the simple verb or the word from which the verbal form comes.

Rules for Accents 3.

An acute accent may stand on the third-last syllable only if the final syllable is short. Thus γέγραπται and ἑτοιμάσατε. If a word has an acute accent on the third-last syllable of a word when the final syllable of the word is short, the accent recedes to the second-last syllable when the final syllable of the word becomes long. Thus ἄγγελος in the nominative case, but ἀγγέλου in the genitive.

A circumflex accent may stand on the second-last syllable only if the last syllable is short. Thus βοῶντος, but προσώπου. If there is a circumflex accent in the nominative when the final syllable is short, that circumflex changes to an acute when the final syllable becomes long. Thus ἐκεῖνος, but ἐκείνου.

An acute accent on the final syllable of a word should be changed to a grave accent before a word which is not an enclitic unless a punctuation mark intervenes. The enclitics will be explained in Lesson 12. Thus far in this grammar the following enclitics have been seen: μου, μοι, and με of the first person pronoun, and σου, σοι, and σε of the second person pronoun; all forms of the present indicative of the verb εἰμί except the second person singular (εἶ). Thus ἀρχὴ τοῦ, καθὼς γέγραπται, and τὴν ὁδόν, but ἀδελφοί μου, υἱός σου, and ἄνθρωποί εἰσιν. τοῦ, γέγραπται, and ὁδόν are not enclitics; therefore the acute accent on ἀρχή, καθώς, and τήν is changed to a grave accent. But μου, σου, and εἰσιν are enclitics; therefore the acute accent on ἀδελφοί, υἱός, and ἄνθρωποί remains.

Contrast the word αὐτόν in Mk 1:10 with the word αὐτὸν in Mk 1:26. The αὐτόν of Mk 1:10 occurs before a punctuation mark; therefore even though the following word (καί) is not an enclitic, the final syllable of αὐτόν retains the acute accent. The αὐτόν of Mk 1:26 occurs immediately before a non-enclitic (τὸ—the fact that it has a grave accent is irrelevant) with no intervening punction; hence its acute accent on the final syllable is changed to a grave accent.

Vocabulary for Lesson 11.

ὑπέρ [Prep 2] Governs the genitive and the accusative cases. With the genitive: *on behalf of, in favor of, in place of.* With the accusative: *above; more than.*

———

ἄγω [V 2, DV 5, VP 1] *I lead, I conduct.*

βαπτίζω [βαπτίσω] [V 5, DV 33, VP 1] *I baptize; I wash.*

δοξάζω [δοξάσω] [V 5, VP 1] *I glorify.*

κράζω [κράξω] [V 3, DV 163, VP 1] *I shout, I cry out.*

πείθω [V 5, DV 235, VP 1] *I persuade.* This irregular verb has special idiomatic meanings in the perfect active and in the passive; cf. Lesson 58.

πειράζω [πειράσω] [V 5, VP 1] *I test; I tempt; I attempt.*

———

ἐλπίς, ἐλπίδος, ἡ [N 14f] *hope.*

λαμπάς, λαμπάδος, ἡ [N 14f] *lamp.*

παῖς, παιδός, ὁ/ἡ [N 14m and 14f] *boy; girl; child; servant.*

πατρίς, πατρίδος, ἡ [N 14f] *native place.*

πούς, ποδός, ὁ [N 14m and N 33] *foot.*

σφραγίς, σφραγίδος, ἡ [N 14f] *seal.*

———

ὅτι [Conj] This frequently-used word has three basic meanings: 1) *because*, as an introduction to a causal clause; 2) quotation marks (". . ."), as an introduction to a direct quotation; 3) *that*, as an introduction to an indirect quotation. These meanings can be distinguished only by means of the context.

Exercises for Lesson 11.

I. Translate into English:
    1. ὁ παῖς οὐκ εἶχε πόδας. (Mt 18:8)

2. οἱ ἄνθρωποι ἔκραζον. (Mk 3:11)

3. λέγω ὅτι αὐτὸς ἁμαρτωλός ἐστιν ὅτι ἡ καρδία αὐτοῦ πονηρά ἐστιν. [Cf. Lesson 24, Vocabulary, for the meaning of ἁμαρτωλός.]

4. ὃς γὰρ οὐκ ἔστιν καθ᾽ ἡμῶν, ὑπὲρ ἡμῶν ἐστιν. (Mk 9:40) [καθ᾽ ἡμῶν = κατὰ ἡμῶν: κατὰ loses the final –α before the initial η of ἡμῶν, and the –τ of κατ᾽ becomes –θ because it becomes "assimilated" to the following rough breathing at the beginning of ἡμῶν.]

5. διὰ τὸν διάβολον ἐπείραζον τὸν θεόν. (Acts 15:10)

6. ὁ Ἰησοῦς ἔρχεται εἰς τὴν πατρίδα αὐτοῦ. (Mk 6:1)

7. αὐτὸς ὑμᾶς βαπτίσει. (Mt 3:11)

8. οὐκ ἔστιν δοῦλος ὑπὲρ τὸν κύριον αὐτοῦ. (Mt 10:24)

9. οἱ ἀδελφοὶ ἔπειθον αὐτούς. (Acts 13:43)

10. ἡ γὰρ σφραγίς μου ὑμεῖς ἐστε. (1 Cor 9:2)

11. λέγουσιν ὅτι ἐβλέπομεν τὸν Κύριον.

12. ἄγουσιν οὖν τὸν Ἰησοῦν ἀπὸ τοῦ οἴκου. (Jn 18:28)

13. οὐκ ἔρχεται ὁ λῃστὴς μετὰ λαμπάδων. (Jn 18:3)

14. ἐγὼ οὐ δοξάσω αὐτόν. (Jn 8:54)

15. εἶχεν ἐλπίδα εἰς τὸν θεόν. (Acts 24:15)

16. αὐτὸς ἁμαρτωλὸς ὅτι ἡ καρδία αὐτοῦ πονηρά ἐστιν. [Cf. Lesson 24, Vocabulary, for the meaning of ἁμαρτωλός.]

17. ὁ θεὸς ἐδόξαζε τὸν παῖδα αὐτοῦ Ἰησοῦν. (Acts 3:13)

II. Translate into Greek:
  1. These are the ones on behalf of whom I was speaking. (Jn 1:30)
  2. A disciple is not above the Lord. (Mt 10:24)
  3. I am leading him to Jesus. (Jn 19:4) [To translate "to Jesus" use πρός with accusative—cf. Lesson 14, Vocabulary.]

III. Mk 2:1-5.

The Meaning of the Present Active
Imperative. λύω, Present Active
Imperative. The Nouns ποιμήν, εἰκών,
μήν, and αἰών. The Reflexive Pronouns
ἐμαυτοῦ, σεαυτοῦ, and ἑαυτοῦ. Rules
for Accents 4.

Lesson 12

The Meaning of the Present Active Imperative.

The present stem normally conveys the aspect of an action as not
terminated. (Cf. Lesson 9.) In the indicative mood this use of the
present stem conveys the idea of an action which is present in terms
of primary time if there is no augment, and of an action which is
past in terms of primary time if there is. In the imperative mood of
the present the aspect conveyed is that of an action not terminated.
In practice this means that the present of the imperative mood
usually conveys the idea of a general precept, i.e., a rule of conduct
to be followed in more than one situation.

The student will by now have seen that the word "present" as
used in New Testament Greek is ambiguous. In itself the word
"present" normally refers to primary time, i.e., "present" as
opposed to past and future. But in New Testament Greek it also
indicates the type of stem which conveys the idea of an action not
terminated. The first meaning of "present" is present in the sense
of "present tense", whereas the second meaning of present is
present in the sense of "present system", i.e., a system which
conveys the present aspect. They are intrinsically related, of course.
All verbs in the present tense belong to the present system, i.e., have
a present root and express the present aspect; but not all verbs in the
present system express present time. There is no uniformity in
usage in New Testament grammars, but continued attention to the
precise meaning of the word "present" in its context should help
bring into focus the student's knowledge of the Greek verbal system.

For the meaning of the active voice cf. Lesson 9.

For the meaning of the imperative mood cf. Lesson 4.

λύω, Present Active Imperative.

The present tense, imperative mood, active voice of λύω (V 1, VP 1):

	Present Tense, Active Voice, Imperative Mood	
	Singular	Plural
2nd Person	λῦ–ε	λύ–ετε
3rd Person	λυ–έτω	λυ–έτωσαν
	[You] Loosen!	[You] Loosen!
	Let him [her, it] loosen!	Let them loosen!

The word λύω has been translated here as *loosen* in order to avoid the ambiguities inherent in the use of *loose*. (In English the phrase *Let him loose!* can mean *Allow him to be loose*, as well as *He should set loose someone else*. In the present context only the latter meaning is appropriate.)

The first person of the imperative mood does not exist. Its place is taken by the use of the subjunctive mood in the first person, usually in the plural, to express exhortation: *Let us loosen* [*him, her, it, them*, etc.]. (Cf. Lesson 71.)

In line with the interpretation given above of the imperative mood in the present system, a translation of [*You*] *keep loosening!*, or [*You*] *continue to loosen!* could be defended. But the full force of the present imperative can be seen only when it is contrasted with the aorist imperative. (Cf. Lesson 19.)

The Nouns ποιμήν, εἰκών, μήν, and αἰών.

Nasal roots of third declension nouns end in –ν. (The nasal cosonants are –μ and –ν.) There are two categories: 1) nouns which show a variation in the length of the vowel in the stem; 2) nouns which show no variation in the length of the vowel in the stem.

Nouns which show a variation in the length of the vowel in the stem are declined as follows (ποιμήν, *shepherd*; εἰκών, *image*) (cf. N 18m and N 20f):

	Singular	Plural
n	ποιμήν	ποιμένες
v	ποιμήν	ποιμένες
g	ποιμένος	ποιμένων
d	ποιμένι	ποιμέσι(ν)
a	ποιμένα	ποιμένας

	Singular	Plural
n	εἰκών	εἰκόνες
v	εἰκών	εἰκόνες
g	εἰκόνος	εἰκόνων
d	εἰκόνι	εἰκόσι(ν)
a	εἰκόνα	εἰκόνας

The root of ποιμήν is ποιμεν–; the root of εἰκών is εἰκον–. These roots are found by dropping the genitive singular ending. In the dative plural the ν of the root is omitted before the σ of the ending.

Nouns which do not show a variation in the length of the vowel in the stem are declined as follows (μήν, *month*; αἰών, *age*) (cf. N 19 and N 21m):

	Singular	Plural
n	μήν	μῆνες
v	μήν	μῆνες
g	μηνός	μηνῶν
d	μηνί	μησί(ν)
a	μῆνα	μῆνας

	Singular	Plural
n	αἰών	αἰῶνες
v	αἰών	αἰῶνες
g	αἰῶνος	αἰώνων
d	αἰῶνι	αἰῶσι(ν)
a	αἰῶνα	αἰῶνας

The root of μήν is μην–; the root of αἰών is αἰων–. In the dative plural the ν is omitted before the σ of the ending.

The Reflexive Pronouns ἐμαυτοῦ, σεαυτοῦ, and ἑαυτοῦ.

A reflexive pronoun is a pronoun which refers back to the subject, expressed or implicit, of the sentence or clause in which it occurs. The nominative case does not occur. The neuter in the first and second person singular is not found in the New Testament (cf. Pro).

	First Person, Singular		
	Masculine	Feminine	Neuter
g	ἐμαυτοῦ	ἐμαυτῆς	—
d	ἐμαυτῷ	ἐμαυτῇ	—
a	ἐμαυτόν	ἐμαυτήν	—

First Person, Plural

	Masculine	Feminine	Neuter
g	ἑαυτῶν	ἑαυτῶν	ἑαυτῶν
d	ἑαυτοῖς	ἑαυταῖς	ἑαυτοῖς
a	ἑαυτούς	ἑαυτάς	ἑαυτά

Second Person, Singular

	Masculine	Feminine	Neuter
g	σεαυτοῦ	σεαυτῆς	—
d	σεαυτῷ	σεαυτῇ	—
a	σεαυτόν	σεαυτήν	—

Second Person, Plural

	Masculine	Feminine	Neuter
g	ἑαυτῶν	ἑαυτῶν	ἑαυτῶν
d	ἑαυτοῖς	ἑαυταῖς	ἑαυτοῖς
a	ἑαυτούς	ἑαυτάς	ἑαυτά

Third Person, Singular

	Masculine	Feminine	Neuter
g	ἑαυτοῦ	ἑαυτῆς	ἑαυτοῦ
d	ἑαυτῷ	ἑαυτῇ	ἑαυτῷ
a	ἑαυτόν	ἑαυτήν	ἑαυτό

Third Person, Plural

	Masculine	Feminine	Neuter
g	ἑαυτῶν	ἑαυτῶν	ἑαυτῶν
d	ἑαυτοῖς	ἑαυταῖς	ἑαυτοῖς
a	ἑαυτούς	ἑαυτάς	ἑαυτά

<u>It should be noted that the plural forms are the same for all three persons</u>.

λέγομεν ἑαυτοῖς (ἑαυταῖς).
We speak to ourselves.

λέγετε ἑαυτοῖς (ἑαυταῖς).
You speak to yourselves.

λέγουσιν ἑαυτοῖς (ἑαυταῖς).
They speak to themselves.

Strictly speaking, the forms ἑαυτοῦ, ἑαυτῆς, or ἑαυτῶν should always be used when there is question of a reflexive usage in the third person involving possession. But as was noted above in Lesson 8, the persons who composed New Testament Greek did not always write according to strict rules: the genitive case of the non-reflexive third person pronoun is often used to express a reflexive idea.

> ἔβλεπε τὸν οἶκον αὐτοῦ.
> *He was seeing his* (i.e., his own) *house.*

Strict usage would have demanded the following:

> ἔβλεπε τὸν οἶκον ἑαυτοῦ.
> *He was seeing his own house.*

A third way of expressing the reflexive idea occurs in the New Testament: the third person non-reflexive pronoun with a rough breathing:

> ἔβλεπε τὸν οἶκον αὑτοῦ.
> *He was seeing his own house.*

In the last two examples there is no ambiguity as regards the meaning, because the forms are reflexive. In the first example the form is ambiguous, but the context normally shows that it is to be understood in a reflexive (or non-reflexive!) way.

Rules for Accents 4.

In the previous lessons, in "Rules for Accents 3", a distinction was made between most words which have been seen so far in the vocabulary listings and a small selection of words called "enclitics". Enclitics are words which tend to transfer their accent to the preceding word if this word is capable of receiving it. (The word "enclitic" comes from a Greek verb meaning *to lean on*.) As was indicated above in Lesson 11, the enclitics seen thus far are μου, μοι, and με of the first person pronoun; σου, σοι, and σε of the second person pronoun; and the forms of the present tense of the indicative mood of εἰμί except for the second person singular. The pronominal forms are weak counterparts to the accented forms of the same case, and normally indicate less emphasis on the person in question.

Contrast ἀπ' ἐμοῦ (Mk 7:6) with ἄγγελόν μου (Mk 1:2); Τί ἐμοὶ καὶ σοί (Mk 5:7—the interrogative pronoun τί never has a grave accent) with 'Ακολούθει μοι (Mk 2:14); ζητοῦσίν σε (Mk 1:37) with πρὸς σέ (Mk 9:17). Cf. also ἔνοχός ἐστιν (Mk 3:29) and πολλοί ἐσμεν (Mk 5:9) for examples involving the verb εἰμί.

Vocabulary for Lesson 12.

ἐπί [Prep 3] Governs the genitive, dative, and accusative cases. With genitive: *on*; *before* [spatial]; *over* [either spatial or in the transferred meaning *about*]; *at the time of*. With the dative: *at*; *on*; *on the basis of*. With the accusative: *on*; *with regard to*; *against*; *at* [temporal]. There is no sharp distinction among the various cases with regard to the meaning *on*.

___

λιμήν, λιμένος, ὁ [N 18m] *harbor*.

ποιμήν, ποιμένος, ὁ [N 18m] *shepherd*.

___

βραχίων, βραχίονος, ὁ [N 20m] *arm*; [*divine*] *power*.

γείτων, γείτονος, ὁ/ἡ [N 20m and N 20f] *neighbor*.

δαίμων, δαίμονος, ὁ [N 20m] *demon*; [*evil*] *spirit*.

εἰκών, εἰκόνος, ἡ [N 20f] *image*.

ἡγεμών, ἡγεμόνος, ὁ [N 20m] *leader*; *governor*.

χιών, χιόνος, ἡ [N 20f] *snow*.

___

"Ελλην, "Ελληνος, ὁ [N 19] *Greek*.

μήν, μηνός, ὁ [N 19] *month*.

___

ἀγών, ἀγῶνος, ὁ [N 21m] *struggle*.

αἰών, αἰῶνος, ὁ [N 21m] *age*; *epoch*.

ἀμπελών, ἀμπελῶνος, ὁ [N 21m] *vineyard*.

χειμών, χειμῶνος, ὁ [N 21m] *winter*; [*winter*] *storm*.

χιτών, χιτῶνος, ὁ [N 21m] *tunic*.

———

ἐμαυτοῦ [Pro] *of my own*.

ἑαυτῶν [Pro] *of our own*.

σεαυτοῦ [Pro] *of your* [sg.] *own*.

ἑαυτῶν [Pro] *of your* [pl.] *own*.

ἑαυτοῦ [Pro] *of his* [*her, its*] *own*.

ἑαυτῶν [Pro] *of their own*.

———

ἤ [Conj] *or*; *than*. When used in comparisons ἤ takes the same
case after as before.

Exercises for Lesson 12.

I. Translate into English:
1. οἱ γείτονες ἔλεγον· οὗτός ἐστιν. (Jn 9:8)
2. ὁ υἱὸς τοῦ ἀνθρώπου ἔχει ἐξουσίαν ἐπὶ τῆς γῆς. (Mk 2:10)
3. οὐκ ἔχομεν ἄρτον μεθ᾽ ἑαυτῶν. [μεθ᾽ = μετά before a vowel with a rough breathing. Cf. Lesson 11, Sentence 4.]
4. τὸ ἱμάτιον αὐτοῦ ἦν ἐπὶ τῆς χιόνος.
5. ἔχετε τὸν αὐτὸν ἀγῶνα ὃν ἐβλέπετε ἐν ἐμοὶ καὶ νῦν ἀκούετε ἐν ἐμοί. (Phil 1:30)
6. ἀπὸ σεαυτοῦ σὺ τοῦτο λέγεις; (Jn 18:34)
7. ἔξει ζωὴν ἐν τῷ αἰῶνι ὃς ἔρχεται. (Mk 10:30) [ἔρχεται is a present tense with a future meaning. This usage is found also in English, e.g., "I am coming tomorrow". The context determines whether the present form has a present meaning or a future meaning.]
8. οἱ στρατιῶται οὐκ ἔχουσιν χιτῶνας.
9. διδάσκαλε, ἐπ᾽ ἀληθείας λέγεις. (Mk 12:32) [Cf. Lesson 22, Vocabulary, for the meaning of διδάσκαλος.]

10. ἐν τῷ χειμῶνι χιών ἐστιν.
11, ὁ Χριστός ἐστιν εἰκὼν τοῦ θεοῦ. (2 Cor 4:4)
12. ὁ Ἕλλην ἔλεγεν ἐν ἑαυτῷ. (Mk 16:3)
13. ἐγώ εἰμι ὁ ποιμὴν ὁ καλός. (Jn 10:11)
14. μετὰ τοῦτον τὸν μῆνα ἔσται ἐν τῷ οἴκῳ αὐτῆς.
15. ἔρχεται ὁ ἄνθρωπος ἐπὶ τῷ ὀνόματι τοῦ Κυρίου. (Mk
    13:6) [Cf. Lesson 16, Vocabulary, for the meaning of
    ὄνομα.]
16. ἔχω ὑπ' ἐμαυτὸν στρατιώτας. (Lk 7:8)
17. ἐπὶ ἡγεμόνων ἔσεσθε. (Mk 13:9)
18. ὁ κύριος ἔχει ἀμπελῶνα ἐν ἐκείνῃ τῇ γῇ.
19. οὐκ ἦν λιμὴν ἐπὶ τῆς νήσου.
20. οὐκ ἔχετε ἄρτον μεθ' ἑαυτῶν. [μεθ' = μετά before a
    vowel with a rough breathing. Cf. Lesson 11, Sentence
    4.]
21. μετὰ βραχίονος ἦγεν αὐτοὺς ἐκ τῆς γῆς. (Acts 13:17)
22. ἔρχεται εἰς ἐκκλησίαν ἢ εἰς οἶκον.
23. οἱ δαίμονες οὐκ ἤκουον αὐτόν.
24. ἐδίδασκεν τοὺς Ἕλληνας. (Jn 7:35) [Cf. Lesson 20,
    Vocabulary, for meaning of διδάσκω.]
25. οὐκ ἔχουσιν ἄρτον μεθ' ἑαυτῶν.
26. ἔρχεται ἐπὶ τὸν τόπον. (Lk 19:5)

II. Translate into Greek:
    1. Let love be upon the earth and in the hearts of men.
       (Mt 9:4; Lk 2:14)
    2. The Lord is the good shepherd and he will be with his
       people. (Jn 10:11)
    3. I say that Jesus is the image of God and the glory of
       men. (1 Cor 11:7)

III. Mk 2:6-12.

The Meaning of the Present Active
Subjunctive. λύω, Present Active
Subjunctive. The Nouns πατήρ, ῥήτωρ,
and σωτήρ. The Reciprocal Pronoun
ἀλλήλων. Rules for Accents 5.

Lesson 13

The Meaning of the Present Active Subjunctive.

In the present system the subjunctive conveys the viewpoint of an
action being considered as not terminated. This basic viewpoint is
usually elaborated by other indications in the text so that the action
is viewed as continuing or repeated, or is viewed as customary, or is
considered as describing the action signified by the meaning of the
verb. (It should be recalled that only the indicative mood conveys the
present of primary time.)

For the meaning of the active voice cf. above, Lesson 9.

For the meaning of the subjunctive mood cf. above, Lesson 5.
Although the purpose clause is perhaps the most important use of
the subjunctive mood in the New Testament, other uses will be
presented in future lessons.

λύω, Present Active Subjunctive.

The present subjunctive active of λύω is conjugated as follows (cf. V
1, VP 1):

	Active Voice, Subjunctive Mood, Present Tense	
	Singular	Plural
1st Person	λύ–ω	λύ–ωμεν
2nd Person	λύ–ῃς	λύ–ητε
3rd Person	λύ–ῃ	λύ–ωσι(ν)

The iota subscript in the second and third person singular
should be noted.

The Nouns πατήρ, ῥήτωρ, and σωτήρ.

Liquid stems of third declension nouns end in −λ and −ρ. (The consonants −λ and −ρ are known as "liquids".) But the λ-stem occurs in the New Testament only in the rare word ἅλς, ἁλός, ὁ, *salt*. The ρ-stem is divided into two categories: 1) those nouns which show a variation in the length of the vowel in the stem; 2) those nouns which show no variation in the length of the vowel in the stem.

Nouns which show a variation in the length of the vowel in the stem are divided into two types. One, exemplified by πατήρ, *father*, has abbreviated forms in the genitive singular and dative singular and plural; the other, ῥήτωρ, *orator*, has no such abbreviated forms (cf. N 24m and N 33, N 26):

	Singular	Plural
n	πατήρ	πατέρες
v	πάτερ	πατέρες
g	πατρός	πατέρων
d	πατρί	πατράσι(ν)
a	πατέρα	πατέρας

The second stem vowel of πατήρ, ε, is dropped in the genitive and dative singular and in the dative plural. The −ασι of the dative plural is a result of phonological changes proper to the Greek language.

	Singular	Plural
n	ῥήτωρ	ῥήτορες
v	ῥῆτορ	ῥήτορες
g	ῥήτορος	ῥητόρων
d	ῥήτορι	ῥήτορσι(ν)
a	ῥήτορα	ῥήτορας

	Singular	Plural
n	σωτήρ	σωτῆρες
v	σωτήρ	σωτῆρες
g	σωτῆρος	σωτήρων
d	σωτῆρι	σωτῆρσι(ν)
a	σωτῆρα	σωτῆρας

The Reciprocal Pronoun ἀλλήλων.

The reciprocal pronoun in the New Testament is limited to the masculine gender (cf. Pro):

	Masculine	Plural Feminine	Neuter
g	ἀλλήλων	—	—
d	ἀλλήλοις	—	—
a	ἀλλήλους	—	—

ἔβλεπον εἰς ἀλλήλους οἱ μαθηταί.
The disciples were looking at each other.

Rules for Accents 5.

The following syllable patterns are normative for the use of accents involving enclitics:

		Preceding Word	Enclitic
a.	i.	– – –́	–
	ii.	– –́	–
	iii.	–́	–
b.	i.	– – –́	– –
	ii.	– –́	– –
	iii.	–́	– –

   a. If a word has an acute accent on the final syllable, the accent of a one-syllable enclitic is absorbed into the accent:

a. i.	ἀδελφοί	σου	(Mk 3:32)
ii.	ὁδόν	σου	(Mk 1:2)
iii.	μή	με	(Mk 5:7)

   b. If a word has an acute accent on the final syllable, the accent of a two-syllable enclitic is absorbed into the accent:

b. i.	δυνατόν	ἐστιν	(Mk 14:35)
ii.	δειλοί	ἐστε	(Mk 4:40)
iii.	δέ	εἰσιν	(Mk 4:15)

Other enclitic patterns will be presented in subsequent lessons.

Vocabulary for Lesson 13.

παρά [Prep 3] Governs the genitive, dative, and accusative cases. With the genitive: *from the side of* [only with persons]. With the dative: *alongside of* [usually with persons]; *according to the judgment of*; *in the house of*. With the accusative: *at*; *alongside*; *against*; *other than*.   *with (d)*

γαστήρ, γαστρός, ἡ [N 24f, N 33] *belly*; *womb*.   *internal*

θυγάτηρ, θυγατρός, ἡ [N 24f, N 33] *daughter*.

μήτηρ, μητρός, ἡ [N 24f, N 33] *mother*.

πατήρ, πατρός, ὁ [N 24m, N 33] *father*.

ἀλέκτωρ, ἀλέκτορος, ὁ [N 26] *rooster*.

ῥήτωρ, ῥήτορος, ὁ [N 26] *orator*.

νιπτήρ, νιπτῆρος, ὁ [N 25] *basin*.

σωτήρ, σωτῆρος, ὁ [N 25] *savior*.

ἀλλήλων [Pro] *each other*.

νῦν [Adv 2] *now* [in the temporal sense]; also in a non-temporal sense: *given things as they stand*; *since this is the situation*.

Exercises for Lesson 13.

I. Translate into English:
   1. ὁ νιπτὴρ ἔσται ἐπὶ τῆς τραπέζης.

2. ἔρχεται ὁ πονηρὸς ἄνθρωπος παρὰ τῶν κακῶν *evil morally* *bad (inept)*
   ἡγεμόνων. (Mk 14:43)
3. ὁ πατὴρ ἡμῶν ὃς ἐν τοῖς οὐρανοῖς ἀγαθός ἐστιν. (Mt 6:9)
4. ἔστω νῦν ἐν τῷ οἴκῳ αὐτοῦ. (Mt 5:38)
5. ἡ θυγάτηρ μου ἐν τῷ οἴκῳ ἐστίν. (Mk 5:35)
6. ἐν ἀληθείᾳ οὗτος ἦν ὁ σωτὴρ τοῦ κόσμου. (Mt 22:16; Jn 4:42)
7. ἦσαν παρ' ἡμῖν παῖδες ἀγαθοί. (Mt 22:25)
8. ἔρχεται ἵνα βλέπῃ τὸν ἀδελφὸν αὐτοῦ.
9. οἱ μαθηταὶ ἔλεγον πρὸς ἀλλήλους. (Mk 4:41)
10. οὗτοί εἰσιν ἀδελφοί μου καὶ ἀδελφαί μου καὶ μήτηρ μου. (Mk 3:35)
11. νῦν ἣν ἔχεις οὐκ ἔστιν ἡ γυνή σου. (Jn 4:18)
12. ἡ μήτηρ ἔχει παῖδα ἐν γαστρί. (Mk 13:17) *no article; idiom*
13. οὗτοι οἱ ῥήτορες οὐκ ἀγαθοί εἰσιν.
14. ὁ οἶκος ἦν παρὰ τὴν ὁδόν. (Mk 4:15)
15. ἦν ἀλέκτωρ παρὰ τὸν οἶκον.

II. Translate into Greek:
   1. This is my mother and this is my father and these are my brothers and these are my sisters. (Mk 3:34-35)
   2. The shepherds were speaking to each other on the road. (Lk 2:15; Mk 4:41; Mk 8:3)
   3. Jesus comes alongside the house with his disciples. (Mk 2:13)

III. Mk 2:13-18.

The Meaning of the Present Active Optative.
λύω, Present Active Optative. The Nouns
πόλις and ἰχθύς. The Possessive Pronouns
ἐμός, ἡμέτερος, σός, and ὑμέτερος.
Rules for Accents 6.

Lesson 14

The Meaning of the Present Active Optative.

In the present system the optative conveys the view of an action not terminated. This basic viewpoint is usually elaborated by other indications in the text so that the action is viewed as continuing or repeated, or is viewed as customary, or is considered as describing the action conveyed by the meaning of the verb. (Only the indicative mood conveys the present of primary time.)

For the meaning of the active voice cf. above, Lesson 9.

For the meaning of the optative mood cf. above, Lesson 6. The optative mood is much less important than the subjunctive, and is used mainly to express wishes. Thus it refers indirectly to the future of primary time.

λύω, Present Active Optative.

The present optative active of λύω is conjugated as follows (cf. V 1, VP 1):

	Active Voice, Optative Mood, Present Tense	
	Singular	Plural
1st Person	λύ–οιμι	λύ–οιμεν
2nd Person	λύ–οις	λύ–οιτε
3rd Person	λύ–οι	λύ–οιεν

The Nouns πόλις and ἰχθύς.

A large group of nouns of the third declension has a root ending in
−ι. This ι changes to ε before an ending beginning with a vowel and
in the dative plural (πόλις, *city*) (cf. N 28f):

	Singular	Plural
n	πόλις	πόλεις
v	πόλι	πόλεις
g	πόλεως	πόλεων
d	πόλει	πόλεσι(ν)
a	πόλιν	πόλεις

There are special endings in the genitive and accusative
singular and nominative, vocative, and accusative plural. This
group should be carefully distinguished from the nouns of the type
ἐλπίς presented in Lesson 11.

A smaller group of nouns in the third declension has a root
ending in −υ. This υ remains unchanged throughout the declension
(ἰχθύς, *fish*) (cf. N 27m):

	Singular	Plural
n	ἰχθύς	ἰχθύες
v	ἰχθύ	ἰχθύες
g	ἰχθύος	ἰχθύων
d	ἰχθύϊ	ἰχθύσι(ν)
a	ἰχθύν	ἰχθύας

The Possessive Pronouns ἐμός, ἡμέτερος, σός, and ὑμέτερος.

Possessive pronouns are pronomial adjectives, agreeing with the
word they modify in gender, number, and case. They are declined
like ἅγιος, ἁγία, ἅγιον or ἀγαθός, ἀγαθή, ἀγαθόν.

	Singular	Plural
1st Person	ἐμός, ἐμή, ἐμόν	ἡμέτερος, ἡμετέρα, ἡμέτερον
2nd Person	σός, σή, σόν	ὑμέτερος, ὑμετέρα, ὑμέτερον

ἔβλεπε τὴν ἡμετέραν τράπεζαν.
He was seeing our table.

ἔβλεπε τὰς ἡμετέρας τραπέζας.
He was seeing our tables.

There is no possessive pronoun for the third person in New Testament Greek. This is supplied by the use of αὐτός in the genitive case.

To show possession, there is a tendency to use the genitive case of the personal pronoun instead of the possessive pronoun, although the latter is always legitimate. Thus, *He was seeing our table*, should probably preferably be translated ἔβλεπε τὴν τράπεζαν ἡμῶν instead of ἔβλεπε τὴν ἡμετέραν τράπεζαν, although the latter translation is correct.

Rules for Accents 6.

Further syllable patterns which are normative for the use of accents involving enclitics:

		Preceding Word	Enclitic
c.	i.	– – ˆ	–
	ii.	– ˆ	–
	iii.	ˆ	–
d.	i.	– – ˆ	– –
	ii.	– ˆ	ʼ– –
	iii.	ˆ	– –

c. If a word has a circumflex accent on the final syllable, the accent of a one-syllable enclitic is absorbed into this accent:

c.	i.	δεξιῶν	μου	(Mk 10:40)
	ii.	φωνεῖ	σε	(Mk 10:49)
	iii.	δῶς	μοι	(Mk 6:25)

d. If a word has a circumflex accent on the final syllable, the accent of a two-syllable enclitic is absorbed into this accent:

d. i.   πονηροῦ   ἐστιν   (Mt 5:37)
   ii.   ἡμῶν   ἐστιν   (Mk 9:40)
   iii.   ποῦ   ἐστιν   (Mk 14:14)

Vocabulary for Lesson 14.

πρός [Prep 3] Governs the genitive, dative, and accusative cases.
    With the genitive: *for* [advantage]. With the dative: *near*
    [temporal and spatial]. With the accusative: *towards*; *with*;
    near; *against*; *for* [purpose]. In the New Testament the use of
    πρός is limited, with few exceptions, to the accusative case.
___

ἀνάστασις, ἀναστάσεως, ἡ [N 28f] *resurrection*.

γνῶσις, γνώσεως, ἡ [N 28f] *knowledge*.

δέησις, δεήσεως, ἡ [N 28f] *supplication, petition*.

δύναμις, δυνάμεως, ἡ [N 28f] *power*.

θλῖψις, θλίψεως, ἡ [N 28f] *suffering*; *calamity*; *tribulation*.

κρίσις, κρίσεως, ἡ [N 28f] *judgment*.

παράκλησις, παρακλήσεως, ἡ [N 28f] *encouragement*; *warning*;
    prayer.

πίστις, πίστεως, ἡ [N 28f] *faith*.

πόλις, πόλεως, ἡ [N 28f] *city*.
___

ἰσχύς, ἰσχύος, ἡ [N 27f] *strength*; *vigor*.

ἰχθύς, ἰχθύος, ὁ [N 27m] *fish*.

ὀσφῦς, ὀσφύος, ἡ [N 27f] *loins*. This word is singular in Greek,
    plural in English.

στάχυς, στάχυος, ὁ [N 27m] *head of grain.*

———

ἐμός, -ή, -όν [Pro] *my, mine.*

ἡμέτερος, -α, -ον [Pro] *our.*

σός, -ή, -όν [Pro] *your, yours* (sg.).

ὑμέτερος, -α, -ον [Pro] *your, yours* (pl.).

———

Χριστός, -οῦ, ὁ [N 6m] *Christ.*

———

μέν [Conj] This word indicates contrast or emphasis and is often
   better left untranslated. It is frequently used in combination
   with another conjunction, e.g., μέν . . . δέ, *on the one hand .
   . . on the other hand;* μέν . . . ἀλλά, *indeed . . . but.* μέν is
   postpositive.

Exercises for Lesson 14.

I. Translate into English:
   1. οἱ στρατιῶται ἔλεγον πρὸς ἀλλήλους. (Mk 8:16)
   2. ἦν ἱμάτιον περὶ τὴν ὀσφὺν αὐτοῦ. (Mk 1:6)
   3. τοῦτο γάρ ἐστι πρὸς τῆς ἡμετέρας ἐλπίδος. (Acts 27:34)
   4. ὁ μὲν Κύριος Ἰησοῦς ἔρχεται εἰς τὸν οὐρανόν, ὁ δὲ
      μαθητὴς αὐτοῦ ἔρχεται πρὸς τὸν οἶκον αὐτοῦ. (Mk
      16:19)
   5. ἦσαν ἰχθύες ἐν τῷ νιπτῆρι.
   6. ἔσονται γὰρ αἱ ἡμέραι ἐκεῖναι θλῖψις. (Mk 13:19)
   7. ὁ ἄγγελος λέγει πρὸς αὐτάς. (Lk 1:13)
   8. ἔλεγεν αὐτῷ ὅτι σὺ εἶ ὁ Χριστός. (Mk 8:29)
   9. ὁ θεὸς ἤκουε τὰς δεήσεις αὐτῶν. (Lk 1:13)
   10. οἱ μαθηταὶ τοῦ Ἰησοῦ ἤσθιον τοὺς στάχυας. (Lk 6:1)
   11. ἦσαν δὲ πρὸς τοῖς οἴκοις ἄνδρες καὶ γυναῖκες. (Mk
      5:11) [Cf. Lesson 37, Vocabulary, for the meaning of
      ἀνήρ.]
   12. ἡ κρίσις ἔσται κατὰ τὸν ἡμέτερον λόγον. (Acts 18:14)

13. ἀδελφοί, εἴ ἐστιν ἐν ὑμῖν λόγος παρακλήσεως πρὸς τὸν λαόν, λέγετε. (Acts 13:15) [Cf. Lesson 15, Vocabulary, for the meaning of εἰ.]

14. ὁ παῖς ἔρχεται πρὸς αὐτόν. (Mk 1:40)

15. ἔχει ὁ ἅγιος ἀγάπην πρὸς τὸν θεὸν ἐξ ὅλης τῆς ἰσχύος αὐτοῦ. (Mk 12:30)

16. οὐκ ἔστι γνῶσις τοῦ Ἰησοῦ ἐν ἐκείνῃ τῇ πόλει. (Lk 1:77)

17. ἡ κρίσις ἡ ἐμὴ δικαία ἐστίν. (Jn 5:30)

18. ἔρχεται ὁ κριτὴς εἰς τὴν πόλιν. (Mk 14:16)

19. οὐ διὰ τὸν σὸν λόγον πίστιν ἔχομεν. (Jn 4:42)

20. οἱ ἐχθροὶ τοῦ Ἰησοῦ λέγουσιν ἀνάστασιν μὴ εἶναι. (Mk 12:18) [Cf. Lesson 30, Vocabulary, for the meaning of ἐχθρός.]

21. ἔρχεται ὁ Μεσσίας μετὰ δυνάμεως καὶ δόξης. (Mk 13:26)

22. ὁ Ἰησοῦς βλέπει τὴν πίστιν αὐτῶν. (Mk 2:5)

23. ἡμετέρα ἐστὶν ἡ βασιλεία τοῦ θεοῦ. (Lk 6:20)

24. ἔρχεται ὁ Κύριος ἐν ἡμέρᾳ κρίσεως. (Mt 10:15)

II. Translate into Greek:

1. Jesus comes with his disciples into the city to speak to the people about God. (Mt 26:36; Mk 5:14; Mk 8:30)

2. Jesus sees the faith of the crowd and says that God is good. (Mk 2:5; Mk 8:29)

3. The disciples of Christ have knowledge of the resurrection. (1 Cor 8:1)

III. Mk 2:19-24.

The Meaning of the Present Active
Infinitive. λύω, Present Active Infinitive.
The Nouns βασιλεύς and νοῦς. The
Interrogative Pronoun τίς. Rules for
Accents 7.

Lesson 15

The Meaning of the Present Active Infinitive.

In the present system the infinitive conveys the view of an action not
terminated. This basic viewpoint is usually elaborated by other
indications in the text so that the action is viewed as continuing or
repeated, or is viewed as customary, or is considered as describing
what is signified by the meaning of the verb. (Only the indicative
mood conveys the present of primary time.) In the accusative with
the infinitive construction (cf. above, Lesson 8) the infinitive
expresses relative time, with reference to what is prior,
contemporaneous, or subsequent to the time of the main verb, when
the accusative with the infinitive follows a verb of saying or
perceiving. The present infinitive expresses time contemporaneous
with the main verb. The reason is that the present infinitive does
not express terminated action (as does the aorist stem, which, in the
accusative with the infinitive, ordinarily expresses previous time),
nor action which is prior (as does the perfect stem, which, in the
accusative with the infinitive, is used, if rarely, to imply prior time),
nor action which is subsequent (as does the future stem, which, in
the accusative with the infinitive, is used to express subsequent
time). In other contructions the present infinitive expresses non-
terminated action with no implication of relative time.

For the meaning of the active voice cf. above, Lesson 9.
For the meaning of the infinitive mood cf. above, Lesson 4.

λύω, Present Active Infinitive.

The present active infinitive of λύω is λύ–ειν (cf. V 1, VP 1).

The Nouns βασιλεύς and νοῦς.

A group of nouns of the third declension has a root ending in
–ευ. The υ of the ευ drops before a vowel. In the accusative plural
the ending is –εις instead of –εας (βασιλεύς, *king*) (cf. N 29):

	Singular	Plural
n	βασιλεύς	βασιλεῖς
v	βασιλεῦ	βασιλεῖς
g	βασιλέως	βασιλέων
d	βασιλεῖ	βασιλεῦσι(ν)
a	βασιλέα	βασιλεῖς

A smaller group of nouns of the third declension has a root
ending in ο which is contracted with several of the endings (νοῦς,
mind) (cf. N 27m and N 33):

	Singular	Plural
n	νοῦς	νόες
v	νοῦ	νόες
g	νοός	νοῶν
d	νοΐ	νουσί(ν)
a	νοῦν	νόας

The Interrogative Pronoun τίς.

The interrogative pronoun is declined as follows:

	Masculine	Singular Feminine	Neuter
n	τίς	τίς	τί
g	τίνος	τίνος	τίνος
d	τίνι	τίνι	τίνι
a	τίνα	τίνα	τί

	Masculine	Plural Feminine	Neuter
n	τίνες	τίνες	τίνα
g	τίνων	τίνων	τίνων
d	τίσι(ν)	τίσι(ν)	τίσι(ν)
a	τίνας	τίνας	τίνα

It should be noted that the accent is always acute and that it is always found over the (first) iota. The masculine and feminine forms are identical.

The pronoun is used much as the interrogative pronoun in English:

τίς ἐστιν;
Who is he?

τί αὐτὴ λέγει;
What does she say?

τίς may also be used as an adjective:

τίς βασιλεύς ἐστιν;
Which king is he?

ἐκ τίνος πόλεώς ἐστιν;
Of what city is he?

Rules for Accents 7.

Further syllable patterns which are normative for the use of accents involving enclitics:

		Preceding Word	Enclitic
e.	i.	– ´– –	–
	ii.	´– –	–
f.	i.	– ´– –	– ´–
	ii.	´– –	– ´–
g.	i.	– ´– –	– ` –
	ii.	´– –	– ` –

e. An acute accent on the next-to-last syllable of a word preceding a single-syllable enclitic suffices for the accentuation both of the word on which it stands and the enclitic. The accent of the

enclitic is not placed on the final syllable of the preceding word:
acute accents on successive syllables of the same word are never
found:

e.   i.   πλησίον   σου   (Mk 12:31)

      ii.   μήτηρ   σου   (Mk 3:32)

f. As was stated in rule 7.e above, an acute accent on the next-
to-last syllable of a word preceding a single-syllable enclitic suffices
for the accentuation both of the word on which it stands and the
enclitic. But the situation changes when a word having an acute
accent on the next-to-last syllable is followed by an enclitic of <u>two</u>
syllables. In this case an accent is placed on the final syllable of the
enclitic. This is done to avoid having three successive unaccented
syllables involving an enclitic.

f.   i.   Ἠλίας   ἐστίν   (Mk 6:15)

      ii.   οἴκῳ   ἐστίν   (Mk 2:1)

g. The acute accent on the final syllable of an enclitic
functions according to the rules of the acute accent, i.e., if there is
no punctuation following the enclitic and the following word is not
an enclitic the acute accent is changed into a grave accent:

g.   i.   τοιούτων   ἐστὶν   (Mk 10:14)

      ii.   χρόνος   ἐστὶν   (Mk 9:21)

Vocabulary for Lesson 15.

ἀντί [Prep 1] Governs the genitive case: *in place of; for; on behalf of.*

ἀρχιερεύς, –έως, ὁ [N 29] *high priest.*

βασιλεύς, –έως, ὁ [N 29] *king.*

γονεύς, –έως, ὁ [N 29] *parent.*

γραμματεύς, –έως, ὁ [N 29] *scribe.*

ἱερεύς, –έως, ὁ [N 29] *priest.*

———

βοῦς, βοός, ὁ [N 27m, N 27f, N 33] *ox; cow.*

νοῦς, νοός, ὁ [N 27m, N 33] *mind; intelligence.*

χοῦς, χοός, ὁ [N 27m, N 33] *dust.*

———

θέλω [V 6, DV 77, VP 1] *I wish.* This word frequently governs the
infinitive. But it can also govern a ἵνα clause with the
subjunctive. This ἵνα clause is <u>not</u> a purpose clause, but a
noun clause, as will be explained in Lesson 75. The imperfect
has an irregular augment: ἠ instead of ἐ (ἤθελον). The
future is not found in the New Testament.

μέλλω [V 6, DV 123, VP 1] *I am about to.* This verb is followed by an
infinitive, usually either present or future. The imperfect can
have either the regular augment ἐ or the irregular augment
ἠ.

———

τίς, τίς, τί [Pro] *who?; what?* τί also has the idiomatic meaning
why? in certain contexts, as will be explained in Lesson 73.

———

εἰ [Conj] *if.* This conjunction is used to introduce a subordinate
clause of a condition in the indicative mood; it is also used as
one of the words introducing an indirect question.

Exercises for Lesson 15.

I. Translate into English:
1. εἰ σὺ εἶ ὁ Χριστός, λέγε ἡμῖν. (Jn 10:24)
2. τίς ὑμῶν οὐ λύει τὸν βοῦν αὐτοῦ; (Lk 13:15)
3. ἡμεῖς οὐκ ἔχομεν κακὸν ἀντὶ κακοῦ ἀπὸ τοῦ θεοῦ.
   (Rom 12:17) [Cf. Lesson 26, Vocabulary, for the
   meaning of κακός.]
4. οἱ παῖδες ἤθελον εἶναι γονεῖς ἀγαθοί. (Mk 9:35)
5. ὁ στρατιώτης ἤμελλε κράζειν.
6. τίνα με λέγουσιν οἱ ἄνθρωποι εἶναι; (Mk 8:27) say/perceive accrtinf
7. ὁ χοῦς ἦν ἐπὶ τὴν τράπεζαν.
8. τίς ἐστιν βασιλεὺς ταύτης τῆς πόλεως;
9. ὁ ἱερεὺς ἔρχεται εἰς τὸ ἱερὸν ἵνα λέγῃ τῷ θεῷ.

10. ἔρχεται πρὸς τὸν Ἰησοῦν ὁ ἀρχιερεύς, ὁ δὲ γραμματεὺς οὐκ ἔρχεται.

11. διὰ τί ἔρχεται ὁ Ἰησοῦς εἰς τοῦτον τὸν οἶκον; (Mk 2:18)

12. ὑμεῖς δὲ νοῦν Χριστοῦ ἔχετε. (1 Cor 2:16)

13. ὁ ἱερεὺς ἤθελε βαπτίζειν τοὺς γονεῖς τῶν παίδων.

II. Translate into Greek:

1. The king wishes to hear the prophet, but the prophet does not wish to speak before the king.

2. If the king wishes to be first in the kingdom, let him hear the voice of God. (Mk 4:23; Mk 10:44)

3. For the son of man was about to have mercy on the woman who has hope. (Jn 11:51; Mk 4:25)

III. Mk 2:25 – 3:3.

The Meaning of the Present Active
Participle. λύω, Present Active Participle.
The Noun πνεῦμα. The Indefinite Pronoun
τις. Rules for Accents 8.

Lesson 16

The Meaning of the Present Active Participle.

Two examples of the use of participles in English are: 1) *A voice crying in the wilderness.* . . .; 2) *Hearing the voice, I* . . . .
      The Greek participle may be described as a verbal adjective. Like a verb, a participle in Greek has aspect and voice and may take an object. Like an adjective, a participle agrees with a noun or pronoun in gender, number, and case. (Cf. Lesson 7.) In the parsing of a participle, all these factors must be taken into account.
      The present participle conveys the view of an action which is not terminated. The action of the present participle is almost always simultaneous with the action of the main verb precisely because the action is viewed as not terminated. (Cf. the reasoning involved in the simultaneity of the present infinitive given in Lesson 15.)
      For the meaning of the active voice cf. above, Lesson 9.
      For the meaning of the participle cf. above, Lesson 7.

λύω, Present Active Participle.

The present active participle of λύω is declined as follows (cf. V 1, VP 1, Adj 7):

	Masculine	Singular Feminine	Neuter
n	λύ–ων	λύ–ουσα	λῦ–ον
v	λύ–ων	λύ–ουσα	λῦ–ον
g	λύ–οντος	λυ–ούσης	λύ–οντος
d	λύ–οντι	λυ–ούσῃ	λύ–οντι
a	λύ–οντα	λύ–ουσαν	λῦ–ον

	Masculine	Plural Feminine	Neuter
n	λύ–οντες	λύ–ουσαι	λύ–οντα
v	λύ–οντες	λύ–ουσαι	λύ–οντα
g	λυ–όντων	λυ–ουσῶν	λυ–όντων
d	λύ–ουσι(ν)	λυ–ούσαις	λύ–ουσι(ν)
a	λύ–οντας	λυ–ούσας	λύ–οντα

The Noun πνεῦμα.

Neuter nouns constitute a numerous group in the third declension.
A particularly large part of this group is composed of nouns with a
nominative ending in –μα and the stem ending in ατ– (πνεῦμα, *spirit*)
(cf. N 16):

	Singular	Plural
n	πνεῦμα	πνεύματα
v	πνεῦμα	πνεύματα
g	πνεύματος	πνευμάτων
d	πνεύματι	πνεύμασι(ν)
a	πνεῦμα	πνεύματα

The stem is πνευματ–. In the dative plural the τ is dropped
before the σ.

The Indefinite Pronoun τις.

The indefinite pronoun τις is the equivalent of a number of
expressions in English: *someone, somebody, anyone, anybody,
some, any, a certain person*, etc.

The declension is exactly the same as for the interrogative
pronoun τίς except that the indefinite pronoun τις is an enclitic, i.e.,
it has no accent or an accent on the second syllable. (Cf. Pro.)

	Masculine	Singular Feminine	Neuter
n	τις	τις	τι
g	τινός	τινός	τινός
d	τινί	τινί	τινί
a	τινά	τινά	τι

	Masculine	Plural Feminine	Neuter
n	τινές	τινές	τινά
g	τινῶν	τινῶν	τινῶν
d	τισί(ν)	τισί(ν)	τισί(ν)
a	τινάς	τινάς	τινά

Inasmuch as τις is an enclitic, the rules for the accents of enclitics given in Lessons 11 and following apply.

Like the interrogative τίς, the indefinite τις can be used as an adjective or as a substantive:

> ... τινες τῶν γραμματέων ...
> *some of the scribes ...*

> ... βασιλεύς τις ...
> *... some king or other ...*

Rules for Accents 8.

Further syllable patterns which are normative for the use of accents involving enclitics:

		Preceding Word	Enclitic
h.	i.	– $\hat{\ }$ ´	–
	ii.	$\hat{\ }$ ´	–
i.	i.	– $\hat{\ }$ ´	– –
	ii.	$\hat{\ }$ ´	– –

h. A circumflex accent on the next-to-last syllable of a word preceding a single-syllable enclitic does not suffice for the accentuation of the enclitic. The enclitic loses its acute accent to the word in which the circumflex accent is found, the accent being placed on the final syllable. Thus there is a sequence of circumflex-acute on successive syllables of the same word:

i.	ζητοῦσίν	σε	(Mk 1:37)
ii.	οἶδά	σε	(Mk 1:24)

i. A circumflex accent on the next-to-last syllable of a word
preceding a two-syllable enclitic results in the same sequence of
circumflex-acute on successive syllables as in the pattern "h":

    i.   ἐκεῖνοί   εἰσιν   (Mk 4:20)
    ii.   οὗτοί   εἰσιν   (Mk 4:18)

Vocabulary for Lesson 16.

ἀνά [Prep 1] Governs the accusative case. With words meaning
    number or measure it has a distributive sense: *each, apiece*.
    With the word μέσον and the genitive it means *through* in a
    spatial sense, the accusative neuter singular of the adjective
    μέσος being used as a noun.

___

αἷμα, αἵματος, τό [N 16] *blood*.

βάπτισμα, βαπτίσματος, τό [N 16] *baptism*.

βρῶμα, βρώματος, τό [N 16] *food*.

θέλημα, θελήματος, τό [N 16] *will; decision*.

ὄνομα, ὀνόματος, τό [N 16] *name*.

παράπτωμα, παραπτώματος, τό [N 16] *sin; trespass*.

πνεῦμα, πνεύματος, τό [N 16] *spirit*.

ῥῆμα, ῥήματος, τό [N 16] *word; event*.

σπέρμα, σπέρματος, τό [N 16] *seed; descendant(s)*.

στόμα, στόματος, τό [N 16] *mouth*.

σῶμα, σώματος, τό [N 16] *body*.

τις, τις, τι [Pro] *some; any; someone; anyone; a certain one; a
    certain*.

___

μέσος, −η, −ον [Adj 1] *middle*.

οὕτως / οὕτω [Adv 3] *thus.*

Exercises for Lesson 16.

I. Translate into English:
1. διὰ τί οὗτος οὕτως λέγει; (Mk 2:7)
2. Ἀνδρέας ἐστὶν τὸ ὄνομα αὐτοῦ. (Lk 1:63)
3. τοῦτό ἐστιν τὸ θέλημα τοῦ πατρός μου. (Jn 6:40)
4. ἔρχεται ὁ προφήτης ἀνὰ μέσον τοῦ ὄχλου ἐν ὀνόματι τοῦ Κυρίου. (Mk 7:31; Mk 11:9)
5. γυνή τις ἔκραζεν ἐκ τοῦ ὄχλου. (Lk 11:27)
6. ὁ βαπτιστὴς ἡμᾶς βαπτίσει ἐν πνεύματι ἁγίῳ. (Mk 1:8)
7. ὁ στρατιώτης ἔρχεται διὰ μέσου αὐτῶν. (Lk 4:30)
8. ὑμεῖς παραπτώματα ἔχετε.
9. εἶπεν ὁ Ἰησοῦς· τοῦτό ἐστιν τὸ αἷμά μου. (Mk 14:24)
10. οἱ προφῆται εἶχον στόμα ἵνα λέγωσιν τὴν ἀλήθειαν περὶ τοῦ θελήματος τοῦ θεοῦ. (Lk 21:15)
11. τοῦτο τὸ βάπτισμα οὐκ ἐξ οὐρανοῦ ἦν. (Mk 11:30)
12. εἶπεν ὁ Ἰησοῦς· τοῦτό ἐστιν τὸ σῶμά μου. (Mk 14:22)
13. ἔρχεται ὁ ὄχλος ἵνα βρῶμα ἔχῃ.
14. τὰ σπέρματα τῶν πατέρων υἱοὶ καὶ θυγατέρες εἰσίν.
15. ὑμεῖς ἔχετε ῥήματα ζωῆς ἐκ τοῦ θεοῦ. (Jn 6:68)
16. ὁ Ἰησοῦς ἔρχεται κηρύσσων τὸ εὐαγγέλιον καὶ λέγων ὅτι ἐγγίζει ἡ βασιλεία τοῦ θεοῦ. (Mk 1:14) [Cf. Lesson 19, Vocabulary, for the meaning of ἐγγίζω.]

II. Translate into Greek:
1. The unclean spirits saw Jesus and cried out against him. (Mk 3:6; Mk 3:11) [Cf. Lesson 24, Vocabulary, for the Greek word for "unclean".]
2. And some of the prophets were saying that the word of the king was evil. (Mk 15:35)
3. This is the will of the one baptizing me. (Jn 6:39)

III. Mk 3:4-10.

The Meaning of the Future Active
Infinitive. λύω, Future Active Infinitive.
The Meaning of the Future Active
Participle. λύω, Future Active Participle.
The Noun τέρας. The Demonstrative
Pronoun ὅδε. Present Verbal Stems Ending
in –σσ. Rules for Accents 9.

Lesson 17

The Meaning of the Future Active Infinitive.

The future infinitive is used relatively rarely in the New Tesament.
It is found principally as a complement to a verb. It always conveys
the view of an action in some way subsequent. (Cf. above, Lesson 9.)
Thus, when used in the accusative with the infinitive construction,
it indicates subsequent time with respect to the time of the main
verb. (Cf. above, Lesson 15.)
  For the meaning of the active voice cf. above, Lesson 9.
  For the meaning of the infinitive mood cf. above, Lesson 4.

λύω, Future Active Infinitive.

The future active infinitive of λύω is formed by adding the present
ending to the future stem (cf. Lesson 11, and V 1, VP 1). The future
active infinitive of λύω is thus λύσειν.

> λέγει τὸν Χριστὸν λύσειν τὸν δοῦλον.
> *He says that Christ will loose the slave.*

> εἶπε τὸν Χριστὸν λύσειν τὸν δοῦλον.
> *He said that Christ would loose the slave.*

Contrast with the use of the present infinitive:

> λέγει τὸν Χριστὸν λύειν τὸν δοῦλον.
> *He says that Christ is loosing the slave.*

The Meaning of the Future Participle.

The future participle is relatively rare in the New Testament. It always expresses action which is viewed as being subsequent. (Cf. above, Lesson 9 and Lesson 16.) It is occasionally used to express purpose because purpose is inherently related to subsequent action.

> ὁ Χριστὸς ἔρχεται λύσων τὸν δοῦλον.
> *Christ comes in order to loose the slave.*

λύω, Future Active Participle.

The future active participle of λύω is formed by adding the endings of the present participle to the future stem (cf. V 1, VP 1, Adj 7). The rules for the modification of the stem for verbs in special categories are the same as for the indicative and infinitive (cf. Lesson 11).
        For the meaning of the active voice cf. Lesson 9.

	Masculine	Singular Feminine	Neuter
n	λύσ–ων	λύσ–ουσα	λῦσ–ον
v	λύσ–ων	λύσ–ουσα	λῦσ–ον
g	λύσ–οντος	λυσ–ούσης	λύσ–οντος
d	λύσ–οντι	λυσ–ούσῃ	λύσ–οντι
a	λύσ–οντα	λύσ–ουσαν	λῦσ–ον

	Masculine	Plural Feminine	Neuter
n	λύσ–οντες	λύσ–ουσαι	λύσ–οντα
v	λύσ–οντες	λύσ–ουσαι	λύσ–οντα
g	λυσ–όντων	λυσ–ουσῶν	λυσ–όντων
d	λύσ–ουσι(ν)	λυσ–ούσαις	λύσ–ουσι(ν)
a	λύσ–οντας	λυσ–ούσας	λύσ–οντα

        This concludes the presentation of the present and future tenses of the active voice of the verb λύω.

The Noun τέρας.

A small group of third-declension neuter nouns ends in –ας with the stem in –ατ– (τέρας, *marvel, wonder*) (cf. N. 17):

	Singular	Plural
n	τέρας	τέρατα
v	τέρας	τέρατα
g	τέρατος	τεράτων
d	τέρατι	τέρασι(ν)
a	τέρας	τέρατα

In some texts the nominative, vocative, and accusative singulars are found as τέρα instead of τέρας.

The Demonstrative Pronoun ὅδε.

A demonstration pronoun meaning *this* in addition to οὗτος is ὅδε. Its meaning is the same as that of οὗτος, but it is not used nearly as frequently.

		Singular	
	Masculine	Feminine	Neuter
n	ὅδε	ἥδε	τόδε
g	τοῦδε	τῆσδε	τοῦδε
d	τῷδε	τῆδε	τῷδε
a	τόνδε	τήνδε	τόδε

		Plural	
	Masculine	Feminine	Neuter
n	οἵδε	αἵδε	τάδε
g	τῶνδε	τῶνδε	τῶνδε
d	τοῖσδε	ταῖσδε	τοῖσδε
a	τούσδε	τάσδε	τάδε

There is a tendency to use the neuter plural of ὅδε as a substantive (τάδε, *these things*).

Present Verbal Stem Endings in –σσ.

A sizeable category of verbs in the New Testament has roots ending with a double sigma (–σσ–) in the present indicative active (e.g., ταράσσω). These verbs have a palatal root and the double sigma is merely the end result of a sound change which takes place only in the present system; in the other tenses the palatal is normally clearly visible. Thus, the future of ταράσσω is ταράξω (cf. V 3).

Rules for Accents 9.

Further syllable patterns which are normative for the use of accents involving enclitics:

	Preceding Word	Enclitic

j. i.   – ´ – ´

    ii.   ´ – ´   –

k. i.   – ´ – ´   – – –

    ii.   ´ – ´   – –

j. and k. An acute accent on the third-last syllable of a word preceding a single-syllable or a double-syllable enclitic results in the placing of the accent of the enclitic on the last syllable of this word.

j. i.   συνθλίβοντά   σε   (Mk 5:31)

    ii.   δύνασαί   με   (Mk 1:40)

k. i.   ἀσύνετοί   ἐστε   (Mk 7:18)

    ii.   φάντασμά   ἐστιν   (Mk 6:49)

Vocabulary for Lesson 17.

πρό [Prep 1] Governs the genitive case: *before*, in a temporal or, less frequently, spatial, sense.

———

ἅλας, ἅλατος, τό [N 17] *salt*.

κέρας, κέρατος, τό [N 17] *horn*; *might* (the latter is a transferred sense from the basic meaning of the word, *horn*).

πέρας, πέρατος, τό [N 17] *end*; *boundary*; *conclusion*.

τέρας, τέρατος, τό [N 17, N 33] *wonder*; *marvel*.

ὅδε, ἥδε, τόδε [Pro] *this*.

διατάσσω [διά + τάσσω] [V 3, DV 303] *I command* [governs the
dative case]; *I arrange*.

κηρύσσω [V 3] *I proclaim; I preach*.

ταράσσω [V 3] *I trouble; I frighten*.

ὑποτάσσω [ὑπό + τάσσω] [V 3, DV 303] *I subject*.

φυλάσσω [V 3, DV 335] *I protect; I guard; I keep; I observe* (a law,
etc.).

ὡς [Conj] This conjunction has many meanings. The most
important are: 1) *when*, to introduce a temporal clause. 2) *as*,
to establish a comparison between nouns and adjectives,
taking "the same case after as before". 3) *about*, with
numbers, to indicate approximation.

Exercises for Lesson 17.

I. Translate into English:
1. ὁ νεανίας ἔλεγεν· τὸν νόμον ἐφύλασσον.
2. τάδε λέγει τὸ πνεῦμα τὸ ἅγιον. (Acts 21:11)
3. ὁ δὲ ἱερεὺς πρὸ τῆς πόλεώς ἐστιν. (Acts 14:13)
4. ὁ Μεσσίας ἐστὶ κέρας ἐν τῷ οἴκῳ τοῦ βασιλέως.
5. ὡς δὲ εἶπε τούτους τοὺς λόγους ὁ Ἰησοῦς ἔβλεπε τὴν
　　γυναῖκα.
6. ἐδίωκον τοὺς προφήτας πρὸ ἡμῶν.
7. ὁ θεὸς ὑποτάξει τὸν θάνατον ὑπὸ τοὺς πόδας τοῦ
　　Χριστοῦ. (Eph 1:22)
8. ἔσονται τέρατα ἐν τοῖς οὐρανοῖς.
9. ἡ λαῖλαψ ἐτάρασσε τὴν θάλασσαν. [Cf. Lesson 21,
　　Vocabulary, for the meaning of θάλασσα.]
10. οἱ ἄνθρωποι οἱ ἀγαθοὶ ἔσονται ὡς ἄγγελοι ἐν τοῖς
　　οὐρανοῖς. (Mk 12:25)
11. ὁ Ἰησοῦς διέτασσεν τοῖς μαθηταῖς αὐτοῦ. (Mt 11:1)

12. ὑμεῖς ἐστε τὸ ἅλας τῆς γῆς. (Mt 5:13)

13. μετὰ ταῦτα ὁ Ἰησοῦς ἔρχεται κηρύσσων τὸ
    εὐαγγέλιον. (Mk 1:14)

14. ἔρχονται ἐκ τῶν περάτων τῆς γῆς ἀκούσοντες τὸ
    εὐαγγέλιον τοῦ Ἰησοῦ. (Mt 12:42)

II. Translate into Greek:
    1. Some of the prophets were frightening the people. (Acts
       15:24)
    2. Jesus goes into this city in order to preach. (Mk 1:38)
    3. They hear the word of God and keep it. (Lk 11:28)

III. Mk 3:11-17.

The Meaning of the Aorist Tense. λύω,
Aorist Active Indicative. The Noun ἔθνος.
The Relative Pronoun ὅστις. The Unreal or
Contrary-to-Fact Condition. Rules for
Accents 10.

Lesson 18

The Meaning of the Aorist Tense.

- rev ch 9
- cf p 454

The aorist aspect conveys the viewpoint of an action as terminated
(cf. Lesson 9). In the indicative mood this aspect combined with
other elements in the context usually means that the action in
question is past. Thus there are two tenses of the indicative mood
which convey past action in primary time: the imperfect, which
conveys the idea of repeated or continuing action in past time (cf.
Lesson 10) and the aorist, <u>which conveys the idea of an action in past
time which is terminated, i.e., not repeated or continuing</u> (cf.
Lesson 9). In a given context this aorist indicative can convey a
variety of nuances, depending on the meaning of the verb and other
factors in the context. But the viewpoint of terminated action
conveyed by the stem will normally be present, explicitly or
implicitly.

　　Thus, as was mentioned above (cf. Lesson 9), the present stem
and its aspect is in counterpoint with the aorist stem and its aspect:
where one is used the other is often being implicitly rejected. These
two aspects, present and aorist, are far more frequently used in New
Testament Greek than the other two, the future and the perfect. The
reason for this is that the present and aorist are normally more
important for narrative and for exposition. From a rhetorical point
of view, verbs formed from the present stem and verbs formed from
the aorist stem each have specific functions in a passage. It is
important to note and to bear in mind that the rhetorical functions
are a consequence of the syntactical functions, and not vice versa.
(Cf. Appendix, "The Greek Verb in the New Testament", p. 454.)

λύω, Aorist Active Indicative.

There are two principal forms of the aorist tense, with no difference in meaning. The more common type is found in the verb λύω and is called a "weak" or "first" aorist. The other, in contrast, is called a "strong" or "second" aorist. (The "strong" or "second" aorist will be explained in Lesson 43.)

Both principal forms of the aorist tense, like the imperfect, have the augment in the indicative mood. It is formed exactly as for the imperfect. The augment is the sign (morphene) which indicates past time. Other moods have the aorist "tense", i.e., aorist stem with the accompanying connotation of action viewed as terminated. The precise force of the aorist in these moods will be explained as occasion demands.

For the meaning of the active voice cf. above, Lesson 9.

For the meaning of the indicative mood cf. above, Lesson 2.

The "weak" or "first" aorist stem is formed by the addition of a σ to the root (λυ–) plus the use of special endings. Thus the aorist stem of λύω is λυσ–. In the indicative mood, as was stated above, the augment is formed as for the imperfect.

The first aorist indicative active of λύω is as follows (cf. V 1, VP 1):

	Active Voice, Indicative Mood, Aorist Tense	
	Singular	Plural
1st Person	ἔ–λυσ–α	ἐ–λύσ–αμεν
2nd Person	ἔ–λυσ–ας	ἐ–λύσ–ατε
3rd Person	ἔ–λυσ–ε(ν)	ἔ–λυσ–αν

I loosed	We loosed
You (sg.) loosed	You (pl.) loosed
He (She, It) loosed	They loosed

For those verbs which end in a consonant, the rules for the addition of the σ to form the aorist are exactly the same as the rules for the addition of the σ to form the future. Thus the following forms: γράφω, γράψω, ἔγραψα; ἁγιάζω, ἁγιάσω, ἡγίασα; κηρύσσω, κηρύξω, ἐκήρυξα.

It should be noted at once, however, that not all verbs with a regularly-formed future indicative have a regularly-formed aorist indicative, and vice versa. Thus, for example, ἄγω, ἄξω, ἤγαγον (irregular aorist), and ἐλπίζω, ἐλπιῶ, ἤλπισα (irregular future).

Not all the verbs seen thus far in this grammar have aorists which are regularly formed according to the paradigm of λύω. For example, ἄγω has a first aorist which is regularly formed, ἦξα, but this form is not nearly as common as another, ἤγαγον, which will be explained in Lesson 43. The aorist of the verbs already seen will be introduced in the exercises, provided that the verbs are not irregular.

The Noun ἔθνος.

A large group of neuter nouns of the third declension end in −ος in the nominative and have a stem ending in −εσ (ἔθνος, *nation*):

	Singular	Plural
n	ἔθνος	ἔθνη
v	ἔθνος	ἔθνη
g	ἔθνους	ἐθνῶν
d	ἔθνει	ἔθνεσι(ν)
a	ἔθνος	ἔθνη

Because of the relative importance of this paradigm it is advisable to explain in some detail the reason behind the various forms.

Three recurring phenomena of Greek phonology are in evidence in this paradigm: 1) the alternation of the stem ἐθνοσ− in the nominative, vocative, and accusative singulars with the stem ἐθνεσ− used everywhere else; 2) the dropping of σ between two vowels (found in all the forms with the stem ἐθνεσ− except the dative plural, and this is not really an exception, for the earlier form here was ἔθνεσ−σι); 3) the contraction of two juxtaposed vowels (ἔθνεος > ἔθνους; ἔθνεα > ἔθνη; ἐθνέων > ἐθνῶν).

The Relative Pronoun ὅστις.

An alternative form of the relative pronoun is found composed of the relative pronoun ὅς joined to the indefinite pronoun τις. At times this longer form seems to preserve something of the connotation of its meaning in classical Greek of a generalizing nature, *whoever*. But usually there seems to be no difference in meaning between the form ὅς (which is much more frequent in the New Testament) and ὅστις.

Only a few of the possible forms of ὅστις are found in the New Testament.

	Masculine	Singular Feminine	Neuter
n	ὅστις	ἥτις	ὅτι
g	ὅτου	—	—
d	—	—	—
a	—	—	—

	Masculine	Plural Feminine	Neuter
n	οἵτινες	αἵτινες	ἅτινα
g	—	—	—
d	—	—	—
a	—	—	—

The Unreal or Contrary-to-Fact Condition.

The following type of sentence is called an unreal or contrary-to-fact conditional sentence: *If you had been here, my brother would not have died.* Both clauses are "contrary to the facts": Jesus was not present, and Martha's brother Lazarus died. Thus in relation to what actually happened the clauses are "unreal".

In Greek this type of sentence has εἰ with a past tense of the indicative in the subordinate clause (protasis), and a past tense of the indicative (usually with ἄν) in the main clause (apodosis).

εἰ ἔκραξεν, ἐφύλαξα ἂν αὐτόν.
If he had cried out, I would have protected him.

εἰ ἔκραζεν, ἐφύλασσον ἂν αὐτόν.
If he were crying out, I would be protecting him.

The aorist indicative often seems to be used if the unreality is presented as being in the past, while the imperfect indicative often seems to be used if the unreality is presented as being in the present. This practical rule of thumb explains the temporal aspects of the translations given above: the first example uses aorist tenses and is translated as a contrary-to-fact condition in the past time, while the second example uses imperfect tenses and is translated as a contrary-to-fact condition in the present time. But the student should be alert to the various factors which can call for a different interpretation of the uses of tenses in regard to the temporal value. Here, as elsewhere, the context is decisive.

The negatives used, when necessary, are οὐ or μή. μή is usually employed in the subordinate clause introduced by εἰ. If the main clause is also negative, it uses οὐ.

Rules for Accents 10.

Further syllable patterns which are normative for the use of accents involving enclitics:

		Preceding Word	Enclitic	Enclitic
1.	i.	´ –	– ´	– –
	ii.	– ´	– ´	–
	iii.	– ´	´	– –

1. When more than one enclitic follows a word, the combination of preceding word and enclitics is called an "enclitic chain". In an enclitic chain the intermediate enclitic or enclitics always have an acute accent on the unique syllable of a monosyllabic enclitic (example iii) or the final syllable of a two-syllable enclitic (examples i and ii). The enclitic in the final position has no accent.

1.	i.	ὅτι	εἰσίν	τινες (Mk 9:1)
	ii.	καλόν	ἐστίν	σε (Mk 9:45)
	iii.	καλόν	σέ	ἐστιν (Mk 9:47)

The word σέ in example iii is the enclitic form of the second person singular personal pronoun and not the strong form as can be seen from the fact that the accent on the final syllable of καλόν is acute and not grave.

There are exceptions to all the rules concerning enclitics given above and in the previous lessons. An enclitic may receive an accent when it immediately follows a punctuation mark (e.g., ἔστιν δὲ [Jn 5:2]; τινὲς δὲ [Jn 7:44]). Further, after some words the enclitic forms of εἰμί retain their accent (e.g., Οὐκ εἰμὶ [Jn 3:28]). But after οὐκ and ἀλλά the third person singular is accented ἔστιν (e.g., οὐκ ἔστιν [Jn 1:47]; ἀλλ' ἔστιν [Jn 7:28]).

The concludes the presentation of the rules for accents involving enclitics.

Vocabulary for Lesson 18.

ἔμπροσθεν [Prep 1] Governs the genitive case: *in front of*. This word is also an adverb with the meaning *in front* [Adv 1].

———

γένος, γένους, τό [N 31] *race; sort; offspring*.

ἔθνος, ἔθνους, τό [N 31] *nation*; [in plural] *Gentiles*.

ἔθος, ἔθους, τό [N 31] *custom*.

ἔτος, ἔτους, τό [N 31] *year*.

μέρος, μέρους, τό [N 31] *part*; [in plural] *parts, region*.

ὄρος, ὄρους, τό [N 31, N 33] *mountain*. In the genitive plural the forms ὀρῶν and ὀρέων are found.

πλῆθος, πλήθους, τό [N 31] *multitude; abundance*.

σκεῦος, σκεύους, τό [N31] *vessel*; [in plural] *goods*.

σκότος, σκότους, τό [N 31] *darkness*.

ψεῦδος, ψεύδους, τό [N 31] *lie*.

———

ὅρος, ὅρου, ὁ [N 6m] *boundary*.

———

ὅστις, ἥτις, ὅτι [Pro] *who; whoever*.

ἄν [Part] ἄν is usually not translated by a particular word. It indicates contingency and its translation depends on the general sense of contingency conveyed by the passage as a whole in which it is found.

Exercises for Lesson 18.

I. Translate into English:
1. σκότος ἦν ἐφ' ὅλην τὴν γῆν. (Mk 15:33)
2. τοῦτο ὃ ἤκουσαν ἐκήρυξαν ἐπὶ τοῦ οἴκου. (Mt 10:27)
3. ἔρχεται ὁ Ἰησοῦς ἔμπροσθεν τοῦ πλήθους. (Mk 2:12)
4. περὶ γὰρ ἐμοῦ ἐκεῖνος ἔγραψεν. (Jn 5:46)
5. ἐν τῷ θεῷ ἐσμεν· αὐτοῦ γὰρ καὶ γένος ἐσμέν. (Acts 17:28)
6. εἰ τὸ σπέρμα τοῦ θεοῦ ἦν, ἅγιος ἂν ἦν. (1 Jn 3:9)
7. ὁ ἄνθρωπος ἐν τοῖς ὄρεσιν ἦν. (Mk 5:5)
8. τὸ ψεῦδος ἐκ τῆς ἀληθείας οὐκ ἔστιν. (1 Jn 2:21)
9. εἰ ἐδόξασε τὸν θεόν, ἐβάπτισα ἂν αὐτόν.
10. πλῆθος ἔρχεται πρὸς αὐτόν. (Mk 3:8)
11. οὐ κωλύω αὐτοὺς οἵτινες ἔχουσιν τὸ πνεῦμα τὸ ἅγιον ὡς καὶ ἡμεῖς. (Acts 10:47)
12. ὁ Ἰησοῦς ἔρχεται κατὰ τὸ ἔθος εἰς τὸ ὄρος. (Lk 22:39)
13. τὸ γὰρ ἱερὸν τοῦ θεοῦ ἅγιόν ἐστιν, οἵτινές ἐστε ὑμεῖς. (1 Cor 3:17)
14. λέγει ὁ Ἰησοῦς· οὐχ ἕξεις μέρος μετ' ἐμοῦ. (Jn 13:8)
15. τὰ σκεύη τούτου τοῦ ἀνθρώπου ἦν ἐν τῷ οἴκῳ. (Lk 17:31)
16. ἔρχεται ἔμπροσθεν ἄγων τοὺς στρατιώτας. (Lk 19:28)
17. οὐκ ἔρχεται εἰς ὁδὸν ἐθνῶν. (Mt 10:5)
18. οἱ γόνεις ἔρχονται κατ' ἔτος εἰς τὸ ἱερόν. (Lk 2:41) [κατ' ἔτος: literally, "according to year", i.e., "yearly" or "each year".]
19. ὁ θεὸς ἡγίασε τοὺς μαθητὰς ἐν τῇ ἀληθείᾳ. (Jn 17:17) [Cf. Lesson 36, Vocabulary, for the meaning of ἁγιάζω.]

II. Translate into Greek:
1. The prophet baptized in the desert in order that his disciples might be holy. (Mk 1:4.8)
2. There were signs among the nations as the prophet had written [use aorist]. (Acts 15:12; Jn 5:46)
3. Now there was a certain good man before Jesus. (Lk 14:2)

III. Mk 3:18-24.

> The Meaning of the Aorist Active
> Imperative. λύω, Aorist Active Imperative.
> The Adjective πᾶς. The Numeral εἷς.
> Rules for Accents 11.

Lesson 19

The Meaning of the Aorist Active Imperative.

The aorist stem normally conveys the aspect of an action as
terminated. (Cf. Lesson 9.) In the indicative mood this use of the
aorist stem, always accompanied by the augment, usually conveys
the idea of an action which is past in terms of primary time. In the
imperative mood of the aorist the aspect conveyed is that of an action
terminated. In practice this means that the aorist of the imperative
mood usually conveys the idea of a command for a specific case, i.e.,
a rule of conduct to be followed in one situation. The reason for this
is that the use of the aorist means an action is viewed as terminated,
that is to say, an action not open-ended. Thus it is in implicit
contrast with the use of the present imperative. (Cf. Lesson 12 and
Lesson 18.)
       For the meaning of the active voice cf. above, Lesson 9.
       For the meaning of the imperative mood cf. above, Lesson 4.

       γράφε πολλάκις.
       Write often.

       γράψον παραχρῆμα.
       Write immediately.

It would be possible to have a sentence γράψον πολλάκις,
Write often, but the choice of the aorist instead of the present would
indicate that the author is thinking of the command as referring to
a specific type of correspondence, so that the command fits under
the notion of rule of conduct to be followed in a certain situation.

λύω, Aorist Active Imperative.

The aorist active imperative of λύω is conjugated as follows (cf. V 1, VP 1):

	Aorist Tense, Active Voice, Imperative Mood	
	Singular	Plural
2nd Person	λῦσ–ον	λύσ–ατε
3rd Person	λυσ–άτω	λυσ–άτωσαν

The Adjective πᾶς.

A common adjective of the third and first declensions is πᾶς, *all*, *every*. The masculine and neuter are declined according to the third declension, and the feminine according to the first (cf. Adj 12).

	Masculine	Singular Feminine	Neuter
n	πᾶς	πᾶσα	πᾶν
v	πᾶς	πᾶσα	πᾶν
g	παντός	πάσης	παντός
d	παντί	πάσῃ	παντί
a	πάντα	πᾶσαν	πᾶν

	Masculine	Plural Feminine	Neuter
n	πάντες	πᾶσαι	πάντα
v	πάντες	πᾶσαι	πάντα
g	πάντων	πασῶν	πάντων
d	πᾶσι(ν)	πάσαις	πᾶσι(ν)
a	πάντας	πάσας	πάντα

The Numeral εἷς.

The numeral εἷς, *one*, is declined as follows:

	Masculine	Feminine	Neuter
n	εἷς	μία	ἕν
g	ἑνός	μιᾶς	ἑνός
d	ἑνί	μιᾷ	ἑνί
a	ἕνα	μίαν	ἕν

Rules for Accents 11.

In contrast to enclitics, which get their full meaning from what precedes, there is a category of words called proclitics, which get their full meaning from what follows. The most important proclitics are these four forms of the article: ὁ, ἡ, οἱ, and αἱ; the prepositions εἰς, ἐκ (ἐξ), and ἐν; the conjunctions εἰ and ὡς; and the negative οὐ. Under certain conditions these words can receive an acute accent (e.g., Mk 4:23: εἴ τις, where εἰ receives the accent of the indefinite pronoun τις; and in Mt 5:37 οὐ is found twice accented, οὒ οὔ, because of the peculiar emphasis it needs in the context, with the acute accent over the first οὐ becoming a grave, according to the normal rules for accents). But these exceptions are rare and are not really parallel to the frequency with which enclitics receive accents; they should cause no difficulty to the student who is aware that proclitics normally do not have accents and only on rare occasions do in fact have them, and then for reasons which are evident.

Vocabulary for Lesson 19.

ἐνώπιον [Prep 1] Governs the genitive case: *in front of*; *in the presence of.*

___

ἅπας, ἅπασα, ἅπαν [Adj 12] This is a strengthened form of πᾶς; it can be an indication of elevated style: *every* [last one]; *each* [and every].

πᾶς, πᾶσα, πᾶν [Adj 12] The precise translation of this word often poses a challenge. The following norms should provide general guidelines. I. πᾶς as an adjective. A. Without the article. 1. In the singular: *each, every*. 2. In the plural: *all.* B. With the article. 1. In the singular: *the whole, the entire.* 2. In the plural: *all the.* II. πᾶς as a noun: *everyone, everything, all.* When used as adjectives, ἅπας and πᾶς do not follow the normal usage of adjectives with regard to attributive and predicative meanings.

[handwritten margin note: w/ art = modified by; art]

___

εἷς, μία, ἕν [Adj 19] *one.*

μηδείς, μηδεμία, μηδέν [Adj 19, Neg] As an adjective: *no*. As noun: *no one; nothing.* μηδείς, in contrast to οὐδείς, is used where the negative μή would be used.

οὐδείς, οὐδεμία, οὐδέν [Adj 19, Neg] As an adjective: *no*. As noun: *no one*; *nothing*. οὐδείς, in contrast to μηδείς, is used where the negative οὐ would be used.

———

ἀπολύω [ἀπό + λύω] [V 1, VP 1] *I release; I send away.*

ἐγγίζω (ἐγγίσω) [V 5, 18; DV 69; VP 1] *I draw near.* It governs either the simple dative or a preposition with its case. The perfect has a present meaning.

καθίζω (καθίσω) [V 5, DV 140, VP 1] *I sit.* This is normally an intransitive verb, i.e., it does not govern an object.

συνάγω [σύν + ἄγω] [V 2, DV 5, VP 1] *I call together; I collect.*

ὑπάγω [ὑπό + ἄγω] [V 2, DV 5, VP 1] *I depart; I go.*

———

παραχρῆμα [Adv 2] *immediately.*

πολλάκις [Adv 2] *often; frequently.*

Exercises for Lesson 19.

I. Translate into English:
1. ὁ ὄχλος ἐκάθισεν ἐπὶ τὴν γήν. (Mk 11:7)
2. ἔσται σοι δόξα ἐνώπιον πάντων. (Lk 14:10)
3. ὁ Ἰησοῦς πολλάκις συνῆγε τοὺς μαθητὰς αὐτοῦ εἰς ἐκεῖνον τὸν τόπον. (Jn 18:2)
4. οὐδεὶς ἀγαθὸς εἰ μὴ εἷς ὁ θεός. (Mk 10:18)
5. συνάξω πάντας τοὺς καρπούς μου. (Lk 12:17) [Cf. Lesson 22, Vocabulary, for the meaning of καρπός.]
6. πᾶς ὁ ὄχλος ἔρχεται πρὸς αὐτόν. (Mk 2:13)
7. ἡ γυνὴ λέγει τῷ Ἰησοῦ πᾶσαν τὴν ἀλήθειαν. (Mk 5:33)
8. ἡ γυνὴ λέγει τῷ Ἰησοῦ πάντα. (Mk 4:34)
9. πάντες γὰρ αὐτὸν ἔβλεψαν. (Mk 6:50)
10. πάντες οἱ μαθηταὶ ἦσαν σὺν τῷ Ἰησοῦ. (Mt 11:13)
11. αὕτη ἡ χαρὰ ἔσται παντὶ τῷ λαῷ. (Lk 2:10) [Cf. Lesson 22, Vocabulary, for the meaning of λαός.] χαρα
12. πᾶσα σάρξ βλέψει τὸν σωτῆρα. (Lk 3:6)
13. οἱ μαθηταὶ ἤγγισαν εἰς τὴν πόλιν. (Mt 21:1)
14. ἅπαντες γὰρ εἶχον τὸν Ἰησοῦν ὅτι προφήτης ἦν. (Mk 11:32)

15. ἅπαντες γὰρ ὑμεῖς εἷς ἐστε ἐν Χριστῷ Ἰησοῦ. (Gal 3:28)
16. ὁ μαθητὴς ἐβάπτισεν αὐτὸν καὶ τοὺς αὐτοῦ ἅπαντας παραχρῆμα. (Acts 16:33)
17. ἄλλοι δὲ ἔλεγον ὅτι προφήτης ὡς εἷς τῶν προφητῶν ἐστιν. (Mk 6:15)
18. ὕπαγε εἰς τὸν οἶκόν σου πρὸς τοὺς σούς. (Mk 5:19)
19. εἰς τὸν αἰῶνα ἐκ σοῦ μηδεὶς καρπὸν ἐσθίοι. (Mk 11:14)
20. ἀπόλυσον αὐτούς. (Mk 6:36)
21. ὁ μαθητὴς ἀπέλυσεν αὐτούς. (Mk 8:9)

II. Translate into Greek:
   1. Send her away, for she is crying out in our presence. (Mt 15:23)
   2. You (pl.) say to them: "The kingdom of God is approaching you". (Lk 10:9)
   3. The disciples stayed (literally, "sat") in the city according to the word of the Lord. (Lk 24:49)

III. Mk 3:25-31.

The Meaning of the Aorist Active Subjunctive. λύω, Aorist Active Subjunctive. The Adjective ἑκών. The Numerals δύο, τρεῖς, and τέσσαρες. Rules for Accents 12.

Lesson 20

The Meaning of the Aorist Active Subjunctive.

In the aorist system the subjunctive conveys the view of an action which is terminated. <u>This basic viewpoint is usually elaborated by other indications in the text so that the action is viewed as being consummated or affirmed in its entirety</u>. Again, the use of the aorist subjunctive is often in implicit contrast with the present subjunctive, which conveys the idea of an action as continuing or customary, or which places particular emphasis on description (cf. above, Lesson 13).

It should be recalled that only the indicative mood conveys the past of primary time.

For the meaning of the active voice cf. above, Lesson 9.

For the meaning of the subjunctive mood cf. above, Lesson 5. Although the purpose clause is perhaps the most important use of the subjunctive mood in the New Testament, other uses will be presented in future lessons.

λύω, Aorist Active Subjunctive.

The aorist subjunctive active of λύω is conjugated as follows (cf. V 1, VP 1):

Aorist Tense, Active Voice, Subjunctive Mood

	Singular	Plural
1st Person	λύσ–ω	λύσ–ωμεν
2nd Person	λύσ–ῃς	λύσ–ητε
3rd Person	λύσ–ῃ	λύσ–ωσι(ν)

ἔρχεται ὁ βασιλεὺς ἵνα βλέψῃς αὐτόν.
The king comes in order that you may see him.

ἔρχεται ὁ Ἰησοῦς ἵνα βλέπῃς τὸν θεόν.
Jesus comes in order that you may see God.

The first example uses the aorist and simply indicates the action of seeing in its entirety. If the author is thinking of a continuing act he does not choose to imply this by using the present tense of the subjunctive. Hence, by implication, one can probably assume he is thinking of only one act of "seeing", although the context would have to be determinative for this interpretation.

The second example uses the present to connote a continued act of seeing God.

The Adjective ἑκών.

Another type of adjective having endings from the third and first declensions has a stem ending in οντ– (ἑκών, *willing*) (cf. Adj 7):

	Masculine	Singular Feminine	Neuter
n	ἑκών	ἑκοῦσα	ἑκόν
v	ἑκών	ἑκοῦσα	ἑκόν
g	ἑκόντος	ἑκούσης	ἑκόντος
d	ἑκόντι	ἑκούσῃ	ἑκόντι
a	ἑκόντα	ἑκοῦσαν	ἑκόν

	Masculine	Plural Feminine	Neuter
n	ἑκόντες	ἑκοῦσαι	ἑκόντα
v	ἑκόντες	ἑκοῦσαι	ἑκόντα
g	ἑκόντων	ἑκουσῶν	ἑκόντων
d	ἑκοῦσι(ν)	ἑκούσαις	ἑκοῦσι(ν)
a	ἑκόντας	ἑκούσας	ἑκόντα

This is the same paradigm as that of the present participle of εἰμί and the present and future active participles of λύω.

The Numerals δύο, τρεῖς, and τέσσαρες.

The numeral δύο, *two*, is declined as follows (cf. Adj 22):

	Masculine	Feminine	Neuter
n	δύο	δύο	δύο
g	δύο	δύο	δύο
d	δυσί(ν)	δυσί(ν)	δυσί(ν)
a	δύο	δύο	δύο

The numeral τρεῖς, *three*, is declined as follows (cf. Adj 22):

	Masculine	Feminine	Neuter
n	τρεῖς	τρεῖς	τρία
g	τριῶν	τριῶν	τριῶν
d	τρισί(ν)	τρισί(ν)	τρισί(ν)
a	τρεῖς	τρεῖς	τρία

The numeral τέσσαρες, *four*, is declined as follows (cf. Adj 22):

	Masculine	Feminine	Neuter
n	τέσσαρες	τέσσαρες	τέσσαρα
g	τεσσάρων	τεσσάρων	τεσσάρων
d	τέσσαρσι(ν)	τέσσαρσι(ν)	τέσσαρσι(ν)
a	τέσσαρας	τέσσαρας	τέσσαρα

Rules for Accents 12.

The accentuation of nouns and adjectives differs from the accentuation of verbs in that the latter is more regular. There is no rule which enables one to predict the accentuation of the nominative singular of nouns and adjectives. The placing of the accent with these words must be memorized.

In cases other than the nominative singular, the accent of nouns and adjectives tends to remain on the same syllable as in the (masculine) nominative insofar as this is possible according to the lengths of the syllables involved. Thus ἅγιος becomes ἁγία in the feminine nominative singular because the final –α is long. For the same reason, the genitive masculine and neuter singular is ἁγίου, and the dative masculine and neuter singular is ἁγίῳ. But the neuter nominative/accusative singular is ἅγιον because the final syllable is short. Final –οι and –αι are considered short for purposes of accentuation, even though they are diphthongs. Thus ἅγιοι and ἅγιαι are the forms of ἅγιος in the masculine and feminine nominative plural, and ἅγια is the form in the neuter nominative plural (the final −α of the neuter nominative/accusative plural is short, in contrast to the final −α of the feminine nominative singular).

In the first and second declensions, accents which remain on the same syllable as in the nominative tend to change from the acute to the circumflex on the final syllable when this becomes long. Thus ἀδελφός becomes ἀδελφοῦ, ἀδρελφῷ, ἀδελφῶν, and ἀδελφοῖς (but the accusative masculine plural ending −ους never takes the circumflex even though it contains a long diphthong).

Vocabulary for Lesson 20.

ὀπίσω [Prep 1] Governs the genitive case: *after* [in both a spatial and a temporal sense]. This word is also an adverb with the meaning *behind* (cf. Adv 1).

–––

ἄκων, ἄκουσα, ἄκον [Adj 7] *unwilling.*

ἑκών, ἑκοῦσα, ἑκόν [Adj 7] *willing.*

NB: English idiom often demands that ἑκών and ἄκων be translated adverbially, that is *willingly* and *unwillingly*.

–––

δύο, δύο, δύο [Adj 22] *two.*

τέσσαρες, τέσσαρες, τέσσαρα [Adj 22] *four.*

τρεῖς, τρεῖς, τρία [Adj 22] *three.*

–––

εἰρήνη, −ης, ἡ [N 1] *peace.*

οἰκία, −ας, ἡ [N 2] *house.*

τέκνον, −ου, τό [N 7] *child; son, daughter.*

ψυχή, −ῆς, ἡ [N 1] *soul; self; life.*

ὥρα, −ας, ἡ [N 2] *hour.*

–––

διδάσκω [V 2, 21; DV 61; VP 1] *I teach.* This verb takes a double accusative, i.e., the accusative for the person taught and the accusative for the thing taught, often both at the same time.

εὐαγγελίζω (εὐαγγελίσω) [εὐ + ἀγγελίζω—εὐ is an adverb meaning *well*. Cf. Lesson 79. The augment is formed by lengthening the ε to η, the prefix ευ remaining unchanged.] [V 5, DV 102, VP 1] *I preach the good news*. This verb takes the accusative for the person being evangelized, and is usually found as a middle deponent. Cf. Lesson 45.

πιστεύω [V 1, VP 1] *I believe (in)*. This verb is used absolutely, or with a noun in the dative or the accusative case, or with a preposition and its object.

σῴζω (σώσω) [V 5, DV 301, VP 1] *I save*. The iota subscript is found in the present system only.

_____

ὅτε [Conj] *when*. This conjunction is used with the indicative mood.

Exercises for Lesson 20.

I. Translate into English.
  1. πιστεύετε ἐν τῷ εὐαγγελίῳ. (Mk 1:15)
  2. ὅτε ἐγγίζουσιν εἰς τὴν πόλιν, λέγει ὁ Ἰησοῦς τοῖς μαθηταῖς αὐτοῦ, Ὑπάγετε εἰς τὸν οἶκον ἐκεῖνον. (Mk 11:2)
  3. ἔβλεψα τέσσαρας ἀγγέλους. (Apoc 7:1)
  4. ἔρχεται ὁ Ἰησοῦς εἰς τὸν οἶκον τοῦ μαθητοῦ ἵνα σώσῃ τὸν υἱὸν αὐτοῦ. (Mk 3:20)
  5. καὶ οἱ τρεῖς εἰς τὸ ἕν εἰσιν. (1 Jn 5:8) [εἰς τὸ ἕν, "for the one": εἰς has the meaning of purpose, literally, "for the one".]
  6. ὁ θεὸς εὐηγγέλισεν τοὺς ἑαυτοῦ δούλους τοὺς προφήτας. (Apoc 10:7)
  7. περὶ δὲ τῆς ἡμέρας ἐκείνης ἢ τῆς ὥρας οὐδεὶς λέγει. (Mk 13:32)
  8. ἔσονται οἱ δύο εἰς σάρκα μίαν. (Mk 10:8) [εἰς σάρκα μίαν, literally, *for one flesh*; in the context, *one flesh*.]
  9. νῦν ἀπολύεις τὸν δοῦλόν σου ἐν εἰρήνῃ. (Lk 2:29)
  10. ἕξεις ἀγάπην τοῦ θεοῦ σου ἐξ ὅλης τῆς καρδίας σου καὶ ἐξ ὅλης τῆς ψυχῆς σου. (Mk 12:30)
  11. ἔρχεται ὁ μαθητὴς ἄκων.
  12. ἔρχεται ὁ μαθητὴς ἑκών.

13. ἐδίδασκεν γὰρ αὐτοὺς ὁ ᾽Ιησοῦς ὡς ἐξουσίαν ἔχων. (Mk 1:22)

14. ἄλλους ἔσωσεν. (Mk 15:31)

15. πᾶς ὁ λαὸς ἔλεγεν, Τὸ αἷμα ἐφ᾽ ἡμᾶς καὶ ἐπὶ τὰ τέκνα ἡμῶν. (Mt 27:25)

16. ἄνθρωπος εἶχεν τέκνα δύο. (Mt 21:28)

17. ἔρχεται ὁ μαθητὴς ὀπίσω τοῦ ᾽Ιησοῦ. (Mk 8:34)

II. Translate into Greek:
1. He believed in the gospel in order to save his soul. (Mk 1:15, Mk 8:35)
2. The four women are coming in order to teach in the house.
3. And if there should be a son of peace in that house, your peace will be upon him. (Lk 10:6) ["If" is translated here by the Greek word ἐάν with the subjunctive mood; cf. Lesson 21.]

III. Mk 3:32 – 4:4.

The Meaning of the Aorist Active Optative.
λύω, Aorist Active Optative. The Adjective
εὐθύς. The Conjunction ἐάν and Its Use in
Conditional Clauses. Rules for Accents 13.

Lesson 21

The Meaning of the Aorist Active Optative.

In the aorist system the optative conveys the view of a wish which is terminated. <u>This basic viewpoint is usually elaborated by other indications in the text so that the action is viewed as being a wish which is consummated or affirmed in its entirety.</u> Again, the use of the aorist optative is often in implicit contrast with the present optative, which conveys the idea of an action which is wished as continuing or customary, or of an idea which places particular emphasis on description (cf. above, Lesson 14).

It should be recalled that only the indicative mood conveys the past of primary time.

For the meaning of the active voice cf. above, Lesson 9.

For the meaning of the optative mood cf. above, Lesson 6.

λύω, Aorist Active Optative.

The aorist active optative of λύω is conjugated as follows (cf. V 1, VP 1):

Active Voice, Optative Mood, Aorist Tense

	Singular	Plural
1st Person	λύσ–αιμι	λύσ–αιμεν
2nd Person	λύσ–αις	λύσ–αιτε
3rd Person	λύσ–αι	λύσ–αιεν

γράψαι παραχρῆμα πρὸς ἐμέ.
May he write me at once!

γράφοι πολλάκις πρὸς ἐμέ.
May he write me often!

The first example uses the aorist of the optative mood in order
to express a wish with regard to an action viewed in its entirety.
The aorist "tense" of itself does not convey the unicity of this action—
of itself the aorist tense or aspect here conveys simply the action as
terminated. But this, together with the implications conveyed by the
adverb παραχρῆμα, suggests that the author is thinking of a unique
action. [It should be noted again that the word "tense" is
ambiguous—cf. above, Lesson 12. In the indicative mood it refers to
primary time; in the other moods it refers to the aspect of the action
conveyed by the stem: terminated (aorist), not terminated (present),
subsequent (future), or prior (perfect).]

The second example uses the present "tense" of the optative
mood in order to express repeated action. The present tense or
aspect of itself does not directly convey the idea of repetition—of itself
the present stem suggests an action not terminated or open. This,
with the accompanying adverb πολλάκις suggests that the author is
thinking of repeated action.

The Adjective εὐθύς.

A sizeable group of adjectives of the first and third declensions has a
stem ending in –υ (εὐθύς, *straight* [cf. Adj 14]):

	Masculine	Singular Feminine	Neuter
n	εὐθύς	εὐθεῖα	εὐθύ
v	εὐθύς	εὐθεῖα	εὐθύ
g	εὐθέως	εὐθείας	εὐθέως
d	εὐθεῖ	εὐθείᾳ	εὐθεῖ
a	εὐθύν	εὐθεῖαν	εὐθύ

	Masculine	Plural Feminine	Neuter
n	εὐθεῖς	εὐθεῖαι	εὐθέα
v	εὐθεῖς	εὐθεῖαι	εὐθέα
g	εὐθέων	εὐθειῶν	εὐθέων
d	εὐθέσι(ν)	εὐθείαις	εὐθέσι(ν)
a	εὐθεῖς	εὐθείας	εὐθέα

For phonological reasons the υ is replaced by ε before a vowel
and in the dative plural.

The Conjunction ἐάν and Its Use in Conditional Clauses.

The conjunction ἐάν is formed from εἰ and ἄν. It is used to introduce the "if clause" (the "protasis") of some conditional sentences. The mood in the protasis is the subjunctive. The main clause of such a conditional sentence (the "apodosis") may contain a present indicative, a future indicative, an imperative, etc. ἐάν is also found in some indefinite relative clauses, although ἄν is more often found in such a construction:

ἐὰν μὴ δοξάσῃ θεόν, ἁμαρτίαν ἕξει.
If he does not glorify God, he will have sin.

ἐὰν μὴ δοξάσῃ θεόν, ἁμαρτίαν ἔχει.
If he does not glorify God, he has sin.

ὃς ἐὰν μὴ δοξάσῃ θεόν, ἁμαρτίαν ἔχει.
Whoever does not glorify God, has sin.

ὃς ἂν μὴ δοξάσῃ θεόν, ἁμαρτίαν ἔχει.
Whoever does not glorify God, has sin.

The difference in tense in the main verbs of the first two examples—future and present—does not reflect any significant difference in meaning. Similarly, the difference between ὃς ἐάν and ὃς ἄν in the last two examples does not reflect any significant difference in meaning.

Rules for Accents 13.

In the genitive plural, nouns of the first declension have a circumflex accent over the final syllable regardless of the position of the accent in the nominative singular: ἀγαπῶν from ἀγάπη; στρατιωτῶν from στρατιώτης.

Vocabulary for Lesson 21.

ἕνεκα [also ἕνεκεν and εἵνεκεν] [Prep 1] Governs the genitive case:
    for the sake of.
___

βαρύς, -εῖα, -ύ [Adj 14] *heavy; serious.*

βραχύς, –εῖα, –ύ [Adj 14] *short; brief.*

εὐθύς, –εῖα, –ύ [Adj 14] *straight; upright.*

θῆλυς, –εια, –υ [Adj 14] *female.*

ὀξύς, –εῖα, –ύ [Adj 14] *sharp; swift, quick.*

πραΰς, –εῖα, –ύ [Adj14] *meek; gentle.*

ταχύς, –εῖα, –ύ [Adj 14] *swift; fast.*

———

ἀπόστολος, –ου, ὁ [N 6m] *apostle.*

δικαιοσύνη, –ης, ἡ [N 1] *justice; uprightness.*

θάλασσα, –ης, ἡ [N 3] *sea.*

καιρός, –οῦ, ὁ [N 6m] *proper time; present time.*

κεφαλή, –ῆς, ἡ [N 1] *head.*

πλοῖον, –ου, τό [N 7] *boat.*

πρόσωπον, –ου, τό [N 7] *face.*

———

ἐάν [Conj] *if.* This conjunction is used with the subjunctive mood, in contrast to the conjunction εἰ, which is used with the indicative mood.

Exercises for Lesson 21.

I. Translate into English:
1. ἐν ἐκείνῳ τῷ καιρῷ ἤκουσεν ὁ ὄχλος τὸν προφήτην. (Mt 14:1)
2. καὶ ὃς ἂν θέλῃ ἐν ὑμῖν εἶναι πρῶτος ἔστω ὑμῶν δοῦλος. (Mt 20:27)
3. ὁ δὲ Ἰησοῦς πραΰς ἐστιν. (Mt 11:29)
4. ἐπὶ ἡγεμόνων καὶ βασιλέων ἔσεσθε ἕνεκεν ἐμοῦ. (Mk 13:9)
5. οὐ γὰρ βλέπεις εἰς τὸ πρόσωπον ἀνθρώπων. (Mk 12:14)
6. οἱ γὰρ νόμοι τοῦ Κυρίου βαρεῖς οὐκ εἰσίν.

7. ἡ μάχαιρα ὀξεῖα ἦν. [Cf. Lesson 31, Vocabulary, for the meaning of μάχαιρα.]
8. τῶν δὲ ἀποστόλων τὰ ὀνόματά ἐστιν ταῦτα. (Mt 10:2)
9. καὶ ἐὰν μὲν ᾖ ἡ οἰκία ἀγαθή, ἔρχεται ἡ εἰρήνη ὑμῶν ἐπ᾽ αὐτήν. (Mt 10:13) [ἔρχεται—present tense with future meaning.]
10. πᾶς ὁ ὄχλος πρὸς τὴν θάλασσαν ἐπὶ τῆς γῆς ἦσαν. (Mk 4:1)
11. βλέπει ἄγγελον πρὸς τῇ κεφαλῇ. (Jn 20:12)
12. ἡ γὰρ καρδία σου οὐκ ἔστιν εὐθεῖα ἔμπροσθεν τοῦ θεοῦ. (Acts 8:21)
13. ἔρχεται ὁ προφήτης πρὸς ὑμᾶς ἐν ὁδῷ δικαιοσύνης. (Mt 21:32)
14. ἐὰν δὲ ὁ ὀφθαλμός σου πονηρὸς ᾖ, ὅλον τὸ σῶμά σου ἐν τῷ σκότει ἔσται. (Mt 6:23)
15. καὶ μετὰ βραχὺ ἔβλεψα τὸν ἄνθρωπον. (Lk 22:58)
16. ἦν τὸ πλοῖον ἐν μέσῳ τῆς θαλάσσης. (Mk 6:47)
17. ἔστω δὲ πᾶς ἄνθρωπος ταχὺς εἰς τὸ ἀκούειν. (Jas 1:19)
18. οὐκ ἔστιν ἄρσεν καὶ θηλὺ ἐν Χριστῷ Ἰησοῦ. (Gal 3:28) [Cf. Lesson 76, John 10:6, p. 415, for the meaning of θηλὺ.]
   ἄρσην – male

II. Translate into Greek:
   1. No one is a good prophet unless God be with him. (Jn 3:2)
   2. Jesus goes in the boat to a deserted place in order not to be with the crowd. (Mk 6:32)
   3. And the rest of the women were saying these things to the apostles on the same day. (Lk 24:10) [Cf. Lesson 22, Vocabulary, for the meaning of "the rest".]

III. Mk 4:5-12.

The Meaning of the Aorist Active Infinitive
and Participle. λύω, Aorist Active
Infinitive and Participle. The Adjective
μέγας. Rules for Accents 14.

Lesson 22

The Meaning of the Aorist Active Infinitive and Participle.

In the aorist system the infinitive conveys the view of an action
which is terminated. <u>In the infinitive mood this basic viewpoint is
usually elaborated by other indications in the text so that the action
is viewed as consummated or viewed in its entirety</u>. (Only the
indicative mood conveys the past of primary time.) In the accusative
with the infinitive construction (cf. above, Lesson 8) the aorist
infinitive normally expresses relative time, with reference to what is
prior to the time of the main verb, in implicit contrast to the present
infinitive, which expresses time contemporaneous with the main
verb.

For the meaning of the active voice cf. above, Lesson 9.
For the meaning of the infinitive mood cf. above, Lesson 4.

The aorist participle conveys the view of an action which is
terminated. The action of the aorist participle is thus seen as being
prior to the action of the main verb precisely because the action is
viewed as terminated, in contrast with the action of the present
participle. (Cf. the reasoning involved in the simultaneity of the
present infinitive given in Lesson 16.)

For the meaning of the active voice cf. above, Lesson 9.
For the meaning of the participial mood cf. above, Lesson 7.

λύω, Aorist Active Infinitive and Participle.

The aorist infinitive active of λύω is λῦσ–αι (cf. V 1, VP 1).

The aorist participle active of λύω is declined as follows (cf. V 1, VP 1, Adj 12):

	Masculine	Singular Feminine	Neuter
n	λύσ–ας	λύσ–ασα	λῦσ–αν
v	λύσ–ας	λύσ–ασα	λῦσ–αν
g	λύσ–αντος	λυσ–άσης	λύσ–αντος
d	λύσ–αντι	λυσ–άσῃ	λύσ–αντι
a	λύσ–αντα	λύσ–ασαν	λῦσ–αν

	Masculine	Plural Feminine	Neuter
n	λύσ–αντες	λύσ–ασαι	λύσ–αντα
v	λύσ–αντες	λύσ–ασαι	λύσ–αντα
g	λυσ–άντων	λυσ–ασῶν	λυσ–άντων
d	λύσ–ασι(ν)	λυσ–άσαις	λύσ–ασι(ν)
a	λύσ–αντας	λυσ–άσας	λύσ–αντα

The aorist "tense" in the infinitive mood may be used to describe action which <u>in itself</u> is continued or repeated:

> θέλει γράψαι πολλάκις.
> *He wishes to write often.*

But the fact that the aorist "tense" of the infinitive is used and not the present "tense" indicates that the writer or speaker <u>is viewing</u> the many acts of writing in their entirety, i.e., as in some way terminated or closed. If the writer or speaker had wished to emphasize the repeated or continuous nature of the action he would have used the present infinitive:

> θέλει γράφειν πολλάκις.
> *He wishes to write often.*

The Adjective μέγας.

The irregular adjective μέγας, *great, large* (cf. Adj 22):

	Masculine	Singular Feminine	Neuter
n	μέγας	μεγάλη	μέγα
v	μέγας	μεγάλη	μέγα
g	μεγάλου	μεγάλης	μεγάλου
d	μεγάλῳ	μεγάλῃ	μεγάλῳ
a	μέγαν	μεγάλην	μέγα

	Masculine	Plural Feminine	Neuter
n	μεγάλοι	μεγάλαι	μεγάλα
v	μεγάλοι	μεγάλαι	μεγάλα
g	μεγάλων	μεγάλων	μεγάλων
d	μεγάλοις	μεγάλαις	μεγάλοις
a	μεγάλους	μεγάλας	μεγάλα

There are thus two stems for this important word: μεγα– and μεγαλ–.

Rules for Accents 14.

Feminine adjectives of the first declension have a circumflex accent on the ending of the genitive plural, even when the accent in the nominative singular is not on the final syllable, provided the stem used in the feminine is different from the stem used in the masculine and neuter. If the stem used in the feminine is not different, the accent on the feminine genitive plural is on the same syllable as in the masculine and neuter. Thus πᾶσα > πασῶν (compare masculine and neuter πάντων), ἑκοῦσα > ἑκουσῶν (compare masculine and neuter ἑκόντων), εὐθεῖα > εὐθειῶν (compare masculine and neuter εὐθέων). But ἁγία > ἁγίων (compare masculine and neuter ἁγίων).

Vocabulary for Lesson 22.

χωρίς [Prep 1] Governs the genitive case: *without*; *besides*. This
   word also occurs as an adverb meaning *separately* [Adv 3].

––

μέγας, μεγάλη, μέγα [Adj 22] *great*; *large*.

–––

ἀρχή, –ῆς, ἡ [N 1] *beginning*; *ruling power*.

διδάσκαλος, –ου, ὁ [N 6m] *teacher.*

ἐντολή, –ῆς, ἡ [N 1] *commandment.*

θρόνος, –ου, ὁ [N 6m] *throne.*

καρπός, –οῦ, ὁ [N 6m] *fruit.*

σάββατον, –ου, τό [N 7; N 33] *Sabbath* [This word is often found in the plural form but with the same meaning as in the singular. The irregular dative σάββασιν usually replaces σαββάτοις.]

συναγωγή, –ῆς, ἡ [N 1] *synagogue; assembly.*

χαρά, –ᾶς, ἡ [N 2] *joy; happiness.*

_____

δώδεκα [Adj 21] *twelve.*

λοιπός, –ή, –όν [Adj 1] I. As adjective: *remaining.* II. As adverb: (τὸ) λοιπόν or τοῦ λοιποῦ [Adv 3]: *henceforth.* III. As noun: λοιπόν, –οῦ, τό [N 7] *the rest.*

πρεσβύτερος, –α, –ον [Adj 2] *elder.* This word is usually used as a substantive [N 6m].

_____

ἰδού [Inter] *look!*

_____

καθώς [Conj] *as; inasmuch as.* This conjunction is used when comparing verbs, i.e., clauses, in contrast to ὡς, which is used more in comparisons between nouns and adjectives. Cf. above, Lesson 17, for the presentation of ὡς in the vocabulary.

Exercises for Lesson 22.

I. Translate into English:
1. ταῦτα λέγω ὑμῖν ἵνα ἡ χαρὰ ἡ ἐμὴ ἐν ὑμῖν ᾖ. (Jn 15:11)
2. ἤγγισεν ὁ καιρὸς τῶν καρπῶν. (Mt 21:34)
3. ἔρχονται πρὸς τὸν Ἰησοῦν οἱ ἀρχιερεῖς καὶ οἱ γραμματεῖς καὶ οἱ πρεσβύτεροι. (Mk 11:27)
4. ἦτε ἐν τῷ καιρῷ ἐκείνῳ χωρὶς Χριστοῦ. (Eph 2:12)

5. οἱ δὲ λέγουσιν αὐτοῖς καθὼς λέγει ὁ Ἰησοῦς. (Mk 11:6)

6. Ἀρχὴ τοῦ εὐαγγελίου Ἰησοῦ Χριστοῦ υἱοῦ θεοῦ. (Mk 1:1)

7. λέγει πρὸς τοὺς λοιποὺς ἀποστόλους. (Acts 2:37)

8. καὶ αὐτὸς ἐδίδασκεν ἐν ταῖς συναγωγαῖς αὐτῶν. (Lk 4:15)

9. ἦν γὰρ ἡ παῖς ἐτῶν δώδεκα. (Mk 5:42)

10. καὶ ἰδοὺ φωνὴ ἐκ τῶν οὐρανῶν λέγουσα, Οὗτός ἐστιν ὁ υἱός μου. (Mt 3:17)

11. τὸ σάββατον διὰ τὸν ἄνθρωπόν ἐστιν καὶ οὐχ ὁ ἄνθρωπος διὰ τὸ σάββατον. (Mk 2:27)

12. καὶ κράξας φωνῇ μεγάλῃ λέγει, Τί ἐμοὶ καὶ σοί, Ἰησοῦ υἱὲ τοῦ θεοῦ; (Mk 5:7) [φωνῇ μεγάλῃ—a dative of manner, indicating the manner in which something takes place; translate: *with a loud* (i.e., *great) voice.*]

13. τὸ λοιπόν, ἀδελφοί, ἀγαθοὶ ἔστε. (Phil 3:1)

14. οὐκ εἰμὶ ὡς οἱ λοιποὶ τῶν ἀνθρώπων. (Lk 18:11)

15. αὕτη ἐστὶν ἡ μεγάλη καὶ πρώτη ἐντολή. (Mt 22:38)

16. οὐκ ἔστιν μαθητὴς ὑπὲρ τὸν διδάσκαλον. (Mt 10:24)

17. ὁ οὐρανὸς θρόνος ἐστιν τοῦ θεοῦ. (Mt 5:34)

II. Translate into Greek:
1. The child will be great in the presence of the Lord. (Lk 1:15)
2. In the beginning was the Word that we all saw. (Jn 1:1)
3. I am an apostle and a teacher of the Gentiles in faith and truth. (1 Tim 2:7)

III. Mk 4:13-20.

The Meaning of the Perfect Active
Indicative. λύω, Perfect Active Indicative.
The Formation of the Reduplication. The
Adjective πολύς. Rules for Accents 15.

Lesson 23

The Meaning of the Perfect Active Indicative.

The perfect forms a whole system distinct from that of the present
and aorist systems (which are complementary) and the future
system (which, like the perfect system, is independent). The perfect
system expresses the view of an action as being in some way prior.
(Cf. Lesson 20.) In the indicative mood the perfect tense is normally
combined with other elements in the context, including the
meaning of the verb itself, to indicate the continuing, present result
of a prior action. This is an expression of primary time. Only in the
indicative does the perfect express primary time.
        For the meaning of the active voice cf. above, Lesson 9.
        For the meaning of the indicative mood cf. above, Lesson 2.

λύω, Perfect Active Indicative.

There are two types of stem in which the perfect system is found in
the active voice: 1) the "weak" (the more frequently found), which
has a −κ as a distinguishing element immediately before the
endings; 2) the "strong", which does not have a −κ before the same
endings. The meaning is the same for both weak and strong perfect
active stems. This distinction is found only in the active voice.
        Also common to both weak and strong perfect active forms
and of the perfect tense (in the middle and passive voices as well) is
the "reduplication", a doubling of initial elements in the verbal root.
There is a variety of ways in which reduplication is formed, as will
be explained below. The most common way, for verbs beginning
with a single consonant, is to repeat the single consonant with the
vowel ε and prefix these two letters to the verbal root (not to the

prefix, if the verb is compound). For λύω the perfect active indicative is as follows (cf. V 1, VP 1).

Active Voice, Indicative Mood, Perfect Tense

	Singular	Plural
1st Person	λέλυκ–α	λελύκ–αμεν
2nd Person	λέλυκ–ας	λελύκ–ατε
3rd Person	λέλυκ–ε(ν)	λελύκ–ασι(ν)
		[λέλυκ–αν]

I have loosed	*We have loosed*
You (sg.) *have loosed*	*You* (pl.) *have loosed*
He (*She, It*) *has loosed*	*They have loosed*

The form λέλυκαν is found at times. This is the use of the aorist active indicative third person plural ending –αν instead of the proper perfect ending –ασι(ν).

The strong perfect has no κ, as was stated above. The precise letter which appears before the ending to form the strong perfect varies with the verb and is ordinarily related to the final consonant of the verbal root. The following example is of the strong perfect of the verb γράφω, which has a φ (cf. V 4, DV 53, VP 1). There is no rule which enables one to state in advance which verbs have weak perfects and which strong.

Active Voice, Indicative Mood, Perfect Tense

	Singular	Plural
1st Person	γέγραφ–α	γεγράφ–αμεν
2nd Person	γέγραφ–ας	γεγράφ–ατε
3rd Person	γέγραφ–ε(ν)	γεγράφ–ασι(ν)

I have written	*We have written*
You (sg.) *have written*	*You* (pl.) *have written*
He (*She, It*) *has written*	*They have written*

As was stated above, the Greek perfect indicative indicates the continuing result of a prior action:

ἀπολέλυκα τοὺς δούλους.
I have freed the slaves [and they are now free as a result of my past action].

ὃ γέγραφα, γέγραφα.
What I have written, I have written [and it now stands as I
wanted it to stand when I wrote it in the past].

The Formation of the Reduplication.

The formation of the reduplication is independent of the categories
of weak or strong perfect active. It is also found in the middle and
passive voices with no change of rules for its formation. The
formation of the reduplication depends on how the verbal root
begins, not how it ends. Each verb usually has only one type of
reduplication. Reduplication normally takes place at the beginning
of the root, not, if the verb is compound, at the beginning of the
prefix.

    1) Most verbs beginning with a single consonant form the
reduplication by repeating the single consonant with the vowel ε and
prefix these two letters to the root: λύω > λέλυκα; πιστεύω >
πεπίστευκα.

    2) If the root begins with a χ, φ, or θ, the consonant in the
reduplicating syllable is κ, π, or τ respectively (that is, the basic
sound without the aspiration): χράομαι > κέχρημαι [the endings
are of the middle voice]; φεύγω > πέφευγα; θύω > τέθυκα.

    3) Roots beginning with π, β, κ, γ, τ or δ followed by λ, μ, ν or ρ
form the reduplication by prefixing the first consonant followed by
an ε: γράφω > γέγραφα.

    4) In roots beginning with two consonants other than those
indicated in Rule 3, or with a "double consonant" (ξ, ζ, ψ), the
reduplication is formed by prefixing an ε with a smooth breathing:
ξενίζω > ἐξένικα.

    5) Roots beginning with ρ form the reduplication by prefixing
ἐρ– (more usual) or ῥε– (less usual): ῥίζομαι > ἐρριζωμένοι [the
ending is of the middle or passive participle]; ῥαντίζω >
ῥεραντισμένοι [the ending is of the middle or passive participle].

    6) Roots beginning with a vowel form the reduplication by
lengthening the vowel, as is done for the formation of the augment
in the imperfect and aorist indicative. Thus ἑτοιμάζω > ἡτοίμακα.
Note that with these verbs the augment and the reduplication look
alike. They are not to be confused. The reduplication is found in all
moods of the perfect system, whereas the augment is found only in
the indicative (in the pluperfect).

    7) A number of verbs have an irregular reduplication. These
verbs will be studied in future lessons. There are not many.

At this stage the student is advised to learn actively only rules 1, 2, and 6. Passive knowledge of the other rules is sufficient for the present.

The Adjective πολύς.

The irregular adjective πολύς, *much, many* (cf. Adj 22):

	Masculine	Singular Feminine	Neuter
n	πολύς	πολλή	πολύ
v	πολύς	πολλή	πολύ
g	πολλοῦ	πολλῆς	πολλοῦ
d	πολλῷ	πολλῇ	πολλῷ
a	πολύν	πολλήν	πολύ

	Masculine	Plural Feminine	Neuter
n	πολλοί	πολλαί	πολλά
v	πολλοί	πολλαί	πολλά
g	πολλῶν	πολλῶν	πολλῶν
d	πολλοῖς	πολλαῖς	πολλοῖς
a	πολλούς	πολλάς	πολλά

There are two roots, πολυ– and πολλο–. Use of the article with this adjective is relatively rare, but it does occur.

Rules for Accents 15.

In the first declension the α in the ending –ας (i.e., in the genitive singular and accusative plural) is always long. Thus τὰς κώμας in Mk 6:6 (the ω does not have a circumflex, showing that the α in the accusative plural ending is long) and ἀπ᾽ ἀγορᾶς in Mk 7:4 (the circumflex accent over the α of the genitive singular ending shows that it is long). But when an accent occurs over the α of these endings it is circumflex only in the genitive; in the accusative plural it is acute or grave. Thus ἀπ᾽ ἀγορᾶς in Mk 7:4 but τὰς φωνὰς in Acts 13:27. (Cf. the acute accent over α in the article.) Contrast the circumflex accent over the α in ἡμᾶς and ὑμᾶς.

Vocabulary for Lesson 23.

πλήν [Prep 1] Governs the the genitive case: *except*. This word is
    also used as a conjunction, meaning *however* [Conj].

___

πολύς, πολλή, πολύ [Adj 22] *much; many*.

___

γραφή, –ῆς, ἡ [N 1] *writing; Scripture*.

ἐπαγγελία, –ας, ἡ [N 2] *promise*.

λίθος, –ου, ὁ [N 6m] *stone*.

παιδίον, –ου, τό [N 7] *infant; child*.

σοφία, –ας, ἡ [N 2] *wisdom*.

χρόνος, –ου, ὁ [N 6m] *time*.

___

δεξιός, –ά, –όν [Adj 2] *right* [as opposed to left].

ἔσχατος, –η, –ον [Adj 1] *last*.

μακάριος, –α, –ον [Adj 2] *blessed; happy*.

μόνος, –η, –ον [Adj 1] *only; alone*.

___

ἑτοιμάζω (ἑτοιμάσω) [V 5, VP 1] *I prepare*.

θύω [V 1, DV 129, VP 1] *I sacrifice*.

ξενίζω (ξενίσω) [V 5, VP 1] *I receive as a guest; I surprise* [ξένος
    means *guest* and *stranger*—cf. Vocabulary, Lesson 45.
    Hence the rather odd pairing of meanings.]

ῥαντίζω (ῥαντίσω) [V 5, DV 269, VP 1] *I sprinkle*.

___

τέ [Conj] This is a weak form of καί and is an enclitic: *and*. τε is
    postpositive.

___

τότε [Adv 2] *then; at that time*.

Exercises for Lesson 23.

I. Translate into English:
1. ἡμῖν γάρ ἐστιν ἡ ἐπαγγελία καὶ τοῖς τέκνοις ἡμῶν.
   (Acts 2:39)
2. ἄνθρωποί τινες ἐξένισαν ἀγγέλους. (Heb 13:2)
3. τότε λέγει αὐτοῖς ὁ Ἰησοῦς, Ὑπάγετε. (Mt 4:10)
4. οὐκ ἦσαν ἄλλοι πλὴν αὐτῶν. (Mk 12:32)
5. εἴ τις θέλει πρῶτος εἶναι, ἔστω ἔσχατος. (Mk 9:35)
6. παιδία, ἐσχάτη ὥρα ἐστίν. (1 Jn 2:18)
7. πλὴν οὐχ ὡς ἡμεῖς θέλομεν ἀλλ' ὡς ὑμεῖς. (Mt 26:39)
8. ἑτοίμασον τὴν ὁδὸν Κυρίου. (Mk 1:3)
9. τὴν βίβλον καὶ πάντα τὸν λαὸν ἐράντισεν. (Heb 9:19)
10. ἐδίδασκον αὐτὸν ἐν παραβολαῖς πολλά. (Mk 4:2)
11. ἡ ὁδὸς τοῦ Κυρίου ἑτοίμη ἐστίν. [Cf. Lesson 24,
    Vocabulary, for the meaning of ἑτοίμη.]
12. ἡ πίστις ὑμῶν οὐκ ἔστιν ἐν σοφίᾳ ἀνθρώπων ἀλλ' ἐν
    δυνάμει θεοῦ. (1 Cor 2:5)
13. καὶ ἔρχεται ὁ Ἰησοῦς πρὸς τοὺς μαθητὰς αὐτοῦ καὶ
    βλέπει ὄχλον πολὺν περὶ αὐτούς. (Mk 9:14)
14. τὰ ἔθνη οὐ θύουσιν θεῷ. (1 Cor 10:20)
15. μετὰ δὲ πολὺν χρόνον ἔρχεται ὁ Κύριος τῶν δούλων
    ἐκείνων. (Mt 25:19)
16. ὁ μαθητὴς ἐπίστευσε τῇ γραφῇ καὶ τῷ λόγῳ ὃν εἶπεν
    ὁ Ἰησοῦς. (Jn 2:22)
17. ἑτοιμάσουσιν τοὺς λίθους οἱ ἐργάται.
18. μακάριοι οἱ ὀφθαλμοὶ οἱ βλέποντες ἃ βλέπετε. (Lk
    10:23)
19. ὁ Ἰησοῦς ἐστιν ἐν δεξιᾷ τοῦ θεοῦ. (Rom 8:34)
20. ἦν τὰ πλοῖα ἐν μέσῳ τῆς θαλάσσης καὶ ὁ Ἰησοῦς
    μόνος ἐπὶ τῆς γῆς. (Mk 6:47)
21. οἱ δοῦλοι συνῆγον πάντας, πονηρούς τε καὶ ἀγαθούς.
    (Mt 22:10)

II. Translate into Greek:
1. He said that the law was not against the promise of
   God. (Gal 3:21)   having cried out
2. The father of the children, crying out, says "I believe",
   and they are all happy. (Mk 9:24)
3. The Scripture does not say that the Christ is from that city.
   (Jn 7:42)

III. Mk 4:21-28.

Lesson 24

The Meaning of the Pluperfect Active Indicative.

The pluperfect indicative expresses a prior action in primary time and normally, by means of the context, conveys the idea of a <u>past</u> result of this prior action. Thus it differs from the perfect indicative, which expresses a prior action and normally, by means of the context, conveys the idea of a <u>present</u> result of this prior action. (The distinctive element of the perfect stem—prior action—is thus characteristic of both tenses.) The pluperfect tense exists only in the indicative mood.

For the meaning of the active voice cf. above, Lesson 9.

For the meaning of the indicative mood cf. above, Lesson 2.

λύω, Pluperfect Active Indicative.

The pluperfect indicative active of λύω is formed from the perfect stem with special endings <u>and an augment which may be omitted</u> (cf. V 1, VP 1):

Active Voice, Indicative Mood, Pluperfect Tense

	Singular	Plural
1st Person	(ἐ)–λελύκ–ειν	(ἐ)–λελύκ–ειμεν
2nd Person	(ἐ)–λελύκ–εις	(ἐ)–λελύκ–ειτε
3rd Person	(ἐ)–λελύκ–ει	(ἐ)–λελύκ–εισαν

I had loosed	*We had loosed*
You (sg.) *had loosed*	*You* (pl.) *had loosed*
He (*She, It*) *had loosed*	*They had loosed*

The augment is formed according to the rules for the augment for the imperfect and the aorist. It is found only in the pluperfect.

ὃ ἐγεγράφει ἐγεγράφει.
What he had written he had written. ["What he had written" and "he had written" express of themselves priority; the context would suggest the emphasis placed on the result.]

The Adjective αἰώνιος.

One category of second declension adjectives has the same form for the masculine and feminine (αἰώνιος, *eternal*) (cf. Adj 5):

	Masculine	Singular Feminine	Neuter
n	αἰώνιος	αἰώνιος	αἰώνιον
v	αἰώνιε	αἰώνιε	αἰώνιον
g	αἰωνίου	αἰωνίου	αἰωνίου
d	αἰωνίῳ	αἰωνίῳ	αἰωνίῳ
a	αἰώνιον	αἰώνιον	αἰώνιον

	Masculine	Plural Feminine	Neuter
n	αἰώνιοι	αἰώνιοι	αἰώνια
v	αἰώνιοι	αἰώνιοι	αἰώνια
g	αἰωνίων	αἰωνίων	αἰωνίων
d	αἰωνίοις	αἰωνίοις	αἰωνίοις
a	αἰωνίους	αἰωνίους	αἰώνια

Many adjectives in this category are compound adjectives, i.e., adjectives formed from two elements. For example: ἔκφοβος, composed of ἐκ and φόβος [a substantive], or εὔκαιρος, composed of εὐ and καιρός [a substantive]. The most common type of adjective in this category is the one composed of an adjective with the prefix of an alpha privative. (See following section.)

The Alpha Privative.

A common way to form a compound adjective is to prefix an ἀ (called an "alpha privative") to negate the force of the adjective's meaning: δυνατός, *powerful* > ἀδύνατος, *impossible*. (In English the prefixes in-, im-, and un- perform the same function.) The Greek adjective δυνατός, *powerful*, can have the three normal endings for an adjective in the first and second declensions, –ός, –ή, –όν. But when it becomes negated through the prefixing of an alpha privative it has the same ending for the masculine and feminine: –ος, –ος, –ον. The alpha privative ususally makes the accent recessive, i.e., the accent will be on the third-last syllable when this is possible. Thus the accent for πιστός, *faithful*, moves to the third-last syllable in the word ἄπιστος, *faithless*.

Rules for Accents 16.

In the first declension, if the final α of the nominative singular is short, the α of the accusative singular ending is short; if the α of the nominative singular is long, the α of the accusative singular ending is long. Thus the final α of ἀλήθεια is short, and the accusative singular is accordingly ἀλήθειαν. But the final α of βασιλεία is long, and the accusative singular is accordingly βασιλείαν. Cf. Mk 5:33 and Mk 4:30.

As was noted above, the accent in words formed with an alpha privative tends to be recessive. Thus δυνατός, δυνατή, δυνατόν becomes ἀδύνατος, ἀδύνατος, ἀδύνατον.

Vocabulary for Lesson 24.

μέχρι(ς) [Prep 1] Governs the genitive case: *until; as far as*. This word is also used to form a conjunction with οὗ, with the meaning *until*.

———

ἄδικος, ἄδικος, ἄδικον [Adj 5] *unjust; evil*.

αἰώνιος, αἰώνιος, αἰώνιον [Adj 5] *eternal*.

ἀκάθαρτος, ἀκάθαρτος, ἀκάθαρτον [Adj 5] *unclean*.

ἄκαρπος, ἄκαρπος, ἄκαρπον [Adj 5] *fruitless*.

ἁμαρτωλός, ἁμαρτωλός, ἁμρτωλόν [Adj 5] *sinful*. [This is not an adjective formed with an alpha privative.] This word is often used as a noun, *sinner* [N 6m].

ἄνομος, ἄνομος, ἄνομον [Adj 5] *lawless; not under the law.*

ἄπιστος, ἄπιστος, ἄπιστον [Adj 5] *unfaithful; unbelieving.*

ἔνοχος, ἔνοχος, ἔνοχον [Adj 5] *subject to; guilty of; liable to; liable to the penalty of* [dative of person, genitive of thing].

ἔρημος, ἔρημος, ἔρημον [Adj 5] *deserted.* This word is also used as a noun, *desert* [N 6f]; cf. Lesson 8.

ἕτοιμος, ἕτοιμος, ἕτοιμον [Adj 5] *ready; prepared.* The feminine in −η is also found.

οὐράνιος, οὐράνιος, οὐράνιον [Adj 5] *heavenly.*

───

ἀμήν [Part] *amen; truly* [Hebrew word].

───

πάλιν [Adv 2] *again; furthermore.*

πῶς [Adv 3] *how?*

Exercises for Lesson 24.

I. Translate into English:
1. ἦν ἐν τῇ συναγωγῇ αὐτῶν ἄνθρωπος ἐν πνεύματι ἀκαθάρτῳ. (Mk 1:23)
2. ὑμεῖς οὐχ ἕτοιμοί ἐστε.
3. ὁ δὲ θεὸς τῆς εἰρήνης μετὰ πάντων ὑμῶν. ἀμήν. (Rom 15:33)
4. ἦν πιστὸς μέχρι θανάτου. (Phil 2:8)
5. ὁ θεός, οὐκ εἰμὶ ὡς οἱ λοιποὶ τῶν ἀνθρώπων, οἱ ἄδικοι καὶ ἁμαρτωλοί εἰσιν. (Lk 18:11)
6. τὸ βάπτισμα ἐξ οὐρανοῦ ἦν ἢ ἐξ ἀνθρώπων; (Mk 11:30)
7. οἱ δὲ πάλιν ἔκραξαν. (Mk 15:13)
8. ἤμεθα ἐν τῷ οἴκῳ ἀπὸ τῆς πρώτης ἡμέρας μέχρι ταύτης τῆς ὥρας. (Acts 10:30)
9. ἔστε πίστοι τῷ Χριστῷ ἵνα μὴ ἦτε ἄκαρποι. (Tit 3:14)
10. διὰ τοῦτο οὐκ ἐπίστευσαν, ὅτι πάλιν εἶπεν ὁ προφήτης. . . (Jn 12:39)
11. κηρύσσετε τὸ εὐαγγέλιον μέχρις οὗ ὁ Κύριος πάλιν ᾖ μετὰ ἡμῶν. (Mk 16:15)

12. μὴ ἴσθι ἄνομος θεοῦ. (1 Cor 9:21)
13. πῶς ἔσται τοῦτο; (Lk 1:34)
14. αὐτὸς ἔνοχός ἐστιν αἰωνίου ἁμαρτίας. (Mk 3:29)
15. γύναι, μὴ ἴσθι ἄπιστος. (Jn 20:27)
16. ὁ προφήτης ἦν ἐπ᾽ ἐρήμοις τόποις. (Mk 1:45)
17. ἔνοχος θανάτου ἐστίν. (Mt 26:66)

II. Translate into Greek:
1. There was a man by the road who had a spirit of an unclean demon. (Lk 4:33)
2. The just are going into eternal life. (Mt 25:46)
3. How do the women not under the law believe my words? (Jn 5:47)

III. Mk 4:29-36.

The Meaning of the Perfect Active
Infinitive, Participle, and Subjunctive.
λύω, Perfect Active Infinitive, Participle,
and Subjunctive. The Adjective ἀληθής.
Rules for Accents 17.

Lesson 25.

The Meaning of the Perfect Active Infinitive, Participle, and Subjunctive.

The perfect infinitive, participle, and subjunctive all express the
aspect characteristic of the perfect stem: prior action. And verbs in
all three moods usually express the present result of this prior
action in conjunction with various factors in the context, including
the meaning of the verbs in question. But the present result of a
prior action in the infinitive and participial moods is not that of
primary time but that of relative time in relation to the verbs on
which they depend. The perfect subjunctive is rare, and stresses the
state resulting from a prior action. The relation of this state to
primary time must be discerned from the main verb of the sentence.

For the meaning of the active voice cf. above, Lesson 9.

For the meaning of the infinitive, participial, and subjunctive
moods cf. above, Lessons 4, 5, and 7.

λύω, Perfect Active Infinitive, Participle, and Subjunctive.

The perfect infinitive active of λύω is λελυκ-έναι (cf. V 1, VP 1). An
example of a strong perfect is γεγραφ-έναι:

> λέγουσιν αὐτὸν γεγραφέναι ἐκεῖνο ὃ γέγραφεν.
> *They say that he has written what he has written.*

> αὐτὴ εἶπεν αὐτὸν γεγραφέναι ἐκεῖνο ὃ γέγραφεν.
> *She said that he had written what he had written.*

The relation to primary time of the state of "being written" as a result of a prior action depends on the main verbs λέγουσιν and εἶπεν.

The perfect active participle of λύω is declined as follows (cf. V 1, VP 1, Adj 17):

	Masculine	Singular Feminine	Neuter
n	λελυκ–ώς	λελυκ–υῖα	λελυκ–ός
v	λελυκ–ώς	λελυκ–υῖα	λελυκ–ός
g	λελυκ–ότος	λελυκ–υίας	λελυκ–ότος
d	λελυκ–ότι	λελυκ–υίᾳ	λελυκ–ότι
a	λελυκ–ότα	λελυκ–υῖαν	λελυκ–ός

	Masculine	Plural Feminine	Neuter
n	λελυκ–ότες	λελυκ–υῖαι	λελυκ–ότα
v	λελυκ–ότες	λελυκ–υῖαι	λελυκ–ότα
g	λελυκ–ότων	λελυκ–υιῶν	λελυκ–ότων
d	λελυκ–όσι(ν)	λελυκ–υίαις	λελυκ–όσι(ν)
a	λελυκ–ότας	λελυκ–υίας	λελυκ–ότα

It should be noted that the nominative and accusative neuter singular are easily confused with the nominative masculine singular of the second declension.

τὸ παιδίον τεθνηκός ἐστιν.
The child is dead [literally, *the one having died*].

The perfect subjunctive active of λύω is formed by the use of the perfect participle active with the subjunctive of εἰμί (cf. V 1, VP 1, VP 17):

Active Voice, Subjunctive Mood, Perfect Tense

	Singular	Plural
1st Person	λελυκώς(–υῖα, –ός) ὦ	λελυκότες (–υῖαι, –ότα) ὦμεν
2nd Person	λελυκώς(–υῖα, –ός) ᾖς	λελυκότες (–υῖαι, –ότα) ἦτε
3rd Person	λελυκώς(–υῖα, –ός) ᾖ	λελυκότες (–υῖαι, –ότα) ὦσι(ν)

The perfect active subjunctive is rarely used in the New Testament.

There is no example of a perfect active imperative or optative in the New Testament.

This lesson terminates the presentation of the active voice of λύω.

The Adjective ἀληθής.

One category of third declension adjectives has a root ending in –εσ and has the same form in the masculine and feminine (ἀληθής, *true*) (cf. Adj 15):

	Masculine	Singular Feminine	Neuter
n	ἀληθής	ἀληθής	ἀληθές
v	ἀληθές	ἀληθές	ἀληθές
g	ἀληθοῦς	ἀληθοῦς	ἀληθοῦς
d	ἀληθεῖ	ἀληθεῖ	ἀληθεῖ
a	ἀληθῆ	ἀληθῆ	ἀληθές

	Masculine	Plural Feminine	Neuter
n	ἀληθεῖς	ἀληθεῖς	ἀληθῆ
v	ἀληθεῖς	ἀληθεῖς	ἀληθῆ
g	ἀληθῶν	ἀληθῶν	ἀληθῶν
d	ἀληθέσι(ν)	ἀληθέσι(ν)	ἀληθέσι(ν)
a	ἀληθεῖς	ἀληθεῖς	ἀληθῆ

The form ἀληθῆ is from ἀληθέσα > ἀληθέα (tendency of σ between vowels to disappear) > ἀληθῆ (the latter being a contraction of εα to η). The genitive singular is from ἀληθέσος > ἀληθέος (disappearance of σ) > ἀληθοῦς (contraction of εο into ου). The dative singular is from ἀληθέσι (disappearance of σ between vowels). The form ἀληθεῖς is from ἀληθέσες > ἀληθέες, with the contraction of εε into ει.

Rules for Accents 17.

The α of the nominative and accusative neuter plural endings of the second declension is always short. Thus σημεῖα is the nominative and accusative plural form for σημεῖον. Cf. Mk 16:17.

Vocabulary for Lesson 25.

ἕως [Prep 1] Governs the genitive case: *until*. This word is also used as a conjunction meaning *while* or *until*, often with ὅτου, οὗ, or ἄν [Conj].

———

ἀληθής, ἀληθής, ἀληθές [Adj 15] *true* [sincere]; *true* [authentic].

ἀσεβής, ἀσεβής, ἀσεβές [Adj 15] *impious*.

ἀσθενής, ἀσθενής, ἀσθενές [Adj 15] *weak*; *ill*.

ἀσφαλής, ἀσφαλής, ἀσφαλές [Adj 15] *safe*.

μονογενής, μονογενής, μονογενές [Adj 15] *only* [child]

πλήρης, πλήρης, πλῆρες [Adj 15] *full*; *complete*.

συγγενής, συγγενής, συγγενές [Adj 15] *related*. As a noun, *relative* [N 30].

ὑγιής, ὑγιής, ὑγιές [Adj 15] *whole*; *healthy*.

ψευδής, ψευδής, ψευδές [Adj 15] *false*. As a noun, *liar* [N 30].

———

οὐδέ . . . οὐδέ and μηδέ . . . μηδέ [Conj, Neg]. Used in pairs, as here, these words mean *neither . . . nor*. The οὐδέ pair is used where οὐ would be used, and the μηδέ pair is used where μή would be used. The words are also used individually, with οὐδέ meaning *and not* and used where οὐ would be used, and μηδέ meaning *and not* and used where μή would be used.

Exercises for Lesson 25

I. Translate into English:
1. ἴσθι ὑγιὴς ἀπὸ τῆς νόσου σου. (Mk 5:34)
2. διδάσκαλε, λέγομεν ὅτι ἀληθὴς εἶ. (Mk 12:14)
3. λέγε μηδὲ τοῖς φίλοις σου μηδὲ τοῖς ἀδελφοῖς. [Cf. Lesson 32, Vocabulary, for the meaning of φίλοις.]
4. ὁ παῖς ἔλεγεν οὐδὲ τοῖς φίλοις αὐτοῦ οὐδὲ τοῖς ἀδελφοῖς.
5. θέλω χωρὶς τοῦ Χριστοῦ εἶναι ὑπὲρ τῶν ἀδελφῶν μου καὶ συγγενῶν μου κατὰ σάρκα. (Rom 9:3)

6. φύλασσε τοὺς παῖδας ἕως αὐτὸς ἀπολύει τὸν ὄχλον. (Mk 6:45)

7. φύλασσε τοὺς παῖδας ἕως οὗ ἀπολύσῃ τὸν ὄχλον. (Mt 14:22)

8. φύλασσε τοὺς παῖδας ἕως ἂν ἀπολύσῃ τὸν ὄχλον. (Mk 9:1)

9. ἦσαν προφῆται ψευδεῖς ἐν τῇ πόλει.

10. ὁ Ἰησοῦς πλήρης ἦν πνεύματος ἁγίου. (Lk 4:1)

11. ἔσομαι μεθ' ὑμῶν ἕως τῆς ἡμέρας ἐκείνης. (Mk 14:25)

12. εἶχεν θυγατέρα μονογενῆ ὡς ἐτῶν δώδεκα. (Lk 8:42)

13. λέγεις αὐτὸν ἡτοιμακέναι τὴν τράπεζαν;

14. ἔλεγεν ὁ προφήτης περὶ τῶν ἀσεβῶν ἀνθρώπων.

15. ἤμην τοῖς ἀσθενέσιν ἀσθενής. (1 Cor 9:22)

16. λέγω τῷ ἱερεῖ τῷ τεθυκότι.

17. οὐδὲ βλέπω τὸ ἀσφαλές. (Acts 21:34)

II. Translate into Greek:
  1. I say that the true prophets have not cried out. (Jn 1:15)
  2. The ones sending me are true, the ones not hearing me are false. (Jn 8:26)
  3. There was darkness over the whole world until the first hour. (Mk 15:33)

III. Mk 4:37 – 5:3.

The Meaning of the Middle Voice. λύω,
Present Middle Indicative. The Noun
μάρτυς. Rules for Accents 18.

Lesson 26

The Meaning of the Middle Voice.

Greek grammar has three voices: active, middle, and passive. The
active voice indicates that the grammatical subject of the sentence is
the real agent of the action. The passive voice indicates that the
grammatical subject of the sentence is in some way or other the
recipient of the agent. In Greek there are separate sets of forms to
express the active voice. (Cf. above, Lessons 9-25, for the active voice
of λύω.) The passive voice will be presented in future lessons. (Cf.
below, Lessons 36-42, for the passive voice of λύω.) There is a
separate set of forms to express the middle voice as well, although
some of these forms are identical with some of the forms of the
passive voice.

The middle voice indicates that the verb has some special
relation to its subject beyond the relation of an active verb to its
subject. This relation can be of various kinds and will become
clearer through the examples of the middle voice given below and in
subsequent lessons. In the New Testament the number of instances
of the middle voice is greatly reduced in comparison with the middle
voice in previous periods of the Greek language. But examples of
the middle voice do occur. Further, the forms of the middle voice
serve as the forms for many "deponent" verbs, i.e., verbs with active
meanings but middle forms (cf. below, Lesson 45).

For the meaning of the indicative mood in the present tense cf.
above, Lesson 9.

λύω, Present Middle Indicative.

The present middle indicative of λύω is conjugated as follows (cf. V
1, VP 2):

Middle Voice, Indicative Mood, Present Tense

	Singular	Plural
1st Person	λύ–ομαι	λυ–όμεθα
2nd Person	λύ–η	λύ–εσθε
3rd Person	λύ–εται	λύ–ονται

I loose [with relation to myself]

We loose [with relation to ourselves]

You (sg.) *loose* [with relation to yourself]

You (pl.) *loose* [with relation to yourselves]

He (She, It) looses [with relation to himself, herself, itself]

They loose [with relation to themselves]

The form λύη is a contraction of λύεσαι (λύεσαι > λύεαι > λύηι > λύη).

There are no examples in the New Testament of the use of λύω in the middle voice. But the verb νίπτω, *I wash*, has a number of examples of a clear use of the middle voice. Contrast the following examples:

ὁ Χριστὸς νίπτει τοὺς πόδας τῶν ἀποστόλων.
Christ washes the feet of the apostles.

ὁ ἀνὴρ νίπτεται.
The man washes [*himself*]. [This Greek sentence can also be translated: *The man has himself washed*, i.e., causes himself to be washed.]

In the second example the verb νίπτεται is in the middle voice. It has no expressed object, the object being implied from the middle voice itself. But there are examples in the New Testament of a verb in the middle voice having a direct object in the accusative case:

ὁ ἀνὴρ νίπτεται τὸ πρόσωπον αὐτοῦ.
The man washes his face.

The Noun μάρτυς.

The noun μάρτυς, *witness*, is declined as follows (cf. N 33):

	Singular	Plural
n	μάρτυς	μάρτυρες
v	μάρτυς	μάρτυρες
g	μάρτυρος	μαρτύρων
d	μάρτυρι	μάρτυσι(ν)
a	μάρτυρα	μάρτυρας

The root of μάρτυς is μαρτυρ–. There are no other words in this category in the New Testament.

Rules for Accents 18.

The α of the neuter nominative and accusative plural ending of adjectives of the second declension is always short, just as is the corresponding α of the noun (cf. above, Rules for Accents 17). Thus ἅγια in 1 Cor 7:14. Contrast this with ἁγία (feminine nominative singular) in Rom 11:16 (twice). Cf. above, Rules for Accents 12 and 15.

Vocabulary for Lesson 26.

ἔξω [Prep 1] Governs the genitive case: *out of; outside of.* This word is also used as an adverb: *outside* [Adv 1].
___

μάρτυς, μάρτυρος, ὁ [N 33] *witness; martyr.*
___

παραβολή, –ῆς, ἡ [N 1] *parable; symbol.*

σωτηρία, –ας, ἡ [N 2] *salvation; liberation.*

φόβος, –ου, ὁ [N 6m] *fear.*

φυλακή, –ῆς, ἡ [N 1] *guard; prison.*
___

κακός, –ή, –όν [Adj 1] *evil; bad.* As a neuter noun: *injury* [N 7].

μικρός, –ά, –όν [Adj 2] *small.* As an adverb (μικρόν): *a little while* [Adv 2].

ὅσος, –η, –ον [Adj 1] *as much as; as many as.*

τυφλός, –ή, –όν [Adj 1] *blind*.

––––

ἀπέχω [ἀπό + ἔχω] [V 2, DV 109, VP 1-2, 4] active transitive: *I receive*; active intransitive: *I am distant*; middle: *I abstain from*; *I avoid* [with genitive].

ἄρχω [V 2, DV 28, VP 1-2] active: *I rule* [with genitive]; middle: *I begin*.

βαπτίζω [βαπτίσω] [V 5, DV 33, VP 1-2] active: cf. Lesson 11; middle: *I get [myself] baptized*; *I wash [myself]*.

νίπτω [V 4-5, DV 207, VP 1-2] active: *I wash [something else or someone else]*; middle: *I wash [myself]*.

παρέχω [παρά + ἔχω] [V 2, DV 109, VP 1-2, 4] active: *I cause*; *I bring about*; middle: *I offer* [from my own means].

ῥαντίζω [ῥαντίσω] [V 5, DV 269, VP 1-2] active: cf. Lesson 23; *sprinkle* middle: *I wash [myself]*.

φυλάσσω [V 3, DV 335, VP 1-2] active: cf. Lesson 17; *protect guard keep observe* middle: *I avoid*; *I observe* [a law, a rule, etc.].

––––

ἐκεῖ [Adv 1] *there*.

ὧδε [Adv 1] *here*.

Exercises for Lesson 26.

I. Translate into English:
1. οὐδὲν κακὸν εὑρίσκομεν ἐν τῷ ἀνθρώπῳ τούτῳ. (Acts 23:9)
2. εἰ τυφλοὶ ἦτε, οὐκ ἂν εἴχετε ἁμαρτίαν. (Jn 9:41)
3. καλόν ἐστιν ἡμᾶς ὧδε εἶναι. (Mk 9:5)
4. εἰ οὐ βαπτίζονται οὐκ ἐσθίουσιν. (Mk 7:4)
5. καὶ οὐκ ἔστιν ἐν ἄλλῳ οὐδενὶ ἡ σωτηρία. (Acts 4:12)
   [Cf. Lesson 70, Repetition of Negatives, for an explanation of the two negatives in this sentence.]
6. ἴσθι ἐκεῖ ἕως ἂν λέγω σοι. (Mt 2:13)
7. ἄρχεται ὁ Ἰησοῦς διδάσκειν αὐτοὺς πολλά. (Mk 6:34)

8. αὐτὸ τὸ βιβλίον καὶ πάντα τὸν λαὸν ἐράντισεν. (Heb 9:19)
9. φυλάσσομαι ἀπὸ πάσης ἀδικίας. (Lk 12:15)
10. ἀπέχετε τὴν παράκλησιν ὑμῶν. (Lk 6:24)
11. εἰ οὐ ῥαντίζονται οὐκ ἐσθίουσιν. (Mk 7:4, critical apparatus)
12. ἐάν τίς μου ἀκούσῃ τῶν ῥημάτων καὶ μὴ φυλάξῃ, ἄδικός ἐστιν. (Jn 12:47) [τίς is the indefinite pronoun; it has an acute accent because it is found in an enclitic chain. Cf. Lesson 18, Rules for Accents 10.)
13. ἡ δὲ καρδία αὐτῶν ἀπέχει ἀπ᾽ ἐμοῦ. (Mt 15:8)
14. ἀπεχόμεθα αἵματος. (Acts 15:29)
15. ὁ Ἰησοῦς ἑαυτὸν παρέχεται ἡγεμόνα. (Tit 2:7)
16. ὁ θεὸς παρέχει ἡμῖν πάντα. (1 Tim 6:17)
17. οἱ στρατιῶται οὐχ εὑρίσκουσιν αὐτοὺς ἐν τῇ φυλακῇ. (Acts 5:22)
18. ὑμεῖς μάρτυρες τούτων. (Lk 24:48)
19. καὶ ἐδίδασκεν αὐτοὺς ἐν παραβολαῖς πολλά. (Mk 4:2)
20. ὁ δὲ Ἰησοῦς ἔξω ἐπ᾽ ἐρήμοις τόποις ἦν. (Mk 1:45)
21. ἅπαντες ὅσοι εἶχον ἀσθενεῖς ἦγον αὐτοὺς πρὸς αὐτόν. (Lk 4:40) [ἀσθενεῖς is an adjective used as a noun: *sick people*.]
22. ὁ δὲ Ἰησοῦς ἔρχεται ἔξω τῆς πόλεως. (Mt 21:17)
23. Κύριε, σύ μου νίπτεις τοὺς πόδας; (Jn 13:6)
24. οὐ γὰρ νίπτονται τὰς χεῖρας αὐτῶν ὅτε ἄρτον ἐσθίουσιν. (Mt 15:2)
25. ἔτι χρόνον μικρὸν μεθ᾽ ὑμῶν εἰμι. (Jn 7:33) [Cf. Lesson 28, Vocabulary, for the meaning of ἔτι. Cf. Lesson 79 for the use of μίκρον in the accusative case expressing duration of time.]

II. Translate into Greek:
1. You will be my witnesses in this city if you will be faithful. (Lk 24:48)
2. The children begin to cry out if their parents are distant.
3. God causes faith for all through the resurrection of Jesus. (Acts 17:31)

III. Mk 5:4-12.

λύω, **Imperfect Middle Indicative and Present Middle Imperative. The Comparative Adjective** μείζων. **The Two Ways of Expressing Adjectival Comparison. Other Uses of the Comparative Adjective. Rules for Accents 19.**

Lesson 27

λύω, **Imperfect Middle Indicative and Present Middle Imperative.**

The imperfect middle indicative of λύω is conjugated as follows (cf. V 1, VP 2):

Indicative Mood, Middle Voice, Imperfect Tense

	Singular	Plural
1st Person	ἐ–λυ–όμην	ἐ–λυ–όμεθα
2nd Person	ἐ–λύ–ου	ἐ–λύ–εσθε
3rd Person	ἐ–λύ–ετο	ἐ–λύ–οντο

I was loosing [with relation to myself]	*We were loosing* [with relation to ourselves]
You (sg.) *were loosing* [with relation to yourself]	*You* (pl.) *were loosing* [with relation to yourself]
He (She, It) was loosing [with relation to himself, herself, itself]	*They were loosing* [with relation to themselves]

The form ἐλύου is a contraction of ἐλύεσο (ἐλύεσο > ἐλύεο > ἐλύου).

The augment (found only in the indicative mood) is formed in the same way as is the augment of the imperfect indicative active (cf. above, Lesson 10). The augment is found only <u>in the past tenses</u> of the indicative mood, i.e., imperfect, aorist, pluperfect.

For the meaning of the middle voice cf. above, Lesson 26.

For the meaning of the indicative mood cf. above, Lesson 9.
For the meaning of the imperfect tense cf. above, Lesson 10.
The present middle imperative of λύω is conjugated as follows
(cf. V 1, VP 2):

Imperative Mood, Middle Voice, Present Tense

	Singular	Plural
2nd Person	λύ–ου	λύ–εσθε
3rd Person	λυ–έσθω	λυ–έσθωσαν

You (sg.) *loosen!* [with relation to yourself]	*You* (pl.) *loosen!* [with relation to yourselves]
Let him [*her, it*] *loosen* [with relation to himself, herself, itself]	*Let them loosen!* [with relation to themselves]

The form λύ–ου is a contraction from λύεσο (λύεσο > λύεο > λύου).

The word *loosen* is used here in the imperative instead of
loose to avoid the ambiguity in the English expression *Let him
loose!* The latter can mean *Let him loosen!*, as above, or *Let him go
loose!*, which is a passive use of the imperative and is to be
distinguished from the middle used here.
For the meaning of the middle voice cf. above, Lesson 26.
For the meaning of the present tense in the imperative mood
cf. above, Lesson 12.

The Comparative Adjective μείζων.

The adjective μείζων, *greater*, is declined as follows (cf. Adj 11):

	Masculine	Singular Feminine	Neuter
n	μείζων	μείζων	μεῖζον
v	μείζων	μείζων	μεῖζον
g	μείζονος	μείζονος	μείζονος
d	μείζονι	μείζονι	μείζονι
a	μείζονα/μείζω	μείζονα/μείζω	μεῖζον

	Masculine	Plural Feminine	Neuter
n	μείζονες/μείζους	μείζονες/μείζους	μείζονα/μείζω
v	μείζονες/μείζους	μείζονες/μείζους	μείζονα/μείζω
g	μειζόνων	μειζόνων	μείζονων
d	μείζοσι(ν)	μείζοσι(ν)	μείζοσι(ν)
a	μείζονας/μείζους	μείζονας/μείζους	μείζονα/μείζω

There are two roots involved. The one common to all forms is μειζον–. The alternative forms come from the stem μειζοσ–. In the masculine and feminine accusative singular the form μείζω is from μείζοσα > μείζοα > μείζω, with οα contracting to ω. This is the same explanation for the formation of the neuter nominative and accusative plural forms. The masculine and feminine nominative and accusative plural form μείζους is from μείζοσες > μείζοες > μείζους, with the οε contracting to ου.

This is an "irregular" way of forming a comparative adjective in Greek, being used for a relatively small number of words. But the words in question are frequently used; the most important of them are given in the vocabulary for this lesson. The "regular" way of forming a comparative adjective will be given in Lesson 29.

The Two Ways of Expressing Adjectival Comparison.

There are two ways of expressing comparison involving adjectives in Greek: 1) with the simple genitive; 2) with the comparative particle ἤ.

> 1) with the genitive:
> οὐκ ἔστιν δοῦλος μείζων τοῦ κυρίου αὐτοῦ.
> *A slave is not greater than his lord.*

> 2) with the comparative particle ἤ.
> οὐκ ἔστιν δοῦλος μείζων ἢ ὁ κύριος αὐτοῦ.
> *A slave is not greater than his lord.*

Other Uses of the Comparative Adjective.

The comparative form of the adjective is also used for a statement of the positive degree in a reinforced form:

μείζων ἐστίν.
He is somewhat large.

The comparative form can also be used for the superlative degree:

μείζων ἐστίν.
He is the largest.

The context is determinative for the precise force of the comparative.

Rules for Accents 19.

In the nouns of the third declension the α of the masculine and feminine accusative singular and plural is always short. Thus: σάρκα, σάρκας; Ἄραβα, Ἄραβας; μῆνα, μῆνας; αἰῶνα, αἰῶνας; ῥήτορα, ῥήτορας.

Similarly, the α of the neuter nominative and accusative singular and plural is always short. Thus: βάπτισμα, βαπτίσματα; πνεῦμα, πνεύματα; σῶμα, σώματα; τέρατα; ἅλατα; κέρατα.

Vocabulary for Lesson 27.

ἄχρι(ς) [Prep 1] Governs the genitive case: *until*; *as far as*. This word is also used as a conjunction, sometimes with οὗ, meaning *until* , followed by either the indicative or subjunctive moods[Conj].

βελτίων, βελτίων, βέλτιον [Adj 11] *better* [comparative form of ἀγαθός; cf. also κρείσσων].

ἐλάσσων, ἐλάσσων, ἔλασσον / ἐλάττων, ἐλάττων, ἔλαττον [Adj 11] *smaller* [comparative form of μικρός].

ἥσσων, ἥσσων, ἧσσον [Adj 11] *worse; less* [comparative form of κακός].

κρείσσων, κρείσσων, κρεῖσσον / κρείττων, κρείττων, κρεῖττον [Adj 11] *better*[comparative form of ἀγαθός; cf. also βελτίων].

μείζων, μείζων, μεῖζον [Adj 11] *greater; larger* [comparative form of μέγας].

πλείων, πλείων, πλεῖον [Adj 11] *more* [comparative form of πολύς].

χείρων, χείρων, χεῖρον [Adj 11] *worse* [comparative form of κακός].
___
γενεά, –ᾶς, ἡ [N 2] *generation; age.*

θηρίον, –ου, τό [N 7] *wild beast.*

ναός, –οῦ, ὁ [N 6m] *temple; shrine.*

τιμή, –ῆς, ἡ [N 1] *honor; price.*

χρεία, –ας, ἡ [N 2] *need; necessity.*
___
δεύτερος, –α, –ον [Adj 2] *second.*

ὅμοιος, –α, –ον [Adj 2] *like, equal to* [with dative].

τρίτος, –η, –ον [Adj 1] *third.*
___
οὔτε . . . οὔτε and μήτε . . . μήτε [Conj, Neg] *neither . . . nor.*
When used separately and not in pairs οὔτε and μήτε each
means *and not; nor; not.* These words are distinguished
according to the criteria for using οὐ and μή.

Exercises for Lesson 27.

I. Translate into English:
1. μὴ ἴσθι ἁμαρτωλὸς ἵνα μὴ χεῖρόν σοί τι ᾖ. (Jn 5:14)
2. νίπτου.
3. ἔστιν γὰρ ὥρα τρίτη τῆς ἡμέρας. (Acts 2:15)
4. οὐκ εἰσὶν ἡμῖν πλεῖον ἢ ἰχθύες δύο. (Lk 9:13)
5. προφήτης ἐν τῇ ἰδίᾳ πατρίδι τιμὴν οὐκ ἔχει. (Jn 4:44)
6. ἐνίπτετο τοὺς πόδας.
7. αὐτοὶ ἔρχονται οὐκ εἰς τὸ κρεῖσσον ἀλλὰ εἰς τὸ
   ἧσσον. (1 Cor 11:17)
8. τίνι εἰσὶν ὅμοιοι οἱ ἄνθρωποι τῆς γενεᾶς ταύτης; (Lk
   7:31)

9. ἔρχεται ὁ προφήτης μὴ ἐσθίων ἄρτον μήτε ἔχων οἶνον.
   (Lk 7:33) [Cf. Lesson 30, Vocabulary, for the meaning of
   οἶνον.]

10. οὗτος ὁ παῖς ἐλάσσων ἐστὶν ἢ ἐκεῖνος.

11. ὁ δὲ Ἰησοῦς ἔλεγεν περὶ τοῦ ναοῦ τοῦ σώματος αὐτοῦ.
    (Jn 2:21)

12. λέγουσιν μὴ εἶναι ἀνάστασιν μήτε ἄγγελον μήτε
    πνεῦμα. (Acts 23:8)

13. αὐτὸς βελτίων ἐστὶν ἐμοῦ.

14. καὶ ἦν ἐν τῇ ἐρήμῳ μετὰ τῶν θηρίων. (Mk 1:13)

15. κύριε, οὔτε οἶκον ἔχεις.

16. μείζων τούτων ἄλλη ἐντολὴ οὐκ ἔστιν. (Mk 12:31)

17. ηὔξανεν ὁ λαὸς ἄχρι οὗ ἦν βασιλεὺς ἕτερος. (Acts
    7:18)

18. ἡ δὲ δευτέρα ἐντολὴ ὁμοία τῇ πρώτῃ ἐστίν. (Mt
    22:39)

19. οὔτε οὗτος ἁμαρτωλός ἐστιν οὔτε οἱ γονεῖς αὐτοῦ. (Jn
    9:3)

20. ἄχρι γὰρ νόμου ἁμαρτία ἦν ἐν κόσμῳ. (Rom 5:13)

21. Ἡ γενεὰ αὕτη γενεὰ πονηρά ἐστιν. (Lk 11:29)

22. Ὁ κύριος αὐτοῦ χρείαν ἔχει. (Mk 11:3)

II. Translate into Greek:
    1. He begins to eat better bread if he has need of it.
    2. Honor and glory to God alone, the king of the ages. (1 Tim
       1:17)
    3. She is smaller than that woman but larger than this one.

III. Mk 5:13-21.

λύω, **Present Middle Subjunctive and Optative. The Superlative Adjective. The Conjunction ὅταν and Its Use. Rules for Accents 20.**

Lesson 28

λύω, Present Middle Subjunctive and Optative.

The present middle subjunctive of λύω is conjugated as follows (cf. V 1, VP 2):

	Middle Voice, Subjunctive Mood, Present Tense	
	Singular	Plural
1st Person	λύ–ωμαι	λυ–ώμεθα
2nd Person	λύ–η	λύ–ησθε
3rd Person	λύ–ηται	λύ–ωνται

The form λύη is a contraction from λύησαι: λύησαι > λύηαι > λύηι > λύη.

For the meaning of the subjunctive mood in the present tense cf. above, Lesson 13, as well as Lesson 5.

For the meaning of the middle voice cf. above, Lesson 26.

The present middle optative of λύω is conjugated as follows (cf. V1, VP 2):

	Middle Voice, Optative Mood, Present Tense	
	Singular	Plural
1st Person	λυ–οίμην	λυ–οίμεθα
2nd Person	λύ–οιο	λύ–οισθε
3rd Person	λύ–οιτο	λύ–οιντο

The form λύοιο comes from λύοισο.

For the meaning of the optative mood in the present tense cf. above, Lesson 14, as well as Lesson 6.

For the meaning of the middle voice cf. above, Lesson 26

The Superlative Adjective.

The forms for the comparative degree of several adjectives were given in Lesson 27 in connection with the paradigm of the third declension adjective μείζων. The superlative degree of μείζων is μέγιστος. It is declined exactly like ἀγαθός (cf. above, Lesson 4). Other superlatives are given in the vocabulary section of this lesson.

The use of the superlative degree of an adjective is not frequent in the New Testament. As was noted above in Lesson 27, the comparative degree occasionally is used for the superlative. The superlative degree can be used to indicate explicit supremacy in some area (τοῦτο τὸ μέγιστόν ἐστιν—*This is the greatest*) or simply to indicate a heightened degree of the positive (τοῦτο μέγιστόν ἐστιν—*This is very great*).

The Conjunction ὅταν and Its Use.

The word ὅταν comes from a combination of ὅτε, *when*, and ἄν, the particle indicating contingency. This conjunction is frequently used with the subjunctive when there is question of a repeated or continued action in the present or future:

> ὅταν ἐν τῷ κόσμῳ ὦ, φῶς εἰμι τοῦ κόσμου.
> *When I am in the world, I am the light of the world.*

[For the meaning of φῶς cf. below, Lesson 37, Vocabulary.]

But it is also (rarely) used with the indicative when there is question of a repeated action in the past: ~~Sant~~ ἂν   Mk 6:56

> ὅταν ἔβλεπον αὐτόν, ἔκραζον.
> *Whenever they saw him, they cried out.*

Rules for Accents 20.

Nouns declined like πόλις (cf. Lesson 14) have an acute accent on the third-last syllable in the genitive singular and plural despite the fact that the last syllable is long. They thus are exceptions to the rule enunciated in Rules for Accents 3 in Lesson 11.

Vocabulary for Lesson 28.

ἐπάνω [Prep 1] Governs the genitive case: *upon*; *over*. This word is also used as an adverb: *upon* [Adv 1].

___

ἐλάχιστος, –η, –ον [Adj 1] *least*; *very small* [superlative of μικρός and ἐλάσσων / ἐλάττων].

κράτιστος, –η, –ον [Adj 1] *best*; *very good* [superlative of ἀγαθός and κρείσσων / κρείττων / βελτίων]. This word is also used in formal address: *most excellent*.

μέγιστος, –η, –ον [Adj 1] *greatest*; *very large* [superlative of μέγας and μείζων].

πλεῖστος, –η, –ον [Adj 1] *most*; *large* [superlative of πολύς and πλείων / πλέων].

___

ἐπιθυμία, –ας, ἡ [N 2] *desire*.

θύρα, –ας, ἡ [N 2] *door*.

μνημεῖον, –ου, τό [N 7] *tomb*; *monument*.

πρόβατον, –ου, τό [N 7] *sheep*.

τέλος, –ους, τό [N 31] *end*; *goal*.

___

ἄξιος, –α, –ον [Adj 2] *worthy of* [with genitive].

ἱκανός, –ή, –όν [Adj 1] *fit*; *sufficient*; *large*; *considerable*; *able*.

καινός, –ή, –όν [Adj 1] *new*.

ὀλίγος, –η, –ον [Adj 1] *small*; *few* [in plural]. The neuter accusative singular of this word, ὀλίγον, is used as an adverb in all three adverbial categories, with the meanings *a little* [space], *a little* [time], *a little* [quality, e.g., *he loves little*] [Adv 1, 2, 3].

___

ὅταν [Conj] *when*; *whenever*.

___

ἔτι [Adv 2] *still*; *further*.

Exercises for Lesson 28.

I. Translate into English:
1. τί ἔτι χρείαν ἔχομεν μαρτύρων; (Mk 14:63) [Cf. Lesson 73 for the meaning of τί, *why?*.]
2. ὑμεῖς ἐκ τοῦ πατρὸς τοῦ διαβόλου ἐστὲ καὶ τὰς ἐπιθυμίας τοῦ πατρὸς ὑμῶν θέλετε. (Jn 8:44)
3. ἀγαθὲ δοῦλε, ὅτι πιστὸς ἦς, ἴσθι ἐξουσίαν ἔχων ἐπάνω πόλεων. (Lk 19:17)
4. ὅταν ἐν τῷ κόσμῳ ὦ, φῶς εἰμι τοῦ κόσμου. (Jn 9:5) [Cf. Lesson 37, Vocabulary, for the meaning of φῶς.]
5. καὶ ἐὰν ᾖ ἡ οἰκία ἀξία, ἔρχεται ἡ εἰρήνη ὑμῶν ἐπ᾽ αὐτήν. (Mt 10:13)
6. οἱ ἄνθρωποι ἔρχονται ἐπάνω. (Lk 11:44)
7. καὶ τῆς βασιλείας αὐτοῦ οὐκ ἔσται τέλος. (Lk 1:33)
8. εἶπεν οὖν πάλιν ὁ Ἰησοῦς, Ἀμὴν ἀμὴν λέγω ὑμῖν ὅτι ἐγώ εἰμι ἡ θύρα τῶν προβάτων. (Jn 10:7)
9. ἐκεῖνος ὁ ἡγεμὼν μέγιστος πάντων ἐστίν.
10. ὀλίγοι εἰσὶν οἱ εὑρίσκοντες τὴν ὁδόν. (Mt 7:14)
11. καὶ ὄχλος τῆς πόλεως ἱκανὸς ἦν σὺν αὐτῇ. (Lk 7:12)
12. ὅστις οὖν λύει μίαν τῶν ἐντολῶν τούτων τῶν ἐλαχίστων καὶ διδάσκει οὕτως τοὺς ἀνθρώπους, ἐλάχιστος ἔσται ἐν τῇ βασιλείᾳ τῶν οὐρανῶν. (Mt 5:19)
13. ἐκεῖ ἦν μνημεῖον καινόν. (Jn 19:41)
14. κράτιστε Ἀνδρέα, γράψω τὴν ἀλήθειαν.
15. ἔρχεται πρὸς αὐτὸν ὄχλος πλεῖστος. (Mk 4:1)

II. Translate into Greek:
1. And the men of the crowd were as sheep not having a shepherd. (Mk 6:34)
2. For the worker is worthy of his bread. (Mt 10:10)
3. Good and faithful servant, you were faithful over a few things, now you will be over many things. (Mt 25:23)

III. Mk 5:22-30.

λύω, **Present Middle Participle and Infinitive. Regular Forms of the Comparative Adjective. Rules for Accents 21.**

Lesson 29

λύω, **Present Middle Participle and Infinitive.**

The present middle participle of λύω is declined as follows (cf. V 1, VP 2, and Adj 1):

	Masculine	Singular Feminine	Neuter
n	λυ–όμενος	λυ–ομένη	λυ–όμενον
v	λυ–όμενε	λυ–ομένη	λυ–όμενον
g	λυ–ομένου	λυ–ομένης	λυ–ομένου
d	λυ–ομένῳ	λυ–ομένῃ	λυ–ομένῳ
a	λυ–όμενον	λυ–ομένην	λυ–όμενον

	Masculine	Plural Feminine	Neuter
n	λυ–όμενοι	λυ–όμεναι	λυ–όμενα
v	λυ–όμενοι	λυ–όμεναι	λυ–όμενα
g	λυ–ομένων	λυ–ομένων	λυ–ομένων
d	λυ–ομένοις	λυ–ομέναις	λυ–ομένοις
a	λυ–ομένους	λυ–ομένας	λυ–όμενα

For the meaning of the present tense of the participle cf. above, Lesson 16, as well as Lesson 7.

For the meaning of the middle voice cf. above, Lesson 26.

The present middle infinitive of λύω is λύ–εσθαι (cf. V 1, VP 2).

For the meaning of the present tense of the infinitive cf. above, Lesson 15, as well as Lesson 4.

For the meaning of the middle voice cf. above, Lesson 26.

Regular Forms of the Comparative Adjective.

The comparison of the adjectives ἀγαθός, κακός, μέγας, μικρός, and πολύς given in Lessons 27 and 28 is irregular. The regular forms of the comparison of adjectives are as follows:

1) For the comparative degree the endings −τερος, −τέρα, −τερον are added to the stem of the adjective in the positive degree. Thus: καινός, *new*: καινότερος, καινοτέρα, καινότερον, *newer*; ἀκριβής, *strict*: ἀκριβέστερος, ἀκριβεστέρα, ἀκριβέστερον, *stricter*.

2) For the superlative degree the endings −τατος, −τάτη, −τατον are added to the stem of the adjective in the positive degree. Thus: καινός, *new* [stem, καινο−]: καινότατος, καινοτάτη, καινότατον, *newest* [stem, ἀκριβεσ−]: ἀκριβής, ἀκριβέστατος, ἀκριβεστάτη, ἀκριβέστατον, *strictest*.

If the final syllable of the stem is constituted by an o and this o is in turn preceded by a short syllable (i.e., a syllable with a short vowel), the final o of the root is lengthened to ω. Thus: σοφός, *wise*; σοφώτερος, *wiser*; σοφώτατος, *wisest*.

As a practical rule for forming the comparative and superlative, adjectives of the second declension add the comparative and superlative endings to the neuter nominative singular less the final ν (contracted adjectives are an exception); adjectives of the third declension add the comparative and superlative endings to the neuter nominative singular. Thus: καινόν > καινο > καινο + τερος > καινότερος; ἀκριβές > ἀκριβεσ + τερος > ἀκριβέστερος.

μικρός also has regular forms for the comparative and superlative in addition to the irregular forms in Lessons 27 and 28.

Rules for Accents 21.

In one-syllable words of the third declension the accent is placed on the last syllable in the genitive and dative singular and plural. Otherwise it remains on the same syllable as in the nominative:

Nominative, Vocative, Accusative	Genitive and Dative
ns μήν	gs μηνός
vs μήν	ds μηνί
as μῆνα	gp μηνῶν
np μῆνες	dp μησί(ν)
vp μῆνες	
ap μῆνας	

The accent on the genitive plural is circumflex, whereas elsewhere on the final syllable it is acute.

There are some exceptions to this general rule: οὖς, *ear*, has ὤτων in the genitive plural; παῖς, *child*, has παίδων in the genitive plural; φῶς, *light*, has φώτων in the genitive plural. πᾶς has πάντων and πᾶσι(ν) in the genitive and dative plural of the masculine and neuter. The feminine, not being monosyllabic in the nominative singular, does not come under the rule.

Vocabulary for Lesson 29.

ἔξωθεν [Prep 1] Governs the genitive case: *from outside; outside.* This word is also used as an adverb with the meaning *from outside, outside* [Adv 1].

ἀγρός, –οῦ, ὁ [N 6m] *field; country* [i.e., rural area].

ἄρχων, –οντος, ὁ [N 22] *ruler; leader.*

βιβλίον, –ου, τό [N 7] *book.*

διαθήκη, –ης, ἡ [N 1] *covenant; testament.*

μαρτυρία, –ας, ἡ [N 2] *testimony.*

ὀργή, –ῆς, ἡ [N 1] *anger.*

περιτομή, –ῆς, ἡ [N 1] *circumcision; those who are circumcised.*

προσευχή, –ῆς, ἡ [N 1] *prayer; entreaty.*

ἀκριβής, –ής, –ές [Adj 15] *strict.*

διάβολος, –ος, –ον [Adj 5] *slanderous.* This word is also used as a noun: *devil; slanderer* [N 6m].

πέντε [Adj 21] *five.*

πτωχός, –ή, –όν [Adj 1] *poor.*

σοφός, –ή, –όν [Adj 1] *wise.*

ἤδη [Adv 2] *now; already.*

ὅπου [Adv 1 and 2] *where; while.* This word is also a conjunction, at times used with ἄν or ἐάν: *wherever; whenever* [Conj].

Exercises for Lesson 29.

I. Translate into English:
1. οὗτος ἔρχεται εἰς μαρτυρίαν ἵνα πάντες πιστεύσωσιν δι᾽ αὐτοῦ. (Jn 1:7)
2. θέλω δὲ ὑμᾶς σοφοὺς εἶναι εἰς τὸ ἀγαθόν. (Rom 16:19)
3. τίς ἐστιν ἄρχων τούτων τῶν στρατιωτῶν;
4. ἔξωθεν τοῦ ναοῦ ἦν ὁ ἱερεύς.
5. καὶ ἔρχεται εἰς τὸν τόπον ὅπου ἦν ὁ προφήτης βαπτίζων. (Jn 10:40)
6. ἡ ζωὴ τοῦ προφήτου ἀκριβεστάτη ἦν. (Acts 26:5)
7. ἡ περιτομὴ τῆς καρδίας ἐν πνεύματί ἐστιν. (Rom 2:29)
8. ὁ παῖς ἦν ἔξωθεν.
9. μακάριοι οἱ πτωχοὶ τῷ πνεύματι, ὅτι αὐτῶν ἐστιν ἡ βασιλεία τῶν οὐρανῶν. (Mt 5:3)
10. καὶ ἔσται ὁ οἶκός μου οἶκος προσευχῆς. (Lk 19:46)
11. ἐκεῖνοι ἔρχονται εἰς τὸν ἴδιον ἀγρόν. (Mt 22:5)
12. οἱ μαθηταὶ αὐτοῦ ἔλεγον ὅτι Ἔρημός ἐστιν ὁ τόπος, καὶ ἤδη ὥρα πολλή. (Mk 6:35)
13. ἔχω γὰρ πέντε ἀδελφούς. (Lk 16:28)
14. ὁ θεὸς ἔγραψεν τὸ ὄνομα αὐτοῦ ἐν τῷ βιβλίῳ τῆς ζωῆς. (Apoc 13:8)
15. τοῦτό ἐστιν ἡ καινὴ διαθήκη ἐν τῷ αἵματί μου. (Lk 22:20)
16. διὰ ταῦτα ἔρχεται ἡ ὀργὴ τοῦ θεοῦ. (Col 3:6)
17. καὶ ἐξ ὑμῶν εἷς διάβολός ἐστιν. (Jn 6:70)
18. ἔσται γὰρ ὀργὴ τῷ λαῷ τούτῳ. (Lk 21:23)
19. ὁ δὲ ἀγρός ἐστιν ὁ κόσμος, τὸ δὲ καλὸν σπέρμα αὐτοί εἰσιν οἱ υἱοὶ τῆς βασιλείας. (Mt 13:38)
20. ὁ οἶκός μου οἶκος προσευχῆς ἔσται πᾶσιν τοῖς ἔθνεσιν. (Mk 11:17)
21. καὶ Μωϋσῆς αὐτό τε τὸ βιβλίον καὶ πάντα τὸν λαὸν ἐράντισεν. (Heb 9:19)

II. Translate into Greek:
1. My testimony about those things which I heard is true. (Jn 5:31)

    2. These are the prayers of the holy ones who are before the shrine. (Apoc 5:8)
    3. Jesus comes into the house of the ruler and sees the crowd and anger comes into his heart. (Mt 9:23)

III. Mk 5:31-39.

λύω, Future Middle Indicative, Infinitive, and Particle. The Use of μᾶλλον to Form the Comparative Degree of Adjectives. The Use of the Conjunction ὥστε. The Result Clause. Rules for Accents 22.

Lesson 30

λύω, Future Middle Indicative, Infinitive, and Participle.

The future tense of the middle voice in all three of the moods which are found in the New Testament—indicative, infinitive, and participle—is formed by adding the endings of the present tense of the middle voice onto the future stem.

For the meaning of the future indicative cf. above, Lesson 11 as well as Lesson 8. For the meaning of the future infinitive cf. Lessons 17 and 8. For the meaning of the future participle cf. Lessons 17 and 8. For the meaning of the middle voice cf. Lesson 16.

The future middle indicative of λύω is conjugated as follows (cf. V 1, VP 2):

	Middle Voice, Indicative Mood, Future Tense	
	Singular	Plural
1st Person	λύσ–ομαι	λυσ–όμεθα
2nd Person	λύσ–ῃ	λύσ–εσθε
3rd Person	λύσ–εται	λύσ–ονται

I shall loose [with relation to myself]	*We shall loose* [with relation to ourselves]
You (sg.) *will loose* [with relation to yourself]	*You* (pl.) *will loose* [with relation to yourselves]
He (She, It) will loose [with relation to himself, herself, itself]	*They will loose* [with relation to themselves]

The form λύσῃ is a contraction from λύσεσαι (λύσεσαι >
λύσεαι > λύσηι > λύῃ).

φυλάξομαι τὰς ἐντολὰς τοῦ θεοῦ.
I shall observe the commandments of God.

2):
The future middle infinitive of λύω is λύσ–εσθαι (cf. V 1, VP

λέγω αὐτὸν φυλάξεσθαι τὰς ἐντολὰς τοῦ θεοῦ.
I say that he will observe the commandments of God.

The future middle participle of λύω is declined as follows (cf.,
V 1, VP 2, Adj 1):

Middle Voice, Participial Mood, Future Tense
Singular

	Masculine	Feminine	Neuter
n	λυσ–όμενος	λυσ–ομένη	λυσ–όμενον
v	λυσ–όμενε	λυσ–ομένη	λυσ–όμενον
g	λυσ–ομένου	λυσ–ομένης	λυσ–ομένου
d	λυσ–ομένῳ	λυσ–ομένῃ	λυσ–ομένῳ
a	λυσ–όμενον	λυσ–ομένην	λυσ–όμενον

Plural

	Masculine	Feminine	Neuter
n	λυσ–όμενοι	λυσ–όμεναι	λυσ–όμενα
v	λυσ–όμενοι	λυσ–όμεναι	λυσ–όμενα
g	λυσ–ομένων	λυσ–ομένων	λυσ–ομένων
d	λυσ–ομένοις	λυσ–ομέναις	λυσ–ομένοις
a	λυσ–ομένους	λυσ–ομένας	λυσ–όμενα

The future participle is occasionally used to express purpose
(cf. above, Lesson 17):

ἔρχεται ὁ μαθητὴς φυλαξόμενος τὰς ἐντολάς.
The disciple is coming to observe the commandments.

The Use of μᾶλλον to Form the Comparative Degree of Adjectives.

It is possible to form the comparative degree of adjectives through
the use of the adverb μᾶλλον, *more,* in addition to the ways of

forming the comparative degree of the adjective given above in Lessons 27, 28, and 29:

κάλον ἐστὶ μᾶλλον ἀγάπην ἔχειν ἢ ὀργήν.
It is better to have love than anger.

The Use of the Conjunction ὥστε. The Result Clause.

The word ὥστε is often used to introduce a main clause in which the verb is usually in the indicative mood:

ὥστε ὁ υἱὸς τοῦ ἀνθρώπου κύριός ἐστι καὶ τοῦ σαββάτου.
And so the son of man is lord also of the Sabbath.

This use of ὥστε to introduce a principal clause must be carefully distinguished from its use to introduce a subordinate clause indicating the result of an action. That is, an action which is caused but not foreseen by the agent. In this construction, known as a "result clause", the verb in the ὥστε clause is in the infinitive mood, and the subject of the infinitive is in the accusative case:

εἶπεν λόγους σοφοὺς ὥστε τὸν ὄχλον κρᾶξαι διὰ χαράν.
He spoke wise words with the result that the crowd cried out
    because of joy.

He didn't speak in order to have the crowd cry out with joy: such a sentence would use a purpose clause (for example, ἵνα with the subjunctive) to express the idea that the agent had this in mind when he spoke. He spoke, and as a matter of fact his words resulted in the crowd's crying out, although this was not his intention.

If the subject of the ὥστε clause is the same as the subject of the main clause the subject of the ὥστε clause is ordinarily not expressed:

λέγει λόγους κακοὺς ὥστε εἶναι κακόν.
He is speaking evil words with the result that he is evil.

In rare instances the indicative is used instead of the infinitive, perhaps to emphasize the reality of the result. (Cf. Jn 3:16.)

Rules for Accents 22.

The word γυνή, *woman*, follows the rules for monosyllables of the third declension. Thus γυνή, γύναι (irregular), γυναικός, γυναικί, γυναῖκα, γυναῖκες, γυναῖκες, γυναικῶν, γυναιξί(ν), γυναῖκας.

Vocabulary for Lesson 30.

πέραν [Prep 1] Governs the genitive case: *beyond*; *on the other side*, This word also occurs as an adverb, *across* [Adv 1], in the phrase τὸ πέραν, literally, *the across*, i.e., *the other side*.

This preposition concludes the presentation of the principal prepositions used in the Greek New Testament. Other prepositions will be presented as the need arises.

ἄνεμος, –ου, ὁ [N 6m] *wind*.

ἀρνίον, –ου, τό [N 7] *lamb*; *sheep*.

διδαχή, –ῆς, ἡ [N 1] *teaching*; *instruction*.

ἥλιος, –ου, ὁ [N 6m] [the] *sun*.

μέλος, –ους, τό [N 31] *member* [of the body].

οἶνος, –ου, ὁ [N 6m] *wine*.

παρρησία, –ας, ἡ [N 2] *boldness*; *frankness*; *freedom in speaking*.

ποτήριον, –ου, τό [N 7] *cup*; *chalice*.

ὑπομονή, –ῆς, ἡ [N 1] *perseverance*; *patience*.

δυνατός, –ή, –όν [Adj 1] *possible*; *powerful*.

ἐχθρός, –ά, –όν [Adj 2] *hating*. As a noun this word means *enemy* [N 6m].

ποῖος, –α, –ον [Adj 2] *what?, which?, what sort of?*

ὥστε [Conj] Introducing a principal clause: *and so*; introducing a
subordinate clause: *so that; with the result that*. At times
this conjunction seems to have a purpose function: *in order
that*.
___

γέ [Part] An enclitic which adds emphasis to the word with which it
is associated.
___

οὐχι [Neg] Emphatic form of οὐ, *not*. This word is usually used to
introduce questions for which an affirmative answer is
expected.
___

μᾶλλον [Adv 3] *more*.

Exercises for Lesson 30.

I. Translate into English:
1. βλέπω δὲ ἕτερον νόμον ἐν τοῖς μέλεσίν μου. (Rom 7:23)
2. ὁ νεκρὸς ἄνθρωπος ἄρχεται λέγειν ὥστε πάντας φόβον
   ἔχειν. (Lk 7:15)
3. οὐχὶ σὺ εἶ ὁ Χριστός; (Lk 23:39)
4. δίκαιόν ἐστιν ἐνώπιον τοῦ θεοῦ ὑμῶν ἀκούειν μᾶλλον
   ἢ τοῦ θεοῦ; (Acts 4:19)
5. διδάσκαλε, ποία ἐντολὴ μεγάλη ἐν τῷ νόμῳ; (Mt 22:36)
6. οἱ μαθηταὶ ἔρχονται εἰς τὸ πέραν χωρὶς ἄρτων. (Mt
   16:5)
7. ὁ δὲ Ἰησοῦς εἶπεν αὐτῷ, Πάντα δύνατα τῷ πιστεύοντι.
   (Mk 9:23)
8. εἰ ἄλλοις οὐκ εἰμὶ ἀπόστολος, ἀλλά γε ὑμῖν εἰμι. (1 Cor
   9:2)
9. ἦν λαῖλαψ μεγάλη ἀνέμου. (Mk 4:37)
10. καὶ ἄλλος ἄγγελος ἔρχεται ἐκ τοῦ οὐρανοῦ, καὶ τὸ
    πρόσωπον αὐτοῦ ὡς ὁ ἥλιος. (Apoc 10:1)
11. οἱ μαθηταὶ εὕρισκον τὸν Ἰησοῦν πέραν τῆς
    θαλάσσης. (Jn 6:25)
12. εἰ σὺ εἶ ὁ Χριστός, λέγε ἡμῖν παρρησίᾳ. (Jn 10:24)
    [The dative is a dative of manner.]
13. καὶ οἱ ἅγιοι ἄνθρωποι ἦσαν ἐνώπιον ἀγγέλων ἁγίων
    καὶ ἐνώπιον τοῦ ἀρνίου. (Apoc 14:10)
14. λέγει ἡ μήτηρ τοῦ Ἰησοῦ πρὸς αὐτόν, Οἶνον οὐκ
    ἔχουσιν. (Jn 2:3)
15. τοῦτο τὸ ποτήριον ἡ καινὴ διαθήκη ἐν τῷ αἵματί
    μου. (Lk 22:20)

16. ὥστε κύριός ἐστιν ὁ υἱὸς τοῦ ἀνθρώπου καὶ τοῦ σαββάτου. (Mk 2:28)
17. ὁ Χριστὸς ἔρχεται ἵνα διὰ τῆς ὑπομονῆς καὶ διὰ τῆς παρακλήσεως τῶν γραφῶν τὴν ἐλπίδα ἔχωμεν. (Rom 15:4)
18. υἱὲ διαβόλου, ἐχθρὲ πάσης δικαιοσύνης. (Acts 13:10)
19. τί ἐστιν τοῦτο; διδαχὴ καινὴ κατ᾽ ἐξουσίαν. (Mk 1:27)

II. Translate into Greek:
  1. They will begin to speak if they have the boldness.
  2. You, O man of God, pursue justice, faith, love, endurance. (1 Tim 6:11)
  3. For the body is not one member, but many. (1 Cor 12:14)

III. Mk 5:40 – 6:6.

λύω, **Aorist Middle Indicative and Imperative. The Adjectives** διπλοῦς **and** χρυσοῦς. **Rules for Accents 23.**

Lesson 31

λύω, **Aorist Middle Indicative and Imperative.**

For the meaning of the aorist indicative cf. above, Lesson 18 and Lesson 2. For the meaning of the middle voice cf. Lesson 26.

The aorist middle indicative of λύω is conjugated as follows (cf. V 1, VP 2):

Middle Voice, Indicative Mood, Aorist Tense

	Singular	Plural
1st Person	ἐ–λυσ–άμην	ἐ–λυσ–άμεθα
2nd Person	ἐ–λύσ–ω	ἐ–λύσ–ασθε
3rd Person	ἐ–λύσ–ατο	ἐ–λύσ–αντο

I loosed [with relation to myself]	*We loosed* [with relation to ourselves]
You (sg.) *loosed* [with relation to yourself]	*You* (pl.) *loosed* [with relation to your-selves]
He (*She, It*) *loosed* [with relation to himself, herself, itself]	*They loosed* [with relation to them-selves]

The form ἐλύσω is the result of a contraction: ἐλύσασο > ἐλύσαο > ἐλύσω.

The stem used is that of the aorist active, the formation of the augment is the same as that for the aorist active (cf. above, Lesson 18).

ἤρξατο κράζειν.
He began to cry out.

For the meaning of the aorist imperative cf. above, Lesson 19 and also Lesson 4. For the meaning of the middle voice cf. above, Lesson 26.

The aorist middle imperative of λύω is conjugated as follows (cf. V 1, VP 2):

Middle Voice, Imperative Mood, Aorist Tense

	Singular	Plural
2nd Person	λῦσ–αι	λύσ–ασθε
3rd Person	λυσ–άσθω	λυσ–άσθωσαν

You (sg.) *loosen!* [with relation to yourself]	*You* (pl.) *loosen!* [with relation to yourselves]
Let him (her, it) loosen! [with relation to himself, herself itself]	*Let them loosen!* [with relation to themselves]

The word *loosen* is used here in the imperative instead of *loose* to avoid the ambiguity in the English expression *Let him loose!* Cf. above, Lesson 27.

φυλαξάσθω αὐτὴ τὴν ἐντολήν.
Let her observe the command!

The Adjectives διπλοῦς and χρυσοῦς.

A limited number of adjectives of the first and second declensions show contracted forms (e.g., διπλοῦς, διπλῆ, διπλοῦν), *double*, from the root διπλο– [cf. Adj 3], and χρυσοῦς, χρυσῆ, χρυσοῦν, *golden*, from the root χρυσε– [Adj 3]. The results of the contraction are the same.

Singular

	Masculine	Feminine	Neuter
n	διπλοῦς	διπλῆ	διπλοῦν
v	διπλοῦς	διπλῆ	διπλοῦν
g	διπλοῦ	διπλῆς	διπλοῦ
d	διπλῷ	διπλῇ	διπλῷ
a	διπλοῦν	διπλῆν	διπλοῦν

	Masculine	Plural Feminine	Neuter
n	διπλοῖ	διπλαῖ	διπλᾶ
v	διπλοῖ	διπλαῖ	διπλᾶ
g	διπλῶν	διπλῶν	διπλῶν
d	διπλοῖς	διπλαῖς	διπλοῖς
a	διπλοῦς	διπλᾶς	διπλᾶ

Explanation of the contractions: ο + ο > ου (διπλοῦς, διπλοῦν, διπλοῦ); ο + ω > ω (διπλῷ, διπλῶν); ο + οι > οι (διπλοῖ, διπλοῖς). ο + α usually results in ω; but here, in the nominative, vocative, and accusative neuter plural, the result is α because of the influence from the ending α in these forms elsewhere. The feminine is explained by the fact that ο plus a long vowel or a diphthong is normally absorbed.

As was stated above, the contractions between a root vowel ε and the above endings yield the same results.

Rules for Accents 23.

Contracted adjectives of the first and second declensions have a circumflex accent on the last syllable of every form. Cf. the declension of διπλοῦς above, in this lesson.

Vocabulary for Lesson 31.

ἁπλοῦς, ἁπλῆ, ἁπλοῦν [Adj 3] *single; healthy.*

διπλοῦς, διπλῆ, διπλοῦν [Adj 3] *double.*

τετραπλοῦς, τετραπλῆ, τετραπλοῦν [Adj 3] *fourfold.*

χαλκοῦς, χαλκῆ, χαλκοῦν [Adj 3] *bronze.*

χρυσοῦς, χρυσῆ, χρυσοῦν [Adj 3] *golden.*

διακονία, -ας, ἡ [N 2] *service; help.*

διάκονος, -ου, ὁ/ἡ [N 6m and N 6f] *servant; minister.*

θυσία, -ας, ἡ [N 2] *sacrifice; act of offering.*

κρίμα, –ατος, τό [N 16] *judgment; verdict; condemnation.*

μάχαιρα, –ης, ἡ [N 3, N 33] *sword; knife.* The genitive singular is irregular. So is the dative singular (–ῃ instead of -ᾳ).

μισθός, –οῦ, ὁ [N 6m] *wages; reward.*

συνείδησις, –εως, ἡ [N 28f] *conscience; awareness.*

φυλή, –ῆς, ἡ [N 1] *tribe; nation.*

———

ἀληθινός, –ή, –όν [Adj 1] *true; real; dependable.*

ἰσχυρός, –ά, –όν [Adj 2] *strong.*

———

διό [Conj] *therefore.*

———

ἄρα [Part] *consequently, then, therefore.* This word is to be distinguished carefully from ἆρα [Part, Neg], an interrogative particle expecting a negative answer, and ἀρά, –ᾶς, ἡ [N 2], *curse.*

Exercises for Lesson 31.

I. Translate into English:
1. διὸ ὁ ἀγρὸς ἐκεῖνος ἀγρὸς αἵματός ἐστιν. (Mt 27:8)
2. ἡ διακονία ἡμῶν διακονία πρὸς τὸν Κύριόν ἐστιν.
3. ἀρξάσθωσαν φυλάσσεσθαι τὰς ἐντολάς.
4. Κύριε, ἰδοὺ μάχαιραι ὧδε δύο. (Lk 22:38)
5. ὑμεῖς ἐστε ἄξιοι διπλῆς τιμῆς. (1 Tim 5:17)
6. ἄρα ἔσται ἡ πίστις ἐπὶ τῆς γῆς; (Lk 18:8)
7. ἡ χαλκῆ μάχαιρα ἦν ἐπὶ τῆς τραπέζης. (Lk 22:21)
8. ἡ συνείδησις αὐτῶν ἀσθενής ἐστιν. (1 Cor 8:7)
9. λέγω ἐκεῖνον τὸν ἐργάτην ἄξιον εἶναι μισθοῦ τετραπλοῦ. (Lk 10:7)
10. ἡ θυσία τοῦ ἱερέως οὐκ ἀξία ἦν ἐνώπιον τοῦ θεοῦ. (Acts 4:19)
11. ἐκ τοῦ στόματος αὐτοῦ ἔρχεται ἀρὰ ἐπὶ τὸν θεόν. (Jas 3:10)
12. ἦν τὸ φῶς τὸ ἀληθινόν. (Jn 1:9)
13. τίς ἄρα μείζων ἐστὶν ἐν τῇ βασιλείᾳ τῶν οὐρανῶν; (Mt 18:1)

14. ἔρχεται δὲ ὁ ἰσχυρότερός μου. (Lk 3:16)
15. ἐὰν οὖν ᾖ ὁ ὀφθαλμός σου ἁπλοῦς, ὅλον τὸ σῶμα σου
    ἐν τῷ φωτὶ ἔσται. (Mt 6:22)
16. ὁ δὲ μείζων ὑμῶν ἔσται ὑμῶν διάκονος. (Mt 23:11)
17. ἦν ἐκεῖ ὄχλος πολὺς ἐκ παντὸς ἔθνους καὶ ἐκ πάντων
    φυλῶν καὶ λαῶν καὶ γλωσσῶν. (Apoc 7:9)
18. οὐδὲ ἔχεις φόβον τοῦ θεοῦ, ὅτι ἐν τῷ αὐτῷ κρίματι εἶ;
    (Lk 23:40)

II. Translate into Greek:
    1. Jesus says that his judgment is true. (Jn 8:16)
    2. If he were a minister of God, he would not be saying these
       things. (Rom 13:4)
    3. One of the twelve comes and with him a crowd from the
       elders with swords. (Mk 14:43)

III. Mk 6:7-16.

λύω, **Aorist Middle Subjunctive and Optative. The Adjective ἀργυροῦς. Rules for Accents 24.**

Lesson 32

λύω, Aorist Middle Subjunctive and Optative.

For the meaning of the aorist subjunctive cf. above, Lesson 20, and also Lesson 5. For the meaning of the middle voice cf. Lesson 26.

The aorist middle subjunctive of λύω is conjugated as follows (cf. V 1, VP 2):

	Middle Voice, Subjunctive Mood, Aorist Tense	
	Singular	Plural
1st Person	λύσ–ωμαι	λυσ–ώμεθα
2nd Person	λύσ–ῃ	λύσ–ησθε
3rd Person	λύσ–ηται	λύσ–ωνται

The form λύσῃ is a contraction of λύσησαι (λύσησαι > λύσηαι > λύσηι > λύσῃ). It should be noted that this form is the same as the aorist active subjunctive third person singular. Hence the form must be analyzed according to the context.

ἔρχεται ἵνα ἄρξηται λέγειν.
He is coming in order that he may begin to speak.

For the meaning of the aorist optative cf. above, Lesson 21, and also Lesson 6. For the meaning of the middle voice cf. Lesson 26.

The aorist middle optative of λύω is conjugated as follows (cf. V 1, VP 2):

	Middle Voice, Optative Mood, Aorist Tense	
	Singular	Plural
1st Person	λυσ–αίμην	λυσ–αίμεθα
2nd Person	λύσ–αιο	λύσ–αισθε
3rd Person	λύσ–αιτο	λύσ–αιντο

The form λύσαιο comes from λύσαισο.

The Adjective ἀργυροῦς.

Another category of contracted adjectives of the first and second declensions has a root ending in ε preceded by a ρ. The feminine of this type contracts to α instead of η (e.g., ἀργυροῦς, ἀργυρᾶ, ἀργυροῦν, *silver* [Adj 4]). For an explanation of the contractions cf. Lesson 31. *Made of silver*

	Masculine	Singular Feminine	Neuter
n	ἀργυροῦς	ἀργυρᾶ	ἀργυροῦν
v	ἀργυροῦς	ἀργυρᾶ	ἀργυροῦν
g	ἀργυροῦ	ἀργυρᾶς	ἀργυροῦ
d	ἀργυρῷ	ἀργυρᾷ	ἀργυρῷ
a	ἀργυροῦν	ἀργυρᾶν	ἀργυροῦν

	Masculine	Plural Feminine	Neuter
n	ἀργυροῖ	ἀργυραῖ	ἀργυρᾶ
v	ἀργυροῖ	ἀργυραῖ	ἀργυρᾶ
g	ἀργυρῶν	ἀργυρῶν	ἀργυρῶν
d	ἀργυροῖς	ἀργυραῖς	ἀργυροῖς
a	ἀργυροῦς	ἀργυρᾶς	ἀργυρᾶ

This concludes the presentation of the various categories of nouns and adjectives. All nouns and adjectives in the New Testament either can be subsumed under one of the various categories presented in this and the previous lessons, or else need special attention by reason of unusual forms. Such words needing special attention by reason of unusual forms will be presented in future lessons.

Rules for Accents 24.

In verbs, the accentuation is more regular than in nouns and adjectives (cf. above, Rules for Accents 12, Lesson 20). In verbs, the accent tends to go as far from the last syllable as possible, to the third-last syllable or, if that is not possible, to the second-last syllable, according to the general rules for the accentuation of these syllables (cf. above, Rules for Accents 3, Lesson 11). Thus the word γέγραπται in Mk 1:2 is accented on the third-last syllable because the last syllable is short (final αι is normally considered short). But ἀποστέλλω and κατασκευάσει in the same verse are accented on the second-last syllable because the last syllable is long.

But there are are exceptions to this general rule. One such exception involves the accent on the active infinitive aorist: the accent remains on the second-last syllable even though the last syllable is considered short for purposes of accent. Thus ἀπολῦσαι in Mk 10:2 has the accent on the second-last syllable, even though there is a third-last syllable, and the accent is circumflex, indicating not only that the syllable −λυ− is long, but that the syllable −σαι is considered short.

Vocabulary for Lesson 32.

ἀργυροῦς, −ᾶ, −οῦν [Adj 4] *silver* [i.e., *made of silver*].

πορφυροῦς, −ᾶ, −οῦν [Adj 4] *purple*.

σιδηροῦς, −ᾶ, −οῦν [Adj 4] *iron* [i.e., *made of iron*].
___
ἀδελφή, −ῆς, ἡ [N 1] *sister*.

ἀδικία, −ας, ἡ [N 2] *wrong-doing; injustice*.

ἔλεος, −ους, τό [N 31] *mercy; compassion*.

ἑορτή, −ῆς, ἡ [N 1] *feast*.

κώμη, −ης, ἡ [N 1] *village*.

μυστήριον, −ου, τό [N 7] *secret; mystery*.

πάσχα, τό [N 32] *Passover; Passover lamb*.
___
πλούσιος, −α, −ον [Adj 2] *rich*.

φίλος, −η, −ον [Adj 1] *loving*. This word is also a noun [N 6m]:
     friend.
___
οὐκέτι [Adv 2, Neg] *no longer*.

ποῦ [Adv 1] *where?*; *to what place?*; *whither?*.

Exercises for Lesson 32.

I. Translate into English:
1. ἔρχεται ἵνα ἄρξηται λέγειν.
2. ὁ ποιμὴν ἔχει ῥάβδον σιδηρᾶν. (Apoc 2:27)
3. ἄνθρωπός τις ἦν πλούσιος ὃς εἶχεν δοῦλον. (Lk 16:1)
4. ἔλεος θέλω καὶ οὐ θυσίαν. (Mt 9:13)
5. ἐν μεγάλῃ δὲ οἰκίᾳ οὐκ ἔστιν μόνον σκεύη χρυσᾶ καὶ
    ἀργυρᾶ. (2 Tim 2:20)
6. ὁ Ἰησοῦς ἤγγισεν εἰς τὴν κώμην. (Lk 24:28)
7. ὥστε οὐκέτι εἰσὶν δύο ἀλλὰ σὰρξ μία. (Mt 19:6)
8. οὗτος ἀληθής ἐστιν καὶ ἀδικία ἐν αὐτῷ οὐκ ἔστιν. (Jn
    7:18)
9. ὁ Ἰησοῦς εἶχεν ἱμάτιον πορφυροῦν. (Jn 19:2)
10. καὶ αἱ ἀδελφαὶ αὐτοῦ οὐχὶ πᾶσαι πρὸς ἡμᾶς εἰσιν;
    (Mt 13:56)
11. ἦν δὲ ἐγγὺς τὸ πάσχα, ἡ μεγάλη ἑορτή. (Jn 6:4) [Cf.
    Lesson 41, Vocabulary, for the meaning of ἐγγύς.]
12. ἰδοὺ μυστήριον ὑμῖν λέγω. (1 Cor 15:51)
13. τίς ἐξ ὑμῶν ἕξει φίλον. . .(Lk 11:5)
14. ποῦ ἡ πίστις ὑμῶν; (Lk 8:25)

II. Translate into Greek:
1. The prophet says that there is no injustice with God.
    (Rom 9:14)
2. God is rich in mercy because of his great love. (Eph 2:4)
3. Where are the wise of this world? (1 Cor 1:20)

III. Mk 6:17-26.

λύω, **Aorist Middle Participle and Infinitive. The Noun χάρις. Rules for Accents 25.**

Lesson 33

λύω, **Aorist Middle Participle and Infinitive.**

For the meaning of the aorist participle and infinitive cf. above, Lesson 22, as well as Lessons 4 and 7 For the meaning of the middle voice cf. Lesson 26.

The aorist middle participle of λύω is declined as follows (cf. V 1, VP 2, Adj 1):

Middle Voice, Participial Mood, Aorist Tense
Singular

	Masculine	Feminine	Neuter
n	λυσ–άμενος	λυσ–αμένη	λυσ–άμενον
v	λυσ–άμενε	λυσ–αμένη	λυσ–άμενον
g	λυσ–αμένου	λυσ–αμένης	λυσ–αμένου
d	λυσ–αμένῳ	λυσ–αμένῃ	λυσ–αμένῳ
a	λυσ–άμενον	λυσ–αμένην	λυσ–άμενον

Plural

	Masculine	Feminine	Neuter
n	λυσ–άμενοι	λυσ–άμεναι	λυσ–άμενα
v	λυσ–άμενοι	λυσ–άμεναι	λυσ–άμενα
g	λυσ–αμένων	λυσ–αμένων	λυσ–αμένων
d	λυσ–αμένοις	λυσ–αμέναις	λυσ–αμένοις
a	λυσ–αμένους	λυσ–αμένας	λυσ–άμενα

ἡ γυνὴ βαπτισαμένη ἤρξατο δοξάζειν τὸν θεόν.
Having had herself baptized, the woman began to glorify God.

The aorist middle infinitive of λύω is λύσ–ασθαι (cf. V 1, VP 2, Adj 1).

θέλω νίψασθαι νῦν ἐν ἐκείνῳ τῷ νιπτῆρι.
I wish to wash now in that basin.

The Noun χάρις.

The important noun χάρις, *grace*, is declined like ἐλπίς, but with some exceptions (cf. N 13f and N 33):

	Singular	Plural
n	χάρις	χάριτες
v	χάρις	χάριτες
g	χάριτος	χαρίτων
d	χάριτι	χάρισι(ν)
a	χάριν / χάριτα	χάριτας

Rules for Accents 25.

The diphthongs –οι and –αι, when final, are regarded as short for purposes of accent, except in the optative (cf. above, Rules for Accents 2, Lesson 10). Thus in the optative aorist active third person singular the form is λύσαι, whereas in the infinitive aorist active the form is λῦσαι. (In both these forms the υ of λύω is long. But in some forms of its conjugation it is short.)

Vocabulary for Lesson 33.

χάρις, χάριτος, ἡ [N 13f, 33] *grace; kindness.*

———

ἀκοή, –ῆς, ἡ [N 1] *report; hearing.*

ἀσθένεια, –ας, ἡ [N 2] *weakness; illness.*

δένδρον, –ου, τό [N 7] *tree.*

νεφέλη, –ης, ἡ [N 1] *cloud.*

πορνεία, –ας, ἡ [N 2] *sexual immorality.*

σταυρός, οῦ, ὁ [N 6m] *cross.*

χήρα, –ας, ἡ [N2] *widow.*

χώρα, –ας, ἡ [N 2] *region; neighborhood.*

———
δέκα [Adj 21] *ten.*

ἐκλεκτός, –ή, –όν [Adj 1] *chosen.*

καθαρός, –ά, –όν [Adj 2] *clean; innocent.*

πνευματικός, –ή, –όν [Adj 1] *spiritual; pertaining to spirit; pertaining to the Spirit.*

πόσος, –η, –ον [Adj 1] *how much?; how many?.*

———
οὐαί [Inter] *alas!* This word is also found as an indeclinable feminine noun [N 32]: *disaster.*

———
σήμερον [Adv 2] *today.*

Exercises for Lesson 33.

I. Translate into English:
1. καὶ ποιμένες ἦσαν ἐν τῇ χώρᾳ τῇ αὐτῇ. (Lk 2:8)
2. καὶ ἰδοὺ φωνὴ ἐκ τῆς νεφέλης λέγουσα, Οὗτός ἐστιν ὁ υἱός μου ὁ ἀγαπητός. (Mt 17:5)
3. Κύριε, τίς ἐπίστευσεν τῇ ἀκοῇ ἡμῶν; (Rom 10:16)
4. σήμερον σωτηρία τῷ οἴκῳ τούτῳ ἐστίν. (Lk 19:9)
5. ἦσαν δέκα δένδρα πρὸ τῆς οἰκίας.
6. εἰ οὖν τὸ φῶς τὸ ἐν σοὶ σκότος ἐστίν, τὸ σκότος πόσον. (Mt 6:23) [Cf. Lesson 37, Vocabulary, for the meaning of φῶς.]
7. χάρις ὑμῖν καὶ εἰρήνη ἀπὸ θεοῦ πατρὸς ἡμῶν καὶ Κυρίου Ἰησοῦ Χριστοῦ. (Rom 1:7)
8. διὰ δὲ τὰς πορνείας ἕκαστος τὴν ἑαυτοῦ γυναῖκα ἐχέτω, καὶ ἑκάστη τὸν ἴδιον ἄνδρα ἐχέτω. (1 Cor 7:2)
9. αὕτη ἡ ἀσθένεια οὐκ ἔστιν πρὸς θάνατον ἀλλ᾽ ὑπὲρ τῆς δόξης τοῦ θεοῦ. (Jn 11:4)
10. ἐκεῖνοι ἐσθίουσιν τὰς οἰκίας τῶν χηρῶν. (Lk 20:47)
11. ἴσθι ἐξουσίαν ἔχων ἐπάνω δέκα πόλεων. (Lk 19:17)
12. καὶ πάντες τὸ αὐτὸ πνευμάτικον βρῶμα ἤσθιον. (1 Cor 10:3)

13. οὐαὶ δὲ ταῖς ἐν γαστρὶ ἐχούσαις ἐν ἐκείναις ταῖς
    ἡμέραις. (Mt 24:19)
14. μακάριοι οἱ καθαροὶ τῇ καρδίᾳ ὅτι αὐτοὶ τὸν θεὸν
    βλέψουσιν. (Mt 5:8)
15. ὁ σταυρὸς τοῦ Ἰησοῦ δύναμίς ἐστιν.
16. ἄλλους ἔσωσεν, σωσάτω ἑαυτόν, εἰ οὗτός ἐστιν ὁ
    Χριστὸς τοῦ θεοῦ ὁ ἐκλεκτός. (Lk 23:35)

II. Translate into Greek:
    1. And behold all things will be clean for us. (Lk 11:41)
    2. Faith is from hearing, and hearing is through the words of
       Christ. (Rom 10:17)
    3. Today if you hear his voice you will have salvation. (Heb
       3:7)

III. Mk 6:27-36.

λύω, **Perfect Middle Indicative, Pluperfect Middle Indicative, and Perfect Middle Participle. The Perfect Middle of Stems Ending in Palatals, Labials, Dentals, Liquids, and Nasals. Rules for Accents 26.**

Lesson 34

λύω, **Perfect Middle Indicative, Pluperfect Middle Indicative, and Perfect Middle Participle.**

For the meaning of the perfect indicative cf. above, Lesson 23, and also Lesson 2. For the meaning of the middle voice cf. Lesson 26.

The perfect middle indicative of λύω is conjugated as follows (cf. V 1, VP 2):

Middle Voice, Indicative Mood, Perfect Tense

	Singular	Plural
1st Person	λέλυ–μαι	λελύ–μεθα
2nd Person	λέλυ–σαι	λέλυ–σθε
3rd Person	λέλυ–ται	λέλυ–νται

I have loosed [with relation to myself]

You (sg.) *have loosed* [with relation to yourself]

He (*She, It*) *has loosed* [with relation to himself, herself, itself]

We have loosed [with relation to ourselves]

You (pl.) *have loosed* [with relation to yourselves]

They have loosed [with relation to themselves]

The formation of the reduplication is the same as that for the active voice (cf. above, Lesson 23).

ἀπολέλυμαι τοὺς δούλους.
I have freed the slaves for myself [and they remain freed].

For the meaning of the pluperfect cf. above, Lesson 24, and also Lesson 2. For the meaning of the middle voice cf. Lesson 26.

The pluperfect middle indicative of λύω is conjugated as follows (cf. V 1, VP 2):

Middle Voice, Indicative Mood, Pluperfect Tense

	Singular	Plural
1st Person	(ἐ)–λελύ–μην	(ἐ)–λελύ–μεθα
2nd Person	(ἐ)–λέλυ–σο	(ἐ)–λέλυ–σθε
3rd Person	(ἐ)–λέλυ–το	(ἐ)–λέλυ–ντο

I had loosed [with relation to myself]	*We had loosed* [with relation to ourselves]
You (sg.) *had loosed* [with relation to yourself]	*You* (pl.) *had loosed* [with relation to yourselves]
He (She, It) had loosed [with relation to himself, herself, itself]	*They had loosed* [with relation to themselves]

ἀπελελύμην τοὺς δούλους.
I had freed the slaves for myself [and they remained free].

The augment can be treated the same way as in the pluperfect active, that is, it can be used or omitted with no difference in meaning (cf. above, Lesson 24).

For the meaning of the perfect participle cf. above, Lesson 25, and also Lesson 7.

The perfect middle participle of λύω is formed as follows (cf.V 1, VP 2, Adj 1):

Middle Voice, Participial Mood, Perfect Tense

	Masculine	Feminine	Neuter
n	λελυ–μένος	λελυ–μένη	λελυ–μένον
v	λελυ–μένε	λελυ–μένη	λελυ–μένον
g	λελυ–μένου	λελυ–μένης	λελυ–μένου
d	λελυ–μένῳ	λελυ–μένῃ	λελυ–μένῳ
a	λελυ–μένον	λελυ–μένην	λελυ–μένον

Singular

	Masculine	Plural Feminine	Neuter
n	λελυ–μένοι	λελυ–μέναι	λελυ–μένα
v	λελυ–μένοι	λελυ–μέναι	λελυ–μένα
g	λελυ–μένων	λελυ–μένων	λελυ–μένων
d	λελυ–μένοις	λελυ–μέναις	λελυ–μένοις
a	λελυ–μένους	λελυ–μένας	λελυ–μένα

The reduplication is the same as in the perfect active participle. The endings are the normal endings for the first and second declension adjectives. But the accent does not recede as the accent on verb forms normally does: it is on the second-last syllable even when the last syllable is short, instead of on the third-last.

The meaning of the perfect tense of the participial mood is the same as elsewhere (cf. Lesson 25). The middle voice has the meaning indicated above in Lesson 26.

ἀπολελυμένος τὸν δοῦλον, ὁ δεσπότης μακάριος ἦν.
Having freed the slave for himself, the master was happy.

The Perfect Middle of Stems Ending in Palatals, Labials, Dentals, Liquids, and Nasals.

The fact that the endings of forms in the perfect middle system begin with a consonant causes no problem when the stem to which they are added ends with a vowel, as is true for λύω. But when the stem ends with a consonant, certain sound changes occur. They are illustrated in the following sets of forms.

For stems ending in a palatal (κ, γ, χ), form changes are as follows (the paradigm is from the verb φυλάσσω, perfect stem πεφυλακ–):-

Middle Voice, Indicative Mood, Perfect Tense

	Singular	Plural
1st Person	πεφύλαγ–μαι	πεφυλάγ–μεθα
2nd Person	πεφύλαξαι	πεφύλαχ–θε
3rd Person	πεφύλακ–ται	πεφυλαγ–μένοι (–αι, –α) εἰσί(ν)

Middle Voice, Indicative Mood, Pluperfect Tense

	Singular	Plural
1st Person	(ἐ)–πεφυλάγ–μην	(ἐ)–πεφυλάγ–μεθα
2nd Person	(ἐ)–πεφύλαξο	(ἐ)–πεφύλαχ–θε
3rd Person	(ἐ)–πεφύλακ–το	πεφυλαγ–μένοι (–αι, –α) ἦσαν

The combination of a palatal (in this case, –κ) with the endings of the perfect middle system results in the following changes in sound: κ + μ > γμ; κ + σ > ξ; κ + τ > κτ. In the second person plural the σ disappears and the κ becomes assimilated to the θ with the result χθ. In the third person plural the use of the participle is required by the fact that the combination of consonant plus –ντ– was not part of the sound system of the language.

For stems ending in a labial (π, β, φ), form changes are as follows (the paradigm is from the verb γράφω, perfect stem γεγραφ–):

Middle Voice, Indicative Mood, Perfect Tense

	Singular	Plural
1st Person	γέγραμ–μαι	γεγράμ–μεθα
2nd Person	γέγραψαι	γέγραφ–θε
3rd Person	γέγραπ–ται	γεγραμ–μένοι (–αι, –α) εἰσί(ν)

Middle Voice, Indicative Mood, Pluperfect Tense

	Singular	Plural
1st Person	(ἐ)–γεγράμ–μην	(ἐ)–γεγράμ–μεθα
2nd Person	(ἐ)–γέγραψο	(ἐ)–γέγραφ–θε
3rd Person	(ἐ)–γέγραπ–το	γεγραμ–μένοι (–αι, –α) ἦσαν

The combination of a labial (in this case, –φ) with the endings of the perfect middle system results in the following changes in sound: φ + μ > μμ; φ + σ > ψ; φ + τ > πτ. In the second person plural the σ disappears and the φ becomes assimilated to the θ with the result φθ. In the third person plural the use of the participle is required by the fact that the combination of consonant plus –ντ– was not part of the sound system of the language.

For stems ending in a dental (τ, δ, θ), form changes are as follows (the paradigm is from the verb βαπτίζω, perfect stem βεβαπτιδ–):

Middle Voice, Indicative Mood, Perfect Tense

	Singular	Plural
1st Person	βεβάπτισ–μαι	βεβαπτίσ–μεθα
2nd Person	βεβάπτισαι	βεβάπτισ–θε
3rd Peson	βεβάπτισ–ται	βεβαπτισ–μένοι (–αι, –α) εἰσί(ν)

Middle Voice, Indicative Mood, Pluperfect Tense

	Singular	Plural
1st Person	(ἐ)–βεβαπτίσ–μην	(ἐ)–βεβαπτίσ–μεθα
2nd Person	(ἐ)–βεβάπτισο	(ἐ)–βεβάπτισ–θε
3rd Person	(ἐ)–βεβάπτισ–το	βε–βαπτισ–μένοι (–αι, –α) ἦσαν

The combination of a labial (in this case, –δ) with the endings of the perfect middle system results in the following changes in sound: δ + μ > σμ; δ + σ > σ; δ + τ > στ. In the second person plural the δ changes to σ to avoid the occurrence of two θ's in succession. In the third person plural the use of the participle is required by the fact that the combination of consonant plus –ντ– was not part of the sound system of the language.

For words whose perfect stems ends in a liquid (λ, ρ) or a nasal (μ, ν) the following rules obtain:
    The liquids have no σ before θ in the second person plural (for example, ἐσταλ–, the perfect stem of στέλλω, *I send*, has ἔσταλθε in the second person plural, both in the perfect and pluperfect endings). Otherwise the liquids have no changes in the final consonant of the stem except for the use of the participle in the third person plural required by the fact that the combination of consonant plus –ντ– was not part of the sound system of the language.
    The nasals change ν to μ before μ in the first person singular and plural and in the participle (e.g., for the nasal stem ἐξηραν–, from the verb ξηραίνω, *I dry up*, the first person singular and plural are ἐξήραμμαι and ἐξηράμμεθα, ἐξηράμμην and ἐξηράμμεθα, with the participle being ἐξηραμμένοι). The σ drops in the second person plural (ἐξήρανθε). The participle is used in the third person plural as for the other consonant stems listed above, and for the same reason.

Rules for Accents 26.

In verb forms having the augment, the accent does not move beyond the augment. (This rule is relevant only for compound verbs.) Thus, the form ἀπεῖχεν (Mt 14:24) from the compound verb ἀπέχω, the form ἐνεῖχεν (Mk 6:19) from the compound verb ἐνέχω, and the form κατεῖχεν (Lk 4:42) from the verb κατέχω.

Vocabulary for Lesson 34.

ἀστήρ, -έρος, ὁ [N 24m, N33] *star*. [The dative plural is ἄστροις.]

παρουσία, -ας, ἡ [N 2] *coming; presence*.

———

ἐλεύθερος, -α, -ον [Adj 2] *free*.

———

ἄρτι [Adv 2] *now, just now; at once*.

εὐθέως [Adv 2] *immediately*.

Exercises for Lesson 34.

I. Translate into English:
   1. καὶ περὶ τὴν κεφαλὴν τῆς γυναῖκος ἦσαν δώδεκα ἄστερες. (Apoc 12:1)
   2. ἀλλ' οὐκ ἔσται εὐθέως τὸ τέλος. (Lk 21:9)
   3. πῶς οὖν βλέπεις ἄρτι; (Jn 9:19)
   4. οὕτως ἔσται ἡ παρουσία τοῦ υἱοῦ τοῦ ἀνθρώπου. (Mt 24:27)
   5. ἄρα γε ἐλεύθεροί εἰσιν οἱ υἱοί. (Mt 17:26)

II. Translate into Greek:
   1. Lord, what will be the signs of your coming? (Mt 24:3)
   2. If we have the truth we are free.
   3. How many stars are there in the heavens?

III. Mk 6:37-40.

λύω, **Perfect Middle Imperative,**
Infinitive, Subjunctive, and Optative. The
Noun χείρ. **Rules for Accents 27.**

Lesson 35

λύω, **Perfect Middle Imperative, Infinitive, Subjunctive, and Optative.**

There are no perfect middle imperatives, infinitives, subjunctives, or optatives in the New Testament. The forms given in this lesson are to help the student fill out the other forms of the middle which are used, and to prepare for the presentation of the perfect passive. Cf. below, Lesson 42.

The perfect middle imperative of λύω is conjugated as follows (cf. V 1, VP 2):

Middle Voice, Imperative Mood, Perfect Tense

	Singular	Plural
2nd Person	λέλυ–σο	λέλυ–σθε
3rd Person	λελύ–σθω	λελύ–σθωσαν

The perfect middle infinitive of λύω is λελύ–σθαι (cf. V 1, VP 2). The perfect middle infinitive of φυλάσσω is πεφυλάχ–θαι; of γράφω, γεγράφ–θαι; of βαπτίζω, βεβαπτίσ–θαι; of στέλλω, ἐστάλ–θαι.

The perfect middle subjunctive and optative are formed by placing the perfect middle participle with the present subjunctive and optative respectively of εἰμί (cf. V 1, VP 2, Adj 1):

Middle Voice, Subjunctive Mood, Perfect Tense

	Singular	Plural
1st Person	λελυμένος, −η, −ον ὦ	λελυμένοι, −αι, −α ὦμεν
2nd Person	λελυμένος, −η, −ον ᾖς	λελυμένοι, −αι, −α ἦτε
3rd Person	λελυμένος, −η, −ον ᾖ	λελυμένοι, −αι, −α ὦσι(ν)

Middle Voice, Optative Mood, Perfect Tense

	Singular	Plural
1st Person	λελυμένος, −η, −ον εἴην	λελυμένοι, −αι, −α εἴημεν
2nd Person	λελυμένος, −η, −ον εἴης	λελυμένοι, −αι, −α εἴητε
3rd Person	λελυμενος, −η, −ον εἴη	λελυμένοι, −αι, −α εἴησαν

There is no perfect middle optative in the New Testament. The forms of the optative given above are to help students orientate themselves in the periphrastic conjugations in which a form of the verb εἰμί is used with a participle.

The meaning of these moods in the perfect tense of the middle voice can be inferred from the meaning of the perfect active tense of these moods (cf. Lesson 25 and, for the optative, Lesson 14 for the present tense) together with the meaning of the middle voice (cf. Lesson 26).

This concludes the presentation of the middle voice of λύω (Lessons 26-35). The fact that the middle voice has been given attention quantitatively comparable to that given to the active voice (Lesson 9-24), and to the passive voice (below, Lessons 36-42), should not be taken as an indication that the middle voice is equal in importance to the other two voices. It is not. But the middle voice does have its role in the New Testament both in its own right and as a means of formulation for certain deponent verbs (as will be explained in Lesson 45). These facts, plus the need to present the middle voice clearly so as to distinguish it from the active and passive voice and enable these two vastly more important voices to be understood better, are the reasons for presenting the middle voice as extensively as has been done here.

The Noun χείρ.

The noun χείρ, *hand*, is declined as follows (cf. N 24f, N 33):

	Singular	Plural
n	χείρ	χεῖρες
v	χείρ	χεῖρες
g	χειρός	χειρῶν
d	χειρί	χερσί(ν)
a	χεῖρα	χεῖρας

The dative plural has a shortened syllable in the root, χερ– instead of χειρ–.

Rules for Accents 27.

In the perfect active participle the accent is on the last syllable in the nominative masculine and neuter and remains on this same syllable (i.e., on the last syllable of the root) throughout the declension of the masculine and neuter. Cf. the paradigms given in Lesson 25 and Adj 17.

Vocabulary for Lesson 35.

χείρ, χειρός, ἡ [N 24f, N 33] *hand*.

ἀργύριον, –ου, τό [N 7] *silver; money*.

ζῷον, –ου, τό [N 7] *animal*.

θυσιαστήριον, –ου, τό [N 7] *altar*.

κοιλία, –ας, ἡ [N 2] *stomach; womb*.

μετάνοια, –ας, ἡ [N 2] *repentance; change of heart*.

πληγή, –ῆς, ἡ [N 1] *plague; blow; calamity*.

πλοῦτος, –ου, ὁ [N 6m] *wealth*. This word is also found as a neuter in the nominative and accusative: τὸ πλοῦτος [N 31].

συνέδριον, –ου, τό [N 7] *Sanhedrin; council*.

χιλίαρχος, –ου, ὁ [N 6m] *(military) officer*, i.e., *tribune*.

λευκός, –ή, –όν [Adj 1] *white*.

νέος, –α, –ον [Adj 2] *new*; *young*. The vowel in the root of this word is never contracted.

περισσός, –ή, –όν [Adj 1] *more*. This word is also found as an adverb: περισσόν [Adv 3]: *to the full*.

———

ὥσπερ [Conj] *as*; *just as*; *like*.

———

καλῶς [Adv 3] *well*.

Exercises for Lesson 35.

I. Translate into English:
1. ἐγὼ ἔρχομαι ἵνα ζωὴν ἔχωσιν καὶ περισσὸν ἔχωσιν. (Jn 10:10)
2. ἔχομεν θυσιαστήριον ἐξ οὗ ἐσθίειν οὐκ ἔχουσιν ἐξουσίαν οἱ ἄλλοι. (Heb 13:10)
3. οὐ γὰρ νίπτονται τὰς χεῖρας αὐτῶν ὅταν ἄρτον ἐσθίωσιν. (Mt 15:2)
4. καὶ καλῶς λέγετε, εἰμὶ γάρ. (Jn 13:13)
5. ὁ θεὸς αὐτῶν ἡ κοιλία. (Phil 3:19)
6. ὁ Χριστὸς ἐν ὑμῖν ἐστιν τὸ πλοῦτος τῆς δόξης τοῦ μυστηρίου ἐν τοῖς ἔθνεσιν. (Col 1:27)
7. ὁ θεός, οὐκ εἰμὶ ὥσπερ οἱ λοιποὶ τῶν ἀνθρώπων. (Lk 18:11)
8. τὸ ἀργύριόν σου σὺν σοὶ εἴη εἰς θάνατον. (Acts 8:20)
9. τὸν νεανίαν τοῦτον ἄγε πρὸς τὸν χιλίαρχον. (Acts 23:17)
10. καὶ εἶπεν ὁ νεώτερος αὐτῶν τῷ πατρί. . . (Lk 15:12)
11. καὶ ἦγον τὸν Ἰησοῦν εἰς τὸ συνέδριον αὐτῶν. (Lk 22:66)
12. τὰ δὲ ἱμάτια αὐτοῦ ἦν λευκά. (Mt 17:2)
13. καὶ ἔβλεψα ἄλλο σημεῖον ἐν τῷ οὐρανῷ μέγα, ἀγγέλους ἔχοντας τὰς ἐσχάτας πληγάς. (Apoc 15:1)
14. ἐγὼ μὲν ὑμᾶς βαπτίζω εἰς μετάνοιαν. (Mt 3:11)
15. τὸ τρίτον ζῷον εἶχε τὸ πρόσωπον ὡς ἀνθρώπου. (Apoc 4:7)
16. τὸ δὲ περισσὸν τούτων ἐκ τοῦ πονηροῦ ἐστιν. (Mt 5:37)

II. Translate into Greek:
    1. Now Jesus was speaking the truth before the Sanhedrin.
       (Jn 8:45)
    2. The just man does not have need of repentance. (Lk
       15:7)
    3. What then will that child be? For even the hand of the Lord
       is with him. (Lk 1:66)

III. Mk 6:41-47.

The Meaning of the Passive Voice. λύω,
Present Passive Indicative, Imperfect
Passive Indicative, Present Passive
Imperative, Subjunctive, Optative,
Infinitive, and Participle. Rules for Accents
28.

Lesson 36

The Meaning of the Passive Voice.

The passive voice indicates that the grammatical subject of a
sentence is in some way or other the recipient of an action. (cf.
above, Lesson 26.) The personal agent of the action is usually
expressed, if he or she or they are expressed at all, by the use of the
preposition ὑπό with the genitive case. (Cf. above, Lesson 10.) ὑπό
with the genitive is usually used to express the agent of an action, if
that agent is a person. If the agent is impersonal, the simple dative
without a preposition is usually used. This simple dative (the dative
of means) is also used with non-passive verbs to express impersonal
agency.
     In Greek the forms of the passive voice are the same as the
forms of the middle voice of all the moods of the present and perfect
systems. Hence the precise force of these verbal forms can be
determined only from the context. In the future and aorist tenses,
on the other hand, the forms of the passive voice are clearly distinct
from the forms of the middle voice. Thus, their precise force can be
determined not only from the context but from the form itself.
     Even though the passive forms of the present and perfect
systems have already been given implicitly above in the presentation
of the middle forms of the present and perfect tenses, inasmuch as
the passive forms are the same as the middle forms in these tenses,
these forms will be repeated in this and the following lessons. This
repetition will help the student realize that even though the forms of
these two voices are the same in these two systems, the meaning is
different. (Cf. Lessons 26-29 above, for the present systems of the
middle voice, and Lessons 34-35 for the perfect systems.)

λύω, Present Passive Indicative, Imperfect Passive Indicative, Present Passive Imperative, Subjunctive, Optative, Infinitive, and Participle.

The present passive indicative of λύω is conjugated as follows (cf. V 1, VP 3):

Passive Voice, Indicative Mood, Present Tense

	Singular	Plural
1st Person	λύ–ομαι	λυ–όμεθα
2nd Person	λύ–η	λύ–εσθε
3rd Person	λύ–εται	λύ–ονται

I am loosed	*We are loosed*
You (sg.) *are loosed*	*You* (pl.) *are loosed*
He (*She, It*) *is loosed*	*They are loosed*

The form λύη is a contraction from λύεσαι (λύεσαι > λύεαι > λύηι > λύη).

For the meaning of the indicative mood cf. above, Lesson 2. For the meaning of the present tense in the indicative mood cf. Lesson 9.

ὁ δοῦλος λύεται ὑπὸ τοῦ δεσπότου αὐτοῦ.
The slave is being let go by his master.

The imperfect passive indicative of λύω is conjugated as follows (cf. V 1, VP 3):

Passive Voice, Indicative Mood, Imperfect Tense

	Singular	Plural
1st Person	ἐ–λυ–όμην	ἐ–λυ–όμεθα
2nd Person	ἐ–λύ–ου	ἐ–λύ–εσθε
3rd Person	ἐ–λύ–ετο	ἐ–λύ–οντο

I was being loosed	*We were being loosed*
You (sg.) *were being loosed*	*You* (pl.) *were being loosed*
He (*She, It*) *was being loosed*	*They were being loosed*

The form ἐλύου is a contraction of ἐλύεσο.

For the meaning of the imperfect tense of the indicative mood cf. above, Lesson 10.

ὁ δοῦλος ἐλύετο ὑπὸ τοῦ δεσπότου αὐτοῦ.
The slave was being let go by his master.

The present passive imperative of λύω is conjugated as follows (cf. V 1, VP 3):

	Passive Voice, Imperative Mood, Present Tense	
	Singular	Plural
2nd Person	λύ–ου	λύ–εσθε
3rd Person	λυ–έσθω	λυ–έσθωσαν

You (sg.) be loosened!   *You (pl.) be loosened!*
Let him (her, it) be loosened! *Let them be loosened!*

The form λύου is a contraction of λύεσο.
The translation *loosen* is used for λύω in line with the same translation used for the active voice of the imperative (cf. above, Lessons 12 and 19).
For the meaning of the present tense of the imperative mood cf. above, Lesson 12, and Lesson 4.

λυέσθω ὁ δοῦλος ὑπὸ τοῦ δεσπότου αὐτοῦ.
Let the slave be let go by his master.

The present passive subjunctive of λύω is conjugated as follows (cf. V 1, VP 3):

	Passive Voice, Subjunctive Mood, Present Tense	
	Singular	Plural
1st Person	λύ–ωμαι	λυ–ώμεθα
2nd Person	λύ–ῃ	λύ–ησθε
3rd Person	λύ–ηται	λύ–ωνται

The form λύῃ is a contraction of λύησαι (λύησαι > λύηαι > λύηι > λύῃ).
For the meaning of the present tense of the subjunctive mood cf. above, Lesson 13, and Lesson 5.

ὁ δοῦλος ἔρχεται ἵνα λύηται ὑπὸ τοῦ δεσπότου αὐτοῦ.
The slave is coming so that he may be let go by his master.

The present passive optative of λύω is conjugated as follows (cf. V 1, VP 3):

Passive Voice, Optative Mood, Present Tense

	Singular	Plural
1st Person	λυ–οίμην	λυ–οίμεθα
2nd Person	λύ–οιο	λύ–οισθε
3rd Person	λύ–οιτο	λύ–οιντο

The form λύοιο comes from λύοισο.
For the meaning of the present tense of the optative mood cf. above, Lesson 14, and Lesson 6.

λύοιτο ὁ δοῦλος ὑπὸ τοῦ δεσπότου αὐτοῦ.
May the slave be let go by his master.

The present passive infinitive of λύω is λύεσθαι (cf. V 1, VP 3).
For the meaning of the present tense of the infinitive mood cf. above, Lesson 15, and Lesson 4.

λέγω τὸν δοῦλον λύεσθαι ὑπὸ τοῦ δεσπότου αὐτοῦ.
I say that the slave is being let go by his master.

The present passive participle of λύω is declined as follows (cf. V 1, VP 3, Adj 1):

Passive Voice, Participial Mood, Present Tense

Singular

	Masculine	Feminine	Neuter
n	λυ–όμενος	λυ–ομένη	λυ–όμενον
v	λυ–όμενε	λυ–ομένη	λυ–όμενον
g	λυ–ομένου	λυ–ομένης	λυ–ομένου
d	λυ–ομένῳ	λυ–ομένῃ	λυ–ομένῳ
a	λυ–όμενον	λυ–ομένην	λυ–όμενον

	Masculine	Plural Feminine	Neuter
n	λυ–όμενοι	λυ–όμεναι	λυ–όμενα
v	λυ–όμενοι	λυ–όμεναι	λυ–όμενα
g	λυ–ομένων	λυ–ομένων	λυ–ομένων
d	λυ–ομένοις	λυ–ομέναις	λυ–ομένοις
a	λυ–ομένους	λυ–ομένας	λυ–όμενα

For the meaning of the present tense in the participial mood cf. above, Lesson 16, and Lesson 7.

The present stem indicates action which is not terminated (cf. above, Lesson 9). In the indicative mood this stem indicates present primary time if there is no augment, and past primary time if there is. The indicative, combined with the present stem, indicates action which is not terminated, i.e., which is open-ended, and hence, often, continued or repeated (cf. Lesson 9 for the present indicative and Lesson 10 for the imperfect). In the other moods the present stem, indicating as it does non-terminated action, has appropriate implications. In the present system the imperative usually conveys the idea of a general precept (cf. Lesson 12). In the present system the subjunctive and optative indicate an action which is viewed as continuing or repeated, or which as customary, or which is being described (cf. Lessons 13 and 14). This can be true of the infinitive as well. But the infinitive and the participle often stand in a relation of contemporaneity with a principal verb on which they depend (cf. Lesson 15 and 16). Students should think their way through the perspectives generated by the aspect (known from the stem), the mood, and the voice, noting how they interact to qualify the meaning of any verb in a given context.

This completes the presentation of the moods of the present passive system of λύω.

Rules for Accents 28.

In the perfect active infinitive the accent is on the second-last syllable even though the final syllable is short: λελυκέναι.

Vocabulary for Lesson 36.

ἀκροβυστία, −ας, ἡ [N 2] *uncircumcision* [often used as a collective noun referring to those who are not Jews].

διδασκαλία, −ας, ἡ [N 2] *teaching*. This word means both the act of teaching and the content of what is taught, as in English.

ἑκατοντάρχης, −ου, ὁ [N 4] *centurion* (Roman military officer). This meaning is also expressed by the word ἑκατόνταρχος, −ου, ὁ [N 6m].

ἐπιστολή, −ῆς, ἡ [N 1] *letter* (in the sense of *epistle*).

πειρασμός, −οῦ, ὁ [N 6m] *test*; *temptation*.

τελώνης, −ου, ὁ [N 4] *tax-gatherer*.

χιλιάς, −άδος, ἡ [N 14f] *thousand*.
———
τεσσαράκοντα / τεσσεράκοντα [Adj 21] *forty*.
———
ἁγιάζω (ἁγιάσω) [V 5, VP 1-3] *I consecrate* (to God); *I purify*; *I make holy*.

βαστάζω (βαστάσω) [V 5, DV 37, VP 1-3] *I carry*; *I tolerate*.

καθαρίζω (καθαρίσω) [V 5, DV 136, VP 1-3) *I cleanse*; *I purify* (ritually).

σκανδαλίζω (σκανδαλίσω) [V 5, VP 1-3] *I cause to stumble*; *I scandalize* (i.e., *I lead into sin*, the more common New Testament meaning, or *I shock*, the more common meaning today; or both together).
———
οὔπω, μήπω [Adv 2, Neg] *not yet*. These words are distinguished according to the principles for distinguishing οὐ and μή.
———
πάντοτε [Adv 2] *always*.

Exercises for Lesson 36.

[handwritten margin note: acc = temporal duration]

I. Translate into English:

1. καὶ ἦν ἐν τῇ ἐρήμῳ τεσσεράκοντα ἡμέρας πειραζόμενος
   ὑπὸ τοῦ διαβόλου. (Mk 1:13) [The word ἡμέρας is in
   the accusative case to express temporal duration; cf.
   Lesson 79.]
2. ὁ θεὸς καθαρίζει τὰς καρδίας αὐτῶν. (Acts 15:9)
3. ὅ τε γὰρ ἁγιάζων καὶ οἱ ἁγιαζόμενοι ἐξ ἑνὸς πάντες.
   (Heb 2:11) [Note that the first word in this sentence is
   the article ὅ; it has an accent because it is followed by an
   enclitic.]
4. ἡ διδασκαλία τοῦ Κυρίου οὐ μόνον διὰ ῥημάτων ἦν.
5. ἀλλ᾽ οὔπω ἐστὶν τὸ τέλος. (Mt 24:6)
6. λέγω μήπω εἶναι τὸ τέλος.
7. πειρασμός ἐστιν ἑκάστῳ ἀνθρώπῳ.
8. καὶ ἐσκανδαλίζοντο ἐν αὐτῷ. (Mt 13:57)
9. ἡ ἐπιστολὴ ἡμῶν ὑμεῖς ἐστε. (2 Cor 3:2)
10. πάντοτε γὰρ τοὺς πτωχοὺς ἔχετε μεθ᾽ ὑμῶν, ἐμὲ δὲ οὐ
    πάντοτε ἔχετε. (Mt 26:11)
11. ἔστω σοι ὥσπερ ὁ τελώνης. (Mt 18:17)
12. ἐν γὰρ Χριστῷ Ἰησοῦ οὔτε περιτομή τι ἰσχύει ουιε
    ἀκροβυστία. (Gal 5:6) [The word τι is an "accusative of
    respect", i.e., an accusative case which indicates that
    "in respect to which" something is being affirmed.
    Here, in respect to "something"; with the negative, in
    respect to "nothing".]
13. μακαρία ἡ κοιλία ἡ βαστάσασά σε. (Lk 11:27)
14. χιλιάδες ἀγγέλων ἦσαν ἔμπροσθεν τοῦ θεοῦ. (Acts 10:4)
15. ἑκατοντάρχου δέ τινος δοῦλος ἀσθενὴς ἦν. (Lk 7:2)

II. Translate into Greek:

1. The disciples of Christ are sanctified by the Spirit of truth.
   (Jn 17:17.19)
2. The cross is carried by the disciples of Christ. (Lk 14:27)
3. The apostles wish to be cleansed from their sins. (1 Jn
   1:7)

III. Mk 6:48-49.

The Weak Aorist Passive and the Strong
Aorist Passive. λύω, Aorist Passive
Indicative and Imperative. The Noun
ἀνήρ.

Lesson 37

The Weak Aorist Passive and the Strong Aorist Passive.

The aorist forms of the passive voice are different from the aorist
forms of the middle voice (cf. above, Lesson 36). The aorist passive
forms are divided into two categories, with no difference of
meaning: 1) "weak" aorist passive (by far the more numerous), and
2) "strong" aorist passive.

    1) Weak aorist passive forms are characterized by a θη as the
aorist passive marker. In the indicative, imperative, and infinitive
this θη is found unchanged; in the subjunctive, the η is absorbed; in
the optative and participle, the η becomes ε,

    2) Strong aorist passive forms do not have this distinctive θ,
but they do have the η where the weak aorist has it. This η in the
strong aorist passive behaves as the η in the weak aorist passive.

    Both weak and strong aorist passives are otherwise
indistinguishable, sharing the same endings in all moods. (The
strong aorist passive will be presented below, in Lesson 41.)

    Because the consonant that indicates the weak aorist passive,
θ, comes immediately after the root of the verb, consonantal changes
are frequently necessary. The following rules should be noted:

    Roots ending in a palatal (κ, γ, χ) have the palatal χ. Thus
ἄγω becomes ἤχθην in the aorist indicative passive.

    Roots ending in a labial (π, β, φ) have the labial φ. Thus πέμπω
becomes ἐπέμφθην in the aorist indicative passive.

    Roots ending in a dental (τ, δ, θ) have a σ. Thus βαπτίζω
becomes ἐβαπτίσθην in the aorist indicative passive.

    Nasal and liquid roots will be treated one by one as they occur,
for they are often irregular. ξηραίνω (cf. above, Lesson 34) becomes
ἐξηράνθην; στέλλω (cf. above, Lesson 34) has a strong aorist passive
which will be presented in a future lesson.

It should be noted that verbs whose present stem ends in σσ have χ before the θ when they are weak aorist passives: φυλάσσω becomes ἐφυλάχθην. [The σσ indicates some kind of guttural.]

λύω, Aorist Passive Indicative and Imperative.

λύω is has a weak aorist passive. In the indicative mood it has an augment, which is formed th same way as other augments (cf. above, Lessons 10, 18, 31). The aorist passive indicative of λύω is formed as follows, the aorist passive stem being λυθη– (the verbal root λυ plus the weak aorist passive marker θη) (cf. V 1, VP 3):

Passive Voice, Indicative Mood, Aorist Tense

	Singular	Plural
1st Person	ἐ–λύθη–ν	ἐ–λύθη–μεν
2nd Person	ἐ–λύθη–ς	ἐ–λύθη–τε
3rd Person	ἐ–λύθη	ἐ–λύθη–σαν

I was loosed	*We were loosed*
You (sg.) *were loosed*	*You* (pl.) *were loosed*
He (*She, It*) was loosed	*They were loosed*

For the meaning of the aorist tense in the indicative mood cf. above, Lesson 18. For the meaning of the passive voice cf. Lessons 26 and 36.

ὁ δοῦλος ἐλύθη ὑπὸ τοῦ δεσπότου αὐτοῦ.
The slave was let go by his master.

The aorist imperative passive of λύω is conjugated as follows (cf. V 1, VP 3):

Passsive Voice, Imperative Mood, Aorist Tense

	Singular	Plural
2nd Person	λύθη–τι	λύθη–τε
3rd Person	λυθή–τω	λυθή–τωσαν

You (sg.) *be loosened*	*You* (pl.) *be loosened*
Let him (*her, it*) *be loosened*	*Let them be loosened*

λύω is translated *loosen* here in keeping with the translation adopted for its use in the imperative mood previously.

The final letters of the 2nd person singular are –θηθι, but the final θ is changed by dissimilation to τ to avoid two consecutive thetas. ("Dissimilation" means the development of a dissimilarity between two identical sounds.) Thus the second θ of –θηθι becomes τ in order to make it dissimilar to the first θ. This phenomenon has already been met in the formation of the reduplication in verbs beginning with an aspirated consonant. Cf. above, Lesson 23, p. 140, #2.

For the meaning of the aorist tense in the imperative mood cf. above, Lesson 19, and Lesson 4. For the meaning of the passive voice cf. Lessons 26 and 36.

λυθήτω ὁ δοῦλος παραχρῆμα ὑπὸ τοῦ δεσπότου αὐτου.
Let the slave be let go by his master at once.

The Noun ἀνήρ.

The noun ἀνήρ, *man* or *husband*, is declined as follows (cf. N 24m, N 33):

	Singular	Plural
n	ἀνήρ	ἄνδρες
v	ἄνερ	ἄνδρες
g	ἀνδρός	ἀνδρῶν
d	ἀνδρί	ἀνδράσι(ν)
a	ἄνδρα	ἄνδρας

Vocabulary for Lesson 37.

ἀνήρ, ἀνδρός, ὁ [N 33] *man; husband.*
———
μαρτύριον, –ου, τό [N 7] *testimony; evidence.*

ξύλον, –ου, τό [N 7] *wood; tree.*

οὖς, ὠτός, τό [N 33] *ear.*

πῦρ, πυρός, τό [N 33] *fire.*

σκηνή, –ῆς, ἡ [N 1] *tent.*

ὕδωρ, ὕδατος, τό [N 33] *water*.

ὑπηρέτης, –ου, ὁ [N 4] *attendant; servant*.

φῶς, φωτός, τό [N 17] *light*.

———

ἑπτά [Adj 21] *seven*.

———

ἀγοράζω (ἀγοράσω) [V 5, VP 1-3] *I purchase; I ransom*.

ἀποκαλύπτω [ἀπό + καλύπτω] [V 4, V 5; DV 43; VP 1-3] *I reveal; I disclose*.

δουλεύω [V 1, VP 1-3] *I serve; I serve as a slave*. This word governs the dative case.

θεραπεύω [V 1, VP 1-3] *I heal; I serve; I take care of*.

θερίζω (θερίσω) [V 5, DV 123, VP 1-3] *I reap*.

κελεύω [V 1, VP 1-3] *I order; I command*.

———

ναί [Part] *yes; surely*.

———

ὁμοίως [Adv 3] *likewise*.

Exercises for Lesson 37.

I. Translate into English:
1. ἡ σκήνη τοῦ μαρτυρίου ἦν τοῖς πατράσιν ἡμῶν ἐν τῇ ἐρήμῳ. (Acts 7:44)
2. ἄρα οὖν αὐτὸς ἐγὼ τῷ μὲν νοΐ δουλεύω νόμῳ θεοῦ, τῇ δὲ σαρκὶ νόμῳ ἁμαρτίας. (Rom 7:25) [The datives τῷ νόι and τῇ σαρκὶ may be considered to be datives of respect, i.e., they are datives used to indicate in which respect the affirmations about "serving" contained in the sentence are true.]
3. ὁμοίως καὶ ὁ δεύτερος καὶ ὁ τρίτος ἕως τῶν ἑπτά. (Mt 22:26)
4. ἠγοράσθητε γὰρ τιμῆς· διὸ δοξάσατε τὸν θεὸν ἐν τῷ σώματι ὑμῶν. (1 Cor 6:20) [τιμῆς is a genitive of price: *of a price*.   Here, idiomatically, *for a price*.]

5. καὶ ἰδοὺ εἷς τῶν δώδεκα ἔρχεται καὶ μετ᾽ αὐτοῦ ὄχλος
   πολὺς μετὰ μαχαιρῶν καὶ ξύλων ἀπὸ τῶν ἀρχιερέων.
   (Mt 26:47)
6. ὅτε οὖν ἔβλεψαν αὐτὸν οἱ ἀρχιερεῖς καὶ οἱ ὑπηρέται
   ἔκραξαν. (Jn 19:6)
7. πολλοὶ ἄνδρες ἦσαν ἐσθίοντες χωρὶς γυναικῶν καὶ
   παιδίων. (Mt 15:38)
8. καὶ ἐθερίσθη ἡ γῆ. (Apoc 14:16)
9. ἔστω δὲ ὁ λόγος ὑμῶν ναὶ ναί, οὒ οὔ. (Mt 5:37)
10. τὰ δὲ ἱμάτια αὐτοῦ ἦν λευκὰ ὡς τὸ φῶς. (Mt 17:2)
11. μακάριος εἶ, ὅτι σὰρξ καὶ αἷμα οὐκ ἀπεκάλυψέν σοι
    ἀλλ᾽ ὁ πατήρ μου ὁ ἐν τοῖς οὐρανοῖς. (Mt 16:17)
12. ἐγὼ μὲν ὑμᾶς βαπτίζω ἐν ὕδατι εἰς μετάνοιαν. (Mt
    3:11)
13. ἐν τῇ ἀναστάσει οὖν τίνος τῶν ἑπτὰ ἔσται γυνή; (Mt
    22:28)
14. αὐτὸς ὑμᾶς βαπτίσει ἐν πνεύματι ἁγίῳ καὶ πυρί. (cf.
    Mt 3:11)
15. ἐν ἐκείνῃ τῇ ὥρᾳ ἐθεράπευσεν πολλοὺς ἀπὸ νόσων καὶ
    πνευμάτων πονηρῶν. (Lk 7:21)
16. εἴ τις ἔχει ὦτα ἀκούειν ἀκουέτω. (Mk 4:23)
17. βλέψας δὲ ὁ Ἰησοῦς ὄχλον περὶ αὐτὸν ἐκέλευσεν
    ἔρχεσθαι εἰς τὸ πέραν. (Mt 8:18) [ἔρχεσθαι is the
    present infinitive of ἔρχεται.]

II. Translate into Greek:
   1. Be healed by my word. [For "by my word" use the simple
      dative without a preposition, the dative of means—cf.
      p. 204.]
   2. The word was heard by the apostles.
   3. God wished to reveal his son in me. (Gal 1:16)

III. Mk 6:50-56.

λύω, **Aorist Passive Subjunctive and Optative. Rules for Accents 29.**

Lesson 38

λύω, Aorist Passive Subjunctive and Optative.

The aorist passive subjunctive of λύω is conjugated as follows (cf. V 1, VP 3). The η of the tense marker θη is absorbed by the long vowel in the subjunctive ending.

	Passive Voice, Subjunctive Mood, Aorist Tense	
	Singular	Plural
1st Person	λυθ–ῶ	λυθ–ῶμεν
2nd Person	λυθ–ῇς	λυθ–ῆτε
3rd Person	λυθ–ῇ	λυθ–ῶσι(ν)

For the meaning of the aorist tense in the subjunctive mood cf. above, Lesson 20, and Lesson 5. For the meaning of the passive voice cf. above, Lessons 26 and 36.

ὁ δοῦλος ἔρχεται ἵνα λυθῇ ὑπὸ τοῦ δεσπότου αὐτοῦ.
The slave is coming in order to be let loose by his master.

The aorist optative passive of λύω is conjugated as follows (cf. V 1, VP 3). The tense marker θη becomes θε in the optative, the ε forming a diphthong with the ι of the optative marker ιη.

	Passive Voice, Optative Mood, Aorist Tense	
	Singular	Plural
1st Person	λυθείην	λυθείημεν
2nd Person	λυθείης	λυθείητε
3rd Person	λυθείη	λυθείησαν

For the meaning of the aorist tense in the optative mood cf. above, Lesson 21, and Lesson 6. For the meaning of the passive voice cf. above, Lessons 26 and 36.

λυθείη ὁ δοῦλος ὑπὸ τοῦ δεσπότου αὐτοῦ.
May the slave be let go by his master.

Rules for Accents 29.

The aorist passive subjunctive has a circumflex accent on every ending because it is the result of a contraction. Cf. the paradigm above of the aorist passive subjunctive of λύω.

Vocabulary for Lesson 38.

ἀνάγκη, −ης, ἡ [N 1] *distress; necessity; need.*

ἀποκάλυψις, −εως, ἡ [N 28f] *revelation; unveiling.*

ἀπώλεια, −ας, ἡ [N 2] *destruction; waste.*

γεωργός, −οῦ, ὁ [N 6m] *farmer; peasant.*

δῶρον, −ου, τό [N 7] *gift; offering.*

ἐπίγνωσις, −εως, ἡ [N 28f] *knowledge.*

κοινωνία, −ας, ἡ [N 2] *fellowship; participation.*

κτίσις, −εως, ἡ [N 28f] *creation.* This word can signify both the act of creation and that which has been created.

προφητεία, −ας, ἡ [N 2] *prophecy.*

ἐπουράνιος, −ος, −ον [Adj 5] *heavenly.*

οἷος, −α, −ον [Adj 2] *such as.*

παλαιός, −ά, −όν [Adj 2] *old; former.*

τέλειος, −α, -ον [Adj 2] *complete; perfect.*

τοσοῦτος, –αύτη, –οῦτον [Adj 1 and Adj 1Pro] *such, so great; so many* (pl.). The form τοσοῦτο is also found in the neuter singular [Adj 1Pro].

———

ἐπεί [Conj] *because; when.*

———

ἴδε [Inter] *look!* [There is no difference in meaning between this word and ἰδού.]

Exercises for Lesson 38.

I. Translate into English:
1. ἀλλὰ ταῦτα τί ἐστιν εἰς τοσούτους; (Jn 6:9)
2. ἀγαπητοί, οὐκ ἐντολὴν καινὴν γράφω ὑμῖν, ἀλλ᾽ ἐντολὴν παλαιὰν ἣν εἴχετε ἀπ᾽ ἀρχῆς. ἡ ἐντολὴ ἡ παλαιά ἐστιν ὁ λόγος ὃν ἠκούσατε. (1 Jn 2:7)
3. εἰς τί ἡ ἀπώλεια αὕτη; (Mt 26:8)
4. οἷος ὁ ἐπουράνιος, τοιοῦτοι καὶ οἱ ἐπουράνιοι. (1 Cor 15:48)
5. ἔσται γὰρ ἀνάγκη μεγάλη ἐπὶ τῆς γῆς καὶ ὀργὴ τῷ λαῷ τούτῳ. (Lk 21:23)
6. Ἴδε ἡ μήτηρ μου καὶ οἱ ἀδελφοί μου. (Mk 3:34)
7. ὥστε αἱ γλῶσσαι εἰς σημεῖόν εἰσιν οὐ τοῖς πιστεύουσιν ἀλλὰ τοῖς ἀπίστοις, ἡ δὲ προφητεία οὐ τοῖς ἀπίστοις ἀλλὰ τοῖς πιστεύουσιν. (1 Cor 14:22)
8. ὁ πατήρ μου ὁ γεωργός ἐστιν. (Jn 15:1)
9. ἔσεσθε οὖν ὑμεῖς τέλειοι ὡς ὁ πατὴρ ὑμῶν ὁ οὐράνιος τελειός ἐστιν. (Mt 5:48)
10. διὰ νόμου ἐπίγνωσις ἁμαρτίας. (Rom 3:20)
11. οἱ ὀφθαλμοί μου ἔβλεψαν τὸ φῶς εἰς ἀποκάλυψιν ἐθνῶν καὶ δόξαν λαοῦ σου. (Lk 2:30-32)
12. τυφλοί, τί γὰρ μεῖζον, τὸ δῶρον ἢ τὸ θυσιαστήριον τὸ ἁγιάζον τὸ δῶρον; (Mt 23:19)
13. ἐκεῖνα τὰ ἀργύρια τιμὴ αἵματός ἐστιν. (Mt 27:6)
14. κηρύξατε τὸ εὐαγγέλιον πάσῃ τῇ κτίσει. (Mk 16:15)
15. οὐχὶ ὁ ἄρτος κοινωνία τοῦ σώματος τοῦ Χριστοῦ ἐστιν; (1 Cor 10:16)

II. Translate into Greek:
1. The witness of Jesus Christ was the spirit of prophecy. (Apoc 19:10)

2. Jesus comes so that each person who wishes may be baptized.
3. The old gifts of God were not just as good as the new.

III. The student has now had the opportunity of carefully working through the first six chapters of Mark's Gospel. It is time to return to the beginning of that Gospel and review the material seen, but now with the advantage of a considerably increased ability to understand the text. The text should now begin to become intelligible to the student in a significant way.

Read Mk 1:1-8, at first without consulting any aids, relying entirely on memory. Then re-read the text, checking any doubtful points against the material already seen in the previous lessons. Finally, read the verses aloud at least three times. The reading aloud should be unhurried, with precision being valued much more than speed.

λύω, **Aorist Passive Participle and
Infinitive. Rules for Accents 30.**

Lesson 39

λύω, Aorist Passive Participle and Infinitive.

The aorist passive participle of λύω is declined as follows (cf. V 1, VP 3, Adj 18). The η in the tense marker θη becomes ε, which is found either as such or as an element underlying the diphthong ει.

Passive Voice, Participial Mood, Aorist Tense

Singular

	Masculine	Feminine	Neuter
n	λυθείς	λυθεῖσα	λυθέ–ν
v	λυθείς	λυθεῖσα	λυθέ–ν
g	λυθέ–ντος	λυθείσης	λυθέ–ντος
d	λυθέ–ντι	λυθείσῃ	λυθέ–ντι
a	λυθέ–ντα	λυθεῖσαν	λυθέ–ν

Plural

	Masculine	Feminine	Neuter
n	λυθέ–ντες	λυθεῖσαι	λυθέ–ντα
v	λυθέ–ντες	λυθεῖσαι	λυθέ–ντα
g	λυθέ–ντων	λυθεισῶν	λυθέ–ντων
d	λυθεῖσι(ν)	λυθείσαις	λυθεῖσι(ν)
a	λυθέ–ντας	λυθείσας	λυθέ–ντα

For the meaning of the aorist tense in the participial mood cf. above, Lesson 22, and Lesson 7. For the meaning of the passive voice cf. Lessons 26 and 36.

> ὁ δοῦλος λυθεὶς ὑπὸ τοῦ δεσπότου αὐτοῦ ἔκραξεν διὰ τὴν χαρὰν αὐτοῦ.
> *The slave, having been let go by his master, shouted because of his joy.*

The aorist passive infinitive of λύω is λυθῆ–ναι (cf. V 1, VP 3):

For the meaning of the aorist tense in the infinitive mood cf. above, Lesson 22, and Lesson 4. For the meaning of the passive voice cf. Lessons 26 and 36.

ὁ δοῦλος ἠθέλησε λυθῆναι ὑπὸ τοῦ δεσπότου αὐτοῦ.
The slave wished to be let go by his master.

Rules for Accents 30

Aorist passive participles have an acute accent on the final syllable of the masculine nominative singular. The accent accordingly tends to remain on this syllable throughout the paradigm. Cf. Rules for Accents 12, Lesson 20.
   The accent of the aorist passive infinitive is on the second-last syllable even though the last syllable is short.

Vocabulary for Lesson 39.

ἀριθμός, –οῦ, ὁ [N 6m] *number.*

ἄφεσις, –εως, ἡ [N 28f] *forgiveness* (of sins); *freeing* (of captives).

βλασφημία, –ας, ἡ [N 2] *blasphemy.*

γάμος, –ου, ὁ [N 6m] *wedding.*

δεσμός, –οῦ, ὁ [N 6m] *bond; chain; prison.*

θυμός, –οῦ, ὁ [N 6m] *rage; fit of anger.*

κόπος, –ου, ὁ [N 6m] *hard work; trouble.*

οἰκοδομή, –ῆς, ἡ [N 2] *building; encouragement.*

πόλεμος, –ου, ὁ [N 6m] *war; conflict.*

πυλών, –ῶνος, ὁ [N 21m] *gate; entrance.*

στέφανος, -ου, ὁ [N 6m] *crown; prize.*

κενός, -ή, -όν [Adj 1] *empty*; *purposeless*; *senseless*.
κρυπτός, -ή, -όν [Adj 1] *hidden*.

ποταπός, -ή, -όν [Adj 1] *what sort of?*, *what kind of?*.

φανερός, -ά, -όν [Adj 2] *manifest*.

πόθεν [Adv 1] *from where?*.

ποτέ [Adv 2] [enclitic] *once*; *ever*.

Exercises for Lesson 39.

I. Translate into English:
1. ἔβλεψα τὴν πόλιν τὴν ἁγίαν ἔχουσαν πυλῶνας δώδεκα.
   (Apoc 21:10.12)
2. ὁ μὲν γάμος ἕτοιμός ἐστιν. . . (Mt 22:8)
3. ἄγουσιν αὐτὸν πρὸς τοὺς ἡγεμόνας τόν ποτε τυφλόν.
   (Jn 9:13)
4. ἦν ἐκ τοῦ ἀριθμοῦ τῶν δώδεκα. (Lk 22:3)
5. τί κόπους παρέχετε τῇ γυναικί; (Mt 26:10) [τί here as
   the idiomatic meaning *why?*. Cf. Lesson 73.]
6. ὅταν δὲ ἀκούσητε πολέμους καὶ ἀκοὰς πολέμων, οὔπω
   τὸ τέλος. (Mk 13:7)
7. ὁ προφήτης ἦν κηρύσσων βάπτισμα μετανοίας εἰς
   ἄφεσιν ἁμαρτιῶν. (Mk 1:4)
8. εἰ οὐκ ἔστιν ἀνάστασις ἐκ τῶν νεκρῶν, κενὸν καὶ τὸ
   κήρυγμα ἡμῶν, κενὴ καὶ ἡ πίστις ὑμῶν. (1 Cor
   15:13-14)
9. πόθεν τούτῳ ἡ σοφία αὕτη καὶ αἱ δυνάμεις; (Mt
   13:54)
10. ἴδε νῦν ἠκούσατε τὴν βλασφημίαν. (Mt 26:65)
11. ἔβλεψα τοὺς πρεσβυτέρους καὶ ἐπὶ τὰς κεφαλὰς αὐτῶν
    στεφάνους χρυσοῦς. (Apoc 4:4)
12. καὶ ἐλύθη ὁ δεσμὸς τῆς γλώσσης αὐτοῦ. (Mk 7:35)
13. διδάσκαλε, ἴδε ποταποὶ λίθοι καὶ ποταπαὶ οἰκοδομαί.
    (Mk 13:1)
14. καὶ πλήρεις ἦσαν πάντες θυμοῦ ἐν τῇ συναγωγῇ
    ἀκούοντες ταῦτα. . . (Lk 4:28)
15. οὐδέν ἐστιν κρυπτὸν ὃ οὐ φανερὸν ἔσται. (Mt 10:26)

II. Translate into Greek:
   1. I say that the bond of his tongue was loosed. (Mk 7:35)
   2. The slaves, having been freed by the crowd, were full of joy.
      (Jn 1:14)
   3. You are about to hear of wars and rumors of wars. (Mk
      13:7)

III. Read Mk 1:9-20, at first without consulting any aids, relying
      entirely on memory. Then re-read the text, checking any
      doubtful points against the material seen in the previous
      lessons. Finally, read the verses aloud at least three times.
      The reading aloud should be unhurried, with precision being
      valued much more than speed.

λύω, **Future Passive Indicative,**
Participle, and Infinitive.

Lesson 40

λύω, **Future Passive Indicative, Participle, and Infinitive.**

The future passive stem of λύω is based on the aorist passive. The
future indicative passive is conjugated as follows (cf. V 1, VP 3):

Passive Voice, Indicative Mood, Future Tense

	Singular	Plural
1st Person	λυθήσ–ομαι	λυθησ–όμεθα
2nd Person	λυθήσ–η	λυθήσ–εσθε
3rd Person	λυθήσ–εται	λυθήσ–ονται

The form λυθήσῃ comes from λυθήσεσαι (λυθήσεσαι >
λυθήσεαι > λυθήσει > λυθήσῃ).

For the meaning of the future tense in the indicative mood cf.
above, Lesson 11, and Lesson 8. For the meaning of the passive voice
cf. Lessons 26 and 36.

ὁ δοῦλος λυθήσεται ὑπὸ τοῦ δεσπότου αὐτοῦ.
The slave will be let go by his master.

The future passive participle of λύω is declined as follows (cf.
V 1, VP 3, Adj 1):

Passive Voice, Participial Mood, Future Tense

	Masculine	Feminine	Neuter
	Singular		
	Masculine	Feminine	Neuter
n	λυθησ–όμενος	λυθησ–ομένη	λυθησ–όμενον
v	λυθησ–όμενε	λυθησ–ομένη	λυθησ–όμενον
g	λυθησ–ομένου	λυθησ–ομένης	λυθησ–ομένου
d	λυθησ–ομένῳ	λυθησ–ομένη	λυθησ–ομένῳ
a	λυθησ–όμενον	λυθησ–ομένην	λυθησ–όμενον

	Masculine	Plural Feminine	Neuter
n	λυθησ–όμενοι	λυθησ–όμεναι	λυθησ–όμενα
v	λυθησ–όμενοι	λυθησ–όμεναι	λυθησ–όμενα
g	λυθησ–ομένων	λυθησ–ομένων	λυθησ–ομένων
d	λυθησ–ομένοις	λυθησ–ομέναις	λυθησ–ομένοις
a	λυθησ–ομένους	λυθησ–ομένας	λυθησ–όμενα

For the meaning of the future tense in the participial mood cf. above, Lesson 17, and Lesson 8. For the meaning of the passive voice cf. Lessons 26 and 36.

ὁ δοῦλος λυθησόμενος ὑπὸ τοῦ δεσπότου αὐτοῦ ἀγαθός
    ἐστιν.
The slave who is about to be let go by his master is good.

The future passive infinitive of λύω is λυθήσ–εσθαι (cf. V 1, VP 3).

For the meaning of the future tense in the infinitive mood cf. above, Lesson 17, and Lesson 8. For the meaning of the passive voice cf. Lessons 26 and 36.

λέγω τὸν δοῦλον λυθήσεσθαι ὑπὸ τοῦ δεσπότου αὐτοῦ.
I say that the slave will be let go by his master.

Vocabulary for Lesson 40.

δεῖπνον, –ου, τό [N 7] *banquet; principal meal.*

δέσμιος, –ου, ὁ [N 6m] *prisoner.*

δηνάριον, –ου, τό [N 7] *denarius* [Roman coin].

εὐλογία, –ας, ἡ [N 2] *blessing; praise.*

ζῆλος, –ου, ὁ [N 6m] *zeal; jealousy.* Also found as ζῆλος, –ους, τό [N 31].

θησαυρός, –οῦ, ὁ [N 6m] *treasure; storeroom.*

ἵππος, -ου, ὁ [N 6m] *horse.*

νυμφίος, –ου, ὁ [N 6m] *bridegroom*.

πλήρωμα, –ατος, τό [N 16] *fullness; fulfilment*.

πλησίον, ὁ [N 32] *neighbor*. As a substantive it remains invariable in all cases and genders. This word is also found as a preposition governing the genitive case [Prep 1]: *near*.

ποταμός, –οῦ, ὁ [N 6m] *river*.

σκοτία, –ας, ἡ [N 2] *darkness*.

χάρισμα, –ατος, τό [N 16] *gift*.

–––

ἑκατόν [Adj 21] *hundred*.

–––

ἐκεῖθεν [Adv 1] *from there*.

οὗ [Adv 1] *where*. This word is used to introduce subordinate clauses including indirect questions, but not direct questions. The reason for this is that it is the genitive of the relative pronoun and thus refers to something which precedes.

Exercises for Lesson 40.

I. Translate into English:
1. πλήρωμα οὖν νόμου ἡ ἀγάπη. (Rom 13:10)
2. κατὰ δὲ ἑορτὴν ἀπέλυεν αὐτοῖς ἕνα δέσμιον. (Mk 15:6)
3. οἱ δὲ μαθηταὶ ἔρχονται εἰς τὸ ὄρος οὗ εἶπεν αὐτοῖς ὁ Ἰησοῦς. (Mt 28:16)
4. καὶ ἔπεμψεν ἄνθρωπός τις τὸν δοῦλον αὐτοῦ τῇ ὥρᾳ τοῦ δείπνου. (Lk 14:16-17) [τῇ ὥρᾳ is a simple dative to indicate time when—cf. Lesson 79.]
5. ὅπου γάρ ἐστιν ὁ θησαυρός σου, ἐκεῖ ἔσται καὶ ἡ καρδία σου. (Mt 6:21)
6. ἀλλ᾽ οὐχ ὡς τὸ παράπτωμα, οὕτως καὶ τὸ χάρισμα. (Rom 5:15)
7. καὶ τίς ἐστίν μου πλησίον; (Lk 10:29) [ἐστίν μου are two enclitics constituting an enclitic chain—cf. Lesson 18.]
8. καὶ ἔβλεψα, καὶ ἰδοὺ ἵππος λευκός. (Apoc 6:2)
9. ἐκ τοῦ αὐτοῦ στόματος ἔρχεται εὐλογία. (Jas 3:10)

10. καὶ ἐβαπτίζοντο ἐν τῷ Ἰορδάνῳ ποταμῷ ὑπ᾽ αὐτοῦ.
    (Mt 3:6)
11. ὃ λέγω ὑμῖν ἐν τῇ σκοτίᾳ, λέγετε ἐν τῷ φωτί. (Mt 10:27)
12. ἓν δηνάριον ἦν μισθὸς μιᾶς ἡμέρας.
13. ὁ δὲ φίλος τοῦ νυμφίου χαρὰν ἔχει διὰ τὴν φωνὴν τοῦ
    νυμφίου. (Jn 3:29)
14. ὁ ζῆλος τοῦ Χριστοῦ μέγας ἦν.
15. μετὰ δὲ δύο ἡμέρας ἔρχεται ἐκεῖθεν ὁ Ἰησοῦς. (Jn 4:43)
16. τίς ἄνθρωπος ἐξ ὑμῶν ἔχει ἑκατὸν πρόβατα; (Lk 15:4)

II. Translate into Greek:
    1. The gospel will be preached to every creature before the end
       of the world. (Mt 24:14; Mk 16:15)
    2. I say that the gospel will be preached to every creature
       before the end of the world. (Mt 24:14; Mk 16:15)
    3. To the slaves who were about to be loosed the soldier spoke
       words of encouragement. (Acts 13:15)

III. Read Mk 1:21-34, at first without consulting any aids, relying
     entirely on memory. Then re-read the text, checking any
     doubtful points against the material already seen in the
     previous lessons. Finally, read the verses aloud at least three
     times. The reading aloud should not be hurried, with
     precision being valued much more than speed.

γράφω, **Aorist Passive Indicative,
Imperative, Subjunctive, Optative,
Participle, and Infinitive.** γράφω, **Future
Passive Indicative, Participle, and
Infinitive.**

Lesson 41

γράφω, Aorist Passive Indicative, Imperative, Subjunctive, Optative, Participle, and Infinitive.

The aorist passive is divided into two categories, as was stated above in Lesson 37: the "weak" aorist passive, in which θη is the aorist passive marker, and the "strong" aorist passive, in which there is no θ in the aorist passive marker, only η. Most verbs having an aorist passive have the weak aorist, like λύω, whose aorist passive forms have been given above, in Lessons 37-39. Most verbs having an aorist passive have the weak aorist, but the strong aorist is of frequent enough occurrence to make it important. Its endings are the same as those of the weak aorist, but it seems useful to present the strong aorist forms in one place. <u>The meaning of the strong aorist is the same as that of the weak; only the forms are different</u>. The stem used to form the strong aorist of various verbs must be learned by memory.

The word γράφω, *I write* (Lesson 9), has a strong aorist passive (cf. V 4, DV 53, VP 4; in addition, for the participle cf. Adj 18). The aorist passive stem is γραφη–.

	Passive Voice, Indicative Mood, Aorist Tense	
	Singular	Plural
1st Person	ἐ–γράφη–ν	ἐ–γράφη–μεν
2nd Person	ἐ–γράφη–ς	ἐ–γράφη–τε
3rd Person	ἐ–γράφη	ἐ–γράφη–σαν

The augment is formed exactly as for the other past tenses of the indicative mood.

Passive Voice, Imperative Mood, Aorist Tense

	Singular	Plural
2nd Person	γράφη–θι	γράφη–τε
3rd Person	γραφή–τω	γραφή–τωσαν

The second person singular imperative ending is –θι. In the weak aorist the presence of the θ causes the θ of the normal ending to be dissimilated into τ: λύθη–τι. In the strong aorist passive γράφη–θι the non-assimilated ending –θι returns.

In the subjunctive mood the aorist passive marker is contracted with the ending.

Passive Voice, Subjunctive Mood, Aorist Tense

	Singular	Plural
1st Person	γραφ–ῶ	γραφ–ῶμεν
2nd Person	γραφ–ῇς	γραφ–ῆτε
3rd Person	γραφ–ῇ	γραφ–ῶσι(ν)

In the optative mood, the η becomes ε and forms a diphthong with the initial vowel ι of the ending.

Passive Voice, Optative Mood, Aorist Tense

	Singular	Plural
1st Person	γραφείην	γραφείημεν
2nd Person	γραφείης	γραφείητε
3rd Person	γραφείη	γραφείησαν

In the participle the aorist passive marker η becomes ε, (The diphthong ει is the result of the lengthening of ε caused by its position.)

Passive Voice, Participial Mood, Aorist Tense

	Masculine	Feminine (Singular)	Neuter
n	γραφ–είς	γραφ–εῖσα	γραφέ–ν
v	γραφ–είς	γραφ–εῖσα	γραφέ–ν
g	γραφέ–ντος	γραφ–είσης	γραφέ–ντος
d	γραφέ–ντι	γραφ–είση	γραφέ–ντι
a	γραφέν–τα	γραφ–εῖσαν	γραφέ–ν

	Masculine	Plural Feminine	Neuter
n	γραφ–έντες	γραφ–εῖσαι	γραφ–έντα
v	γραφ–έντες	γραφ–εῖσαι	γραφ–έντα
g	γραφ–έντων	γραφ–εισῶν	γραφ–έντων
d	γραφ–εῖσι(ν)	γραφ–είσαις	γραφ–εῖσι(ν)
a	γραφ–έντας	γραφ–είσας	γραφ–έντα

The aorist passive infinitive is γραφῆ–ναι.

γράφω, Future Passive Indicative, Participle, and Infinitive.

The strong future passive forms are based on the stem of the strong aorist passive, just as the weak future passive are based on the stem of the weak aorist passive (cf. V 4, DV 53, VP 4; in addition, for the participle, cf. Adj 1). There is no difference in meaning between the futures based on the respective stems.

Passive Voice, Indicative Mood, Future Tense
1st Person	γραφήσ–ομαι	γραφησ–όμεθα
2nd Person	γραφήσ–η	γραφήσ–εσθε
3rd Person	γραφήσ–εται	γραφήσ–ονται

The form γραφήσῃ comes from γραφήσεσαι (γραφήσεσαι > γραφήσεαι > γραφήσηι > γραφήσῃ).

Passive Voice, Participial Mood, Future Tense
	Masculine	Singular Feminine	Neuter
n	γραφησ–όμενος	γραφησ–ομένη	γραφησ–όμενον
v	γραφησ–όμενε	γραφησ–ομένη	γραφησ–όμενον
g	γραφησ–ομένου	γραφησ–ομένης	γραφησ–ομένου
d	γραφησ–ομένῳ	γραφησ–ομένῃ	γραφησ–ομένῳ
a	γραφησ–όμενον	γραφησ–ομένην	γραφησ–όμενον

	Masculine	Plural Feminine	Neuter
n	γραφησ–όμενοι	γραφησ–όμεναι	γραφησ–όμενα
v	γραφησ–όμενοι	γραφησ–όμεναι	γραφησ–όμενα
g	γραφησ–ομένων	γραφησ–ομένων	γραφησ–ομένων
d	γραφησ–ομένοις	γραφησ–ομέναις	γραφησ–ομένοις
a	γραφησ–ομένους	γραφησ–ομένας	γραφησ–όμενα

The future passive infinitive is γραφήσ–εσθαι.

Vocabulary for Lesson 41.

All the verbs given in this lesson's vocabulary have strong aorist passives. The form of the aorist passive is given here by way of exception. Normally it is to be found only in the list of Difficult Verbs, indicated with each verb.

ἀλλάσσω [V 3, DV 13, VP 1-4] [strong aorist passive: ἠλλάγην] *I change: I transform.*

ἀπαλλάσσω [ἀπό + ἀλλάσσω] [V 3, DV 13, VP 1-4] [strong aorist passive: ἀπηλλάγην] *I set free.*

ἀποκαταλλάσσω [ἀπό + κατά + ἀλλάσσω] [V 3, DV 13, VP 1-4] [strong aorist passive: ἀποκατηλλάγην] *I reconcile.*

καταλλάσσω [κατά + ἀλλάσσω] [V 3, DV 13, VP 1-4] [strong aorist passive: κατηλλάγην] *I reconcile.*
–––

ἐκκόπτω [ἐκ + κόπτω] [V 4, V 5; DV 161, VP 1-4] [strong aorist passive: ἐξεκόπην] *I cut off; I remove.*

κόπτω [V 4 and V 5; DV 161; VP 1-4] [strong aorist passive: ἐκόπην] *I cut*; in middle voice: *I lament.*
–––

θλίβω [V 4, DV 126, VP 1-4] [strong aorist passive: ἐθλίβην] *I press.*

κρύπτω [V 4 and V 5; DV 166; VP 1-4] [strong aorist passive: ἐκρύβην] *I hide.*
–––

κλέπτης, –ου, ὁ [N 4] *thief.*

πάθημα, -ατος, τό [N 16] *suffering; passion.*

πέτρα, –ας, ἡ [N 2] *rock.*

ῥαββί, ὁ [N 32] *master* [Hebrew word].

ῥίζα, –ης, ἡ [N 3] *root*.

συκῆ, –ῆς, ἡ [N 1 and N 33] *fig tree*.
———
διότι [Conj] *because; therefore*.
———
ἐγγύς [Adv 1 and Adv 2] *near* [in both local and temporal senses].
This word is also a preposition which governs the genitive
case [Prep 1]: *near*.

Exercises for Lesson 41.

I. Translate into English:
1. ἡ πέτρα δὲ ἦν ὁ Χριστός. (1 Cor 10:4)
2. ὁ Χριστὸς ἔρχεται ἵνα ἀπαλλάξῃ τούτους ἀπὸ τοῦ
   φόβου τοῦ θανάτου. (Heb 2:14-15)
3. ἐγγὺς ἦν ὁ τόπος τῆς πόλεως. (Jn 19:20)
4. ἔκκοψον τὴν συκῆν ταύτην. (Lk 13:7)
5. εἰ γὰρ ἐχθροὶ ὄντες κατηλλάγημεν τῷ θεῷ διὰ τοῦ
   θανάτου τοῦ υἱοῦ αὐτοῦ, πολλῷ μᾶλλον
   καταλλαγέντες σωθησόμεθα ἐν τῇ ζωῇ αὐτοῦ. (Rom
   5:10) [πολλῷ is a dative of respect: "with respect to
   much"; in the context, "by how much more".]
6. καὶ τότε κόψονται πᾶσαι αἱ φυλαὶ τῆς γῆς. (Mt 24:30)
7. ὄντα ὑπὸ τὴν συκῆν ἔβλεψά σε. (Jn 1:48)
8. Ἰησοῦς δὲ ἐκρύβη. (Jn 8:59)
9. διότι ἐγώ εἰμι μετὰ σοῦ. (Acts 18:10)
10. ῥαββί, καλόν ἐστιν ἡμᾶς ὧδε εἶναι. (Mk 9:5)
11. οὐκ ἄξιά εἰσιν τὰ παθήματα τοῦ νῦν καιροῦ πρὸς
    τὴν μέλλουσαν δόξαν ἀποκαλυφθῆναι εἰς ἡμᾶς. (Rom
    8:18)
12. ἐγγύς ἐστιν ἡ βασιλεία τοῦ θεοῦ. (Lk 21:31)
13. ἐν τοῖς οὐρανοῖς κλέπτης οὐκ ἐγγίζει. (Lk 12:33)
14. καὶ οὐκ ἔχουσιν ῥίζαν ἐν ἑαυτοῖς. (Mk 4:17)

II. Translate into Greek:
1. The book was written by the prophet. (Acts 7:42)
2. The book will be written by the prophet. (Acts 7:42)
3. I say that the book was written by the prophet. (Acts 7:42)

III. Mk 1:35 – 2:12.

λύω, Perfect Passive Indicative, Pluperfect
Passive Indicative, Perfect Passive
Imperative, Infinitive, Subjunctive,
Optative, and Participle. The Key Forms of
λύω. The Principal Parts of λύω. Rules
for Accents 31.

Lesson 42

λύω, Perfect Passive Indicative, Pluperfect Passive Indicative, Perfect Passive Imperative, Infinitive, Subjunctive, Optative, and Participle.

The perfect middle forms and the perfect passive forms of λύω are
the same, as was stated above (cf. Lesson 36). Hence the student has
already seen all the forms needed for the expression of the passive
voice in the perfect tense. But the forms will be repeated here in
their entirety with their passive meanings (as was done with the
present passive tense in Lesson 36) so that the distinction between
the middle and passive voices as regards meaning may be drawn
more sharply. The perfect system is much more important in the
passive voice than in the middle. (For λύω cf. V 1, VP 3; in addition,
for the participle, cf. Adj 1).

Passive Voice, Indicative Mood, Perfect Tense

	Singular	Plural
1st Person	λέλυ–μαι	λελύ–μεθα
2nd Person	λέλυ–σαι	λέλυ–σθε
3rd Person	λέλυ–ται	λέλυ–νται

I have been loosed	*We have been loosed*
You (sg.) *have been loosed*	*You* (pl.) *have been loosed*
He (She, It) has been loosed	*They have been loosed*

For the meaning of the perfect tense in the indicative mood cf.
above, Lesson 23. For the meaning of the passive voice cf. Lessons 26
and 36.

ὁ δοῦλος λέλυται ὑπὸ τοῦ δεσπότου αὐτοῦ.
The slave has been let go by his master.

Passive Voice, Indicative Mood, Pluperfect Tense

	Singular	Plural
1st Person	(ἐ)–λελύ–μην	(ἐ)–λελύ–μεθα
2nd Person	(ἐ)–λέλυ–σο	(ἐ)–λέλυ–σθε
3rd Person	(ἐ)–λέλυ–το	(ἐ)–λέλυ–ντο

I had been loosed	*We had been loosed*
You (sg.) *had been loosed*	*You* (pl.) *had been loosed*
He (She, It) had been loosed	*They had been loosed*

For the meaning of the pluperfect tense cf. above, Lesson 24.
For the meaning of the passive voice cf. Lessons 26 and 36.

ὁ δοῦλος ἐλέλυτο ὑπὸ τοῦ δεσπότου αὐτοῦ.
The slave had been let go by his master.

Passive Voice, Imperative Mood, Perfect Tense

	Singular	Plural
2nd Person	λέλυ–σο	λέλυ–σθε
3rd Person	λελύ–σθω	λελύ–σθωσαν

The use of the perfect imperative passive is understandably
rare, and examples depend much on the context for their precise
force. Hence it seems advisable not to give an example using the
verb λύω, no example of which in the perfect passive imperative is
found in the New Testament. But at Mk 4:39 the verb φιμόω, *I
muzzle* (an o contract verb, a category to be explained in Lesson 51)
is used in the perfect passive imperative to give a strong command
of silence to the wind and sea: πεφίμωσο, *Be still!*, i.e., *be in a state
where you have already been muzzled.*

The perfect passive infinitive of λύω is λελύ–σθαι.

For the meaning of the perfect tense in the infinitive mood cf.
above, Lesson 25. For the meaning of the passive voice cf. Lessons 26
and 36.

Passive Voice, Subjunctive Mood, Perfect Tense

	Singular		Plural	
1st Person	λελυ–μένος, –η, –ον	ὦ	λελυ–μένοι, –αι, –α	ὦμεν
2nd Person	λελυ–μένος, –η, –ον	ᾖς	λελυ–μένοι, –αι, -α	ἦτε
3rd Person	λελυ–μένος, –η, –ον	ᾖ	λελυ–μένοι, –αι, –α	ὦσι(ν)

For the meaning of the perfect tense in the subjunctive mood cf. above, Lesson 25. For the meaning of the passive voice cf. Lessons 26 and 36.

ὁ δοῦλος ἔρχεται ἵνα λελυμένος ᾖ ὑπὸ τοῦ δεσπότου.
The slave comes so that he may be (in a state of having been) *let go by his master.*

Passive Voice, Optative Mood, Perfect Tense

	Singular		Plural	
1st Person	λελυ–μένος, –η, –ον	εἴην	λελυ–μένοι, –αι, -α	εἴημεν
2nd Person	λελυ–μένος, –η, -ον	εἴης	λελυ–μένοι, –αι, –α	εἴητε
3rd Person	λελυ–μένος, –η, –ον	εἴη	λελυ–μένοι, –αι, –α	εἴησαν

For the meaning of the perfect tense in the optative mood cf. above, Lessons 6 and 14; for the meaning of the perfect tense in the non-indicative moods, Lesson 25; for the meaning of the passive voice cf. Lessons 26 and 36.

λελυμένος εἴη ὑπὸ τοῦ δεσπότου αὐτοῦ.
May the slave be [in a state of having been] *let go by his*
        master.

By their very nature the subjunctive and optative moods are rarely used in the perfect passive.

Passive Voice, Participial Mood, Perfect Tense

	Masculine	Singular Feminine	Neuter
n	λελυ–μένος	λελυ–μένη	λελυ–μένον
v	λελυ–μένε	λελυ–μένη	λελυ–μένον
g	λελυ–μένου	λελυ–μένης	λελυ–μένου
d	λελυ–μένῳ	λελυ–μένῃ	λελυ–μένῳ
a	λελυ–μένον	λελυ–μένην	λελυ–μένον

	Masculine	Plural Feminine	Neuter
n	λελυ–μένοι	λελυ–μέναι	λελυ–μένα
v	λελυ–μένοι	λελυ–μέναι	λελυ–μένα
g	λελυ–μένων	λελυ–μένων	λελυ–μένων
d	λελυ–μένοις	λελυ–μέναις	λελυ–μένοις
a	λελυ–μένους	λελυ–μένας	λελυ–μένα

For the meaning of the perfect tense in the participial mood cf. above, Lesson 25. For the meaning of the passive voice cf. Lessons 26 and 36.

λελυμένος ὑπὸ τοῦ δεσπότου αὐτοῦ ὁ δοῦλος μακάριος ἦν.
Having been let go by his master, the slave was happy.

The sound changes which result from the juxtaposition of verb stems ending in a consonant and the perfect endings (which begin with a consonant) are the same in the perfect passive as in the perfect middle. Cf. above, Lessons 34 and 35.

The Key Forms of λύω. The Principal Parts of λύω.

This lesson brings to a close the presentation of the forms of the verb λύω and related thematic verbs. A schematic presentation of the key forms of λύω will now be given. These forms are all in the first person singular of the indicative mood. Inasmuch as these forms contain the stems of the four different tense systems in all three voices, knowledge of these key forms makes possible the formation of all possible forms of the verb λύω.

This schematic presentation shows how the middle and passive voices have common forms in the present and perfect, but different forms in the future and aorist.

	Active Voice	Middle Voice	Passive Voice
Present Tense	λύ–ω	λύ–ομαι	λύ–ομαι
Future Tense	λύσ–ω	λύσ–ομαι	λυθήσ–ομαι
Aorist Tense	ἔ–λυσ–α	ἐ–λυσ–άμην	ἐ–λύθη–ν
Perfect Tense	λέλυκ–α	λέλυ–μαι	λέλυ–μαι

This presentation is useful but ungainly and repetitious. For example, if one knows the form λύω one does not need to have a schematic presentation in which the present middle and present passive are given in order to know how to form them. For this reason a more succinct presentation of the useful forms of a verb is desirable. This presentation is called the presentation of the "principal parts" of a verb. Six forms are necessary. For λύω they are:

1. λύ–ω   2. λύσ–ω   3. ἔ–λυσ–α   4. λέλυκ–α   5. λέλυ–μαι   6. ἐ–λύθη–ν

From these six principal forms or principal "parts" all possible voices, moods, and tenses can be formed, whether of λύω or of any other verb: 1. present indicative active; 2. future indicative active; 3. aorist indicative active; 4. perfect indicative active; 5. perfect indicative middle/passive; 6. aorist indicative passive. The first person singular of each tense has been arbitrarily chosen to represent the tense in question. Note that principal part 5 is labeled "middle/passive" because, out of context, the form can be either middle or passive. But in a given context it is either one or the other. For the verb λύω, of course, and for any other regular verb, the strategem of devising a list of "principal parts" is not really necessary for anyone knowledgeable about the rules governing the various forms: the root of λύω is, for all practical purposes, regular. (The length of the υ varies, but this does not affect the orthography of the various forms). This is true for all other verbs whose roots remain invariable throughout the entire system. But there are a number of verbs which are "irregular", and the scheme of the six principal parts is a useful memory device for learning to construct and/or recognize their forms. Beginning with Lesson 43 the principal parts will be used to present such irregular, difficult verbs.

Rules for Accents 31.

In the perfect middle and passive participle all cases have an acute accent on the second-to-last syllable.

Vocabulary for Lesson 42.

ἐλαία, -ας, ἡ [N 2] olive tree; olive.

εὐσέβεια, –ας, ἡ [N 2] *piety; religion*.

εὐχαριστία, –ας, ἡ [N 2] *thanksgiving; gratitude*.

θεμέλιος, –ου, ὁ [N 6m] *foundation*. This word is also found as
θεμέλιον, –ου, τό [N 7].

κληρονόμος, –ου, ὁ [N 6m] *heir*.

λύπη, –ης, ἡ [N 1] *grief, sorrow; affliction*.

νήπιος, –ου, ὁ [N 6m] *infant*.

οἰκουμένη, –ης, ἡ [N 1] *inhabited world*.

παρθένος, -ου, ἡ [N 6f] *virgin*. Also: παρθένος, –ου, ὁ [N 6m] *chaste
man*.

σκάνδαλον, –ου, τό [N 7] *occasion for sin* or *moral shock*.

τροφή, –ῆς, ἡ [N1] *food, nourishment; living*.

τύπος, –ου, ὁ [N 6m] *pattern; figure; mark*.

———

γνωστός, –ή, –όν [Adj 1] *known*. This word is found as a noun:
friend [N 6m].

γυμνός, –ή, –όν [Adj 1] *naked; lightly clad; poorly dressed*.

———

μήποτε [Conj, Neg] *lest perhaps*. Also interrogative: *whether
perhaps*.

———

μηκέτι [Adv 2, Neg] *no longer*. This word is used normally with
verbs which are not in the indicative mood.

Exercises for Lesson 42.

I. Translate into English:
1. καὶ κηρυχθήσεται τοῦτο τὸ εὐαγγέλιον τῆς βασιλείας
ἐν ὅλῃ τῇ οἰκουμένῃ εἰς μαρτύριον πᾶσιν τοῖς
ἔθνεσιν. (Mt 24:14)

2. σὺ δέ, ὦ ἄνθρωπε θεοῦ, δίωκε δὲ δικαιοσύνην,
   εὐσέβειαν, πίστιν, ἀγάπην, ὑπομόνην. (1 Tim 6:11)
3. βλέπετε, ἀδελφοί, μήποτε ἔσται ἔν τινι ὑμῶν καρδία
   πονηρὰ ἀπιστίας. (Heb 3:12)
4. γύναι, ἀπολέλυσαι τῆς ἀσθενείας σου. (Lk 13:12)
5. εἰ γὰρ οἱ ἐκ νόμου κληρονόμοι, κενὴ ἡ πίστις ἡμῶν.
   (Rom 4:14)
6. ὁ δὲ μαθητὴς ἐκεῖνος ἦν γνωστὸς τῷ ἀρχιερεῖ. (Jn
   18:15).
7. οὐχὶ ἡ ψυχὴ πλεῖόν ἐστιν τῆς τροφῆς; (Mt 6:25)
   [πλεῖόν means "something more" in this context.]
8. ὁ θεμέλιος τοῦ οἴκου ἰσχυρὸς ἦν.
9. ἰδοὺ ἡ παρθένος ἐν γαστρὶ ἕξει. (Mt 1:23)
10. λέγεις ὅτι Πλούσιός εἰμι καὶ οὐδὲν χρείαν ἔχω, καὶ σὺ
    εἶ πτωχὸς καὶ τυφλὸς καὶ γυμνός. (Apoc 3:17) [οὐδὲν
    is an accusative of respect; literally, *I have need with
    regard to nothing.*]
11. μηκέτι εἰς τὸν αἰῶνα ἐκ σοῦ μηδεὶς καρπὸν ἐσθίοι.
    (Mk 11:14) [Note that in Greek a double negative does
    not result in a positive assertion, as in English. In
    Greek a double negative emphasizes the negative and
    does not remove it. In the English translation,
    therefore, some other way of emphasizing the negation
    must be found other than a repetition of the negative.]
12. αὐταί εἰσιν αἱ δύο ἐλαῖαι αἳ ἐνώπιον τοῦ κυρίου τῆς
    γῆς εἰσιν. (Apoc 11:4)
13. καὶ ὃ ἐὰν λύσῃς ἐπὶ τῆς γῆς ἔσται λελυμένον ἐν τοῖς
    οὐρανοῖς. (Mt 16:19) [ἔσται λελυμένον is the
    periphrastic construction and means *will be in the
    state of having been loosed*—cf. Lesson 52.]
14. ὁ κληρονόμος ποτὲ νήπιος ἦν. (Gal 4:1)
15. ὁ δὲ Ἰησοῦς εἶπεν, Ὕπαγε ὀπίσω μου· σκάνδαλον
    εἶ ἐμοῦ. (Mt 16:23)
16. καὶ ὑμεῖς οὖν νῦν λύπην ἔχετε. (Jn 16:22)

II. Translate into Greek:
   1. We have prophets who have been tested according to all
      things. (Heb 4:15)
   2. You (pl.) have been tested in all these things.
   3. Now our souls have been disturbed. (Jn 12:27)

III. Mk 2:13 – 3:6.

Strong Aorist Forms in the Active and
Middle Voices. βάλλω, Aorist Active
Indicative, Imperative, Subjunctive,
Optative, Participle, and Infinitive.
Difficult Verbs: βάλλω. Rules for Accents
32.

Lesson 43

Strong Aorist Forms in the Active and Middle Voices.

As was explained in Lesson 37, in the aorist passive there are two
types of forms, "weak" and "strong". A similar distinction is true in
the aorist active and in the aorist middle. In both voices there are
two sets of forms, one called "weak aorist" or "first aorist", and
another called "strong aorist" or "second aorist". The weak or first
aorist has already been seen, with λύω as the paradigm. In this and
the following lesson, the active and middle forms of the strong or
second aorist will be presented. The paradigm used will be βάλλω.

As for the aorist passive, there is no difference in meaning
between the two types of aorist in the active and middle voices.

A few verbs have both first and second aorist forms, but most
verbs have one or the other. First or weak aorist forms are by far the
more numerous, but second or strong aorist forms have
considerable importance.

There is no relation between the strong aorist forms in the
active and middle voices and the strong aorist forms in the passive
voice. A verb can have strong aorist forms in the active and middle
voices without having strong aorist forms in the aorist passive, and
vice versa. But a verb which has a strong aorist active has a strong
aorist middle: the root is the same for both voices.

In this grammar the strong aorist forms of the active and
middle voices will be called "second aorists" to help distinguish
them from the "strong aorists" of the passive. The latter are seldom
called "second aorists".

βάλλω, Aorist Active Indicative, Imperative, Subjunctive, Optative, Participle, and Infinitive.

βάλλω, *I throw*, has the following forms in the second (strong) aorist active (cf. V 6, DV 22, VP 4):

Active Voice, Indicative Mood, Aorist Tense

	Singular	Plural
1st Person	ἔ–βαλ–ον	ἐ–βάλ–ομεν
2nd Person	ἔ–βαλ–ες	ἐ–βάλ–ετε
3rd Person	ἔ–βαλ–ε(ν)	ἔ–βαλ–ον

I threw	*We threw*
You (sg.) *threw*	*You* (pl.) *threw*
He (*She, It*) *threw*	*They threw*

The aorist stem is βαλ–. There is only one λ, in contrast to the present stem, which is βαλλ–. Hence βάλλω qualifies as a "difficult" verb. Its principal parts will accordingly be given in this lesson, the first in a series. These parts are best learned by memory.

The ε is the augment. The rules for its formation are the same as for the imperfect.

The endings are the same as those of the imperfect active indicative. The fact that ἔβαλον is the strong aorist and not the imperfect depends on recognition of the stem, as stated above.

The meaning of the strong aorist indicative active is the same as for the weak aorist active. (Cf. above, Lesson 18, and Lesson 9 for the meaning of the active voice.)

ἔβαλον τὸν ἄνδρα εἰς φυλακήν.
They threw the man into prison.

It is important to note that at times the endings of the first aorist are used with a second aorist stem with no difference in meaning. Thus the sentence given above, *They threw the man into prison*, can also be translated: ἔβαλαν τὸν ἄνδρα εἰς φυλακήν. This use of first aorist endings with second aorist stems is most common in the indicative mood, but it is occasionally found in other moods. The endings of the second aorist are not found with the first aorist.

In the other moods of the second aorist the present endings are used. Thus the aorist imperative active of βάλλω is conjugated as follows (cf. V 6, DV 32, VP 4):

Active Voice, Imperative Mood, Aorist Tense

	Singular	Plural
2nd Person	βάλ–ε	βάλ–ετε
3rd Person	βαλ–έτω	βαλ–έτωσαν

The meaning of the aorist tense in the imperative mood has been presented in Lesson 19. For the meaning of the active voice cf. Lesson 9.

βαλέτωσαν τὸν ἄνδρα εἰς φυλακήν.
Let them throw the man into prison.

The aorist subjunctive active of βάλλω is conjugated as follows (cf. V 6, DV 32, VP 4):

Active Voice, Subjunctive Mood, Aorist Tense

	Singular	Plural
1st Person	βάλ–ω	βάλ–ωμεν
2nd Person	βάλ–ῃς	βάλ–ητε
3rd Person	βάλ–ῃ	βάλ–ωσι(ν)

The meaning of the aorist tense in the subjunctive mood has been presented above, in Lesson 20. For the meaning of the active voice cf. Lesson 9.

ἔρχεται μὴ βάλωσιν αὐτὸν εἰς φυλακήν.
He comes so that they may not throw him into prison.

The aorist optative active of βάλλω is conjugated as follows (cf. V 6, DV 32, VP 4):

Active Voice, Optative Mood, Aorist Tense

	Singular	Plural
1st Person	βάλ–οιμι	βάλ–οιμεν
2nd Person	βάλ–οις	βάλ–οιτε
3rd Person	βάλ–οι	βάλ–οιεν

μὴ βάλοιεν αὐτὸν εἰς φυλακήν.
May they not throw him in prison.

The aorist participle active of βάλλω is declined as follows (cf. V 6, DV 32, VP 4, and Adj 7):

Active Voice, Participial Mood, Aorist Tense
Singular

	Masculine	Feminine	Neuter
n	βαλ–ών	βαλ–οῦσα	βαλ–όν
v	βαλ–ών	βαλ–οῦσα	βαλ–όν
g	βαλ–όντος	βαλ–ούσης	βαλ–όντος
d	βαλ–όντι	βαλ–ούσῃ	βαλ–όντι
a	βαλ–όντα	βαλ–οῦσαν	βαλ–όν

Plural

	Masculine	Feminine	Neuter
n	βαλ–όντες	βαλ–οῦσαι	βαλ–όντα
v	βαλ–όντες	βαλ–οῦσαι	βαλ–όντα
g	βαλ–όντων	βαλ–ουσῶν	βαλ–όντων
d	βαλ–οῦσι(ν)	βαλ–ούσαις	βαλ–οῦσι(ν)
a	βαλ–όντας	βαλ–ούσας	βαλ–όντα

The meaning of the aorist tense in the participial mood has been presented above, in Lesson 22. For the meaning of the active voice cf. Lesson 9.

βαλόντες αὐτὸν εἰς φυλακήν, ἔρχονται εἰς τοὺς οἴκους
    αὐτῶν.
Having thrown him in prison, they go into their houses.

The aorist infinitive active of βάλλω is βαλ–εῖν. Cf. V 6, DV 32, VP 4).
The meaning of the aorist tense in the infinitive mood has been presented above, in Lesson 22. For the meaning of the active voice cf. Lesson 22.

λέγω αὐτὸν βαλεῖν αὐτοὺς εἰς φυλακήν.
I say that he threw them into prison.

The middle forms of the second aorist will be given in Lesson
44.

Difficult Verbs: βάλλω.

βάλλω, *I throw, I hurl* [V 6, DV 32, VP 1-4]

λύω	λύσω	ἔλυσα	λέλυκα	λέλυμαι	ἐλύθην
βάλλω	βαλῶ	ἔβαλον	βέβληκα	βέβλημαι	ἐβλήθην
Mt 3:10	Mt 13:50	Mt 4:6	Jn 13:2	Mt 8:6	Mt 5:13

In this introductory treatment of the "difficult verbs" the
principal parts of λύω are given to help the student make the
transition from the regular to the irregular verbs. They will be
given in the next two lessons as well.

The references to New Testament texts are to occurrences of
some form of the "part" of the verb in question, either of the simple
verb as given here or of a compound verb based on the simple verb.
The reference can be to any mood.

The future of βάλλω follows the regular rules for liquids,
which will be explained in Lesson 48. The double λ is proper to the
present system; the strong aorist active and middle stems have only
one λ, as do the other stems. The α of the root is changed to η and
inverted with the λ in the final three stems.

The selection of "difficult verbs" in this grammar will be to
some extent arbitrary. By intention more verbs are included than in
most lists of "irregular verbs". The norm for selection will be
facility for learning on the part of the student.

Rules for Accents 32.

The accent of the strong aorist active participle is on the last syllable
of the masculine singular. The accent remains on this syllable
throughout the declension of the masculine and neuter, and on the
second-last syllable in the feminine as well (except for the genitive
plural), even when the last syllable is short. Cf. above, Rules for
Accent 12, Lesson 20.

The strong aorist active infinitive has a circumflex on the final syllable.

Vocabulary for Lesson 43.

βάλλω [V 6, DV 32, VP 1-4] *I throw, I hurl; I place.*

ἐκβάλλω [ἐκ + βάλλω] [V 6, DV 32, VP 1-4] *I drive out; I send away.*

ἐπιβάλλω [ἐπί + βάλλω] [V 6, DV 32, VP 1-4] *I lay (hands on).*

περιβάλλω [περί + βάλλω] [V 6, DV 32, VP 1-4] *I put on; I clothe.*

————

ἄκανθα, -ης, ἡ [N 3] *thorn plant*; in plural: *thorns.*

ἀνομία, -ας, ἡ [N 2] *lawlessness; sin.*

γράμμα, -ατος, τό [N 16] *letter* [of the alphabet]; *letter* [i.e., "epistle"— normally in the plural].

διαλογισμός, -οῦ, ὁ [N 6m] *thought; dispute.*

ὑπακοή, -ῆς, ἡ [N 1] *obedience; submission.*

χόρτος, -ου, ὁ [N 6m] *grass, hay.*

————

ἀλλότριος, -α, -ον [Adj 2] *belonging to another; another; strange.*

————

ὡσεί [Conj] *like, as* [used in comparisons]. This word is also found as an adverb [Adv 3: *approximately*].

————

νυνί [Adv 2] *now.* This is an emphatic form of νῦν.

Exercises for Lesson 43.

I. Translate into English:
1. οἱ δὲ ἐπέβαλον τὰς χεῖρας αὐτῷ. (Mk 14:46)
2. ἦν δὲ χόρτος πολὺς ἐν τῷ τόπῳ. (Jn 6:10)
3. καὶ ἦν ἤδη ὡσεὶ ὥρα ἕκτη. (Lk 23:44)
4. αἱ ἄκανθαι ὀξεῖαί εἰσιν.
5. εἰ δὲ τοῖς ἐκείνου γράμμασιν οὐ πιστεύσετε, πῶς τοῖς ἐμοῖς ῥήμασιν πιστευσετε; (Jn 5:47)

6. γυμνὸς ἤμην καὶ περιεβάλετέ με. (Mt 25:36)
7. ὁ ἀρχιερεὺς ἔρχεται εἰς τὰ ἅγια ἐν αἵματι ἀλλοτρίῳ. (Heb 9:25)
8. ἐκ γὰρ τῆς καρδίας ἔρχονται διαλογισμοὶ πονηροί. (Mt 15:19)
9. νυνὶ δὲ μένει πίστις, ἐλπίς, ἀγάπη, τὰ τρία ταῦτα· μείζων δὲ τούτων ἡ ἀγάπη. (1 Cor 13:13)
10. καὶ ἡ ἁμαρτία ἐστὶν ἡ ἀνομία. (1 Jn 3:4)
11. καὶ πολλάκις καὶ εἰς πῦρ αὐτὸν ἔβαλεν. (Mk 9:22)
12. καὶ δαιμόνια πολλὰ ἐξέβαλεν. (Mk 1:34)
13. καὶ δαιμόνια πολλὰ ἐξέβαλλον. (Mk 6:13)
14. δι᾽ οὗ ἔχομεν χάριν εἰς ὑπακοὴν πίστεως ἐν πᾶσιν τοῖς ἔθνεσιν ὑπὲρ τοῦ ὀνόματος αὐτοῦ. (Rom 1:5)
15. ἔγραψα ἐπιστολὴν ἔχουσαν τὸν τύπον τοῦτον. (Acts 23:25)
16. καὶ εἶπεν ὁ Ἰησοῦς τοῖς μαθηταῖς αὐτοῦ περὶ πλοίου ἵνα ὁ ὄχλος μὴ θλίβῃ αὐτόν. (Mk 3:9)
17. ἡμεῖς πάντες ἀλλαγησόμεθα. (1 Cor 15:51).
18. καὶ ὑμᾶς ποτε ὄντας ἐχθρούς, νῦν δὲ ἀποκατήλλαξεν ἐν τῷ σώματι τῆς σαρκὸς αὐτοῦ διὰ τοῦ θανάτου. (Col 1:21-22)
19. ἀμήν· ἡ εὐλογία καὶ ἡ δόξα καὶ ἡ σοφία καὶ ἡ εὐχαριστία καὶ ἡ τιμὴ καὶ ἡ δύναμις τῷ θεῷ ἡμῶν εἰς τοὺς αἰῶνας τῶν αἰώνων· ἀμήν. (Apoc 7:12) [εἰς τοὺς αἰῶνας τῶν αἰώνων means, literally, *until the ages of the ages*, i.e., *for ever and ever*. According to context, αἰών can mean *age* or *eternity*.]

II. Translate into Greek:
   1. And many times he threw them into fire and into water. (Mk 9:22)
   2. For they have not yet been cast into prison. (Jn 3:24)
   3. Keep saying to the mountains: "Be thrown into the sea". (Mt 21:21)

III. Mk 3:7-30.

βάλλω, Aorist Middle Indicative,
Imperative, Subjunctive, Optative,
Participle, and Infinitive. Difficult Verbs:
ἄγω. Rules for Accents 33.

Lesson 44

βάλλω, Aorist Middle Indicative, Imperative, Subjunctive, Optative, Participle, and Infinitive.

The aorist middle indicative of βάλλω is conjugated as follows (cf. V 6, DV 32, VP 4):

Middle Voice, Indicative Mood, Aorist Tense

	Singular	Plural
1st Person	ἐ–βαλ–όμην	ἐ–βαλ–όμεθα
2nd Person	ἐ–βάλ–ου	ἐ–βάλ–εσθε
3rd Person	ἐ–βάλ–ετο	ἐ–βάλ–οντο

I threw [with relation to myself]

You (sg.) *threw* [with relation to yourself]

He (*She, It*) *threw* [with relation to himself, herself, itself]

We threw [with relation to ourselves]

You (pl.) *threw* [with relation to yourselves]

They threw [with relation to themselves]

The form ἐβάλου is a contraction from ἐβάλεσο.
For the meaning of the aorist middle indicative cf. Lesson 31.

τί περιεβάλετο;
What did he/she put on?

The aorist middle imperative of βάλλω is conjugated as follows (cf. V 6, DV 32, VP 4):

Middle Voice, Indicative Mood, Aorist Tense

	Singular	Plural
2nd Person	βαλ–οῦ	βάλ–εσθε
3rd Person	βαλ–έσθω	βαλ–έσθωσαν

Throw! [with relation to yourself]	*Throw!* [with relation to yourselves]
Let him [her, it] throw! [with relation to himself, herself, itself]	*Let them throw!* [with relation to themselves]

The form βαλοῦ is a contraction from βαλέσο.
For the meaning of the aorist middle imperative cf, above, Lesson 31.

περιβαλοῦ τὸ ἱμάτιον ἐκεῖνο.
Put on that garment.

The aorist middle subjunctive of βάλλω is conjugated as follows (cf. V 6, DV 32, VP 4):

Middle Voice, Subjunctive Mood, Aorist Tense

	Singular	Plural
1st Person	βάλ–ωμαι	βαλ–ώμεθα
2nd Person	βάλ–ῃ	βάλ–ησθε
3rd Person	βάλ–ηται	βάλ–ωνται

The form βάλῃ is a contraction from βάλησαι (βάλησαι > βάληαι > βάληι > βάλῃ).
For the meaning of the aorist middle subjunctive cf. above, Lesson 32.

ἔρχεται ἵνα περιβάληται ἐκεῖνο τὸ ἱμάτιον.
He comes in order to put on that garment.

The middle optative of βάλλω is conjugated as follows (cf. V 6, DV 32, VP 4):

Middle Voice, Optative Mood, Aorist Tense

	Singular	Plural
1st Person	βαλ–οίμην	βαλ–οίμεθα
2nd Person	βάλ–οιο	βάλ–οισθε
3rd Person	βάλ–οιτο	βάλ–οιντο

The form βάλοιο comes from βάλοισο.
For the meaning of the aorist middle optative cf. above, Lesson 32.

περιβάλοιτο ἐκεῖνο τὸ ἱμάτιον.
May he put on that garment.

The aorist middle participle of βάλλω is declined as follows (cf. V 6, DV 32, VP 4, Adj 1):

Middle Voice, Participial Mood, Aorist Tense

Singular

	Masculine	Feminine	Neuter
n	βαλ–όμενος	βαλ–ομένη	βαλ–όμενον
v	βαλ–όμενε	βαλ–ομένη	βαλ–όμενον
g	βαλ–ομένου	βαλ–ομένης	βαλ–ομένου
d	βαλ–ομένῳ	βαλ–ομένη	βαλ–ομένῳ
a	βαλ–όμενον	βαλ–ομένην	βαλ–όμενον

Plural

	Masculine	Feminine	Neuter
n	βαλ–όμενοι	βαλ–όμεναι	βαλ–όμενα
v	βαλ–όμενοι	βαλ–όμεναι	βαλ–όμενα
g	βαλ–ομένων	βαλ–ομένων	βαλ–ομένων
d	βαλ–ομένοις	βαλ–ομέναις	βαλ–ομένοις
a	βαλ–ομένους	βαλ–ομένας	βαλ–όμενα

For the meaning of the aorist middle participle cf. above, Lesson 33.

περιβαλομένη ἐκεῖνο τὸ ἱμάτιον, ἔρχεται εἰς τὸν οἶκον.
Having put on that garment, she comes into the house.

The aorist middle infinitive of βάλλω is βαλ–έσθαι (cf. V 6, DV 32, VP 4).

For the meaning of the aorist middle infinitive cf. above, Lesson 33.

λέγω αὐτὴν περιβαλέσθαι ἐκεῖνο τὸ ἱμάτιον.
I say that she has put on that garment.

Difficult Verbs: ἄγω.

ἄγω, *I lead, go* [V 2, DV 5, VP 1-4]

λύω	λύσω	ἔλυσα	λέλυκα	λέλυμαι	ἐλύθην
ἄγω	ἄξω	ἤγαγον	—	ἦγμαι	ἤχθην
Mt 26:46	Acts 22:5	Mt 21:7		Mt 18:20	Lk 18:40

Once again the principal parts of λύω are presented to help in orientation. The perfect active of ἄγω is not found in the New Testament; hence the slot where this ordinarily is found (cf. λέλυκα) is indicated by a dash. The weak aorist ἦξα is found only in compound verbs in the New Testament.

Rules for Accents 33.

The accent on the second person singular of the aorist middle imperative is irregular: βαλοῦ.
The accent on the aorist middle infinitive is also irregular: βαλέσθαι.

Vocabulary for Lesson 44.

ἄγω [V 2, DV 5, VP 1-4] *I lead, go.*

ἀνάγω [ἀνά + ἄγω] [V 2, DV 5, VP 1-4] *I lead up*; passive: *I am led up*; *I set sail.*

ἀπάγω [ἀπό + ἄγω] [V 2, DV 5, VP 1-4] *I lead*; *I lead away by force.*

εἰσάγω [εἰς + ἄγω] [V 2, DV 5, VP 1-4] *I lead in.*

ἐξάγω [ἐκ + ἄγω] [V 2, DV 5, VP 1-4] *I lead out.*

προάγω [πρό + ἄγω] [V 2, DV 5, VP 1-4] transitive: *I precede*; intransitive: *I precede*.

συνάγω [σύν + ἄγω] [V 2, DV 5, VP 1-4] *I gather*, with transitive sense; the passive often means *I gather* in the intransitive sense (e.g., *a crowd gathers*).

———

ἐνιαυτός, –οῦ, ὁ [N 6m] *year*.

κληρονομία, –ας, ἡ [N 2] *inheritance*.

λύχνος, –ου, ὁ [N 6m] *lamp*.

μακροθυμία, –ας, ἡ [N 2] *patience; perseverance*.

μέτρον, –ου, τό [N 7] *measure*.

———

ἕκτος, –η, –ον [Adj 1] *sixth*.

κοινός, –ή, –όν [Adj 1] *common; unclean*.

κωφός, –ή, –όν [Adj 1] *mute; deaf*.

———

ἀληθῶς [Adv 3] *truly*.

πότε [Adv 2] *when?*.

Exercises for Lesson 44.

I. Translate into English:
1. οἱ δὲ ὄχλοι οἱ προάγοντες αὐτὸν ἔκραζον. (Mt 21:9)
2. καὶ ἦν ἤδη ὡσεὶ ὥρα ἕκτη. (Lk 23:44)
3. τότε ὁ Ἰησοῦς ἀνήχθη εἰς τὴν ἔρημον ὑπὸ τοῦ πνεύματος, πειρασθῆναι ὑπὸ τοῦ διαβόλου. (Mt 4:1) [πειρασθῆναι is an infinitive expressing purpose—cf. Lesson 76.]
4. καὶ ἦν ἐκβάλλων δαιμόνιον, καὶ αὐτὸ ἦν κωφόν. (Lk 11:14)
5. ἕως πότε μεθ᾽ ὑμῶν ἔσομαι; (Mt 17:17)
6. ὁ δὲ καρπὸς τοῦ πνεύματός ἐστιν ἀγάπη, χαρά, εἰρήνη, μακροθυμία. . . . (Gal 5:22)

7. οἱ γονεῖς τὸν Ἰησοῦν εἰς τὴν ἁγίαν πόλιν ἀνήγαγον.
   (Lk 2:22)
8. εἰ γὰρ ἐκ νόμου ἡ κληρονομία, οὐκέτι ἐξ ἐπαγγελίας.
   (Gal 3:18)
9. ἀληθῶς θεοῦ υἱὸς ἦν οὗτος. (Mt 27:54)
10. καὶ ἀπήγαγον τὸν Ἰησοῦν πρὸς τὸν ἀρχιερέα. (Mk
    14:53)
11. ἕκαστος ἔχει μέτρον πίστεως ἀπὸ τοῦ θεοῦ. (Rom 12:3)
12. διὰ τί οἱ μαθηταί σου ἐσθίουσιν τὸν ἄρτον κοιναῖς
    χερσίν; (Mk 7:5) [The dative is a dative of means or
    manner.]
13. οὗτος ἦν ἀρχιερεὺς τοῦ ἐνιαυτοῦ ἐκείνου. (Jn 18:13)
14. καὶ οἱ ὑπηρέται εἰσήγαγον τὸν Ἰησοῦν εἰς τὴν
    οἰκίαν τοῦ ἀρχιερέως. (Lk 22:54)
15. καὶ ἰδοὺ δύο τυφλοί, ἀκούσαντες ὅτι Ἰησοῦς παράγει,
    ἔκραξαν. (Mt 20:30)
16. ὁ κύριος ἐξήγαγεν αὐτὸν ἐκ τῆς φυλακῆς. (Acts
    12:17)
17. ὁ λύχνος τοῦ σώματός ἐστιν ὁ ὀφθαλμός. (Mt 6:22)
18. καὶ συνήχθησαν πρὸς αὐτὸν ὄχλοι πολλοί. (Mt 13:2).

II. Translate into Greek:
   1. I shall precede you [sg.] into this city.
   2. We have been led by the Spirit. (Mt 4:1)
   3. I say that Jesus was led out of the house by evil men.

III. Mk 3:31 – 4:20.

Deponent Verbs. Middle Deponents.
Passive Deponents. Usages among
Compound Verbs. Difficult Verbs:
ἔρχομαι. Rules for Accents 34.

Lesson 45

Deponent Verbs. Middle Deponents. Passive Deponents.

In Greek there is a large body of verbs called "deponents". They are verbs which "set aside" (*deponere* in Latin) their active forms, but keep the active meaning for their remaining middle or passive forms. The middle deponents have no active forms but use middle forms to express active meanings. The passive deponents have no active or middle forms, but use passive forms to express active meanings.

For example, the word ἐργάζομαι is a middle deponent, i.e., it is middle in form, but has an active meaning, *I work*. There is no form ἐργάζω in the New Testament. This form is "set aside" so that the middle form takes over its meaning. This is true for all persons and numbers and all moods and tenses of the middle forms of ἐργάζομαι.

The word ἐφοβήθην is an aorist passive indicative in form, but it has an active meaning, *I feared*. In the New Testament there is no form ἐφόβησα. It is "set aside" so that the passive form has its active meaning. This is true for all persons and numbers and all moods and tenses of the passive forms of φοβέομαι. There is no form ἐφοβησάμην either. φοβέομαι simply has no middle forms or middle meaning. It has only passive forms with active meaning.

There is no rule for knowing when a verb is deponent or, if so, whether it is a middle deponent or a passive deponent. The only way these distinctions can be learned is by memory.

The forms of middle and passive deponents are exactly the same as the forms of normal verbs in the middle or passive voices. Hence there is no need here to give the forms of deponent verbs.

Middle deponents set aside their active forms, and use their middle forms to express active meanings. They have no middle meanings. But their passive forms can have truly passive

meanings. Thus, the word ἐθεασάμην is a middle deponent
meaning *I looked at*. But the word ἐθεάθην means *I was looked at*.
     Because the middle and passive forms are the same in the
present and perfect systems of the normal Greek verb, it is
impossible to tell if a verb is a middle or a passive deponent from
these systems alone, if one is judging by forms outside of context.
Only in the future or aorist systems is such a distinction outside of
context possible. In the vocabulary listings in this and subsequent
lessons, the first person singular of the present indicative will be
given as usual, but inasmuch as this abstract listing is ambiguous
as regards whether a verb is middle or passive deponent, the
category to which a deponent verb belongs—middle or passive—will
be indicated. If the vocabulary listing of a verb does not give an
active form for the first person singular of the present indicative, the
verb is deponent. The category, middle or passive deponent, will
then be given by the indication "V 22" (middle deponent) or "V 23"
(passive deponent).
     A schematic arrangement featuring a comparison with λύω
may help illustrate the differences between the "normal" verb
(exemplified by λύω) and middle and passive deponents (exemplified
by θεάομαι and φοβέομαι respectively). (The future will be used
because the middle and passive forms are distinguishable in this
tense system.)

Normal Verb	**Middle Deponent**	**Passive Deponent**
active form		
λύσω		
active meaning		
middle form	**middle form**	
λύσομαι	θεάσομαι	
middle meaning	**active meaning**	
passive form	passive form	**passive form**
λυθήσομαι	θεαθήσομαι	φοβηθήσομαι
passive meaning	passive meaning	**active mean-**
		ing

     Not all middle deponents have passive voices as does θεάομαι.
But at least the passive forms are theoretically "available". For a

passive deponent such as φοβέομαι the passive forms are not even theoretically "available", at least in New Testament Greek.

It is important to note that the word "deponent" is used with different meanings and can vary from author to author. Hence it is advisable to ascertain just what an author means by the word "deponent" before drawing any conclusions in relation to what an author says and to what is said in this grammar.

Usages among Compound Verbs.

A compound verb, as has already been mentioned when the formation of the augment was explained, is one in which a prefix, usually a preposition, is combined with a verb stem to form a verb with a special meaning involving both parts (e.g., εἰσάγω). There is no standard usage regarding the way a compound verb is related to other words in the sentence. Some compound verbs are transitive (e.g., ὁ Ἰησοῦς προῆγεν αὐτούς, *Jesus was preceding them*); others, even the same verb in a different context, are intransitive (e.g., ὁ Ἰησοῦς προῆγεν, *Jesus was preceding*). Some repeat the prefix as a preposition with a specific case (e.g., ὁ Ἰησοῦς εἰσῆλθεν εἰς τὴν πόλιν, *Jesus entered into the city*). Others have a case other than the accusative but without a preposition (e.g., ὁ Ἰησοῦς προσῆλθεν αὐτοῖς, *Jesus approached them*). These varying usages must be learned from the way each verb is treated in the New Testament. But the beginning student is advised not to make too much of the differences as regards ordinary use of the text lest the memory be unduly burdened.

Difficult Verbs: ἔρχομαι.

ἔρχομαι, *I come; I go* [V 2, V 22, DV 99, VP 1-2 and 4]

λύω	λύσω	ἔλυσα	λέλυκα	λέλυμαι	ἐλύθην
ἔρχομαι	ἐλεύσομαι	ἦλθον	ἐλήλυθα	—	—
Mt 13:19	Mt 24:5	Mt 2:2	Lk 5:32		

This verb is a middle deponent in the present and future systems (note the form of the future). In the aorist it is strong but not deponent. The root of the aorist is ἐλθ-. It is important to note that the θ in the root here has nothing to do with the θ of the weak aorist passive forms of the regular verb. The perfect active is strong.

There are no passive forms. The verb is intransitive, i.e., does not take an object.

The accent on the aorist imperative is irregular: ἐλθέ.

The forms ἔρχεται and ἔρχονται given in Lesson 2 and used until now without explanation are the third person present indicative singular and plural of ἔρχομαι.

Rules for Accents 34.

The accent on the aorist imperative active second person singular of ἔρχομαι is irregular: ἐλθέ. Three other common aorist imperative active second person singular forms are similarly irregular: εὑρέ (from εὑρίσκω, *I find*); εἰπέ (from λέγω, *I say*); λαβέ (from λαμβάνω, *I take*). The irregularity disappears when the verbs are used with a prefix, i.e., in a compound verb. Thus: ἔξελθε.

Vocabulary for Lesson 45.

ἀπέρχομαι [ἀπό + ἔρχομαι] [V 2, V 22, DV 99, VP 1-2 and 4] *I go away*.

διέρχομαι [διά + ἔρχομαι] [V 2, V 22, DV 99, VP 1-2 and 4] *I pass through*.

εἰσέρχομαι [εἰς + ἔρχομαι] [V 2, V 22, DV 99, VP 1-2 and 4] *I enter; I share in*.

ἐξέρχομαι [ἐκ + ἔρχομαι] [V 2, V 22, DV 99, VP 1-2 and 4] *I go out*.

ἔρχομαι [V 2, V 22, DV 99, VP 1-2 and 4] *I come; I go*.

κατέρχομαι [κατά + ἔρχομαι] [V 2, V 22, DV 99, VP 1-2 and 4] *I come down; I land*.

παρέρχομαι [παρά + ἔρχομαι] [V 2, V 22, DV 99, VP 1-2 and 4] *I pass (by)*.

προέρχομαι [πρό + ἔρχομαι] [V 2, V 22, DV 99, VP 1-2 and 4] *I go before*.

προσέρχομαι [πρός + ἔρχομαι] [V 2, V 22, DV 99, VP 1-2 and 4] *I go
in; I approach* [with simple dative].

συνέρχομαι [σύν + ἔρχομαι] [V 2, V 22, DV 99, VP 1-2 and 4] *to come
together; to gather together* [intransitive]. It can be used with
the dative with the meaning *to come with, to accompany.*

———
εὐαγγελίζομαι (εὐαγγελίσομαι) [εὐ+ ἀγγελίζομαι—εὖ is an adverb
meaning *well*. Cf. vocabulary entry εὐαγγελίζω, Lesson 20.]
[V 5, V 22; DV 102; VP 2-3] *I preach the good news*. This verb
governs the dative or accusative of persons being evangelized,
and the accusative of content of the good news. Cf. Lesson 20
for the use of the active voice. Hence it is something of an
anomaly, being treated as a regular verb and as a middle
deponent in the New Testament. The deponent usage
predominates.

———
ὄφις, –εως, ὁ [N 28m] *serpent, snake.*

ὀψία, –ας, ἡ [N 2] *evening.*

———
ξένος, –η, –ον [Adj 1] *strange, foreign*. This word is found as a noun
[N 6m]: *stranger, foreigner.*

———
ἐπαύριον [Adv 2] *on the next day.*

μήτι [Adv 2, Neg] This word is used as an interrogative to expect a
negative answer, or to express strong emotion. The simple
form μή is also used with these meanings. The negative οὐ,
when introducing a question, expects an affirmative answer.
οὐχί, the strengthened form of οὐ, is also used in this way.

Exercises for Lesson 45.

I. Translate into English:
  1. μήτι οὗτός ἐστιν ὁ Χριστός; (Jn 4:29)
  2. καὶ ἀπήγαγον τὸν Ἰησοῦν πρὸς τὸν ἀρχιερέα, καὶ
     συνέρχονται πάντες οἱ ἀρχιερεῖς καὶ οἱ πρεσβύτεροι
     καὶ οἱ γραμματεῖς. (Mk 14:53)
  3. καὶ σοῦ δὲ αὐτῆς τὴν ψυχὴν διελεύσεται μάχαιρα. (Lk
     2:35)
  4. σὺν ὀψίᾳ ἔρχεται τὸ σκότος.

5. καὶ γὰρ ἐγὼ ἄνθρωπός εἰμι ὑπὸ ἐξουσίαν, ἔχων ὑπ᾽ ἐμαυτὸν στρατιώτας, καὶ λέγω τούτῳ, Ἔρχου, καὶ ἔρχεται. (Mt 8:9)

6. ξένος ἤμην καὶ συνηγάγετέ με, γυμνὸς καὶ περιεβάλετέ με. (Mt 25:35-36)

7. ὁ οὐρανὸς καὶ ἡ γῆ παρελεύσεται, οἱ δὲ λόγοι μου οὐ παρελεύσονται. (Mt 24:35)

8. τῇ ἐπαύριον βλέπει τὸν Ἰησοῦν ἐρχόμενον πρὸς αὐτόν. (Jn 1:29)

9. καὶ ἀπελθοῦσα εἰς τὸν οἶκον αὐτῆς εὑρίσκει τὸ παιδίον βεβλημένον ἐπὶ τὴν γῆν καὶ τὸ δαιμόνιον ἐξεληλυθός. (Mk 7:30) [Cf. Lesson 67, Vocabulary, for the meaning of εὑρίσκω.]

10. ἔξελθε ἐξ αὐτοῦ καὶ μηκέτι εἰσέλθῃς εἰς αὐτόν. (Mk 9:25) [This is an example of an aorist subjunctive used to convey a negative command—cf. Lesson 72.]

11. καὶ ἐβλήθη ὁ ὄφις ὁ μέγας. (Apoc 12:9)

12. καὶ προσῆλθον αὐτῷ ὄχλοι πολλοὶ ἔχοντες μεθ᾽ ἑαυτῶν τυφλούς, κωφούς, καὶ ἑτέρους πολλούς. (Mt 15:30)

13. καὶ αὐτὸς προελεύσεται ἐνώπιον αὐτοῦ ἐν πνεύματι. (Lk 1:17)

14. καὶ κατῆλθον εἰς τὴν πόλιν ἢ παρὰ τὴν θάλασσαν ἦν. (Acts 8:5; Mt 4:18)

II. Translate into Greek:
    1. I see women coming to us.
    2. You (sg.) have come in spirit and in truth.
    3. They were coming out of the house. (Acts 19:16)

III. Mk 4:21-41.

> Contract Verbs. Rules of Contraction for –ε
> Contracts. Principal Parts of –ε Contracts. φιλέω,
> Present Active Indicative, Imperfect Active
> Indicative, Present Active Imperative, Subjunctive,
> Participle, and Infinitive. Difficult Verbs:
> γίνομαι. Rules for Accents 35.

Lesson 46

Contract Verbs.

Many Greek verbal roots add the vowels –ε, –α, or –o. This vowel
reacts differently in the various tense systems. In the present
system it always contracts with the initial vowel of the endings.
(Hence the denomination, "contract verbs".) In the other tense
systems this vowel is usually (not always) lengthened in some way
or another. Contract verbs are divided into three categories,
according to the vowel with which the verbal root ends: 1) –ε
contracts (e.g., φιλέ–ω, *I love, I like*); 2) –α contracts (e.g., ἀγαπά–ω,
I love); 3) –o contracts (e.g., φανερό–ω, *I manifest*).

These changes in orthography do not affect the meaning: the
meanings of the tenses, moods and voices are the same as for λύω.

Rules of Contraction for –ε Contracts.

The rules of contraction for roots that add ε are as follows:

> ε + ε > ει (e.g., φιλέ–ετε > φιλεῖτε)
> ε + o > ου (e.g., φιλέ–ομεν > φιλοῦμεν)
> ε before a long vowel or a diphthong is absorbed (e.g., φιλέ–ω >
>   φιλῶ; φιλέ–ουσι[ν] > φιλοῦσι[ν]).

In modern vocabulary listings contract verbs are usually
given in their uncontracted form of the first person singular of the
present indicative active (or middle or passive, if the verb is
deponent) in order to facilitate the identification of the category of

contract verb in which the verb falls. Thus the word φιλέω is found
in a vocabulary or dictionary listing, although this form is never
found in the New Testament text. There it is always φιλῶ.

Principal Parts of –ε Contracts.

The contracted forms are found only in the present system (all
moods, all voices). In the other systems the vowel ε added to the root
is usually lengthened to η (exceptions to this rule will be given in
Lesson 47). Thus the principal parts of φιλέω are as follows:

φιλέ–ω φιλή–σω ἐφίλη–σα πεφίλη–κα πεφίλη–μαι ἐφιλή–θην

All the forms outside the present system are conjugated
exactly like λύω. Some contract verbs are irregular, so that their
principal parts must be learned by memory. But unless noted, ε
contracts follow the pattern of φιλέω.

φιλέω, Present Active Indicative, Imperfect Active Indicative, Present Active Imperative, Subjunctive, Participle, and Infinitive.

The present active tenses of φιλέω follow (cf. V 8, VP 1-3 and 5-6; for
the participle cf. also Adj 9):

Active Voice, Indicative Mood, Present Tense

	Singular	Plural
1st Person	φιλῶ	φιλοῦμεν
2nd Person	φιλεῖς	φιλεῖτε
3rd Person	φιλεῖ	φιλοῦσι(ν)

Active Voice, Indicative Mood, Imperfect Tense

	Singular	Plural
1st Person	ἐφίλουν	ἐφιλοῦμεν
2nd Person	ἐφίλεις	ἐφιλεῖτε
3rd Person	ἐφίλει	ἐφίλουν

Active Voice, Imperative Mood, Present Tense

	Singular	Plural
2nd Person	φίλει	φιλεῖτε
3rd Person	φιλείτω	φιλείτωσαν

Active Voice, Subjunctive Mood, Present Tense

	Singular	Plural
1st Person	φιλῶ	φιλῶμεν
2nd Person	φιλῇς	φιλῆτε
3rd Person	φιλῇ	φιλῶσι(ν)

The present optative of contract verbs is not found in the New Testament.

Active Voice, Participial Mood, Present Tense

Singular

	Masculine	Feminine	Neuter
n	φιλῶν	φιλοῦσα	φιλοῦν
v	φιλῶν	φιλοῦσα	φιλοῦν
g	φιλοῦντος	φιλούσης	φιλοῦντος
d	φιλοῦντι	φιλούσῃ	φιλοῦντι
a	φιλοῦντα	φιλοῦσαν	φιλοῦν

Plural

	Masculine	Feminine	Neuter
n	φιλοῦντες	φιλοῦσαι	φιλοῦντα
v	φιλοῦντες	φιλοῦσαι	φιλοῦντα
g	φιλούντων	φιλουσῶν	φιλούντων
d	φιλοῦσι(ν)	φιλούσαις	φιλοῦσι(ν)
a	φιλοῦντας	φιλούσας	φιλοῦντα

The present active infinitive is φιλεῖν.

The rules for accentuation of contracted forms will be given in Rules for Accents 35 below.

Difficult Verbs: γίνομαι.

γίνομαι, *I become* [V 7, 21, 22, 23; DV 49; VP 2-4]

γίνομαι	γενήσομαι	ἐγενόμην	γέγονα	γεγένημαι	ἐγενήθην
Mt 27:24	Mt 18:19	Mt 7:28	Mt 1:22	Jn 2:9	Mt 6:10

This important and complicated verb defies categorization. The basic meanings in both the middle and passive forms are synonymous (*I become, I come to be*, etc.). This seems to be the meaning of the perfect active as well. In the aorist middle the verb is strong, in the aorist passive it is weak. In the perfect active it is strong. The future is a middle form.

Rules for Accents 35.

The basic rules for contract verbs are the same as those for verbs in general. The proper accent for the contracted forms may be determined according to the following principles:
    1) If there is no accent on either of the two elements forming the contraction, the accent remains where it was on the uncontracted form (e.g., ἐφίλε–ον remains ἐφίλουν).
    2) If there is an accent on the first of the two elements forming the contraction the accent falls on the contracted syllable and is circumflex (e.g., φιλέ–ομεν becomes φιλοῦμεν).
    3) If there is an accent on the second of the two elements forming the contraction, the accent falls on the contracted syllable and is acute (e.g., φιλε–έτω becomes φιλείτω).
    It should be noted that the present indicative third person singular active is thus φιλέ–ει > φιλεῖ, while the present imperative second person singular active is φίλε–ε > φίλει.

Vocabulary for Lesson 46.

ἀκολουθέω [V 8; VP 1-3, 5-6] *I follow*. It governs the dative case.

δεῖ [V 8, 19, DV 54; VP 4] *it is necessary; it is proper*. The imperfect is ἔδει, *it was necessary; it was proper*. [It governs the accusative with the infinitive construction.]

δοκέω [V 8; DV 65; VP 1-3, 5-6] *I think; I suppose; I seem*.

ζητέω [V 8; VP 1-3, 5-6] *I seek.*

λαλέω [V 8; VP 1-3, 5-6] *I speak; I proclaim.*

μαρτυρέω [V 8; VP 1-3, 5-6] *I bear witness; I approve.*

περιπατέω [περί + πατέω] [V 8; VP 1-3, 5-6] *I walk; I conduct myself.*

ποιέω [V 8; VP 1-3, 5-6] *I make; I do.*

τηρέω [V 8; VP 1-3, 5-6] *I keep; I keep in custody; I keep back.*

φιλέω [V 8; VP 1-3, 5-6] *I love; I like; I kiss.*

φοβέομαι [V 8, 23; DV 331; VP 2-3, 6] *I fear.*

———

γίνομαι [V 7, 21, 22, 23; DV 49; VP 2-4] *I become.*

παραγίνομαι [παρά + γίνομαι] [V7, 21, 22, 23; DV 49; VP 2-4] *I arrive; I appear.*

———

καθάπερ [Conj] *as; just as.* This conjunction is used to make comparisons between clauses, i.e., segments of sentences involving verbs. This word is also found as an adverb [Adv 3]: *thus.*

———

ὡσαύτως [Adv 3] *likewise.*

Exercises for Lesson 46.

I. Translate into English:
1. καὶ πάντες ἐμαρτύρουν αὐτῷ καὶ ἐλάλουν περὶ τῶν λόγων τῆς χάριτος τῶν ἐκπορευομένων ἐκ τοῦ στόματος αὐτοῦ. (Lk 4:22) [Cf. Lesson 54, Vocabulary, for the meaning of ἐκπορεύομαι.]
2. ἦν δὲ ὁ προφήτης βαπτίζων ἐν τῷ Ἰορδάνῃ ποταμῷ, ὅτι ὕδατα πολλὰ ἦν ἐκεῖ, καὶ παρεγίνοντο καὶ ἐβαπτίζοντο. (Jn 3:23)
3. καὶ ἐλάλει αὐτοῖς τὸν λόγον. (Mk 2:2)
4. ἔδει δὲ τὸν Ἰησοῦν διέρχεσθαι διὰ τῆς χώρας. (Jn 4:4)

5. εἰ υἱὸς εἶ τοῦ θεοῦ, λέγε ἵνα οἱ λίθοι οὗτοι ἄρτοι γένωνται. (Mt 4:3) [ἵνα Noun Clause—cf. Lesson 75.]

6. πάλιν δὲ ἐξελθὼν περὶ ἕκτην ὥραν ἐποίησεν ὡσαύτως. (Mt 20:5)

7. οὐ γὰρ ὑμεῖς ἐστε οἱ λαλοῦντες ἀλλὰ τὸ πνεῦμα τοῦ πατρὸς ὑμῶν τὸ λαλοῦν ἐν ὑμῖν. (Mt 10:20)

8. ὀπίσω μου ἔρχεται ἀνὴρ ὃς ἔμπροσθέν μου γέγονεν, ὅτι πρῶτός μου ἦν. (Jn 1:30)

9. εἰ δὲ θέλεις εἰς τὴν ζωὴν εἰσελθεῖν, τήρησον τὰς ἐντολάς. (Mt 19:17)

10. ταῦτα πάντα ἐλάλησεν ὁ Ἰησοῦς ἐν παραβολαῖς τοῖς ὄχλοις, καὶ χωρὶς παραβολῆς οὐδὲν ἐλάλει αὐτοῖς. (Mt 13:34)

11. ἐγένετο ὁ προφήτης βαπτίζων ἐν τῇ ἐρήμῳ καὶ κηρύσσων βάπτισμα μετανοίας εἰς ἄφεσιν ἁμαρτιῶν. (Mk 1:4)

12. καλῶς πάντα πεποίηκεν· τοὺς κωφοὺς ποιεῖ ἀκούειν. (Mk 7:37)

13. τί ὑμῖν δοκεῖ περὶ τοῦ Χριστοῦ; τίνος υἱός ἐστιν; (Mt 22:42)

14. καὶ μετὰ ταῦτα περιεπάτει ὁ Ἰησοῦς ἐν τῇ χώρᾳ ἐκείνῃ. (Jn 7:1)

15. καθάπερ γὰρ τὸ σῶμα ἕν ἐστιν καὶ μέλη πολλὰ ἔχει, πάντα δὲ τὰ μέλη τοῦ σώματος πολλὰ ὄντα ἕν ἐστιν σῶμα, οὕτως καὶ ὁ Χριστός. (1 Cor 12:12)

16. καὶ ὁ Ἰησοῦς λέγει αὐτῷ, Ἀκολούθει μοι, καὶ ἠκολούθησεν αὐτῷ. (Mt 9:9)

17. ἐγώ εἰμι· μὴ φοβεῖσθε. (Mk 6:50)

18. ποιήσατε οὖν καρποὺς ἀξίους τῆς μετανοίας. (Lk 3:8)

19. ζητεῖτε δὲ πρῶτον τὴν βασιλείαν τοῦ θεοῦ καὶ τὴν δικαιοσύνην αὐτοῦ. (Mt 6:33)

20. καὶ εἰς πάντα τὰ ἔθνη πρῶτον δεῖ κηρυχθῆναι τὸ εὐαγγέλιον. (Mk 13:10)

21. ὁ φιλῶν πατέρα ἢ μητέρα ὑπὲρ ἐμὲ οὐκ ἔστιν μου ἄξιος· καὶ ὁ φιλῶν υἱὸν ἢ θυγατέρα ὑπὲρ ἐμὲ οὐκ ἔστιν μου ἄξιος. (Mt 10:37)

II. Translate into Greek:
    1. If you [pl.] will become faithful, you [pl.] will be happy.
    2. May they not become unfaithful. (Jn 20:27)
    3. I have become wise through the wisdom of Christ.

III. Mk 5:1-20.

φιλέω, Present Middle and Passive
Indicative, Imperfect Middle and Passive
Indicative, Present Middle and Passive
Imperative, Subjunctive, Participle, and
Infinitive. Contraction in –εω Roots of One
Syllable. The Non-Lengthening of ε in the
Non-Contracted Forms of Some –ε
Contracts. Difficult Verbs: καλέω, δέω.

Lesson 47

φιλέω, Present Middle and Passive Indicative, Imperfect Middle and Passive Indicative, Present Middle and Passive Imperative, Subjunctive, Participle, and Infinitive.

The moods of the present middle and passive of φιλέω are as follows
(cf. V 8; VP 1-3, 5-6; for the participle cf. also Adj 1):

Middle and Passive Voices, Indicative Mood, Present Tense

	Singular	Plural
1st Person	φιλοῦμαι	φιλούμεθα
2nd Person	φιλῇ	φιλεῖσθε
3rd Person	φιλεῖται	φιλοῦνται

The form φιλῇ comes from φιλε–έσαι (φιλε–έσαι > φιλε–έαι >
φιλῆι > φιλῇ).

Middle and Passive Voices, Indicative Mood, Imperfect Tense

	Singular	Plural
1st Person	ἐφιλούμην	ἐφιλούμεθα
2nd Person	ἐφιλοῦ	ἐφιλεῖσθε
3rd Person	ἐφιλεῖτο	ἐφιλοῦντο

The form ἐφιλοῦ comes from ἐφιλέ–εσο (ἐφιλέ–εσο > ἐφιλέ–εο >
ἐφιλέ–ου > ἐφιλοῦ).

Middle and Passive Voices, Imperative Mood, Present Tense
	Singular	Plural
2nd Person	φιλοῦ	φιλεῖσθε
3rd Person	φιλείσθω	φιλείσθωσαν

The form φιλοῦ comes from φιλέ–εσο (φιλέ–εσο > φιλέ–εο > φιλέ–ου > φιλοῦ).

Middle and Passive Voices, Subjunctive Mood, Present Tense
	Singular	Plural
1st Person	φιλῶμαι	φιλώμεθα
2nd Person	φιλῇ	φιλῆσθε
3rd Person	φιλῆται	φιλῶνται

The form φιλῇ comes from φιλε–ησαι (φιλε–ησαι > φιλε–ηαι > φιλέ–ηι > φιληῑ > φιλῇ).

Middle and Passive Voices, Participial Mood, Present Tense

Singular
	Masculine	Feminine	Neuter
n	φιλούμενος	φιλουμένη	φιλούμενον
v	φιλούμενε	φιλουμένη	φιλούμενον
g	φιλουμένου	φιλουμένης	φιλουμένου
d	φιλουμένῳ	φιλουμένη	φιλουμένῳ
a	φιλούμενον	φιλουμένην	φιλούμενον

Plural
	Masculine	Feminine	Neuter
n	φιλούμενοι	φιλούμεναι	φιλούμενα
v	φιλούμενοι	φιλούμεναι	φιλούμενα
g	φιλουμένων	φιλουμένων	φιλουμένων
d	φιλουμένοις	φιλουμέναις	φιλουμένοις
a	φιλουμένους	φιλουμένας	φιλούμενα

The present middle/passive infinitive is φιλεῖσθαι.

It is important to bear in mind that the listing of forms under the rubrics "middle/passive" or "middle and passive" does not mean that the occurrence of one of these forms in a text can be both middle and passive at one and the same time. It must be one or the other.

Even if the text is ambiguous and either alternative is possible, they cannot both be possible at the same time in one and the same way.

Contraction in −εω Roots of One Syllable.

In verbs with roots of one syllable in the category of ε contracts, there are exceptions to the rules of contraction given in Lesson 46: not all of the normal contractions take place. The contractions which do not take place are ε + ο, ε + ω, and ε + η. Thus, for the verb πνέω, I blow, one finds πνέοντα instead of πνοῦντα, and πνέῃ instead of πνῇ.

The Non-Lengthening of ε in the Non-Contracted Forms of Some −ε Contracts.

A few contract verbs in −εω do not lengthen the ε in the forms which are not contracted. Memory is the only way of learning these verbs. They are not many, and those which do exist will be noted in the vocabulary. The most important verb in the category is καλέω, I call, which retains the ε unlengthened in the future active/middle and in the aorist active/middle.

Difficult Verbs: καλέω, δέω.

καλέω, I call; I invite; I name [V 8; DV 142; VP 1-3, 5-6]

καλέω	καλέσω	ἐκάλεσα	κέκληκα	κέκλημαι	ἐκλήθην
Mt 22:43	Mt 1:21	Mt 1:25	Lk 14:12	Mt 22:3	Mt 23:8

δέω, I bind [V 8; DV 59; VP 1-3, 5-6]

—	δήσω	ἔδησα	δέδεκα	δέδεμαι	ἐδέθην
	Acts 21:11	Mt 14:3	Acts 22:29	Mt 16:19	Acts 21:13

This verb lengthens the ε in the first two principal parts, but not in the last three.

Vocabulary for Lesson 47.

ἐπικαλέω [ἐπί + καλέω] [V 8; DV 142; VP 1-3, 5-6] active: *I call*;
  middle: *I call upon, I appeal to.*

καλέω [V 8; DV 142; VP 1-3, 5-6] *I call; I invite; I name.*

παρακαλέω [παρά + καλέω] [V 8; DV 142; VP 1-3, 5-6] *I beg; I
  encourage; I console.*

προσκαλέομαι [πρός + καλέομαι] [V 8, 22; DV 142; VP 1-3, 5-6] *I call
  to myself; I invite.*

___

δέω [V 8, DV 59, VP 1-3, 5-6] *I bind.*

___

πλέω [V 8; DV 252; VP 1, 5] *I sail.*

πνέω [V 8; DV 256; VP 1, 5] *I blow.*

___

αἰνέω [future: αἰνέσω] [V 8; DV 6; VP 1-3, 5-6] *I praise; I approve.*

αἰτέω [V 8; VP 1-3, 5-6] *I request; I demand.*

δέομαι [V 8, 23; DV 56; VP 3, 6] *I ask; I implore.* This verb governs
  the genitive for the person who is being asked.

θεωρέω [V 8; VP 1-3, 5-6] *I watch; I observe.*

κρατέω [V 8; VP 1-3, 5-6] *I take hold of; I hold fast.* Governs the
  accusative or the genitive. The genitive is explained by the
  usage, much more common in classical Greek, of considering
  verbs of touching or holding as concerning only a "part" of the
  object touched or held. Thus the "partitive genitive" is used
  to express the idea that only a "part" of the object touched or
  held is really touched or held.

παραιτέομαι [παρά + αἰτέομαι] [V 8, 22; VP 2-3, 6] *I ask for; I keep
  away from; I ask to be excused.*

προσκυνέω [πρός + κυνέω] [V 8; VP 1-3, 5-6] transitive: *I worship*
  [with accusative or dative for the object of worship];
  intransitive: *I bow low.*

___

ἔπειτα [Adv 2] *then, next.*

κακῶς [Adv 3] *badly; wrongly.*

Exercises for Lesson 47.

I. Translate into English:
1. ἔχε με παρῃτημένον. (Lk 14:18)
2. ὃ ἐὰν δήσῃς ἐπὶ τῆς γῆς ἔσται δεδεμένον ἐν τοῖς οὐρανοῖς, καὶ ὃ ἐὰν λύσῃς ἐπὶ τῆς γῆς ἔσται λελυμένον ἐν τοῖς οὐρανοις. (Mt 16:19)
3. οὗτος προσελθὼν τῷ ἡγεμόνι ᾐτήσατο τὸ σῶμα τοῦ Ἰησοῦ. (Mt 27:58)
4. καὶ ἐκάλεσεν τὸ ὄνομα αὐτοῦ Ἰησοῦν. (Mt 1:25)
5. εἰ κακῶς ἐλάλησα, μαρτύρησον περὶ τοῦ κακοῦ. (Jn 18:23)
6. μέλλομεν πλεῖν εἰς ἄλλους τόπους. (Acts 27:2)
7. καὶ ὧδε ἔχει ἐξουσίαν παρὰ τῶν ἀρχιερέων δῆσαι πάντας τοὺς ἐπικαλουμένους τὸ ὄνομά σου. (Acts 9:14)
8. καὶ ἦλθον οἱ ποταμοὶ καὶ ἔπνευσαν οἱ ἄνεμοι. (Mt 7:25)
9. ὁ δὲ πατὴρ αὐτοῦ ἐξελθὼν παρεκάλει αὐτόν. (Lk 15:28)
10. καὶ ἐζήτουν αὐτὸν κρατῆσαι, καὶ ἐφοβήθησαν τὸν ὄχλον. (Mk 12:12)
11. ἔπειτα μετὰ ἔτη τρία ἀνῆλθον εἰς τὴν ἁγίαν πόλιν. (Gal 1:18)
12. καὶ προσκαλεσάμενος πάλιν τὸν ὄχλον ἔλεγεν αὐτοῖς, Ἀκούσατέ μου πάντες. (Mk 7:14)
13. ἡ δὲ ἐλθοῦσα προσεκύνει αὐτῷ. (Mt 15:25)

II. Translate into Greek:
1. They will be called sons of God. (Lk 1:32.35)
2. The soldiers sailed on the third day. (Mt 16:21) [Use the simple dative without a preposition to express the time.]
3. They came in order to worship him. (Mt 2:2)

III. Mk 5:21-43.

Future Active and Middle Systems of Liquid
and Nasal Verbs. στέλλω, Future Active
and Future Middle. Aorist Active and
Middle of Liquid and Nasal Verbs.
στέλλω, Aorist Active and Aorist Middle.
Difficult Verbs: στέλλω, κρίνω,
ἀγγέλλω.

Lesson 48

Future Active and Middle Systems of Liquid and Nasal Verbs.

Contract verbs in –εω have special contracted forms only in the
present system, as was explained above, in Lesson 46. There are
two other categories of verbs, liquid (i.e., with a root ending in λ or ρ)
and nasal (i.e., with a root ending in μ or ν), which in a sense can be
said to make use of the paradigm of –εω contracts to form the future
active and middle voices. This phenomenon results from
phonological changes peculiar to these roots. For example, in the
case of the verb στέλλω, *I send*, the verbal root is στελ–. (For reasons
irrelevant to the present discussion the present stem is στελλ–, with
two lambdas.) The future is not formed by adding σ directly to the
stem, but by adding ε plus the regular endings, which then contract
according to the rules already given for the present system of
contract verbs in ε, so that the future, first person singular is στελῶ,
just as the present, first person singular of φιλέω is φιλῶ.

This same type of reasoning applies to the future of nasal
verbs such as μένω (μενέω > μενῶ).

The same rules, of course, apply to all the moods of the future
active and of the future middle of these two categories of verbs.

στέλλω, Future Active and Future Middle.

The future indicative active and future indicative middle of στέλλω
are conjugated as follows [cf. V 6 and DV 292; στέλλω is found in the
New Testament only as part of a compound verb]:

Active Voice, Indicative Mood, Future Tense

	Singular	Plural
1st Person	στελῶ	στελοῦμεν
2nd Person	στελεῖς	στελεῖτε
3rd Person	στελεῖ	στελοῦσι(ν)

Middle Voice, Indicative Mood, Future Tense

	Singular	Plural
1st Person	στελοῦμαι	στελούμεθα
2nd Person	στελῇ	στελεῖσθε
3rd Person	στελεῖται	στελοῦνται

The form στελῇ comes from στελέ–εσαι (στελέ–εσαι > στελέ–εαι > στελέ–ηι > στελῆι > στελῇ).

The future infinitive and future participle active and middle are formed on the analogy of the indicative from the present forms of φιλέω.

Aorist Active and Middle of Liquid and Nasal Verbs.

Liquid and nasal verbs also have special rules for the formation of the aorist active and middle. But the resulting forms have no resemblance to contract verbs in –εω as do the forms of the future active and middle. The aorist active and middle voices of liquid and nasal verbs are treated here for convenience, inasmuch as they are formed according to special rules, just as their future is formed according to special rules, and it seems appropriate to treat the two phenomena together.

Most verbs have weak aorist active and middle forms, as was explained in Lesson 18. This means that the aorist stem is formed by the addition of a σ to the root. When this σ of the aorist stem is added to the root of liquid and nasal verbs special changes take place: the σ is dropped and the syllable previous to the liquid (or nasal) is lengthened, usually by the formation of a diphthong involving ι. Thus the aorist active indicative of στέλλω is ἔστειλα; the aorist active indicative of μένω is ἔμεινα.

στέλλω, Aorist Active Indicative and Aorist Middle Indicative.

The aorist indicative active and middle of στέλλω are conjugated as follows (cf. V 6 and DV 292):

Active Voice, Indicative Mood, Aorist Tense

	Singular	Plural
1st Person	ἔ–στειλ–α	ἐστείλ–αμεν
2nd Person	ἔ–στειλ–ας	ἐ–στείλ–ατε
3rd Person	ἔ–στειλ–ε(ν)	ἔ–στειλ–αν

Middle Voice, Indicative Mood, Aorist Tense

	Singular	Plural
1st Person	ἐ–στειλ–άμην	ἐ–στειλ–άμεθα
2nd Person	ἐ–στείλ–ω	ἐ–στείλ–ασθε
3rd Person	ἐ–στείλ–ατο	ἐ–στείλ–αντο

The form ἐστείλω comes from ἐστείλασο (ἐστείλασο > ἐστείλαο > ἐστείλω).

The endings are the normal endings for the aorist active and middle indicative. The same endings are used for the aorist active and middle indicative of μένω, based on the stem μειν–.

The stems στειλ– and μειν– are used to form all other moods of the aorist active and middle.

The future and aorist are the only two tense systems in which the liquid and nasal verbs have special forms. In other aspects, of course, liquid and nasal verbs can be irregular.

Difficult Verbs: στέλλω, κρίνω, ἀγγέλλω.

στέλλω, *I send* [V 6; DV 292; VP 1-3, 5-6]

στέλλω	στελῶ	ἔστειλα	ἔσταλκα	ἔσταλμαι	ἐστάλην
Mt 10:16	Mt 24:31	Mt 2:16	Lk 4:18	Lk 13:34	Mt 15:24

The verb στέλλω exists in the New Testament only as part of compound verbs, although these are numerous. The examples of the principle parts given above are of the verb ἀποστέλλω. The future and aorist have been discussed in this lesson. The aorist passive is strong.

κρίνω, *I judge, I discern, I decide* [V 7; DV 165; VP 1-3, 5-6]

κρίνω	κρινῶ	ἔκρινα	κέκρικα	κέκριμαι	ἐκρίθην
Mt 7:1	Heb 10:30	Lk 7:43	Acts 16:15	Jn 3:18	Mt 5:40

The principles for forming the future and aorist active and middle have been discussed in this lesson. The aorist active has a long ι to compensate for the dropping of σ, but the lengthened quality of the ι does not appear in the orthography.

ἀγγέλλω, *I tell* [V 6; DV 2; VP 1-3, 5-6]

ἀγγέλλω	ἀγγελῶ	ἤγγειλα	—	ἤγγελμαι	ἠγγέλην
Acts 14:27	Jn 4:25	Mt 2:8		Gal 3:19	Lk 8:20

The simple verb ἀγγέλλω is rare in the New Testament, but compounds based on it are frequent. The principles for forming the future and aorist active and middle have been discussed in this lesson. The aorist passive is strong.

Vocabulary for Lesson 48.

ἀποστέλλω [ἀπό + στέλλω] [V 6; DV 292; VP 1-3, 5-6] *I send; I send with a mission.*

ἐξαποστέλλω [ἐκ + ἀπό + στέλλω] [V 6; DV 292; VP 1-3, 5-6] *I send off; I send forth.*

————
ἀνακρίνω [ἀνά + κρίνω] [V 7; DV 165; VP 1-3, 5-6] *I examine; I judge.*

ἀποκρίνομαι [ἀπό + κρίνομαι] [V 7, 22, 23; DV 165; VP 2-3, 6]. This verb is primarily a passive deponent, but middle forms are also found with the same active meaning as the passive: *I answer; I declare.*

διακρίνω [διά + κρίνω] [V 7; DV 165; VP 1-3, 5-6] active: *I evaluate; I distinguish;* middle: *I hesitate; I doubt.* The aorist passive also means *I hesitate, I doubt.*

κατακρίνω [κατά + κρίνω] [V 7; DV 165; VP 2-3, 5-6] *I condemn.*

κρίνω [V 7; DV 165; VP 1-3, 5-6] *I judge; I discern; I decide.*

————
ἀγγέλλω [V 6; DV 2; VP 1-3, 5-6] *I tell.*

ἀναγγέλλω [ἀνά + ἀγγέλλω] [V 6; DV 2; VP 1-3, 5-6] *I tell; I report; I preach*.

ἀπαγγέλλω [ἀπό + ἀγγέλλω] [V 6; DV 2; VP 1-3, 5-6] *I inform; I proclaim; I command* [with dative of the person commanded].

ἐπαγγέλλομαι [ἐπί + ἀγγέλλομαι] [V 6, 22; DV 2; VP 2-3, 6] *I promise; I profess*.

καταγγέλλω [κατά + ἀγγέλλω] [V 6; DV 2; VP 1-3, 5-6] *I proclaim; I preach*.

παραγγέλλω [παρά + ἀγγέλλω] [V 6; DV 2; VP 1-3, 5-6] *I order* [dative of person ordered].

ἐπιμένω [ἐπί + μένω] [V 7; DV 125; VP 1-3, 5-6] intransitive: *I remain; I continue*.

μένω [V 7; DV 197; VP 1-3, 5-6] transitive: *I await*; intransitive: *I remain*.

ὑπομένω [ὑπό + μένω] [V 7; DV 197; VP 1-3, 5-6] *I endure; I undergo*.

Exercises for Lesson 48.

I. Translate into English:
1. κατακρινοῦσιν τὸν υἱὸν τοῦ ἀνθρώπου θανάτῳ. (Mk 10:33)
2. κἀκεῖ μείνατε ἕως ἂν ἐξέλθητε ἐκ τῆς πόλεως. (Mt 10:11)
3. τούτους τοὺς δώδεκα ἀπέστειλεν ὁ Ἰησοῦς παραγγείλας αὐτοῖς λέγων, Ἀπαγγείλατε ὅσα ὁ Κύριος πεποίηκεν. (Mt 10:5; Mk 5:19)
4. ὅταν ἔλθῃ ὁ Μεσσίας, ἀναγγελεῖ ἡμῖν ἅπαντα. (Jn 4:25)
5. ὁ δὲ ἀνακρίνων με Κύριός ἐστιν. (1 Cor 4:4)
6. ἀποκριθεὶς δὲ ὁ Ἰησοῦς εἶπεν αὐτοῖς, Ἀμὴν λέγω ὑμῖν, ἐὰν ἔχητε πίστιν καὶ μὴ διακριθῆτε, κἂν τῷ ὄρει τούτῳ λέγητε, Βλήθητι εἰς τὴν θάλασσαν, γενήσεται. (Mt 21:21) [κἂν = καὶ ἂν, i.e., it is an example of crasis.]
7. ὁ δὲ ὑπομείνας εἰς τέλος οὗτος σωθήσεται. (Mt 10:22)

8. ἄνδρες ἀδελφοί, ἡμῖν ὁ λόγος τῆς σωτηρίας ταύτης ἐξαπεστάλη. (Acts 13:26)

9. πιστὸς γὰρ ὁ ἐπαγγειλάμενος. (Heb 10:23)

10. ὁ δὲ ἀποκριθεὶς αὐτοῖς λέγει, Ὦ γενεὰ ἄπιστος, ἕως πότε πρὸς ὑμᾶς ἔσομαι; (Mk 9:19)

11. καὶ πάντες δὲ οἱ προφῆται κατήγγειλαν τὰς ἡμέρας ταύτας. (Acts 3:24)

12. μὴ κρίνετε, ἵνα μὴ κριθῆτε· ἐν ᾧ γὰρ κρίματι κρίνετε κριθήσεσθε. (Mt 7:1-2)

13. ἐλπίζω γὰρ ἐπιμεῖναι πρὸς ὑμᾶς. (1 Cor 16:7)

14. ἔρχεται ἡ γυνὴ ἀγγέλλουσα τοῖς μαθηταῖς ὅτι Ἑώρακα τὸν Κύριον. (Jn 20:18)

15. ἐδεῖτο δὲ αὐτοῦ ὁ ἀνὴρ ἀφ᾽ οὗ ἐξεληλύθει τὰ δαιμόνια εἶναι σὺν αὐτῷ. (Lk 8:38)

16. καὶ ἀπῆλθον οἱ ποιμένες δοξάζοντες καὶ αἰνοῦντες τὸν θεόν ἐπὶ πᾶσιν ἃ ἤκουσαν. (Lk 2:20)

17. πολλοὶ ἐπίστευσαν εἰς τὸ ὄνομα αὐτοῦ, θεωροῦντες αὐτοῦ τὰ σημεῖα ἃ ἐποίει. (Jn 2:23)

II. Translate into Greek:
1. I have sent you so that you may preach the good news.
2. I shall judge those who condemn you.
3. What God promised he is also capable of doing. (Rom 4:21)

III. Mk 6:1-13.

Rules of Contraction for −α Contracts.
Principal Parts of −α Contracts. ἀγαπάω,
Present Active Indicative, Imperfect Active
Indicative, Present Active Imperative,
Subjunctive, Participle, and Infinitive.
Difficult Verbs: ὁράω, ἔχω. **Rules for**
Accents 36.

Lesson 49

Rules of Contraction for −α Contracts.

For an introduction to contract verbs cf. above, Lesson 46.
The rules of contraction for roots ending in α are as follows:

α + ε or η > α (e.g., τιμά–ετε > τιμᾶτε; τιμά–ητε > τιμᾶτε);
α + ο, ω, or ου > ω (e.g., τιμά–ομεν > τιμῶμεν; τιμά–ω >
τιμῶ; τιμά–ουσι[ν] > τιμῶσι[ν]);
α + a diphthong containing ι results in a long vowel
with the ι written as an iota subscript.

A simplified version of the above rules is as follows:
α + any "o" sound (ο, ου, ω) results in ω;
α + any other sound (ε, η) results in α;
if an iota is involved, it becomes subscript.

Principal Parts of −α Contracts.

In the principal parts of ἀγαπάω outside the present system the
vowel which is added to the root is lengthened to η:

ἀγαπά–ω ἀγαπή–σω ἠγάπη–σα ἠγάπη–κα ἠγάπη–μαι ἠγαπή–θην

But if the α that is added to the root is preceded by an ε, ι, or ρ
the α remains and is lengthened to ᾱ, although the lengthening is
not customarily indicated. Thus the principal parts of κοπιάω, *I
work hard, I labor* are as follows:

κοπιά–ω	κοπιά–σω	ἐκοπία–σα
		κεκοπία–κα	κεκοπία–μαι	ἐκοπιά–θην

However, there are exceptions to this rule both ways. For example, χράομαι lengthens the α to η: χρήσομαι. And κλάω lengthens the α to ᾱ: ἔκλασα.

ἀγαπάω, Present Active Indicative, Imperfect Active Indicative, Present Active Imperative, Subjunctive, Participle, and Infinitive.

The present active of ἀγαπάω, *I love*, is conjugated as follows (cf. V 9; VP 1-3, 5-6; for the participle, cf. Adj 8):

Active Voice, Indicative Mood, Present Tense

	Singular	Plural
1st Person	ἀγαπῶ	ἀγαπῶμεν
2nd Person	ἀγαπᾷς	ἀγαπᾶτε
3rd Person	ἀγαπᾷ	ἀγαπῶσι(ν)

Active Voice, Indicative Mood, Imperfect Tense

	Singular	Plural
lst Person	ἠγάπων	ἠγαπῶμεν
!nd Person	ἠγάπας	ἠγαπᾶτε
!rd Person	ἠγάπα	ἠγάπων

Note the following: ἠγάπων: imperfect indicative active first ʼerson singular and third person plural; ἀγαπῶν: present ʼarticiple active masculine and neuter singular. These two forms hould be carefully distinguished by augment and by accent.

Active Voice, Imperative Mood, Present Tense

	Singular	Plural
nd Person	ἀγάπα	ἀγαπᾶτε
rd Person	ἀγαπάτω	ἀγαπάτωσαν

Active Voice, Subjunctive Mood, Present Tense

	Singular	Plural
st Person	ἀγαπῶ	ἀγαπῶμεν
nd Person	ἀγαπᾷς	ἀγαπᾶτε
rd Person	ἀγαπᾷ	ἀγαπῶσι(ν)

The forms of the present subjunctive are the same as the forms of the present indicative. They can be distinguished only from the context.

The present optative active of contract verbs in −αω is not found in the New Testament.

Active Voice, Participial Mood, Present Tense

Singular

	Masculine	Feminine	Neuter
n	ἀγαπῶν	ἀγαπῶσα	ἀγαπῶν
v	ἀγαπῶν	ἀγαπῶσα	ἀγαπῶν
g	ἀγαπῶντος	ἀγαπώσης	ἀγαπῶντος
d	ἀγαπῶντι	ἀγαπώσῃ	ἀγαπῶντι
a	ἀγαπῶντα	ἀγαπῶσαν	ἀγαπῶν

Plural

	Masculine	Feminine	Neuter
n	ἀγαπῶντες	ἀγαπῶσαι	ἀγαπῶντα
v	ἀγαπῶντες	ἀγαπῶσαι	ἀγαπῶντα
g	ἀγαπώντων	ἀγαπώσων	ἀγαπώντων
d	ἀγαπῶσι(ν)	ἀγαπώσαις	ἀγαπῶσι(ν)
a	ἀγαπῶντας	ἀγαπώσας	ἀγαπῶντα

On the possibility of confusing certain forms of the participle with certain forms of the imperfect indicative see the observations above, following the paradigm of the imperfect indicative active.

The present active infinitive is ἀγαπᾶν.

There is no iota subscript in the present active infinitive of contract verbs in −αω because the present infinitive ending itself is a contraction of the original vowels ε–εν. Hence ἀγαπά–ε–εν > ἀγαπᾶ–εν > ἀγαπᾶν.

The rules for accentuation of contract verbs have been given above, in Lesson 46. But special note should be taken of the accent of the neuter participle as explained below in Rules for Accents 36.

The middle/passive forms of the present tense of ἀγαπάω will be given in Lesson 50.

)ifficult Verbs: ὁράω, ἔχω.

ὁράω, transitive: *I see*; intransitive: *I take care* [V 9, DV 222, VP 1-6]

ὁράω	ὄψομαι	εἶδον	ἑώρακα	—	ὤφθην
t 8:4	Mt 5:8	Mt 2:2	Lk 1:22		Mt 17:3
			ἑόρακα		
			Col 2:1		

The future is a middle deponent. The aorist active is strong, ith an irregular augment (the aorist root is ἰδ–). There are two rms of the perfect active, ἑώρακα being the more common. There no perfect middle/passive in the New Testament.

ἔχω, *I have* [cf. Lesson 9] [V 2, DV 109, VP 1-4]

ἔχω	ἔξω	ἔσχον	ἔσχηκα	---	---
8:9	Mt 12:11	Mt 19:16	Mk 5:15		

It will be recalled that the augment of the imperfect of ἔχω is ·egular, εἶχον (cf. above, Lesson 10). The augment of the aorist is ¡ular. Thus the aorist stem is σχ–.

les for Accents 36.

e accent of the neuter nominative, vocative, and accusative gular of the present active participle of ἀγαπάω is probably ısed by analogy with the accentuation of the masculine ninative and vocative singular. The same is true of the responding forms of φιλέω (cf. above, Lesson 46) and of φανερόω below, Lesson 51).

cabulary for Lesson 49.

ἀγαπάω [V 9; VP 1-3, 5-6] *I love*.

ὁράω [V 9, DV 222, VP 1-6] transitive: *I see*; intransitive: *I take care*.

ἐνέχω [ἐν + ἔχω] [V 2, DV 109, VP 1-4] *I am hostile to* [with dative]; passive: *I am subject to.*

ἐπέχω [ἐπί + ἔχω] [V 2, DV 109, VP 1-4] transitive: *I hold firmly*; intransitive: *I pay attention to* [with dative]; *I stay.*

ἔχω [V 2, DV 109, VP 1-4] *I have.* Cf. Lesson 9.

κατέχω [κατά + ἔχω] [V 2, DV 109, VP 1-4] transitive: *I hold fast; I possess; I prevent*; intransitive: *I head toward.*

μετέχω [μετά + ἔχω] [V 2, DV 109, VP 1-4] *I have a share in* [with genitive or a preposition governing genitive].

προσέχω [πρός + ἔχω] [V 2, DV 109, VP 1-4] *I pay attention to, I give myself to* [with accusative or dative]; *I watch out for* [with ἀπό plus genitive].

συνέχω [σύν + ἔχω] [V 2, DV 109, VP 1-4] *I surround.*

ὑπερέχω [ὑπέρ + ἔχω [V 2, DV 109, VP 1-4] *I surpass.*

———

γεννάω [V 9; VP 1-3, 5-6] *I am father to; I give birth to.*

ἐπερωτάω [ἐπί + ἐρωτάω] [V 9; VP 1-3, 5-6] *I ask; I ask for.*

ἐπιτιμάω [ἐπί + τιμάω [V 9, VP 1-3, 5-6] *I order not to; I rebuke* [with dative of person].

ἐρωτάω [V 9, VP 1-3, 5-6] *I ask; I beg.*

θεάομαι [V 9, 22; VP 2-3, 6] *I see; I notice.*

καυχάομαι [V 9, 22; DV 147; VP 2-3, 6] *I boast; I boast about.*

κοπιάω [V 9, VP 1-3, 5-6] *I work hard; I become weary.*

τιμάω [V 9; VP 1-3, 5-6] *I honor.*

———

αὔριον [Adv 2] *tomorrow.*

οὐδέποτε [Adv 2] *never.*

Exercises for Lesson 49.

I. Translate into English:
1. πέντε γὰρ ἄνδρας ἔσχες, καὶ νῦν ὃν ἔχεις οὐκ ἔστιν σου ἀνήρ. (Jn 4:18)
2. καὶ ἐπηρώτα αὐτόν, Τί ὄνομά σοι; (Mk 5:9) [The dative is a dative of possession and functions like a genitive of possession.]
3. δευτέρα αὕτη, Ἀγαπήσεις τὸν πλησίον σου ὡς σεαυτόν. μείζων τούτων ἄλλη ἐντολὴ οὐκ ἔστιν. (Mk 12:31)
4. εἰς τοῦτο γὰρ κοπιῶμεν, ὅτι ἠλπίκαμεν ἐπὶ θεῷ ζῶντι, ὅς ἐστιν σωτὴρ πάντων ἀνθρώπων. (1 Tim 4:10)
5. ἡ δὲ γυνὴ ἐνεῖχεν τῷ προφήτῃ. (Mk 6:19)
6. προσέχετε δὲ τὴν δικαιοσύνην ὑμῶν μὴ ποιεῖν ἔμπροσθεν τῶν ἀνθρώπων πρὸς τὸ θεαθῆναι αὐτοῖς· εἰ δὲ μή γε, μισθὸν οὐκ ἔχετε παρὰ τῷ πατρὶ ὑμῶν τῷ ἐν τοῖς οὐρανοῖς. (Mt 6:1)
7. λέγει αὐτῷ ὁ Ἰησοῦς, Ὅτι ἑώρακάς με πεπίστευκας; μακάριοι οἱ μὴ ἰδόντες καὶ πιστεύσαντες. (Jn 20:29)
8. καὶ ἠρώτησεν αὐτὸν ἅπαν τὸ πλῆθος ἀπελθεῖν ἀπ' αὐτῶν, ὅτι φόβῳ μεγάλῳ συνείχοντο. (Lk 8:37)
9. οὕτως οὐδέποτε εἴδομεν. (Mk 2:12)
10. ὁ δὲ ἀνὴρ ἐπεῖχεν τοῖς ἀποστόλοις. (Acts 3:5)
11. καὶ ἐπετίμησεν αὐτῷ ὁ Ἰησοῦς λέγων, ἔξελθε ἀπ' αὐτοῦ. (Lk 4:35)
12. τίμα τὸν πατέρα σου καὶ τὴν μητέρα σου. (Mk 7:10)
13. καὶ τότε ὄψονται τὸν υἱὸν τοῦ ἀνθρώπου ἐρχόμενον ἐν νεφέλαις μετὰ δυνάμεως πολλῆς καὶ δόξης. (Mk 13:26)
14. ἐγένετο δὲ ἐπὶ τὴν αὔριον συναχθῆναι αὐτῶν τοὺς ἄρχοντας καὶ τοὺς πρεσβυτέρους καὶ τοὺς γραμματεῖς ἐν τῇ ἁγίᾳ πόλει. (Acts 4:5) [Here αὔριον, an adverb, is used as the object of the preposition. Thus the adverb functions as a noun since αὔριον represents ἡ αὔριον ἡμέρα.]
15. ὤφθη δὲ αὐτῷ ἄγγελος ἀπ' οὐρανοῦ. (Lk 22:43)
16. ὁ δὲ καυχώμενος ἐν κυρίῳ καυχάσθω. (2 Cor 10:17)
17. εἰ ἄλλοι τῆς ὑμῶν ἐξουσίας μετέχουσιν, οὐ μᾶλλον ἡμεῖς; (1 Cor 9:12)
18. καὶ οἱ ὄχλοι κατεῖχον τὸν Ἰησοῦν ἵνα μὴ ἀπέλθῃ ἀπ' αὐτῶν. (Lk 4:42)
19. καλὸν αὐτῷ εἰ οὐκ ἐγεννήθη ὁ ἄνθρωπος ἐκεῖνος. (Mk 14:21)

20. πᾶσα ψυχὴ ἐξουσίαις ὑπερεχούσαις ὑποτασσέσθω.
(Rom 13:1)

II. Translate into Greek:
1. Christ will be seen by those honoring him.
2. Seeing the unfaithful man Jesus rebuked him. (1 Cor 7:13;
Mt 17:18)
3. They have had five houses in this city. (Mt 10:23)

III. Mk 6:14-29.

ἀγαπάω, **Present Middle and Passive Indicative, Imperfect Middle and Passive Indicative, Present Middle and Passive Imperative, Subjunctive, Participle, and Infinitive. Difficult Verbs:** λέγω, αἴρω.

Lesson 50

ἀγαπάω, **Present Middle and Passive Indicative, Imperfect Middle and Passive Indicative, Present Middle and Passive Imperative, Subjunctive, Participle, and Infinitive.**

For an explanation of contract verbs cf. Lesson 46.

The moods of the present middle/passive of ἀγαπάω are conjugated as follows (cf. V 9; VP 1-3, 5-6; for the participle cf. also Adj 1):

	Middle and Passive Voices, Indicative Mood, Present Tense	
	Singular	Plural
1st Person	ἀγαπῶμαι	ἀγαπώμεθα
2nd Person	ἀγαπᾶσαι / ἀγαπᾷ	ἀγαπᾶσθε
3rd Person	ἀγαπᾶται	ἀγαπῶνται

The form ἀγαπᾶσαι comes from the form ἀγαπά–εσαι through the contraction of the vowels α + ε to produce ᾶ. The retention of –σαι is not found in classical Greek. The form ἀγαπᾷ comes from the same form ἀγαπά–εσαι and through the omission of σ but through a different set of contractions: ἀγαπά–εσαι > ἀγαπά–εαι > ἀγαπά–αι > ἀγαπᾶι > ἀγαπᾷ.

	Middle and Passive Voices, Indicative Mood, Imperfect Tense	
	Singular	Plural
1st Person	ἠγαπώμην	ἠγαπώμεθα
2nd Person	ἠγαπῶ	ἠγαπᾶσθε
3rd Person	ἠγαπᾶτο	ἠγαπῶντο

The form ἠγαπῶ comes from ἠγαπά–εσο through the omission
of a σ between two vowels and through contraction: ἠγαπά–εσο >
ἠγαπά–εο > ἠγαπά–ω > ἠγαπῶ.

Middle and Passive Voices, Imperative Mood, Present Tense

	Singular	Plural
2nd Person	ἀγαπῶ	ἀγαπᾶσθε
3rd Person	ἀγαπάσθω	ἀγαπάσθωσαν

Middle and Passive Voices, Subjunctive Mood, Present Tense

	Singular	Plural
1st Person	ἀγαπῶμαι	ἀγαπώμεθα
2nd Person	ἀγαπᾷ	ἀγαπᾶσθε
3rd Person	ἀγαπᾶται	ἀγαπῶνται

The form ἀγαπᾷ comes from the form ἀγαπά–ησαι through
the omission of σ and through contraction: ἀγαπά–ησαι > ἀγαπά–
ηαι > ἀγαπά–αι > ἀγαπᾶι > ἀγαπᾷ.

As was noted in Lesson 49, the present indicative and the
present subjunctive are distinguishable only by the context. But it
should also be noted that in the middle/passive the forms of the
second person singular are different. The second person
middle/passive singular can be confused with the third person
singular of the active.

In the New Testament there is no middle/passive present
optative of contract verbs in –αω.

Middle and Passive Voices, Participial Mood, Present Tense

Singular

	Masculine	Feminine	Neuter
n	ἀγαπώμενος	ἀγαπωμένη	ἀγαπώμενον
v	ἀγαπώμενε	ἀγαπωμένη	ἀγαπώμενον
g	ἀγαπωμένου	ἀγαπωμένης	ἀγαπωμένου
d	ἀγαπωμένῳ	ἀγαπωμένῃ	ἀγαπωμένῳ
a	ἀγαπώμενον	ἀγαπωμένην	ἀγαπώμενον

	Masculine	Plural Feminine	Neuter
n	ἀγαπώμενοι	ἀγαπώμεναι	ἀγαπώμενα
v	ἀγαπώμενοι	ἀγαπώμεναι	ἀγαπώμενα
g	ἀγαπωμένων	ἀγαπωμένων	ἀγαπωμένων
d	ἀγαπωμένοις	ἀγαπωμέναις	ἀγαπωμένοις
a	ἀγαπωμένους	ἀγαπωμένας	ἀγαπώμενα

The present infinitive middle/passive is ἀγαπᾶσθαι.

It is important to recall again that the listing of these forms as "middle/passive" does not mean that the occurrence of one of these forms in a text can be both middle and passive at one and the same time. The form in a given context must be one or the other. Even if the text is ambiguous and either alternative is possible a form cannot be both middle and passive at one and the same time in the same way.

Difficult Verbs: λέγω, αἴρω.

λέγω, *I say, I speak* [V 2; DV 179; VP 1-3, 4]

λέγω Mt 1:20	ἐρῶ Mt 7:4	εἶπον Mt 2:8	εἴρηκα Mt 26:75	εἴρημαι Lk 2:24	ἐρρέθην Mt 5:21
					ἐρρήθην Mt 1:22

The aorist active of this important verb is strong, with an irregular augment: the unaugmented root is εἰπ– and the augmented form is the same (hence the unaugmented forms are εἰπεῖν, εἰπών, etc.). The unaugmented form of the aorist passive has only one ρ; as a result the aorist participle masculine nominative singular, for example, is ῥηθείς.

The form εἶπε(ν), *he (she, it) said*, given in Lesson 2, is the third person singular of the aorist indicative active of λέγω.

There is another verb λέγω. It means *I gather* and has different principal parts (cf. DV 117, λέγω II). In the New Testament it is found only in compounded forms.

The aorist imperative active second person singular is accented εἰπέ (cf. above, Rules for Accents 34, Lesson 45).

αἴρω, *I take up* [V 6; DV 8; VP 1-3, 5-6]

αἴρω	ἀρῶ	ἦρα	ἦρκα	ἦρμαι	ἤρθην
Mt 9:16	Mt 4:6	Mt 9:6	Col 2:14	Jn 20:1	Mt 21:21

     This verb has a ι in the present stem. Elsewhere the stem is ἀρ-. In the future the verb follows the rules for a liquid.

Vocabulary for Lesson 50.

λέγω [V 2; DV 179; VP 1-3, 4] *I say; I speak.*

αἴρω [V 6; DV 8; VP 1-3] *I raise; I lift up.*

ἐπαίρω [ἐπί + αἴρω] [V 6; DV 8; VP 1-3] *I raise; I lift up.*

βοάω [V 9; VP 1-3, 5-6] *I call out.*

διψάω [V 9; VP 1-3, 5-6] *I am thirsty.*

ἰάομαι [V 9, V 22; DV 130; VP 1-3, 6] *I heal; I restore.*

κλάω [V 9; DV 156 (note the irregularity: α remains in the aorist—ἔκλασα; cf. Lesson 49); VP 1-3, 5-6] *I break.*

κοιμάομαι [V 9, V 23; VP 3, 6] *I sleep; I fall asleep.*

μεριμνάω [V 9; VP 1-3, 5-6] *I am anxious.* Often used with genitive.

νικάω [V 9; VP 1-3, 5-6] *I conquer; I win.*

πεινάω [V 9; DV 236 (note the irregularity: α remains in the aorist—ἐπείνασα); VP 1-3, 5-6] *I am hungry.*

πλανάω [V 9; VP 1-3, 5-6] *I lead astray; I deceive.*

προσδοκάω [πρός + δοκάω] [V 9; VP 1-3, 5-6] *I wait for.*

τολμάω [V 9; VP 1-3, 5-6] *I dare.*

χράομαι [V 9, 22; DV 342 (α becomes η in the aorist—ἐχρησάμην; cf. Lesson 49); VP 2-3, 6] *I use; I make use of* [with dative].

———
ἅπαξ [Adv 2] *once.*

ὅθεν [Adv 1, 3] *from where; where; whence* [logical inference].

Exercises for Lesson 50.

I. Translate into English:
1. μὴ νικῶ ὑπὸ τοῦ κακοῦ, ἀλλὰ νίκα ἐν τῷ ἀγαθῷ τὸ κακόν. (Rom 12:21)
2. καὶ αὐτὸς ἐπάρας τοὺς ὀφθαλμοὺς αὐτοῦ εἰς τοὺς μαθητὰς αὐτοῦ ἔλεγεν, Μακάριοι οἱ πτωχοί, ὅτι ὑμετέρα ἐστὶν ἡ βασιλεία τοῦ θεοῦ. (Lk 6:20)
3. ὁ φίλος ἡμῶν κεκοίμηται. (Jn 11:11)
4. ὅθεν, ἀδελφοὶ ἅγιοι, δεῖ ἀκολουθῆσαι τῷ Κυρίῳ. (Heb 3:1)
5. μόνον εἰπὲ λόγῳ καὶ ἰαθήσεται ὁ παῖς μου. (Mt 8:8) [λόγῳ is a dative of means: "say by a word", i.e., "say a word".]
6. καὶ ἐάν τις ὑμῖν εἴπῃ, Διὰ τί ποιεῖτε τοῦτο; εἴπατε, Ὁ κύριος αὐτοῦ χρείαν ἔχει. (Mk 11:3)
7. καὶ οὐδεὶς οὐκέτι ἐτόλμα αὐτὸν ἐπερωτῆσαι. (Mk 12:34)
8. μὴ οὖν μεριμνήσητε εἰς τὴν αὔριον, ἡ γὰρ αὔριον μεριμνήσει ἑαυτῆς. (Mt 6:34) [μεριμνήσητε is an aorist subjunctive used in a prohibition—cf. Lesson 72.]
9. ἀμὴν λέγω ὑμῖν ὅτι ὃς ἂν εἴπῃ τῷ ὄρει τούτῳ, Ἄρθητι καὶ βλήθητι εἰς τὴν θάλασσαν, καὶ μὴ διακριθῇ ἐν τῇ καρδίᾳ αὐτοῦ ἀλλὰ πιστεύῃ ὅτι ὃ λαλεῖ γίνεται, ἔσται αὐτῷ. (Mk 11:23)
10. οὐκ ἔστιν θεὸς νεκρῶν· πολὺ πλανᾶσθε. (Mk 12:27)
11. καὶ ἐβόησεν ὁ Ἰησοῦς φωνῇ μεγάλῃ. (Mk 15:34) [φωνῇ μεγάλῃ is a dative of manner.]
12. ὁ Λόγος σὰρξ ἐγένετο ἅπαξ ἐν τούτῳ τῷ κόσμῳ. (Jn 1:14)

II. Translate into Greek:
1. He will come and lead many astray. (Mt 24:5)
2. I was thirsty and there was no water.
3. Being thirsty he came to the water.

III. Mk 6:30-44.

Rules for Contraction of–o Contracts.
Principal Parts of–o Contracts. φανερόω,
Present Active Indicative, Imperfect Active
Indicative, Present Active Imperative,
Subjunctive, Participle, and Infinitive.
Difficult Verbs: φέρω, ἐγείρω.

Lesson 51

Rules for Contraction of–o Contracts.

For an introduction to contract verbs cf. above, Lesson 46.
    The rules of contraction for roots ending in o are as follows:
        o + a long vowel > ω (φανερό–ητε > φανερῶτε)
        o + a short vowel > ου (φανερό–ομεν > φανερούμεν);
        o before ου is absorbed (φανερό–ουσι > φανερούσι);
        o + any diphthong with ι or iota subscript, results in the
            diphthong οι (φανερό–εις > φανεροῖς, φανερό–ης >
            φανεροῖς).
    The final result is always an "o" sound.

Principal Parts of–o Contracts.

In the other principal parts of φανερόω the root is lengthened to ω:

φανερό–ω   φανερώ–σω   ἐφανέρω–σα   πεφανέρω–κα

        πεφανέρω–μαι   ἐφανερώ–θην

φανερόω, Present Active Indicative, Imperfect Active Indicative, Present Active Imperative, Subjunctive, Participle, and Infinitive.

The present active system of φανερόω, *I make manifest*, is as follows
(cf. V 10; VP 1-3, 5-6; for the participle, Adj 10):

Active Voice, Indicative Mood, Present Tense

	Singular	Plural
1st Person	φανερῶ	φανεροῦμεν
2nd Person	φανεροῖς	φανεροῦτε
3rd Person	φανεροῖ	φανεροῦσι(ν)

Active Voice, Indicative Mood, Imperfect Tense

	Singular	Plural
1st Person	ἐφανέρουν	ἐφανεροῦμεν
2nd Person	ἐφανέρους	ἐφανεροῦτε
3rd Person	ἐφανέρου	ἐφανέρουν

Active Voice, Imperative Mood, Present Tense

	Singular	Plural
2nd Person	φανέρου	φανεροῦτε
3rd Person	φανερούτω	φανερούτωσαν

Active Voice, Subjunctive Mood, Present Tense

	Singular	Plural
1st Person	φανερῶ	φανερῶμεν
2nd Person	φανεροῖς	φανερῶτε
3rd Person	φανεροῖ	φανερῶσι(ν)

It should be noted that the singular forms are the same as the singular forms for the indicative.

The present optative of contract verbs is not found in the New Testament.

Active Voice, Participial Mood, Present Tense
Singular

	Masculine	Feminine	Neuter
n	φανερῶν	φανεροῦσα	φανεροῦν
v	φανερῶν	φανεροῦσα	φανεροῦν
g	φανεροῦντος	φανερούσης	φανεροῦντος
d	φανεροῦντι	φανερούσῃ	φανεροῦντι
a	φανεροῦντα	φανεροῦσαν	φανεροῦν

	Masculine	Plural Feminine	Neuter
n	φανεροῦντες	φανεροῦσαι	φανεροῦντα
v	φανεροῦντες	φανεροῦσαι	φανεροῦντα
g	φανερούντων	φανερουσῶν	φανερούντων
d	φανεροῦσι(ν)	φανερούσαις	φανεροῦσι(ν)
a	φανεροῦντας	φανερούσας	φανεροῦντα

The present active infinitive is φανεροῦν.

There is no iota subscript or diphthong with ι in the present active infinitive because the present infinitive ending itself is a contraction of the original vowels ε–εν. Hence, φανερό–ε–εν > φανεροῦ–εν > φανεροῦν.

The rules for accentuation have been given above, in Lesson 46.

The middle/passive voices will be given in Lesson 52.

Difficult Verbs: φέρω, ἐγείρω.

φέρω, *I bring*; *I carry*; *I bear*; *I endure* [V 6, DV 197, VP 1-4]

φέρω	οἴσω	ἤνεγκον	ἐνήνοχα	—	ἠνέχθην
Mt 14:18	Jn 21:18	Mt 14:11	Heb 11:17		Mt 14:11

There are three different roots. The active aorist is strong, although it can have weak endings. The perfect active is also strong. The perfect middle/passive is not found in the New Testament.

ἐγείρω, *I raise up*; *I arise* [V 6, DV 46, VP 1-3]

ἐγείρω	ἐγερῶ	ἤγειρα	—	ἐγήγερμαι	ἠγέρθην
Mt 10:8	Mt 12:11	Mt 3:9		Mt 11:11	Mt 1:24

The future is contracted as is normal for liquid roots. The aorist active has the last syllable of the stem lengthened, as is also normal. There is no perfect active in the New Testament.

Vocabulary for Lesson 51.

ἀναφέρω [ἀνά + φέρω] [V 6, DV 324, VP 1-4] *I offer (sacrifice); I take up.*

διαφέρω [διά + φέρω] [V 6, DV 324, VP 1-4] transitive: *I carry through*; intransitive: *I am different from, I am better than* [with genitive].

προσφέρω [πρός + φέρω] [V 6, DV 324, VP 1-4] *I offer (sacrifice); I bring.*

συμφέρω [σύν + φέρω] [V 6, 19; DV 324; VP 1-4] usually used impersonally: *it is useful, it is profitable; it is better; it is good* [This verb is often found followed by an infinitive or by a ἵνα noun clause—cf. Lesson 75].

φέρω [V 6, DV 324, VP 1-4] *I bring; I carry; I bear; I endure.*

―――

ἐγείρω [V 6, DV 70, VP 1-3] transitive: *I raise up*; intransitive: *I arise.* Note that in the present active and in aorist passive the meaning is sometimes equivalent to the intransitive active: *I arise, I arose.*

―――

δικαιόω [V 10; VP 1-3, 5-6] *I make righteous; I declare righteous.*

θανατόω [V 10; VP 1-3, 5-6] *I put to death.*

κοινόω [V 10; VP 1-3, 5-6] *I make unclean; I defile.*

ὁμοιόω [V 10; VP 1-3, 5-6] *I make like*; passive: *I resemble.*

σταυρόω [V 10; VP 1-3, 5-6] *I crucify.*

τελειόω [V 10; VP 1-3, 5-6] *I make perfect.*

ὑψόω [V 10; VP 1-3, 5-6] *I exalt; I lift up.*

φανερόω [V 10; VP 1-3, 5-6] *I make manifest; I make clear.*

―――

ἄνωθεν [Adv 1, 2] *from above; from the beginning; again.*

μακρόθεν [Adv 1] *far off* [usually found as object of the preposition ἀπό: *from far off, from afar*].

Exercises for Lesson 51.

I. Translate into English:

1. ὥστε ἀδελφοί μου, καὶ ὑμεῖς ἐθανατώθητε τῷ νόμῳ διὰ τοῦ σώματος τοῦ Χριστοῦ. (Rom 7:4)
2. καὶ καθὼς ὁ προφήτης ὕψωσεν τὸν ὄφιν ἐν τῇ ἐρήμῳ, οὕτως ὑψωθῆναι δεῖ τὸν υἱὸν τοῦ ἀνθρώπου, ἵνα πᾶς ὁ πιστεύων ἐν αὐτῷ ἔχῃ ζωὴν αἰώνιον. (Jn 3:14-15)
3. ἄλλος σε οἴσει ὅπου οὐ θέλεις. (Jn 21:18)
4. ἐγερθήσεται γὰρ ἔθνος ἐπ᾽ ἔθνος καὶ βασιλεία ἐπὶ βασιλείαν. (Mt 24:7)
5. οὐχ ὑμεῖς μᾶλλον διαφέρετε αὐτῶν; (Mt 6:26)
6. ἦσαν δὲ ἐκεῖ γυναῖκες πόλλαι ἀπὸ μακρόθεν θεωροῦσαι, αἵτινες ἠκολούθησαν τῷ Ἰησοῦ. (Mt 27:55)
7. καὶ ἀπεκρίθη αὐτῷ εἷς ἐκ τοῦ ὄχλου, Διδάσκαλε, ἤνεγκα τὸν υἱόν μου πρὸς σέ, ἔχοντα πνεῦμα κακόν. (Mk 9:17)
8. εἰ γὰρ νεκροὶ οὐκ ἐγείρονται, οὐδὲ Χριστὸς ἐγήγερται. (1 Cor 15:16)
9. τίνι δὲ ὁμοιώσω τὴν γενεὰν ταύτην; (Mt 11:16)
10. αὐτὸς οὐκ ἔχει καθ᾽ ἡμέραν ἀνάγκην, ὥσπερ οἱ ἀρχιερεῖς, ὑπὲρ τῶν ἰδίων ἁμαρτιῶν θυσίας ἀναφέρειν. (Heb 7:27)
11. δεῖ ὑμᾶς γεννηθῆναι ἄνωθεν. (Jn 3:7)
12. τί οὖν ποιήσω Ἰησοῦν τὸν λεγόμενον Χριστόν; λέγουσιν πάντες, Σταυρωθήτω. (Mt 27:22)
13. τότε προσηνέχθησαν αὐτῷ παιδία. (Mt 19:13)
14. ὁ δὲ ποιῶν τὴν ἀλήθειαν ἔρχεται πρὸς τὸ φῶς, ἵνα φανερωθῇ αὐτοῦ τὰ ἔργα. (Jn 3:21)
15. ἀλλ᾽ ἐγὼ τὴν ἀλήθειαν λέγω ὑμῖν, συμφέρει ὑμῖν ἵνα ἐγὼ ἀπέλθω. (Jn 16:7) [Cf. Lesson 75 for the use of ἵνα to introduce a noun clause.]
16. οὐ τὸ εἰσερχόμενον εἰς τὸ στόμα κοινοῖ τὸν ἄνθρωπον, ἀλλὰ τὸ ἐκπορευόμενον ἐκ τοῦ στόματος τοῦτο κοινοῖ τὸν ἄνθρωπον. (Mt 15:11) [Cf. Lesson 34, Vocabulary, for meaning of ἐκπορεύομαι.]
17. καὶ προσελθὼν ἤγειρεν αὐτὴν κρατήσας τῆς χειρός. (Mk 1:31)
18. οὐδὲν γὰρ ἐτελείωσεν ὁ νόμος. (Heb 7:19)

19. δικαιωθέντες οὖν ἐκ πίστεως εἰρήνην ἔχομεν πρὸς τὸν θεὸν διὰ τοῦ σώματος τοῦ Χριστοῦ. (Rom 5:1)

20. ἀπεκρίθη Ἰησοῦς καὶ εἶπεν αὐτοῖς, Λύσατε τὸν ναὸν τοῦτον καὶ ἐν τρισὶν ἡμέραις ἐγερῶ αὐτόν. (Jn 2:19)

21. ἔγειρε καὶ περιπάτει. (Lk 5:23)

22. δύναμις παρ᾽ αὐτοῦ ἐξήρχετο καὶ ἰᾶτο πάντας. (Lk 6:19)

23. τί ἐποίησεν ὁ ἡγεμών, ὅτε χρείαν ἔσχεν καὶ ἐπείνασεν αὐτὸς καὶ οἱ μετ᾽ αὐτοῦ; (Mk 2:25) [Cf. DV 236 for the form ἐπείνασεν.]

24. ἦσαν γὰρ πάντες προσδοκῶντες αὐτόν. (Lk 8:40)

25. οἴνῳ ὀλίγῳ χρῶ διὰ τὸ σῶμα. (1 Tim 5:23)

26. καὶ ὁ διψῶν ἐρχέσθω. (Apoc 22:17)

II. Translate into Greek:
  1. The soldiers brought the slaves to the king.
  2. Jesus was wishing to make manifest the glory of the Father. (Phil 2:11)
  3. God raised up the Lord Jesus from the dead. (Acts 4:10)

III. Mk 6:45-56.

φανερόω, **Present Middle and Passive Indicative, Imperfect Middle and Passive Indicative, Present Middle and Passive Imperative, Participle, and Infinitive. The Periphrastic Construction. Difficult Verbs:** λαμβάνω, ἀποθνῄσκω.

Lesson 52

φανερόω, Present Middle and Passive Indicative, Imperfect Middle and Passive Indicative, Present Middle and Passive Imperative, Subjunctive, Participle, and Infinitive.

The moods of the present middle and passive systems of φανερόω are conjugated as follows (cf. V 10; VP 1-3, 5-6; for participle, cf. Adj 1):

	Middle and Passive Voices, Indicative Mood, Present Tense	
	Singular	Plural
1st Person	φανεροῦμαι	φανερούμεθα
2nd Person	φανεροῖ	φανεροῦσθε
3rd Person	φανεροῦται	φανεροῦνται

The form φανεροῖ comes from φανερό–εσαι (φανερό–εσαι > φανερό–εαι > φανερό–ηι > φανεροῖ).

	Middle and Passsive Voices, Indicative Mood, Imperfect Tense	
1st Person	ἐφανερούμην	ἐφανερούμεθα
2nd Person	ἐφανεροῦ	ἐφανεροῦσθε
3rd Person	ἐφανεροῦτο	ἐφανεροῦντο

The form ἐφανεροῦ comes from ἐφανερό–εσο (ἐφανερό–εσο > ἐφανερό–εο > ἐφανερό–ου > ἐφανεροῦ).

	Middle and Passive Voices, Imperative Mood, Present Tense	
2nd Person	φανεροῦ	φανεροῦσθε
3rd Person	φανερούσθω	φανερούσθωσαν

The form φανεροῦ comes from φανερό–εσο (φανερό–εσο >
φανερό–ου > φανεροῦ).

	Middle and Passive Voices, Subjunctive Mood, Present Tense	
1st Person	φανερῶμαι	φανερώμεθα
2nd Person	φανεροῖ	φανερῶσθε
3rd Person	φανερῶται	φανερῶνται

The form φανεροῖ comes from φανερό–ησαι (φανερό–ηαι >
φανερό–ηι > φανεροῖ).

The present optative of contract verbs is not found in the New
Testament.

Middle and Passive Voices, Participial Mood, Present Tense
Singular

	Masculine	Feminine	Neuter
n	φανερούμενος	φανερουμένη	φανερούμενον
v	φανερούμενε	φανερουμένη	φανερούμενον
g	φανερουμένου	φανερουμένης	φανερουμένου
d	φανερουμένῳ	φανερουμένη	φανερουμένῳ
a	φανερούμενον	φανερουμένην	φανερούμενον

Plural

	Masculine	Feminine	Neuter
n	φανερούμενοι	φανερούμεναι	φανερούμενα
v	φανερούμενοι	φανερούμεναι	φανερούμενα
g	φανερουμένων	φανερουμένων	φανερουμένων
d	φανερουμένοις	φανερουμέναις	φανερουμένοις
a	φανερουμένους	φανερουμένας	φανερούμενα

The infinitive for the present middle and passive is
φανεροῦσθαι.

It is important to recall that the listing of these forms as
"middle and passive" does not mean that the occurrence of one of
these forms in a text can be both middle and passive at one and the
same time. It must be one or the other. Even if the text is
ambiguous and either alternative is possible, they cannot both be
possible at one and the same time in one and the same way.

The Periphrastic Construction.

In New Testament Greek there are a number of texts in which a
participle (present for the most part, but occasionally a perfect) is
used with a form of the verb εἰμί. Sometimes this combination
seems to be used to emphasize the duration of the action in question
or the duration of the result of the action. But often there seems to be
no reason for using this combination rather than the ordinary form
of the verb without εἰμί. This use of the participle with εἰμί is called
the "periphrastic construction". The construction has already been
seen in the formation of the perfect active, middle, and passive
subjunctive and optative (cf. above, Lessons 25, 35, and 42).

> ὁ μαθητὴς βαπτίζων ἐστὶν ἐν τῷ ποταμῷ.
> *The disciple is baptizing in the river.*

> ὁ μαθητὴς βαπτίζων ἦν ἐν τῷ ποταμῷ.
> *The disciple was baptizing in the river.*

> ὁ μαθητὴς βαπτίζων ἔσται ἐν τῷ ποταμῷ.
> *The disciple will be baptizing in the river.*

Difficult Verbs: λαμβάνω, ἀποθνῄσκω.

λαμβάνω, *I take; I receive* [V 7, DV 176, VP 1-4]

λαμβάνω	λή(μ)ψομαι	ἔλαβον	εἴληφα	εἴλημμαι	ἐλήμφθην
Mt 7:8	Mt 10:41	Mt 5:40	Apoc 3:3	Jn 8:4	Phil 3:12

The future is a middle deponent (in some texts the μ is
omitted). The aorist active is strong. The reduplication in the
perfect system is irregular.

ἀποθνῄσκω, *I die* [V 2, 18; DV 127; VP 1-4]

ἀποθνῄσκω	ἀποθανοῦμαι	ἀπέθανον	τέθνηκα	---	---
Mk 12:20	Rom 5:7	Mt 8:32	Jn 11:44		

The future is a middle deponent with the accentuation proper
to a liquid stem. The aorist active is strong. The iota subscript is
found only in the present system. The perfect has present force: *I
am dead.*

Vocabulary for Lesson 52.

ἀναλαμβάνω [ἀνά + λαμβάνω] [V 7, DV 176, VP 1-4] *I take up; I take.*

ἀπολαμβάνω [ἀπό + λαμβάνω] [V 7, DV 176, VP 1-4] *I get back; I receive* [middle: *I take aside*].

ἐπιλαμβάνομαι [ἐπί + λαμβάνομαι] [V 7, 22; DV 176; VP 2-4] *I take hold of, I seize, I arrest* [with genitive or accusative].

καταλαμβάνω [κατά + λαμβάνω] [V 7, DV 176, VP 1-4] *I obtain; I overtake.*

λαμβάνω [V 7, DV 176, VP 1-4] *I take; I receive.*

παραλαμβάνω [παρά + λαμβάνω] [V 7, DV 176, VP 1-4] *I take; I accept.*

προσλαμβάνομαι [πρός + λαμβάνομαι] [V 7, 22; DV 176; VP 1-4] *I welcome; I take aside.*

συλλαμβάνω [σύν + λαμβάνω] [V 7, DV 176, VP 1-4] *I seize; I become pregnant; I catch (fish).*

———

ἀποθνήσκω [ἀπό + θνήσκω] [V 2, 18; DV 127; VP 1-4] *I die* [perfect has present force: *I am dead*].

———

ἅπτομαι [V 4, 5, 22; DV 22; VP 2-3] *I touch* [with genitive]. In the active voice this verb is found with the meaning *I kindle (a fire)*, but this is rare in the New Testament.

εὐχαριστέω [εὖ + χαριστέω—εὖ is an adverb meaning *well*. Cf. Lesson 79.] The augmented form in the New Testament does not prefix an ε before the root and does not modify the prefix ευ so that as a result the augmented form is the same as the unaugmented] [V 8; VP 1-3, 5-6] *I give thanks.*

θαυμάζω (θαυμάσω) [V 5, DV 120, VP 1-3] transitive: *I admire*; intransitive: *I marvel at, I am amazed* [This verb is usually in the active voice in the New Testament, although the passive voice is occasionally used (cf. Apoc 13:3).].

μισέω [V 8, VP 1-3, 5-6] *I hate.*

ὑπάρχω [ὑπό + ἄρχω] [V 2, DV 28, VP 1-3] *I am*. The neuter plural of the present active participle, ὑπάρχοντα, is used with the meaning *possessions*.

φωνέω [V 8, VP 1-3, 4-5] *I call; I summon*.

εἶτα [Adv 2, 3] *then; moreover*.

πρίν [Conj] *before*. Normally this conjunction takes the accusative with the infinitive, but it is sometimes found with the subjunctive, especially after a negative principal clause.

Exercises for Lesson 52.

I. Translate into English:
1. εἶπεν δὲ αὐτοῖς, Ποῦ ἡ πίστις ὑμῶν; φοβηθέντες δὲ ἐθαύμασαν. (Lk 8:25)
2. καὶ ἐπιλαβόμενος ἰάσατο αὐτὸν καὶ ἀπέλυσεν. (Lk 14:4)
3. καὶ ἦν αὐτῷ εἰρημένον ὑπὸ τοῦ πνεύματος τοῦ ἁγίου μὴ ἰδεῖν θάνατον πρὶν [ἢ] ἂν ἴδῃ τὸν Χριστὸν κυρίου. (Lk 2:26)
4. ἔλαβεν δὲ φόβος πάντας, καὶ ἐδόξαζον τὸν θεὸν λέγοντες ὅτι Προφήτης μέγας ἠγέρθη ἐν ἡμῖν. (Lk 7:16)
5. εἶπεν οὖν πάλιν αὐτοῖς, Ἐγὼ ὑπάγω καὶ ζητήσετέ με, καὶ ἐν τῇ ἁμαρτίᾳ ὑμῶν ἀποθανεῖσθε. (Jn 8:21)
6. καὶ τὸ πνεῦμα φωνῆσαν φωνῇ μεγάλῃ ἐξῆλθεν ἐξ αὐτοῦ. (Mk 1:26)
7. οἱ δὲ παρὰ τὴν ὁδόν εἰσιν οἱ ἀκούσαντες, εἶτα ἔρχεται ὁ διάβολος καὶ αἴρει τὸν λόγον ἀπὸ τῆς καρδίας αὐτῶν, ἵνα μὴ πιστεύσαντες σωθῶσιν. (Lk 8:12)
8. εἰς τὰ ἴδια ἦλθεν, καὶ οἱ ἴδιοι αὐτὸν οὐ παρέλαβον. (Jn 1:11)
9. ὁ μὲν οὖν κύριος Ἰησοῦς μετὰ τὸ λαλῆσαι αὐτοῖς ἀνελήμφθη εἰς τὸν οὐρανὸν καὶ ἐκάθισεν ἐκ δεξιῶν τοῦ θεοῦ. (Mk 16:19)
10. καὶ ἔσεσθε μισούμενοι ὑπὸ πάντων διὰ τὸ ὄνομά μου. ὁ δὲ ὑπομείνας εἰς τέλος οὗτος σωθήσεται. (Mk 13:13)
11. ἔλεγεν γὰρ ἐν ἑαυτῇ, Ἐὰν μόνον ἅψωμαι τοῦ ἱματίου αὐτοῦ σωθήσομαι. (Mt 9:21)
12. ἀπέλαβες τὰ ἀγαθά σου ἐν τῇ ζωῇ σου. (Lk 16:25)
13. καὶ ἰδοὺ ἦλθεν ἀνήρ, καὶ οὗτος ἄρχων τῆς συναγωγῆς ὑπῆρχεν. (Lk 8:41)

14. καὶ προσλαβόμενος αὐτὸν ὁ ἀπόστολος ἤρξατο
    ἐπιτιμᾶν αὐτῷ. (Mt 16:22)
15. ἦραν οὖν τὸν λίθον. ὁ δὲ Ἰησοῦς ἦρεν τοὺς
    ὀφθαλμοὺς καὶ εἶπεν, Πάτερ, εὐχαριστῶ σοι ὅτι
    ἤκουσάς μου. (Jn 11:41)
16. εἶπεν οὖν αὐτοῖς ὁ Ἰησοῦς, Ἔτι μικρὸν χρόνον
    τὸ φῶς ἐν ὑμῖν ἐστιν. περιπατεῖτε ὡς τὸ φῶς ἔχετε,
    μὴ σκοτία ὑμᾶς καταλάβῃ. (Jn 12:35) [μικρὸν
    χρόνον is an accusative to express duration of time—cf.
    Lesson 79.]
17. συλλαβὼν δὲ αὐτὸν ἤγαγε καὶ εἰσήγαγεν εἰς τὴν
    οἰκίαν τοῦ ἀρχιερέως. (Lk 22:54)

II. Translate into Greek:
    1. Manifest yourself! (Jn 7:4)
    2. I have received the witness of the prophet.
    3. We shall die but we shall not go away from the Lord.

III. Now that Mk 1 – 6 have been read twice, the student is prepared
     to begin reading new sections of Mark with ever greater
     comprehension. For the present lesson, Mk 7:1-30 should be
     read, at first without the consultation of any aids, with
     reliance entirely on memory. Then the text should be re-read,
     with any doubtful points being checked against the material
     already seen. Finally, the verses should be read aloud at least
     three times.

γινώσκω, **Aorist Active Indicative,**
Imperative, Subjunctive, Participle, and
Infinitive. βαίνω, **Aorist Active Indicative,**
Imperative, Subjunctive, Participle, and
Infinitive. Difficult Verbs: γινώσκω,
βαίνω.

Lesson 53

γινώσκω, **Aorist Active Indicative, Imperative, Subjunctive, Participle, and Infinitive.**

Several verbs conjugated like λύω have special forms, and are
important enough to merit special treatment.

The verb γινώσκω, *I know*, is an irregular verb but with
regular endings for the irregular stems except for the aorist active
system (there are no aorist middle forms). The aorist active forms of
γινώσκω are as follows (cf. V 2, 18, 21; DV 50; VP 1-3):

	Indicative Mood, Active Voice, Aorist Tense	
	Singular	Plural
1st Person	ἔγνων	ἔγνωμεν
2nd Person	ἔγνως	ἔγνωτε
3rd Person	ἔγνω	ἔγνωσαν

	Imperative Mood, Active Voice, Aorist Tense	
	Singular	Plural
2nd Person	γνῶθι	γνῶτε
3rd Person	γνώτω	γνώτωσαν

	Active Voice, Subjunctive Mood, Aorist Tense	
	Singular	Plural
1st Person	γνῶ	γνῶμεν
2nd Person	γνῷς	γνῶτε
3rd Person	γνῷ / γνοῖ	γνῶσι(ν)

The form γνοῖ as a possible source of confusion with an optative should be noted. The aorist optative is not found in the New Testament.

Active Voice, Participial Mood, Aorist Tense

Singular

	Masculine	Feminine	Neuter
n	γνούς	γνοῦσα	γνόν
v	γνούς	γνοῦσα	γνόν
g	γνόντος	γνούσης	γνόντος
d	γνόντι	γνούσῃ	γνόντι
a	γνόντα	γνοῦσαν	γνόν

Plural

	Masculine	Feminine	Neuter
n	γνόντες	γνοῦσαι	γνόντα
v	γνόντες	γνοῦσαι	γνόντα
g	γνόντων	γνουσῶν	γνόντων
d	γνοῦσι(ν)	γνούσαις	γνοῦσι(ν)
a	γνόντας	γνούσας	γνόντα

The infinitive is γνῶναι.

βαίνω, Aorist Active Indicative, Imperative, Subjunctive, Active Participle, Infinitive.

The simple verb βαίνω *I walk, I go,* is not found in the New Testament, but there are numerous compounds based on it. It is irregular, but with regular endings except in the aorist active. The aorist active has special forms throughout and is conjugated as follows (cf. V 7, DV 31, VP 1-2; for the participle, cf. Adj 12):

Active Voice, Indicative Mood, Aorist Tense

	Singular	Plural
1st Person	ἔβην	ἔβημεν
2nd Person	ἔβης	ἔβητε
3rd Person	ἔβη	ἔβησαν

Active Voice, Imperative Mood, Aorist Tense
	Singular	Plural
2nd Person	βῆθι / βά	βάτε / βῆτε
3rd Person	βάτω / βήτω	βάτωσαν

Active Voice, Subjunctive Mood, Aorist Tense
	Singular	Plural
1st Person	βῶ	βῶμεν
2nd Person	βῇς	βῆτε
3rd Person	βῇ	βῶσι(ν)

The aorist optative is not found in the New Testament.

Active Voice, Participial Mood, Aorist Tense

	Singular		
	Masculine	Feminine	Neuter
n	βάς	βᾶσα	βάν
v	βάς	βᾶσα	βάν
g	βάντος	βάσης	βάντος
d	βάντι	βάσῃ	βάντι
a	βάντα	βᾶσαν	βάν

	Plural		
	Masculine	Feminine	Neuter
n	βάντες	βᾶσαι	βάντα
v	βάντες	βᾶσαι	βάντα
g	βάντων	βασῶν	βάντων
d	βᾶσι(ν)	βάσαις	βᾶσι(ν)
a	βάντας	βάσας	βάντα

The aorist infinitive active is βῆναι.

Difficult Verbs: γινώσκω, βαίνω.

γινώσκω, *I know*; *I learn* [V 2, 18, 21; DV 50; VP 1-3]

γινώσκω	γνώσομαι	ἔγνων	ἔγνωκα	ἔγνωσμαι	ἐγνώσθην
Mt 1:25	Lk 1:18	Mt 7:23	Jn 5:42	1 Cor 8:3	Gal 4:9

Instead of a future active there is a future middle deponent.
The reduplication of the perfect system is irregular. The aorist has
special forms throughout, as is explained in the first part of the
lesson. The perfect active has a present meaning.

βαίνω, *I walk; I go* [V 7, DV 31, VP 1-2]

| βαίνω | βήσομαι | ἔβην | βέβηκα | --- | --- |
| Mt 20:17 | Rom 10:6 | Mt 3:16 | Jn 3:13 | | |

Instead of a future active there is a future middle deponent.
The perfect middle/passive and aorist passive exist only in the
compound forms; none of them are found in the New Testament.
The aorist has special forms throughout as explained above in this
lesson.

Vocabulary for Lesson 53.

ἀναγινώσκω [ἀνά + γινώσκω] [V 2, 18, 21 DV 50; VP 1-3] *I read.*

γινώσκω [V 2, 18, 21; DV 50; VP 1-3] *I know; I learn.*

ἐπιγινώσκω [ἐπί + γινώσκω] [V 2, 18, 21; DV 50; VP 1-3] *I know; I
recognize.*

ἀναβαίνω [ἀνά + βαίνω] [V 7, DV 31, VP 1-2] *I embark; I go up.*

ἐμβαίνω [ἐν + βαίνω] [V 7, DV 31, VP 1-2] *I get into; I embark.* It
should be noted that the prefix of this compound verb is ἐν,
which reappears before an augment (e.g., ἐνέβαινον).

καταβαίνω [κατά + βαίνω] [V 7, DV 31, VP 1-2] *I descend; I fall
down.*

μεταβαίνω [μετά + βαίνω] [V 7, DV 31, VP 1-2] *I leave; I cross over.*

ἀσθενέω [V 8; VP 1-3, 5-6] *I am ill; I am weak.*

βλασφημέω [V 8; VP 1-3, 5-6] *I blaspheme ; I insult.*

διακονέω [V 8; DV 60; VP 1-3, 5-6] *I serve; I provide for.* The augment is formed by lengthening the α (e.g., διηκόνουν). The verb governs the dative case.

εὐλογέω [V 8; VP 1-3, 5-6] *I bless.*

κατοικέω [κατά + οἰκέω] [V 8; VP 1-3, 5-6] transitive: *I live in* [with simple accusative]; intransitive: *I live* [with preposition].

λογίζομαι (λογίσομαι) [V 5, 22; VP 2-3] *I reckon; I think; I classify.*

περισσεύω [V 1, VP 1-3] *I am over; I overflow; I excel.*

πράσσω [V 3, DV 261, VP 1-3] transitive: *I do; I practice;* intransitive: *I act.*

———

δεῦτε [Adv 1] *come!* [literally, *to here! hither!* The word is an adverb despite the usual translation.]

πώς [Adv 3] *somehow.* This is an enclitic. It should be distinguished from the non-enclitic interrogative πῶς.

Exercises for Lesson 53.

I. Translate into English:
1. καὶ μετὰ ἀνόμων ἐλογίσθη. (Lk 22:37)
2. πῶς ἔσται τοῦτο, ἐπεὶ ἄνδρα οὐ γινώσκω; (Lk 1:34)
3. ἔρχομαι πρὸς ὑμᾶς μή πως παθήματα ὑμῶν περισσεύῃ.
4. σῶσον σεαυτὸν καταβὰς ἀπὸ τοῦ σταυροῦ. (Mk 15:30)
5. καὶ ἐζήτουν αὐτὸν κρατῆσαι, καὶ ἐφοβήθησαν τὸν ὄχλον, ἔγνωσαν γὰρ ὅτι πρὸς αὐτοὺς τὴν παραβολὴν εἶπεν. (Mk 12:12)
6. καὶ οἱ ἄγγελοι διηκόνουν αὐτῷ. (Mk 1:13)
7. γνῶθι σεαυτόν.
8. ὃς δ᾽ ἂν βλασφημήσῃ εἰς τὸ πνεῦμα τὸ ἅγιον οὐκ ἔχει ἄφεσιν εἰς τὸν αἰῶνα. (Mk 3:29)
9. ἀπὸ τῶν καρπῶν αὐτῶν ἐπιγνώσεσθε αὐτούς. (Mt 7:16)
10. τότε ἐρεῖ ὁ βασιλεὺς τοῖς ἐκ δεξιῶν αὐτοῦ [*on his right*], Δεῦτε, οἱ εὐλογημένοι τοῦ πατρός μου. (Mt 25:34)
11. περὶ δὲ τῆς ἀναστάσεως τῶν νεκρῶν οὐκ ἀνέγνωτε τὸ ῥηθὲν ὑμῖν ὑπὸ τοῦ θεοῦ; (Mt 22:31)

12. οὐ γὰρ ὃ θέλω τοῦτο πράσσω, ἀλλ᾽ ὃ μισῶ τοῦτο
    ποιῶ. (Rom 7:15)
13. ἐξήγαγεν δὲ αὐτοὺς ἔξω καὶ ἐπάρας τὰς χεῖρας αὐτοῦ
    εὐλόγησεν αὐτούς. (Lk 24:50)
14. καθὼς περισσεύει τὰ παθήματα τοῦ Χριστοῦ εἰς ὑμᾶς,
    οὕτως διὰ τοῦ Χριστοῦ περισσεύει καὶ ἡ
    παράκλησις ἡμῶν. (2 Cor 1:5)
15. βαπτισθεὶς δὲ ὁ Ἰησοῦς εὐθέως ἀνέβη ἀπὸ τοῦ ὕδατος.
    (Mt 3:16)
16. ὅσοι εἶχον ἀσθενοῦντας νόσοις ἤγαγον αὐτοὺς πρὸς
    αὐτόν. (Lk 4:40) [νόσοις is a dative of cause: *ill with
    diseases*.]
17. καὶ μεταβὰς ἐκεῖθεν ἦλθεν εἰς τὴν συναγωγὴν αὐτῶν.
    (Mt 12:9)
18. τότε ἔρχεται καὶ παραλαμβάνει ἕτερα πνεύματα
    πονηρότερα ἑαυτοῦ ἑπτά, καὶ εἰσελθόντα κατοικεῖ
    ἐκεῖ. (Lk 11:26)
19. καὶ ἐμβάντι αὐτῷ εἰς τὸ πλοῖον ἠκολούθησαν αὐτῷ οἱ
    μαθηταὶ αὐτοῦ. (Mt 8:23)

II. Translate into Greek:
    1. If I had known the truth, I would not have come.
    2. The crowd, knowing [it], followed him. (Lk 9:11)
    3. They have descended in order to do the will of God. (Jn
       6:38)

III. Read Mk 7:31 – 8:21, at first without the consultation of any aids,
     relying solely on memory. Then re-read the text, checking
     any doubtful points against the material already seen.
     Finally, read the verses aloud at least three times.

οἶδα: **Perfect Form, Present Meaning.**
οἶδα, **Perfect Active Indicative, Pluperfect**
Active Indicative, Perfect Active Imperative,
Subjunctive, Participle, and Infinitive.
Difficult Verbs: πορεύομαι, πίπτω.

Lesson 54

οἶδα: **Perfect Form, Present Meaning.**

The verb οἶδα is frequently used. It has a perfect form which is
normally translated with a present meaning. It is found principally
in the perfect active system with this present meaning. The future,
εἰδήσω, is found only once in the New Testament.

   The verb οἶδα is etymologically linked with the aorist of ὁράω,
εἶδον. But the student is advised to keep the two verbs separate.

οἶδα, **Perfect Active Indicative, Pluperfect Active Indicative, Perfect**
Active Imperative, Subjunctive, Participle, and Infinitive.

The forms of οἶδα are as follows (cf. V 18, DV 212, VP 1-2; for the
participle cf. also Adj 17):

	Active Voice, Indicative Mood, Perfect Form (Present Meaning)	
	Singular	Plural
1st Person	οἶδα	οἴδαμεν
2nd Person	οἶδας	οἴδατε
3rd Person	οἶδεν	οἴδασι(ν)

	Active Voice, Indicative Mood, Pluperfect Form (Imperfect Meaning)	
	Singular	Plural
1st Person	ᾔδειν	ᾔδειμεν
2nd Person	ᾔδεις	ᾔδειτε
3rd Person	ᾔδει	ᾔδεισαν

Active Voice, Imperative Mood, Perfect Form

	Singular	Plural
2nd Person	ἴσθι	ἴστε
3rd Person	ἴστω	ἴστωσαν

Note that the second person singular is the same form as the second person singular of the present imperative of εἰμί.

Active Voice, Subjunctive Mood, Present Tense (Perfect Form)

	Singular	Plural
1st Person	εἰδῶ	εἰδῶμεν
2nd Person	εἰδῇς	εἰδῆτε
3rd Person	εἰδῇ	εἰδῶσι(ν)

The optative of οἶδα is not found in the New Testament.

Active Voice, Participial Mood, Perfect Form

		Singular	
	Masculine	Feminine	Neuter
n	εἰδώς	εἰδυῖα	εἰδός
v	εἰδώς	εἰδυῖα	εἰδός
g	εἰδότος	εἰδυίας	εἰδότος
d	εἰδότι	εἰδυίᾳ	εἰδότι
a	εἰδότα	εἰδυῖαν	εἰδός

		Plural	
	Masculine	Feminine	Neuter
n	εἰδότες	εἰδυῖαι	εἰδότα
v	εἰδότες	εἰδυῖαι	εἰδότα
g	εἰδότων	εἰδυιῶν	εἰδότων
d	εἰδόσι(ν)	εἰδυίαις	εἰδόσι(ν)
a	εἰδότας	εἰδυίας	εἰδότα

The infinitive is εἰδέναι.

Difficult Verbs: πορεύομαι, πίπτω.

πορεύομαι, *I proceed*; *I travel*; *I live* [V 1, 22, 23; DV 260; VP 2-3]

πορεύομαι   πορεύσομαι   —   —   πεπόρευμαι ἐπορεύθην
Mt 8:9   Lk 11:5   1 Pt 4:3   Mt 2:9

The future is a middle deponent; the aorist, a passive deponent, i.e., the aorist passive form is active in meaning.

πίπτω, *I fall* [V 4, 5, 21; DV 248; VP 1-4]

πίπτω   πεσοῦμαι   ἔπεσον   πέπτωκα   —   —
Mt 17:15   Mt 10:29   Mt 7:25   Acts 15:16

The future is a middle deponent; the aorist is strong.

Vocabulary for Lesson 54.

οἶδα [V 18, DV 212, VP 1-2] *I know.*

εἰσπορεύομαι [εἰς + πορεύομαι] [V 1, 22, 23; DV 260; VP 2-3] *I enter.*

ἐκπορεύομαι [ἐκ + πορεύομαι] [V 1, 22, 23; DV 260; VP 2-3] *I go out.*

πορεύομαι [V 1, 22, 23; DV 260; VP 2-3] *I proceed; I travel; I live.*

ἀναπίπτω [ἀνά + πίπτω] [V 4, 5, 21; DV 248; VP 2-4] *I recline (at a meal); I lean.*

ἐπιπίπτω [ἐπί + πίπτω] [V 4, 5, 21; DV 248; VP 2-4] *I fall upon* [with a simple dative or with a preposition].

πίπτω [V 4, 5, 21; DV 248; VP 2-4] *I fall.*

ἀσπάζομαι (ἀσπάσομαι) [V 5, 22; VP 2-3] *I greet; I welcome.*

βούλομαι [V 6, 23; DV 44; VP 2-3] *I want; I desire; I plan.*

δέχομαι [V 2, 22; DV 58; VP 2-3] *I receive.*

εὔχομαι [V 2, 22; DV 108; VP 2-3] *I pray; I wish.*

μετανοέω [μετά + νοέω] [V 8; VP 1-3, 5-6] *I repent.*

πληρόω [V 10; VP 1-3, 5-6] *I fulfill; I fill; I complete.*

προσδέχομαι [προς + δέχομαι] [V 2, 22; DV 58; VP 2-3] *I wait for; I welcome.*

προσεύχομαι [πρός + εὔχομαι] [V 2, 22; DV 108, VP 2-3] *I pray.*

———

ἔσωθεν [Adv 1] *within; from within.*

Exercises for Lesson 54.

I. Translate into English:
1. καὶ αὐτὸς ἦν προσδεχόμενος τὴν βασιλείαν τοῦ θεοῦ. (Mk 15:43)
2. ὁ δὲ Ἰησοῦς διελθὼν διὰ μέσου αὐτῶν ἐπορεύετο. (Lk 4:30)
3. ὃς ἂν ἓν τῶν τοιούτων παιδίων δέξηται ἐπὶ τῷ ὀνόματί μου, ἐμὲ δέχεται· καὶ ὃς ἂν ἐμὲ δέχηται, οὐκ ἐμὲ δέχεται ἀλλὰ τὸν ἀποστείλαντά με. (Mk 9:37)
4. καὶ ἀποκριθέντες τῷ Ἰησοῦ εἶπαν, Οὐκ οἴδαμεν. (Mt 21:27)
5. καὶ ἐταράχθη ὁ ἀνὴρ ἰδών, καὶ φόβος ἐπέπεσεν ἐπ' αὐτόν. (Lk 1:12)
6. πάντα ταῦτα τὰ πονηρὰ ἔσωθεν ἐκπορεύεται καὶ κοινοῖ τὸν ἄνθρωπον. (Mk 7:23)
7. οὐ τὸ εἰσερχόμενον εἰς τὸ στόμα κοινοῖ τὸν ἄνθρωπον, ἀλλὰ τὸ ἐκπορευόμενον ἐκ τοῦ στόματος τοῦτο κοινοῖ τὸν ἄνθρωπον. (Mt 15:11)
8. καὶ προελθὼν μικρὸν ἔπιπτεν ἐπὶ τῆς γῆς, καὶ προσηύχετο ἵνα εἰ δύνατόν ἐστιν παρέλθῃ ἀπ' αὐτοῦ ἡ ὥρα. (Mk 14:35) [μικρὸν is an accusative expressing distance: *a little way.*]
9. ἡ δὲ γυνὴ φοβηθεῖσα, εἰδυῖα ὃ γέγονεν αὐτῇ, ἦλθεν καὶ εἶπεν τῷ Ἰησοῦ πᾶσαν τὴν ἀλήθειαν. (Mk 5:33)
10. καὶ ἀκούσαντες οἱ μαθηταὶ ἔπεσαν ἐπὶ πρόσωπον αὐτῶν καὶ ἐφοβήθησαν. (Mt 17:6)
11. τότε ἐπληρώθη τὸ ῥηθὲν διὰ τοῦ προφήτου. (Mt 2:17)
12. καὶ ἤρξατο ἀσπάζεσθαι αὐτόν. (Mk 15:18)
13. οὐκ ᾔδειτε ὅτι ἐν τοῖς τοῦ πατρός μου δεῖ εἶναί με; (Lk 2:49)
14. μετανοεῖτε καὶ πιστεύετε ἐν τῷ εὐαγγελίῳ. (Mk 1:15)
15. κριτὴς ἐγὼ τούτων οὐ βούλομαι εἶναι. (Acts 18:15)

16. ἀλλ' ὅταν κληθῇς πορευθεὶς ἀνάπεσε εἰς τὸν ἔσχατον τόπον. (Lk 14:10)
17. καὶ ἦν μετ' αὐτῶν εἰσπορευόμενος καὶ ἐκπορευόμενος εἰς τὴν πόλιν. (Acts 9:28)
18. εὔχεσθε ὑπὲρ ἀλλήλων, ὅπως ἰαθῆτε. (Jas 5:16)

II. Translate into Greek:
1. We know that the testimonies are true with which they witness concerning us. (Jn 5:32) ["with which"—use simple accusative (an accusative of respect).]
2. The women were fearing the prophets, knowing them [to be] just and holy men. (Jn 6:20)
3. And they did not know them but they received them in the name of Jesus.

III. Read Mk 8:22 – 9:1, at first without the consultation of any aids, relying entirely on memory. Then re-read the text, checking any doubtful points against the material already seen. Finally, read the verses aloud at least three times.

Verbs in –μι. δίδωμι, Present Active
Indicative, Imperfect Active Indicative,
Present Active Imperative, Subjunctive,
Participle, and Infinitive. δίδωμι, Aorist
Active Indicative, Imperative, Participle,
and Infinitive. Difficult Verbs: δίδωμι,
ἀποκτείνω. Rules for Accents 37.

Lesson 55

Verbs in –μι.

Verbs in ancient Greek are divided into two major categories: 1)
those whose ending in the first person singular of the present active
indicative is –ω (e.g., λύω); 2) those whose ending in the first person
singular of the present indicative active is –μι (e.g., εἰμί). These
convenient identifications are based on a fundamental difference in
structure between the two categories. Verbs ending in –ω in the first
person singular are known as "thematic verbs" because in the
present, future, and second aorist systems a vowel (ε or o)is
interposed between the root and the endings (for example, λύ–ο–μεν);
the vowel is called a "thematic vowel". Verbs in the second category
do not have a vowel interposed between the root and the endings in
the indicative and imperative (for example, τίθε–μεν); they are
accordingly called "non-thematic verbs". (In both categories the
thematic and non-thematic vowels are at times not immediately
evident because of contractions.)
     After an initial presentation of εἰμί, this grammar has made
a detailed presentation of the verbs in the first category. (Cf. above,
Lesson 9, for the introduction to the distinction between the two
categories.) It is now time to consider in detail the second category,
the category of non-thematic or "–μι" verbs.
     In Greek , verbs in –μι (second category) have distinctive forms
in relation to verbs in –ω (first category) only in the present of all
three voices and in some moods of the aorist systems of the active
and middle voices. In all other systems the forms are the same for
both categories. But even where non-thematic verbs generally have
non-thematic forms there is occasionally found a thematic form or

forms. (For example the thematic forms ἐδίδουν—ἐδίδο–ον >
ἐδίδουν; ἐδίδο–ες—ἐδίδους; ἐδίδου—ἐδίδου in the imperfect active
indicative.)

    A distinctive characteristic of –μι verbs is that the vowel of the
root often changes within a tense system. For example, the verb
δίδωμι has a long root vowel, ω, in the present singular of the
indicative active, but a short root vowel, ο, in the present plural and
most other forms. This change in the quantity of the vowel is known
as "vowel gradation".

δίδωμι, Present Active Indicative, Imperfect Active Indicative, Present Active Imperative, Subjunctive, Participle, and Infinitive.

The –μι verb δίδωμι, *I give*, is conjugated as follows in the present
active system (cf. V 13, 21; DV 62; VP 1-3, 7-8, 11; for the participle cf.
also Adj 20):

Active Voice, Indicative Mood, Present Tense

	Singular	Plural
1st Person	δίδω–μι	δίδο–μεν
2nd Person	δίδω–ς	δίδο–τε
3rd Person	δίδω–σι(ν)	διδό–ασι(ν)

    The vowel gradation (διδ<u>ω</u>– in the singular as contrasted with
διδ<u>ο</u>– in the plural) should be noted.

Active Voice, Indicative Mood, Imperfect Tense

	Singular	Plural
1st Person	ἐ–δίδουν [thematic form]	ἐ–δίδο–μεν
2nd Person	ἐ–δίδους [thematic form]	ἐ–δίδο–τε
3rd Person	ἐ–δίδου [thematic form]	ἐ–δίδο–σαν / ἐ–δίδουν [thematic form]

Active Voice, Imperative Mood, Present Tense

	Singular	Plural
2nd Person	δίδου [thematic form]	δίδο–τε
3rd Person	διδό–τω	διδό–τωσαν

    Contraction in the second person singular (δίδο–ε > δίδου)
precludes distinguishing the stem from the ending by a hyphen.

Active Voice, Subjunctive Mood, Present Tense

	Singular	Plural
1st Person	διδῶ	διδῶ–μεν
2nd Person	διδῷ–ς / διδοῖ–ς	διδῶ–τε
3rd Person	διδῷ / διδοῖ	διδῶ–σι(ν)

Contractions preclude distinguishing the stem from the ending by a hyphen.

The alternate forms in the second and third person singular should be noted, along with the possibility of confusion with the present optative mood.

The present optative mood of δίδωμι is not found in the New Testament.

Active Voice, Participial Mood, Present Tense

Singular

	Masculine	Feminine	Neuter
n	διδούς	διδοῦσα	διδό–ν
v	διδούς	διδοῦσα	διδό–ν
g	διδό–ντος	διδούσης	διδό–ντος
d	διδό–ντι	διδούση	διδό–ντι
a	διδό–ντα	διδοῦσαν	διδό–ν

Plural

	Masculine	Feminine	Neuter
n	διδό–ντες	διδοῦσαι	διδό–ντα
v	διδό–ντες	διδοῦσαι	διδό–ντα
g	διδό–ντων	διδουσῶν	διδό–ντων
d	διδοῦσι(ν)	διδούσαις	διδοῦσι(ν)
a	διδό–ντας	διδούσας	διδό–ντα

The present active infinitive is διδό–ναι.

The presence of a reduplicated element in the present stem should be noted (δι–). The root is δο–.

δίδωμι, Aorist Active Indicative, Imperative, Participle, and Infinitive.

The aorist active system of δίδωμι is conjugated as follows (cf. V 13, 21; DV 62; VP 1-3, 7-8, 11.

Active Voice, Indicativ Mood, Aorist Tense

	Singular	Plural
1st Person	ἔ–δωκ–α	ἐ–δώκ–αμεν
2nd Person	ἔ–δωκ–ας	ἐ–δώκ–ατε
3rd Person	ἔ–δωκ–ε(ν)	ἔ–δωκ–αν / ἔδοσαν

[athematic form]

The possibility of confusion with the perfect active should be noted. [This unusual κ is found also in the aorists of τίθημι and ἵημι.]

Active Voice, Imperative Mood, Aorist Tense

	Singular	Plural
2nd Person	δό–ς	δό–τε
3rd Person	δό–τω	δό–τωσαν

Active Voice, Subjunctive Mood, Aorist Tense

	Singular	Plural
1st Person	δῶ	δῶμεν
2nd Person	δῷς / δοῖς	δῶτε
3rd Person	δῷ / δοῖ / δώῃ	δῶσι(ν)

The possibility of confusion with an optative is clear as regards several of the above forms.

The aorist optative active of δίδωμι occurs in the New Testament only in the third person singular: δώῃ.

Active Voice, Participial Mood, Aorist Tense

Singular

	Masculine	Feminine	Neuter
n	δούς	δοῦσα	δό–ν
v	δούς	δοῦσα	δό–ν
g	δό–ντος	δούσης	δό–ντος
d	δό–ντι	δούσῃ	δό–ντι
a	δό–ντα	δοῦσαν	δό–ν

	Masculine	Plural Feminine	Neuter
n	δό–ντες	δοῦσαι	δό–ντα
v	δό–ντες	δοῦσαι	δό–ντα
g	δό–ντων	δουσῶν	δό–ντων
d	δοῦσι(ν)	δούσαις	δοῦσι(ν)
a	δό–ντας	δούσας	δό–ντα

The aorist active infinitive is δοῦναι (δο–εναι > δοῦναι.)

The aorist indicative active is irregular because of the presence of κ, which is ordinarily the sign of the perfect when occurring at the end of a stem. Inasmuch as the perfect active of δίδωμι also has a κ, the aorist (ἔδωκα) should be distinguished from the perfect (δέδωκα).

The middle and passive voices will be presented in the following lesson.

Difficult Verbs: δίδωμι, ἀποκτείνω.

δίδωμι, *I give* [V 13, 21; DV 62; VP 1-3, 7-8, 11]

δίδωμι	δώσω	ἔδωκα	δέδωκα	δέδομαι	ἐδόθην
Mt 13:8	Mt 4:9	Mt 10:1	Mk 14:44	Mt 13:11	Mt 14:9

The forms peculiar to the verbs in –μι are limited for δίδωμι to the present (all voices) and to the aorist active (except for the indicative) and aorist middle. The aorist active indicative has the endings of the aorist active of λύω but with the irregular stem containing a κ, a fact which makes confusion with the perfect active possible.

ἀποκτείνω, *I kill; I murder* [V 7, DV 168, VP 1-3, 5-6]

ἀποκτείνω	ἀποκτενῶ	ἀπέκτεινα	—	—	ἀπεκτάνθην
Lk 12:4	Mt 17:23	Lk 11:48			Mt 16:21

The form ἀποκτέννω is also found in the present system (cf. Mt 10:28). In the future there is the contracted form proper to a nasal. In the aorist active the absence of the σ is compensated for by

the lengthening of the preceding syllable which makes the stem
similar to the present stem, especially in the moods different from
the indicative. There are no perfect forms in the New Testament.

Rules for Accents 37.

The accent in the present active participle of δίδωμι and the other
verbs in –μι is on the final syllable of the masculine nominative
singular, that is, on the final syllable of the root. It remains on this
syllable throughout the declension.

The accent on the present active infinitive is on the second-
last syllable.

The accent on the present active subjunctive falls on the
lengthened vowel of the stem.

Vocabulary for Lesson 55.

ἀποδίδωμι [ἀπό + δίδωμι] [V 13, 21; DV 62; VP 1-3, 7-8, 11] *I pay; I
give back; I reward.*

δίδωμι [V 13, 21; DV 62; VP 1-3, 7-8, 11] *I give.*

ἐπιδίδωμι [ἐπί + δίδωμι] [V 13, 21; DV 62; VP 1-3, 7-8, 11] *I give; I
deliver.*

παραδίδωμι [παρά + δίδωμι] [V 13, 21; DV 62; VP 1-3, 7-8, 11] *I hand
over; I betray.*

ἀποκτείνω [ἀπό + κτείνω] [V7, DV 168, VP 1-3, 5-6] *I kill; I murder.*

ἀπαρνέομαι [ἀπό + ἀρνέομαι] [V 8, 22; DV 26; VP 2-3, 6] *I deny; I
disown.*

ἀρνέομαι [V 8, 22; DV 26; VP 2-3, 6] *I deny; I disown.*

γαμέω [V 8; VP 1-3, 5-6] *I marry.*

ἐλεέω [V 8, 9; DV 81; VP 1-3, 5-6] *I am merciful.* In the present
system ἐλεάω is also found. This verb can take the
accusative case, without a preposition.

ἐλπίζω [V 5, DV 86, VP 1-3, 5-6] *I hope; I hope in* [the future stem is irregular: ἐλπιῶ].

ἐνδύω [ἐν + δύω] [V 1, DV 67, VP 1-3] active: *I dress* [someone else]; middle: *I dress* [myself].

ἔξεστι(ν) [ἐκ + ἐστι(ν)] [V 16, 19; DV 78; VP 9] [imperfect: ἔξον ἦν] *it is permitted; it is possible.* *impersonal verb*

ἐπιτελέω [ἐπί + τελέω] [V 8; DV 305; VP 1-3, 5-6] *I complete; I accomplish.* The final ε of the root remains unlengthened.

ἡγέομαι [V 8, 22; DV 115; VP 2-3, 6] *I consider; I rule.*

προφητεύω [V 1, VP 1-3] *I prophesy; I preach.*

τελέω [V 8; DV 305; VP 1-3, 5-6] *I finish; I fulfill.* The final ε of the root remains unlengthened.

___

αἰτία, -ας, ἡ [N 2] *cause; charge; guilt; relationship.*

___

λίαν [Adv 3] *greatly.*

Exercises for Lesson 55.

I. Translate into English:
1. προφήτευσον ἡμῖν, Χριστέ. (Mt 26:68)
2. ἐδίδασκεν γὰρ τοὺς μαθητὰς αὐτοῦ καὶ ἔλεγεν αὐτοῖς ὅτι Ὁ υἱὸς τοῦ ἀνθρώπου παραδίδοται εἰς χεῖρας ἀνθρώπων, καὶ ἀποκτενοῦσιν αὐτόν, καὶ ἀποκτανθεὶς μετὰ τρεῖς ἡμέρας ἐγερθήσεται. (Mk 9:31) [παραδίδοται is the present passive indicative third person singular of δίδωμι—cf. Lesson 56.]
3. καὶ οὐκ ἀπεκρίθη αὐτῷ οὐδὲ ἓν ῥῆμα, ὥστε θαυμάζειν τὸν ἡγεμόνα λίαν. (Mt 27:14)
4. ὃς γὰρ ἔχει, δοθήσεται αὐτῷ· καὶ ὃς οὐκ ἔχει, καὶ ὃ ἔχει ἀρθήσεται ἀπ' αὐτοῦ. (Mk 4:25)
5. κύριε, ἐλέησόν μου τὸν υἱόν. (Mt 17:15)
6. ἀλλὰ ἐνδύσασθε τὸν κύριον Ἰησοῦν Χριστόν. (Rom 13:14)

7. εἴ τις θέλει ὀπίσω μου ἐλθεῖν, ἀπαρνησάσθω ἑαυτὸν
   καὶ ἀράτω τὸν σταυρὸν αὐτοῦ καὶ ἀκολουθείτω
   μοι. (Mt 16:24)
8. νυνὶ δὲ καὶ τὸ ποιῆσαι ἐπιτελέσατε. (2 Cor 8:11)
9. κάλεσον τοὺς ἐργάτας καὶ ἀπόδος αὐτοῖς τὸν μισθὸν
   ἀρξάμενος ἀπὸ τῶν ἐσχάτων ἕως τῶν πρώτων. (Mt
   20:8)
10. ἰδοὺ ἀναβαίνομεν εἰς τὴν πόλιν τὴν ἁγίαν, καὶ
    τελεσθήσεται πάντα τὰ γεγραμμένα διὰ τῶν
    προφητῶν τῷ υἱῷ τοῦ ἀνθρώπου. (Lk 18:31)
11. λέγουσιν αὐτῷ οἱ μαθηταὶ αὐτοῦ, Εἰ οὕτως ἐστὶν ἡ
    αἰτία τοῦ ἀνθρώπου μετὰ τῆς γυναικός, οὐ συμφέρει
    γαμῆσαι. (Mt 19:10)
12. καὶ γὰρ ὁ υἱὸς τοῦ ἀνθρώπου οὐκ ἦλθεν
    διακονηθῆναι ἀλλὰ διακονῆσαι καὶ δοῦναι τὴν
    ψυχὴν αὐτοῦ ἀντὶ πολλῶν. (Mk 10:45)
13. ἐκ σοῦ γὰρ ἐξελεύσεται ἡγούμενος. (Mt 2:6)
14. οὐκ ἔξεστίν σοι ἔχειν τὴν γυναῖκα τοῦ ἀδελφοῦ σου.
    (Mk 6:18)
15. καὶ ἐπεδόθη αὐτῷ βιβλίον τοῦ προφήτου. (Lk 4:17)
16. ἰδοὺ ὁ παραδιδούς με ἤγγικεν. (Mk 14:42)
17. ὅστις δ᾽ ἂν ἀρνήσηταί με ἔμπροσθεν τῶν ἀνθρώπων,
    ἀρνήσομαι κἀγὼ αὐτὸν ἔμπροσθεν τοῦ πατρός μου
    τοῦ ἐν τοῖς οὐρανοῖς. (Mt 10:33)
18. καὶ ἤλπιζέν τι σημεῖον ἰδεῖν ὑπ᾽ αὐτοῦ γινόμενον. (Lk
    23:8)

II. Translate into Greek:
   1. And they gave the [loaves of] bread to the one who was with
      them.
   2. We shall kill these soldiers but not those.
   3. You will disown your friends.

III. Read Mk 9:2-29, at first without the consultation of any aids,
    relying entirely on memory. Then re-read the text, checking
    any doubtful points against the material already seen.
    Finally, read the verses aloud at least three times.

δίδωμι, Present Middle and Passive
Indicative, Imperfect Middle and Passive
Indicative, Present Middle and Passive
Imperative, Subjunctive, Participle, and
Infinitive. δίδωμι, Aorist Middle
Indicative. Difficult Verbs: ζάω, ἀνοίγω.
Rules for Accents 38.

Lesson 56

δίδωμι, Present Middle and Passive Indicative, Imperfect Middle and Passive Indicative, Present Middle and Passive Imperative, Subjunctive, Participle, and Infinitive.

The present middle and passive system of δίδωμι is conjugated as follows (cf. V 13, 21; DV 62; VP 1-3, 7-8, 11; for the participle also cf. Adj 1):

	Middle and Passive Voices, Indicative Mood, Present Tense	
	Singular	Plural
1st Person	δίδο–μαι	διδό–μεθα
2nd Person	δίδο–σαι	δίδο–σθε
3rd Person	δίδο–ται	δίδο–νται

	Middle and Passive Voices, Indicative Mood, Imperfect Tense	
	Singular	Plural
1st Person	ἐ–διδό–μην	ἐ–διδό–μεθα
2nd Person	ἐ–δίδο–σο	ἐ–δίδο–σθε
3rd Person	ἐ–δίδο–το	ἐ–δίδο–ντο

	Middle and Passive Voices, Imperative Mood, Present Tense	
	Singular	Plural
2nd Person	δίδο–σο	δίδο–σθε
3rd Person	διδό–σθω	διδό–σθωσαν

Middle and Passive Voices, Subjunctive Mood, Present Tense

	Singular	Plural
1st Person	διδῶ–μαι	διδώ–μεθα
2nd Person	διδῷ	διδῶ–σθε
3rd Person	διδῶ–ται	διδῶ–νται

διδῷ < διδό–ησαι.

The optative mood of the present middle or passive is not found in the New Testament.

Middle and Passive Voices, Participial Mood, Present Tense

Singular

	Masculine	Feminine	Neuter
n	διδό–μενος	διδο–μένη	διδό–μενον
v	διδό–μενε	διδο–μένη	διδό–μενον
g	διδο–μένου	διδο–μένης	διδο–μένου
d	διδο–μένῳ	διδο–μένη	διδο–μένῳ
a	διδό–μενον	διδο–μένην	διδό–μενον

Plural

	Masculine	Feminine	Neuter
n	διδό–μενοι	διδό–μεναι	διδό–μενα
v	διδό–μενοι	διδό–μεναι	διδό–μενα
g	διδο–μένων	διδο–μένων	διδο–μένων
d	διδο–μένοις	διδο–μέναις	διδο–μένοις
a	διδο–μένους	διδο–μένας	διδό–μενα

The present middle and passive infinitive is δίδο–σθαι.

It should be noted once again that the expression "middle and passive" does not mean that a word can be both middle and passive at one and the same time in the same respect in a given context.

δίδωμι, Aorist Middle Indicative.

The aorist middle of δίδωμι is strong and in the New Testament is found only in the indicative. It is conjugated as follows (cf. V 13, 21; DV 62; VP 1-3, 7-8, 11):

Middle Voice, Indicative Mood, Aorist Tense

	Singular	Plural
1st Person	ἐ–δό–μην	ἐ–δό–μεθα
2nd Person	ἔ–δου	ἔ–δο–σθε
3rd Person	ἔ–δο–το	ἔ–δο–ντο

ἔδου < ἔδο–σο.

Difficult Verbs: ζάω, ἀνοίγω.

ζάω, *I am alive; I live* [V 9; DV 110; VP 1-3, 5-6]

ζάω	ζήσομαι	ἔζησα	—	—	—
Acts 17:28	Mt 4:4	Rom 14:9			
	ζήσω				
	Jn 6:51				

The irregularity of this frequently-used word lies in the fact that it is really a verb in either –αω or –ηω, depending on the form used. The present indicative is as follows: ζῶ, ζῇς, ζῇ, ζῶμεν, ζῆτε, ζῶσι(ν). Two forms of the imperfect are found in the New Testament: the first person singular, ἔζων, and the second person plural, ἐζῆτε. The present infinitive is ζῆν, the present participle is ζῶν, ζῶσα, ζῶν (ζῶντος, ζώσης, ζῶντος). The future is also found in the active voice (cf. Jn 6:51).

ἀνοίγω, *I open* [V 2, DV 20, VP 1-3]

ἀνοίγω	ἀνοίξω	ἤνοιξα	ἀνέῳγα	ἤνοιγμαι	ἠνοίχθην
Jn 10:3	Mt 13:35	Jn 9:21	Jn 1:51	Acts 7:56	Apoc 20:12
		ἀνέῳξα		ἀνέῳγμαι	ἀνεῴχθην
		Jn 9:14		Acts 9:8	Mt 3:16
					[variant]
		ἠνέῳξα		ἠνέῳγμαι	ἠνεῴχθην
		Jn 9:17		Apoc 3:8	Mt 3:16

The complexity of this verb is more apparent than real. In the aorist active indicative and the aorist passive indicative there are three types of augment, and in the perfect middle and passive there are three types of reduplication. In each of these parts the first form has one augment or reduplication, the second has two, and the third has three. There is also an alternative form for the aorist passive, ἠνοίγην, which is strong (cf. Mt 20:33 and Mk 7:35).

Rules for Accents 38.

The accent of several verbs in –μι falls on the lengthened vowel of the stem in the present middle and passive subjunctive.

Vocabulary for Lesson 56.

ζάω [V 9; DV 110; VP 1-3, 5-6] *I am alive; I live.*

ἀνοίγω [ἀνά + οἴγω] [V 2, DV 20, VP 1-3] *I open.*

ἀδικέω [α privative + δίκη] [V 8; VP 1-3, 5-6] *I harm; I do wrong.*

ἀναβλέπω [ἀνά + βλέπω] [V 4, DV 43, VP 1-3] *I look up; I regain my sight.* As a prefix ἀνά can mean *up* or *again.*

γνωρίζω (γνωρίσω) [V 5, DV 51, VP 1-3] *I make known.*

γρηγορέω [V 8; VP 1-3, 5-6] *I keep awake; I watch; I am vigilant.*

ἐμβλέπω [ἐν + βλέπω] [V 4, DV 43, VP 1-3] *I look at; I consider* [governs dative case]. The prefix is ἐν and appears in this form before a vowel (e.g., ἐνέβλεπον).

ἐξομολογέω [ἐκ + ὁμολογέω] [V 8; VP 1-3, 5-6] active: *I agree;* middle: *I confess; I acknowledge.*

καταργέω [κατά + ἀργέω] [V 8; VP 1-3, 5-6] *I cancel; I destroy; I abolish.*

κατηγορέω [This is not a compound verb, even though the augment is understood to be expressed by the η as in κατηγόρουν in Mk 15:3.] [V 8; VP 1-3, 5-6] *I accuse* [with genitive of person being accused].

λυπέω [V 8; VP 1-3, 5-6] *I pain, I grieve; I injure.*

ὁμολογέω [V 8; VP 1-3, 5-6] *I profess; I admit.*

φρονέω [V 8; VP 1-3, 5-6] *I think.*

χαρίζομαι (χαρίσομαι) [V 5, 22; DV 340; VP 2-3] *I grant; I deal graciously with* [with dative].

———

μάλιστα [Adv 3] *especially.*

πρωΐ [Adv 2] *early in the morning.*

Exercises for Lesson 56.

I. Translate into English:
1. γρηγορεῖτε οὖν, ὅτι οὐκ οἴδατε τὴν ἡμέραν οὐδὲ τὴν ὥραν. (Mt 25:13)
2. καὶ λέγει αὐτῷ, Ἀμὴν ἀμὴν λέγω ὑμῖν, ὄψεσθε τὸν οὐρανὸν ἀνεῳγότα καὶ τοὺς ἀγγέλους τοῦ θεοῦ ἀναβαίνοντας καὶ καταβαίνοντας ἐπὶ τὸν υἱὸν τοῦ ἀνθρώπου. (Jn 1:51)
3. ἐν ἐκείνῃ τῇ ὥρᾳ ἐθεράπευσεν πολλοὺς ἀπὸ νόσων καὶ πνευμάτων πονηρῶν, καὶ τυφλοῖς πολλοῖς ἐχαρίσατο βλέπειν. (Lk 7:21)
4. οὐκ ἐπ᾽ ἄρτῳ μόνῳ ζήσεται ὁ ἄνθρωπος, ἀλλ᾽ ἐπὶ παντὶ ῥήματι ἐκπορευομένῳ διὰ στόματος θεοῦ. (Mt 4:4)
5. ὑμεῖς λυπηθήσεσθε, ἀλλ᾽ ἡ λύπη ὑμῶν εἰς χαρὰν γενήσεται.
6. τυφλοὶ ἀναβλέπουσιν καὶ κωφοὶ ἀκούουσιν, καὶ νεκροὶ ἐγείρονται καὶ πτωχοὶ εὐαγγελίζονται. (Mt 11:5)
7. καὶ ἐβαπτίζοντο ἐν τῷ Ἰορδάνῃ ποταμῷ ὑπ᾽ αὐτοῦ ἐξομολογούμενοι τὰς ἁμαρτίας αὐτῶν. (Mt 3:6)
8. σὺ εἶ ὁ Χριστὸς ὁ υἱὸς τοῦ θεοῦ τοῦ ζῶντος. (Mt 16:16)
9. νόμον οὖν καταργοῦμεν διὰ τῆς πίστεως; (Rom 3:31)
10. καὶ λίαν πρωΐ ἔρχονται ἐπὶ τὸ μνημεῖον. (Mk 16:2)
11. εἰ μὲν οὖν ἀδικῶ καὶ ἄξιον θανάτου πέπραχά τι, οὐ παραιτοῦμαι τὸ ἀποθανεῖν. (Acts 25:11) [πέπραχα is the perfect tense, from πράσσω.]
12. ὕπαγε ὀπίσω μου· σκάνδαλον εἶ ἐμοῦ, ὅτι οὐ φρονεῖς τὰ τοῦ θεοῦ ἀλλὰ τὰ τῶν ἀνθρώπων. (Mt 16:23)
13. καὶ ἐν τῷ κατηγορεῖσθαι αὐτὸν ὑπὸ τῶν ἀρχιερέων καὶ πρεσβυτέρων οὐδὲν ἀπεκρίνατο. (Mt 27:12)

14. εἰς τοῦτο γὰρ κοπιῶμεν, ὅτι ἠλπίκαμεν ἐπὶ θεῷ ζῶντι, ὅς ἐστιν σωτὴρ πάντων ἀνθρώπων, μάλιστα πιστῶν. (1 Tim 4:10)

15. καὶ ὡς ἦλθεν ἐπὶ τὸν τόπον, ἀναβλέψας ὁ Ἰησοῦς εἶπεν πρὸς αὐτόν, Κατάβηθι, σήμερον γὰρ ἐν τῷ οἴκῳ σου δεῖ με μεῖναι. (Lk 19:5)

16. ὁ δὲ Ἰησοῦς ἐμβλέψας αὐτῷ ἠγάπησεν αὐτόν. (Mk 10:21)

17. ὑμᾶς δὲ εἴρηκα φίλους, ὅτι πάντα ἃ ἤκουσα παρὰ τοῦ πατρός μου ἐγνώρισα ὑμῖν. (Jn 15:15)

II. Translate into Greek:
1. These our sons were dead and now they are alive. (Lk 15:24)
2. And having opened his treasure he offered them a gift. (Mt 2:11)
3. Men would not have possessions if they had not been given them from heaven. (Jn 19:11)

III. Mk 9:30 – 10:12.

τίθημι, **Present Active Indicative, Imperfect Active Indicative, Present Active Imperative, Subjunctive, Participle, and Infinitive.** τίθημι, **Aorist Active Indicative, Imperative, Subjunctive, Participle, and Infinitive. Difficult Verbs:** τίθημι, πίνω.

Lesson 57

τίθημι, **Present Active Indicative, Imperfect Active Indicative, Present Active Imperative, Subjunctive, Participle, and Infinitive.**

The word τίθημι, *I put, I place,* is conjugated as follows in the present system (cf. V 12, 21; DV 309; VP 1-3, 7-8, 11; for the participle cf. also Adj 20). Contractions often preclude distinguishing stem from ending in the paradigms below.

Active Voice, Indicative Mood, Present Tense

	Singular	Plural
1st Person	τίθη–μι	τίθε–μεν
2nd Person	τίθη–ς	τίθε–τε
3rd Person	τίθη–σι(ν)	τιθέ–ασι(ν) / τιθι–ᾶσι(ν)

Active Voice, Indicative Mood, Imperfect Tense

	Singular	Plural
1st Person	ἐ–τίθην	ἐ–τίθε–μεν
2nd Person	ἐ–τίθεις [thematic form]	ἐ–τίθε–τε
3rd Person	ἐ–τίθει [thematic form]	ἐ–τίθε–σαν / ἐτίθουν [thematic form]

Active Voice, Imperative Mood, Present Tense

	Singular	Plural
2nd Person	τίθει [thematic form]	τίθε–τε
3rd Person	τιθέ–τω	τιθέ–τωσαν

Active Voice, Subjunctive Mood, Present Tense
	Singular	Plural
1st Person	τιθῶ	τιθῶμεν
2nd Person	τιθῇς	τιθῆτε
3rd Person	τιθῇ	τιθῶσι(ν)

There is no present optative active in the New Testament.

Active Voice, Participial Mood, Present Tense

Singular
	Masculine	Feminine	Neuter
n	τιθείς	τιθεῖσα	τιθέ–ν
v	τιθείς	τιθεῖσα	τιθέ–ν
g	τιθέ–ντος	τιθείσης	τιθέ–ντος
d	τιθέ–ντι	τιθείσῃ	τιθέ–ντι
a	τιθέ–ντα	τιθεῖσαν	τιθέ–ν

Plural
	Masculine	Feminine	Neuter
n	τιθέ–ντες	τιθεῖσαι	τιθέ–ντα
v	τιθέ–ντες	τιθεῖσαι	τιθέ–ντα
g	τιθέ–ντων	τιθεισῶν	τιθέ–ντων
d	τιθεῖσι(ν)	τιθείσαις	τιθεῖσι(ν)
a	τιθέ–ντας	τιθείσας	τιθέ–ντα

The present infinitive active is τιθέ–ναι.

The reduplicating element τι is part of the present stem. Cf. δί–δωμι and V 21.

The accents peculiar to the present subjunctive, participle, and infinitive should be noted (cf. above, Rules for Accents 37, Lesson 55).

τίθημι, Aorist Active Indicative, Imperative, Subjunctive, Participle, and Infinitive.

The aorist active system of τίθημι is as follows (cf. V 12, 21; DV 309; VP 1-3, 7-8, 11; for the participle cf. also Adj 18):

Active Voice, Indicative Mood, Aorist Tense

	Singular	Plural
1st Person	ἔ–θηκ–α	ἐ–θήκ–αμεν
2nd Person	ἔ–θηκ–ας	ἐ–θήκ–ατε
3rd Person	ἔ–θηκ–ε(ν)	ἔ–θηκ–αν

Active Voice, Imperative Mood, Aorist Tense

	Singular	Plural
2nd Person	θέ–ς	θέ–τε
3rd Person	θέ–τω	θέ–τωσαν

Active Voice, Subjunctive Mood, Aorist Tense

	Singular	Plural
1st Person	θῶ	θῶμεν
2nd Person	θῇς	θῆτε
3rd Person	θῇ	θῶσι(ν)

The aorist optative active is not found in the New Testament.

Active Voice, Participial Mood, Aorist Tense

Singular

	Masculine	Feminine	Neuter
n	θείς	θεῖσα	θέ–ν
v	θείς	θεῖσα	θέ–ν
g	θέ–ντος	θείσης	θέ–ντος
d	θέ–ντι	θείσῃ	θέ–ντι
a	θέ–ντα	θεῖσαν	θέ–ν

Plural

	Masculine	Feminine	Neuter
n	θέ–ντες	θεῖσαι	θέ–ντα
v	θέ–ντες	θεῖσαι	θέ–ντα
g	θέ–ντων	θεισῶν	θέ–ντων
d	θεῖσι(ν)	θείσαις	θεῖσι(ν)
a	θέ–ντας	θείσας	θέ–ντα

The aorist infinitive active is θεῖναι.

The aorist indicative stem has κ whereas the other mood stems do not. Inasmuch as the perfect stem also has a κ (τέθεικα) the absence of any reduplication in the aorist active (indicative) should be noted.

The middle and passive forms will be presented in the following lesson.

Difficult Verbs: τίθημι, πίνω.

τίθημι, *I place, I put* [V 12, 21; DV 309; VP 1-3, 7-8, 11]

τίθημι	θήσω	ἔθηκα	τέθεικα	τέθειμαι	ἐτέθην
Lk 8:16	Mt 12:18	Mt 27:60	Jn 11:34	Mk 15:47	Mk 4:21

The present active and middle/passive, and the aorist active (except for the indicative) have special endings appropriate for –μι verbs.
The middle aorist also has special forms.

πίνω, *I drink* [V 7, DV 246, VP 1-4]

πίνω	πίομαι	ἔπιον	πέπωκα	—	ἐπόθην
Mt 11:18	Mt 20:23	Mt 6:25	Apoc 18:3		1 Cor 15:54

The future is a middle deponent. The aorist is strong. The perfect middle/passive is not found in the New Testament.
The form πεῖν is found at Jn 4:7 for the aorist active infinitive.

Vocabulary for Lesson 57.

ἐπιτίθημι [ἐπί + τίθημι] [V 12, 21; DV 309; VP 1-3, 7-8, 11] *I put on* [with dative case]; *I place.*

παρατίθημι [παρά + τίθημι] [V 12, 21; DV 309; VP 1-3, 7-8, 11] *I place before; I distribute.*

προστίθημι [πρός + τίθημι] [V 12, 21; DV 309; VP 1-3, 7-8, 11] *I add to; I give; I continue.*

τίθημι [V 12, 21; DV 309; VP 1-3, 7-8, 11] *I put; I place.*
___

πίνω [V 7, DV 246, VP 1-4] *I drink.*
___

βασιλεύω [V 1, VP 1-3] *I rule.*

δοκιμάζω (δοκιμάσω) [V 5, VP 1-3] *I test; I discern.*

εὐδοκέω [εὖ + δοκέω] [V 8; DV 65; VP 1-3, 5-6] *I am well; I am pleased with* [with ἐν and the dative]; *I choose.*

καθεύδω [V 1, VP 1-3] *I sleep.*

κατεργάζομαι [κατά + ἐργάζομαι] [V 5, 22; DV 94; VP 2-3] *I do; I produce.*

λατρεύω [V 1, VP 1-3] *I serve; I worship* [with the dative case].

μνημονεύω [V 1, VP 1-3] *I remember* [with the genitive or the accusative case].

πωλέω [V 8; VP 1-3, 5-6] *I sell.*

ὑπακούω [ὑπό + ἀκούω] [V 1, DV 11, VP 1-3] *I listen to; I obey* [usually with the dative case].
___

δεῦρο [Adv 1] *come.* Despite the translation, the word is not a verb.

ταχύ [Adv 2] *quickly.*

τρίς [Adv 2] *three times.*

Exercises for Lesson 57.

I. Translate into English:
1. ὕπαγε ὅσα ἔχεις πώλησον καὶ δὸς τοῖς πτωχοῖς, καὶ ἕξεις θησαυρὸν ἐν οὐρανῷ, καὶ δεῦρο ἀκολούθει μοι. (Mk 10:21)

2. πρὶν ἀλέκτορα φωνῆσαι σήμερον ἀπαρνήσῃ με τρίς. (Lk 22:61)

3. εἶτα πάλιν ἐπέθηκεν τὰς χεῖρας ἐπὶ τοὺς ὀφθαλμοὺς αὐτοῦ. (Mk 8:25)

4. καὶ ἰδοὺ φωνὴ ἐκ τῶν οὐρανῶν λέγουσα, Οὗτός ἐστιν ὁ υἱός μου ὁ ἀγαπητός, ἐν ᾧ εὐδόκησα. (Mt 3:17)

5. ζητεῖτε δὲ πρῶτον τὴν βασιλείαν τοῦ θεοῦ καὶ τὴν δικαιοσύνην αὐτοῦ, καὶ ταῦτα πάντα προστεθήσεται ὑμῖν. (Mt 6:33)

6. καὶ ἰδοὺ ἄνδρες φέροντες ἄνθρωπον καὶ ἐζήτουν αὐτὸν εἰσενεγκεῖν καὶ θεῖναι αὐτὸν ἐνώπιον τοῦ Ἰησοῦ. (Lk 5:18)

7. καὶ εἰς ἣν ἂν πόλιν εἰσέρχησθε καὶ δέχωνται ὑμᾶς, ἐσθίετε τὰ παρατιθέμενα ὑμῖν, καὶ θεραπεύετε τοὺς ἐν αὐτῇ ἀσθενεῖς, καὶ λέγετε αὐτοῖς, Ἤγγικεν ἐφ᾽ ὑμᾶς ἡ βασιλεία τοῦ θεοῦ. (Lk 10:8-9) [εἰς ἣν ἂν πόλιν relative plus ἂν with subjunctive: *into whatever city you may go*. . .]

8. τὸ παιδίον οὐκ ἀπέθανεν ἀλλὰ καθεύδει. (Mk 5:39)

9. καὶ ταχὺ πορευθεῖσαι εἴπατε τοῖς μαθηταῖς αὐτοῦ ὅτι Ἠγέρθη ἀπὸ τῶν νεκρῶν. (Mt 28:7)

10. οὐδεὶς αἴρει τὴν ψυχήν ἀπ᾽ ἐμοῦ, ἀλλ᾽ ἐγὼ τίθημι αὐτὴν ἀπ᾽ ἐμαυτοῦ. ἐξουσίαν ἔχω θεῖναι αὐτήν, καὶ ἐξουσίαν ἔχω πάλιν λαβεῖν αὐτήν· ταύτην τὴν ἐντολὴν ἔλαβον παρὰ τοῦ πατρός μου. (Jn 10:18)

11. οὐ θέλομεν τοῦτον βασιλεῦσαι ἐφ᾽ ἡμᾶς. (Lk 19:14)

12. τὸ ποτήριον ὃ ἐγὼ πίνω πίεσθε καὶ τὸ βάπτισμα ὃ ἐγὼ βαπτίζομαι βαπτισθήσεσθε. (Mk 10:39) [τὸ βάπτισμα and ὃ are accusatives of respect: *with respect to* . . . .]

13. Κύριον τὸν θεόν σου προσκυνήσεις καὶ αὐτῷ μόνῳ λατρεύσεις. (Mt 4:10) [The future tense is an expression of a command.]

14. καὶ ἐφοβήθησαν φόβον μέγαν, καὶ ἔλεγον πρὸς ἀλλήλους, Τίς ἄρα οὗτός ἐστιν ὅτι καὶ ὁ ἄνεμος καὶ ἡ θάλασσα ὑπακούει αὐτῷ; (Mk 4:41)

15. ὃ γὰρ κατεργάζομαι οὐ γινώσκω· οὐ γὰρ ὃ θέλω τοῦτο πράσσω, ἀλλ᾽ ὃ μισῶ τοῦτο ποιῶ. (Rom 7:15)

16. ἀλλὰ ταῦτα λελάληκα ὑμῖν ἵνα ὅταν ἔλθῃ ἡ ὥρα αὐτῶν μνημονεύητε αὐτῶν ὅτι ἐγὼ εἶπον ὑμῖν. (Jn 16:4)

II. Translate into Greek:
    1. All men first put out the good wines; you (pl.) have saved
       the good wines until now. (Jn 2:10)
    2. We placed you (sg.) so that you might go and bear fruits
       and so that your fruits might remain. (Jn 15:16)
    3. Now remain (sg.) in the house itself, eating and drinking
       their food, for workers are worthy of their wage. (Lk
       10:7)

III. Mk 10:13-45.

τίθημι, **Present Middle and Passive Indicative, Imperfect Middle and Passive Indicative, Present Middle and Passive Imperative, Subjunctive, Participle, and Infinitive.** τίθημι, **Aorist Middle Indicative, Imperative, Subjunctive, Participle, and Infinitive.** κεῖμαι, **Present Passive Indicative, Imperfect Passive Indicative, Present Passive Participle and Infinitive. Difficult Verbs:** πείθω, σπείρω.

Lesson 58

τίθημι, **Present Middle and Passive Indicative, Imperfect Middle and Passive Indicative, Present Middle and Passive Imperative, Subjunctive, Participle, and Infinitive.**

The present middle and passive systems of τίθημι are conjugated as follows (cf. V 12, 21; DV 309; VP 1-3, 7-8, 11; for the participle cf. also Adj 1):

	Middle and Passive Voices, Indicative Mood, Present Tense	
	Singular	Plural
1st Person	τίθε–μαι	τιθέ–μεθα
2nd Person	τίθε–σαι	τίθε–σθε
3rd Person	τίθε–ται	τίθε–νται

	Middle and Passive Voices, Indicative Mood, Imperfect Tense	
	Singular	Plural
1st Person	ἐ–τιθέ–μην	ἐ–τιθέ–μεθα
2nd Person	ἐ–τίθε–σο	ἐ–τίθε–σθε
3rd Persion	ἐ–τίθε–το	ἐ–τίθε–ντο

Middle and Passive Voices, Imperative Mood, Present Tense

	Singular	Plural
2nd Person	τίθε–σο	τίθε–σθε
3rd Person	τιθέ–σθω	τιθέ–σθωσαν

Middle and Passive Voices, Subjunctive Mood, Present Tense

	Singular	Plural
1st Person	τιθῶμαι	τιθώμεθα
2nd Person	τιθῇ	τιθῆσθε
3rd Person	τιθῆται	τιθῶνται

τιθῇ < τιθέ–ησαι.

The optative mood of the present middle and passive is not found in the New Testament.

Middle and Passive Voices, Participial Mood, Present Tense

Singular

	Masculine	Feminine	Neuter
n	τιθέ–μενος	τιθε–μένη	τιθέ–μενον
v	τιθέ–μενε	τιθε–μένη	τιθέ–μενον
g	τιθε–μένου	τιθε–μένης	τιθε–μένου
d	τιθε–μένῳ	τιθε–μένη	τιθε–μένῳ
a	τιθέ–μενον	τιθε–μένην	τιθέ–μενον

Plural

	Masculine	Feminine	Neuter
n	τιθέ–μενοι	τιθέ–μεναι	τιθέ–μενα
v	τιθέ–μενοι	τιθέ–μεναι	τιθέ–μενα
g	τιθε–μένων	τιθε–μένων	τιθε–μένων
d	τιθε–μένοις	τιθε–μέναις	τιθε–μένοις
a	τιθε–μένους	τιθε–μένας	τιθέ–μενα

The present middle and passive infinitive is τίθε–σθαι.

It should be noted again that the middle and passive voices are identical in form in the present system but not in meaning: a given form has to be one or the other voice.

τίθημι, Aorist Middle Indicative, Imperative, Subjunctive, Participle, and Infinitive.

The aorist middle system of τίθημι is conjugated as follows (cf. V 12, 21; DV 309; VP 1-3, 7-8, 11; for the participle cf. also Adj 1):

Middle Voice, Indicative Mood, Aorist Tense

	Singular	Plural
1st Person	ἐ–θέ–μην	ἐ–θέ–μεθα
2nd Person	ἔ–θου	ἔ–θε–σθε
3rd Person	ἔ–θε–το	ἔ–θε–ντο

ἔθου < ἔθε–σο.

Middle Voice, Imperative Mood, Aorist Tense

	Singular	Plural
2nd Person	θοῦ	θέ–σθε
3rd Person	θέ–σθω	θέ–σθωσαν

θοῦ < θέ–σο.

Middle Voice, Subjunctive Mood, Aorist Tense

	Singular	Plural
1st Person	θῶμαι	θώμεθα
2nd Person	θῇ	θῆσθε
3rd Person	θῆται	θῶνται

θῇ < θε–ησαι

The aorist middle optative is not found in the New Testament.

Middle Voice, Participial Mood, Aorist Tense
Singular

	Masculine	Feminine	Neuter
n	θέ–μενος	θε–μένη	θέ–μενον
v	θέ–μενε	θε–μένη	θέ–μενον
g	θε–μένου	θε–μένης	θε–μένου
d	θε–μένῳ	θε–μένῃ	θε–μένῳ
a	θέ–μενον	θε–μένην	θέ–μενον

	Masculine	Plural Feminine	Neuter
n	θέ–μενοι	θέ–μεναι	θέ–μενα
v	θέ–μενοι	θέ–μεναι	θέ–μενα
g	θε–μένων	θε–μένων	θε–μένων
d	θε–μένοις	θε–μέναις	θε–μένοις
a	θε–μένους	θε–μένας	θέ–μενα

The aorist middle infinitive is θέ–σθαι.

κεῖμαι, Present Passive Indicative, Imperfect Passive Indicative, Present Passive Participle and Infinitive.

A verb associated with τίθημι is κεῖμαι, *I lie, I am laid.* It tends to replace the perfect passive of τίθημι in the New Testament. For example:

> δεῦτε ἴδετε τὸν τόπον ὅπου ἔκειτο.
> *Come see the place where he was laid.*

κεῖμαι is probably best taken as a true passive, although there is no attestation of any active form. It resembles in some ways a perfect, but is best taken as a present, although it is used in contexts where the perfect of τίθημι could be expected. It is a –μι verb and is conjugated as follows (cf. V 17, DV 148, VP 2; for the participle cf. Adj 1.):

Passive Voice, Indicative Mood, Present Tense

	Singular	Plural
1st Person	κεῖ–μαι	κεί–μεθα
2nd Person	κεῖ–σαι	κεῖ–σθε
3rd Person	κεῖ–ται	κεῖ–νται

Passive Voice, Indicative Mood, Imperfect Tense

	Singular	Plural
1st Person	ἐ–κεί–μην	ἐ–κεί–μεθα
2nd Person	ἔ–κει–σο	ἔ–κει–σθε
3rd Person	ἔ–κει–το	ἔ–κει–ντο

The imperative, subjunctive, and optative moods are not found in the New Testament.

Passive Voice, Participial Mood, Present Tense

Singular

	Masculine	Feminine	Neuter
n	κεί–μενος	κει–μένη	κεί–μενον
v	κεί–μενε	κει–μένη	κεί–μενον
g	κει–μένου	κει–μένης	κει–μένου
d	κει–μένῳ	κει–μένῃ	κει–μένῳ
a	κεί–μενον	κει–μένην	κεί–μενον

Plural

	Masculine	Feminine	Neuter
n	κεί–μενοι	κεί–μεναι	κεί–μενα
v	κεί–μενοι	κεί–μεναι	κεί–μενα
g	κει–μένων	κει–μένων	κει–μένων
d	κει–μένοις	κει–μέναις	κει–μένοις
a	κει–μένους	κει–μένας	κεί–μενα

The present passive infinitive is κεῖ–σθαι.

Difficult Verbs: πείθω, σπείρω.

πείθω, *I persuade* (cf. Lesson 11) [V 5, 18; DV 235; VP 1-3]

πείθω	πείσω	ἔπεισα	πέποιθα	πέπεισμαι	ἐπείσθην
Acts 18:4	Mt 28:14	Acts 12:20	Mt 27:43	Lk 20:6	Acts 17:4

The perfect active is strong. The special feature of this verb is the shifts of meaning which take place in the various parts. The present, future, and aorist active mean *persuade*; the perfect active means *trust*, with the force of a present tense; the passive means *be persuaded, obey*.

σπείρω, *I sow*   [V 6, DV 289, VP 1-3]

σπείρω	—	ἔσπειρα	—	ἔσπαρμαι	ἐσπάρην
Mt 6:26		Mt 25:24		Mt 13:19	Mt 13:20

There are no future active or perfect active forms found in the New Testament. The aorist active is typical of a liquid verb. The aorist passive is strong.

Vocabulary for Lesson 58.

ἀνάκειμαι [ἀνά + κεῖμαι] [V 17, DV 148, VP 2] *I recline; I recline at table* [a normal posture for eating].

κατάκειμαι [κατά + κεῖμαι] [V 17, DV 148, VP 2] *I lie in bed; I recline at table* [a normal posture for eating].

κεῖμαι [V 17, DV 148, VP 2] *I lie; I am placed.*

πείθω [V 5, 18; DV 235; VP 1-3] (cf. Lesson 11) active present, future, and aorist: *I persuade*; active perfect: *I trust in* [present force; governs the accusative case]; passive: *I am persuaded; I obey* [with the dative].

σπείρω [V 6, DV 289, VP 1-3] *I sow.*

ἀθετέω [This is an α privative + a root from τίθημι, but the augment is formed by lengthening the α as in ἠθέτησαν at Lk 7:30.] [V 8; VP 1-3, 5-6] *I reject; I make invalid.*

ἀρέσκω [V 2, DV 23, VP 1-3] *I please* [governs the dative].

διαλογίζομαι [διά + λογίζομαι] (διαλογίσομαι) [V 5, 22; VP 2-3] *I discuss; I reason.*

ἐκτείνω [ἐκ + τείνω] [V 7, DV 304, VP 1-3, 5-6] *I stretch out* [with the direct object in the accusative case].

ἐνεργέω [ἐν + the root of ἔργον] [V 8; VP 1-3, 5-6] transitive: *I effect*; intransitive: *I work.*

καταλύω [κατά + λύω] [V 1, VP 1-3] transitive: *I destroy*; intransitive: *I find lodging.*

κληρονομέω [V 8; VP 1-3, 5-6] *I inherit.*

νηστεύω [V 1, VP 1-3] *I fast.*

ῥύομαι [V 1, 22; DV 275; VP 2-3] *I rescue.*

―――

κάτω [Adv 1] *down; below.*

σφόδρα [Adv 3] *very much; greatly.*

Exercises for Lesson 58.

I. Translate into English:

1. ὁ προφήτης ἐγήγερται ἐκ νεκρῶν, καὶ διὰ τοῦτο ἐνεργοῦσιν αἱ δυνάμεις ἐν αὐτῷ. (Mk 6:14)

2. ἄλλην παραβολὴν παρέθηκεν αὐτοῖς λέγων, Ὡμοιώθη ἡ βασιλεία τῶν οὐρανῶν ἀνθρώπῳ σπείραντι καλὸν σπέρμα ἐν τῷ ἀγρῷ αὐτοῦ. (Mt 13:24)

3. καὶ ἀκούσαντες οἱ μαθηταὶ ἔπεσαν ἐπὶ πρόσωπον αὐτῶν καὶ ἐφοβήθησαν σπόδρα. (Mt 17:6)

4. καὶ θεωρεῖ δύο ἀγγέλους ἐν λευκοῖς, ἕνα πρὸς τῇ κεφαλῇ καὶ ἕνα πρὸς τοῖς ποσίν, ὅπου ἔκειτο τὸ σῶμα τοῦ Ἰησοῦ. (Jn 20:12)

5. ἕκαστος ἡμῶν τῷ πλησίον ἀρεσκέτω εἰς τὸ ἀγαθὸν πρὸς οἰκοδομήν. (Rom 15:2)

6. ὅταν δὲ νηστεύητε, μὴ γίνεσθε ὡς οἱ ὑποκριταί· ἀμὴν λέγω ὑμῖν, ἀπέχουσιν τὸν μισθὸν αὐτῶν. (Mt 6:16)

7. ὁ ἀκούων ὑμῶν ἐμοῦ ἀκούει, καὶ ὁ ἀθετῶν ὑμᾶς ἐμὲ ἀθετεῖ· ὁ δὲ ἐμὲ ἀθετῶν ἀθετεῖ τὸν ἀποστείλαντά με. (Lk 10:16)

8. τοῦτον ἰδὼν ὁ Ἰησοῦς κατακείμενον, καὶ γνοὺς ὅτι ἤδη χρόνον ἔχει, λέγει αὐτῷ, Θέλεις ὑγιὴς γενέσθαι; (Jn 5:6)

9. εἰ υἱὸς εἶ τοῦ θεοῦ, βάλε σεαυτὸν κάτω. (Mt 4:6)

10. πέποιθεν ἐπὶ τὸν θεόν, ῥυσάσθω νῦν εἰ θέλει αὐτόν· εἶπεν γὰρ ὅτι θεοῦ εἰμι υἱός. (Mt 27:43)

11. τότε ἐρεῖ ὁ βασιλεὺς τοῖς ἐκ δεξιῶν αὐτοῦ, Δεῦτε, οἱ εὐλογημένοι τοῦ πατρός μου, κληρονομήσατε τὴν ἡτοιμασμένην ὑμῖν βασιλείαν ἀπὸ τῆς ἀρχῆς τοῦ κόσμου. (Mt 25:34)

12. τίς γὰρ μείζων, ὁ ἀνακείμενος ἢ ὁ διακονῶν; οὐχὶ ὁ ἀνακείμενος; ἐγὼ δὲ ἐν μέσῳ ὑμῶν εἰμι ὡς ὁ διακονῶν. (Lk 22:27)

13. καὶ ἐκτείνας τὴν χεῖρα αὐτοῦ ἐπὶ τοὺς μαθητὰς αὐτοῦ εἶπεν, Ἰδοὺ ἡ μήτηρ μου καὶ οἱ ἀδελφοί μου. (Mt 12:49)

14. εἶπεν δὲ καὶ πρός τινας τοὺς πεποιθότας ἐφ᾽ ἑαυτοῖς ὅτι εἰσὶν δίκαιοι. (Lk 18:9)

15. οἱ δὲ διελογίζοντο ἐν ἑαυτοῖς λέγοντες ὅτι ῎Αρτους οὐκ ἐλάβομεν. (Mt 16:7)

16. ἐὰν ᾖ ἐξ ἀνθρώπων τὸ ἔργον τοῦτο, καταλυθήσεται. (Acts 5:38)

II. Translate into Greek:
1. And one of them was persuaded and followed Jesus.
2. And they stretched out their hands and they became healthy. (Mt 12:13)
3. An unjust man will not inherit the kingdom of God. (1 Cor 6:9)

III. Mk 10:46 – 11:25

ἴστημι, **Principal Parts.** ἴστημι, **Present
Active Indicative, Imperfect Active
Indicative, Present Active Imperative,
Subjunctive, Participle, and Infinitive.**
ἴστημι, **Aorist Active Transitive and Aorist
Active Intransitive.** ἴστημι, **Aorist Active
Indicative Intransitive, Aorist Active
Imperative Intransitive, Aorist Active
Subjunctive Intransitive, Aorist Active
Participle Intransitive, Aorist Active
Infinitive Intransitive.** ἴστημι, **Perfect
Active, Forms and Meaning. Difficult
Verbs:** ἴστημι, πάσχω.

Lesson 59

ἴστημι, **Principal Parts.**

The common and difficult verb ἴστημι, *I stand,* has the following
principal parts:

ἴστημι   στήσω   ἔστησα   ἔστηκα   —   ἐστάθην
                      ἔστην

The active forms of the present active, ἴστημι, as well as the
forms of the future active, στήσω, and the aorist active, ἔστησα, all
have <u>transitive</u> meanings, i.e., they are construed with an object
(e.g., *I stand a book on the shelf* or *I station him in the front line*).
The other aorist active, ἔστην, the perfect active ἔστηκα (along with
the pluperfect active), and all the middle forms have <u>intransitive</u>
meanings, i.e., they are not construed with an object (e.g., *I stood on
the corner for a full hour*). The aorist passive ἐστάθην also
frequently has an intransitive meaning.

Transitive Force	Intransitive Force
ἴστημι	ἔστην
στήσω	ἔστηκα
ἔστησα	all middle forms

ἵστημι, Present Active Indicative, Imperfect Active Indicative, Present Active Imperative, Subjunctive, Participle, and Infinitive.

The present system of ἵστημι is conjugated as follows (cf. V 11, 21; DV 134, VP 1-3, 7-8, 11; for the participle, cf. also Adj 20):

Active Voice, Indicative Mood, Present Tense [Transitive Force]

	Singular	Plural
1st Person	ἵστη–μι	ἵστα–μεν
2nd Person	ἵστη–ς	ἵστα–τε
3rd Person	ἵστη–σι(ν)	ἵστασι(ν) [< ἵστα–ασι]

Active Voice, Indicative Mood, Imperfect Tense [Transitive Force]

	Singular	Plural
1st Person	ἵστη–ν	ἵστα–μεν
2nd Person	ἵστη–ς	ἵστα–τε
3rd Person	ἵστη	ἵστα–σαν

The initial ι is long because it functions as the augment as well as the first letter of the stem.

Active Voice, Imperative Mood, Present Tense [Transitive Force]

	Singular	Plural
2nd Person	ἵστη	ἵστα–τε
3rd Person	ἱστά–τω	ἱστά–τωσαν

Active Voice, Subjunctive Mood, Present Tense [Transitive Force]

	Singular	Plural
1st Person	ἱστῶ	ἱστῶμεν
2nd Person	ἱστῇς	ἱστῆτε
3rd Person	ἱστῇ	ἱστῶσι(ν)

Active Voice, Participial Mood, Present Tense [Transitive Force]

	Masculine	Feminine (Singular)	Neuter
n	ἱστά–ς	ἱστᾶσα	ἱστά–ν
v	ἱστά–ς	ἱστᾶσα	ἱστά–ν
g	ἱστά–ντος	ἱστάσης	ἱστά–ντος
d	ἱστά–ντι	ἱστάσῃ	ἱστά–ντι
a	ἱστά–ντα	ἱστᾶσαν	ἱστά–ν

		Plural	
	Masculine	Feminine	Neuter
n	ἱστά–ντες	ἱστᾶσαι	ἱστά–ντα
v	ἱστά–ντες	ἱστᾶσαι	ἱστά–ντα
g	ἱστά–ντων	ἱστασῶν	ἱστά–ντων
d	ἱστᾶσι(ν)	ἱστάσαις	ἱστᾶσι(ν)
a	ἱστά–ντας	ἱστάσας	ἱστά–ντα

The present active infinitive is ἱστά–ναι (transitive force).

ἵστημι, Aorist Active Transitive and Aorist Active Intransitive.

The forms of the <u>transitive</u> active aorist, ἔστησα, are conjugated like ἔλυσα, in all moods.

The forms of the <u>intransitive</u> active aorist, ἔστην, have a special conjugation (see the following section).

ἵστημι, Aorist Active Indicative Intransitive, Aorist Active Imperative Intransitive, Aorist Active Subjunctive Intransitive, Aorist Active Participle Intransitive, Aorist Active Infinitive Intransitive.

The forms of the <u>intransitive</u> active aorist of ἵστημι, ἔστην, are conjugated as follows (cf. V 11, 21; DV 134; VP 1-3, 7-8, 11; for the participle cf. also Adj 12):

Active Voice, Indicative Mood, Aorist Tense [Intransitive Force]

	Singular	Plural
1st Person	ἔ–στη–ν	ἔ–στη–μεν
2nd Person	ἔ–στη–ς	ἔ–στη–τε
3rd Person	ἔ–στη	ἔ–στη–σαν

It should be noted that the third person plural form, ἔ–στη–σαν, has the same appearance as the third person plural form of the aorist active indicative <u>transitive</u>, ἔ–στη–σ–αν.

Active Voice, Imperative Mood, Aorist Tense [Intransitive Force]

	Singular	Plural
2nd Person	στή–θι	στή–τε
3rd Person	στή–τω	στή–τωσαν

Active Voice, Subjunctive Mood, Aorist Tense [Intransitive Force]

	Singular	Plural
1st Person	στῶ	στῶμεν
2nd Person	στῇς	στῆτε
3rd Person	στῇ	στῶσι(ν)

There is no intransitive active aorist optative in the New Testament.

Active Voice, Participial Mood, Aorist Tense [Intransitive Force]

Singular

	Masculine	Feminine	Neuter
n	στά–ς	στᾶσα	στά–ν
v	στά–ς	στᾶσα	στά–ν
g	στά–ντος	στάσης	στά–ντος
d	στά–ντι	στάσῃ	στά–ντι
a	στά–ντα	στᾶσαν	στά–ν

Plural

	Masculine	Feminine	Neuter
n	στά–ντες	στᾶσαι	στά–ντα
v	στά–ντες	στᾶσαι	στά–ντα
g	στά–ντων	στασῶν	στά–ντων
d	στᾶσι(ν)	στάσαις	στᾶσι(ν)
a	στά–ντας	στάσας	στά–ντα

The intransitive aorist active infinitive is στῆ–ναι.

ἵστημι, Perfect Active, Forms and Meaning.

The perfect active forms have an <u>intransitive</u> meaning, with the present aspect of the perfect emphasized so that for practical purposes the form means *I stand* (intransitive).

There are two forms used in the perfect active, the weak and the strong, with no difference in meaning, but based on two different roots. ἑστηκ– and ἑστα–. Only the weak perfect is found in the indicative (perfect: ἕστηκα; pluperfect: εἱστήκειν—the augment is irregular). Only the strong perfect is found in the infinitive (ἑστάναι). Both the weak and the strong perfect forms are found in the participle (weak: ἑστηκώς, ἑστηκυῖα, ἑστηκός, stem ἑστηκοτ–; strong: ἑστώς, ἑστῶσα, ἑστός, stem ἑστωτ– [Adj 22]).

Both participial forms are found in the subjunctive, which uses the perfect participle with the present subjunctive of εἰμί. The optative perfect is not found in the New Testament.

The middle and passive forms will be presented in the following lesson.

Difficult Verbs: ἵστημι, πάσχω.

ἵστημι, transitive: *I make stand; I establish;* intransitive: *I stand; I come to a halt* [V 11, 21; DV 134; VP 1-3, 7-8, 11]

ἵστημι	στήσω	ἔστησα	ἔστηκα	—	ἐστάθην
Heb 7:28	Mt 25:33	Mt 4:5	Mt 12:47		Mt 2:9
		ἔστην	ἑστώς		
		Lk 6:8	Mt 6:5		

The present active and future active and weak aorist active (ἔστησα) are all transitive: *I stand* in the sense of *I cause to stand, I make stand, I establish.* The strong aorist active (special endings) and perfect active (both weak and strong forms) are intransitive: *I stand* in the sense of *I come to a halt, I am in a place.* The aorist passive, ἐστάθην, is frequently used with this latter, intransitive meaning, although it can also have a normal passive meaning. The perfect active is used with a present meaning in both weak and strong forms. The perfect middle and passive are not found in the New Testament. ἱ is found in the present system but not in the aorist because it is the reduplicating element. There are rough breathings in the present and perfect systems. In brief, this is a difficult verb—the most difficult in the New Testament.

πάσχω, *I suffer* [V 2, DV 231, VP 1-4]

πάσχω	—	ἔπαθον	πέπονθα	—	—
1 Cor 12:26		Mt 16:21	Lk 13:2		

The future is not found in the New Testament. The aorist and the perfect are strong.

Vocabulary for Lesson 59.

ἀνθίστημι [ἀντί + ἵστημι] [V 11, 18, 21; DV 134; VP 1-3, 7-8, 11] *I resist* [governs the dative case].

ἀνίστημι [ἀνά + ἵστημι] [V 11, 18, 21; DV 134; VP 1-3, 7-8, 11] transitive: *I raise; I appoint*; intransitive: *I rise; I stand up.*

ἀφίστημι [ἀπό + ἵστημι] [V 11, 18, 21; DV 134; VP 1-3, 7-8, 11] *I leave; I apostatize* [with the genitive or a preposition and the genitive].

ἐξίστημι [ἐκ + ἵστημι] [V 11, 18, 21; DV 134; VP 1-3, 7-8, 11] transitive: *I amaze*; intransitive: *I am amazed.*

ἐφίστημι [ἐπί + ἵστημι] [V 11, 18, 21; DV 134; VP 1-3, 7-8, 11] *I come up to*; perfect active: *I am present.*

ἵστημι [V 11, 18, 21; DV 134; VP 1-3, 7-8, 11] transitive: *I make stand; I establish*; intransitive: *I stand; I stop.*

καθίστημι [κατά + ἵστημι] [V 11, 18, 21; DV 134; VP 1-3, 7-8, 11] *I put in charge*; passive: *I am made to be; I am appointed.*

παρίστημι [παρά + ἵστημι] [V 11, 18, 21; DV 134; VP 1-3, 7-8, 11] transitive: *I present; I provide*; intransitive: *I stand by* [with the dative case].

συνίστημι [σύν + ἵστημι] [V 11, 18, 21; DV 134; VP 1-3, 7-8, 11] transitive: *I recommend*; intransitive: *I stand with; to stand together* with the dative case].

———

πάσχω [V 2, DV 231, VP 1-4] *I suffer; I experience.*

———

ἐντέλλομαι [ἐν + τέλλομαι] [V 6, 22; DV 306; VP 2-3] *I order* [with the dative case].

ἐπιθυμέω [ἐπί + the root from θυμός] [V 8; VP 1-3, 5-6] *I desire strongly.*

κλείω [V 1, DV 157, VP 1-3] *I shut; I close.*

πάρειμι [παρά + εἰμί] [V 16, DV 78, VP 9] *I am present.*

———

ἐπειδή [Conj] *since; because; when; after.*

———

ἅμα [Adv 2] *at the same time; together.* This word is also found as a preposition governing the dative case [Prep 1]: *together with.*

Exercises for Lesson 59.

I. Translate into English:
1. οὗτοι ἔχουσιν τὴν ἐξουσίαν κλεῖσαι τὸν οὐρανόν. (Apoc 11:6)
2. ἀμὴν λέγω ὑμῖν ὅτι ἐπὶ πᾶσιν τοῖς ὑπάρχουσιν αὐτοῦ καταστήσει αὐτόν. (Mt 24:47)
3. ἰδοὺ ἡ μήτηρ καὶ οἱ ἀδελφοὶ αὐτοῦ εἱστήκεισαν ἔξω ζητοῦντες αὐτῷ λαλῆσαι. (Mt 12:46)
4. ἐγὼ δὲ λέγω ὑμῖν μὴ ἀντιστῆναι τῷ πονηρῷ. (Mt 5:39)
5. ἐπειδὴ γὰρ δι᾽ ἀνθρώπου θάνατος, καὶ δι᾽ ἀνθρώπου ἀνάστασις νεκρῶν. (1 Cor 15:21)
6. καὶ λαβὼν παιδίον ἔστησεν αὐτὸ ἐν μέσῳ αὐτῶν. (Mk 9:36)
7. καὶ ἐπὶ ἡγεμόνων καὶ βασιλέων σταθήσεσθε ἕνεκεν ἐμοῦ εἰς μαρτύριον αὐτοῖς. (Mk 13:9)
8. τοῦτο γάρ ἐστιν τὸ θέλημα τοῦ πατρός μου, ἵνα πᾶς ὁ θεωρῶν τὸν υἱὸν καὶ πιστεύων εἰς αὐτὸν ἔχῃ ζωὴν αἰώνιον, καὶ ἀναστήσω αὐτὸν ἐγὼ ἐν τῇ ἐσχάτῃ ἡμέρᾳ. (Jn 6:40) [The ἵνα-clause is not a purpose clause but a substantive clause, in apposition to τοῦτο and θέλημα. Cf. Lesson 75.]
9. προσεύχεσθε ἅμα ἐν εὐχαριστίᾳ.
10. Ἰησοῦς οὖν ἰδὼν τὴν μητέρα καὶ τὸν μαθητὴν παρεστῶτα ὃν ἠγάπα, λέγει τῇ μητρί, Γύναι, ἴδε ὁ υἱός σου. (Jn 19:26)
11. καὶ ἐρεῖ λέγων ὑμῖν, Οὐκ οἶδα ὑμᾶς πόθεν ἐστέ· ἀπόστητε ἀπ᾽ ἐμοῦ, πάντες ἐργάται ἀδικίας. (Lk 13:27)
12. λέγει οὖν αὐτοῖς ὁ Ἰησοῦς, Ὁ καιρὸς ὁ ἐμὸς οὔπω πάρεστιν, ὁ δὲ καιρὸς ὁ ὑμέτερος πάντοτέ ἐστιν ἕτοιμος. (Jn 7:6)

13. ἐξίσταντο δὲ πάντες οἱ ἀκούοντες αὐτοῦ. (Lk 2:47)
    [ἐξίσταντο is the imperfect of the middle voice of
    ἵστημι; cf. Lesson 60.]

14. ἀμὴν γὰρ λέγω ὑμῖν ὅτι πολλοὶ προφῆται καὶ δίκαιοι
    ἐπεθύμησαν ἰδεῖν ἃ βλέπετε καὶ οὐκ εἶδαν, καὶ
    ἀκοῦσαι ἃ ἀκούετε καὶ οὐκ ἤκουσαν. (Mt 13:17)

15. καὶ ἰδοὺ τρεῖς ἄνδρες ἐπέστησαν ἐπὶ τὴν οἰκίαν ἐν ᾗ
    ἦμεν, ἀπεσταλμένοι ἀπὸ τοῦ ἡγεμόνος πρός με. (Acts
    11:11)

16. συνίστησιν δὲ τὴν ἑαυτοῦ ἀγάπην εἰς ἡμᾶς ὁ θεὸς ὅτι
    Χριστὸς ὑπὲρ ἡμῶν ἀπέθανεν. (Rom 5:8)

17. λέγω δὲ ὑμῖν ὅτι ὁ προφήτης ἤδη ἦλθεν, καὶ οὐκ
    ἐπέγνωσαν αὐτὸν ἀλλὰ ἐποίησαν ἐν αὐτῷ ὅσα
    ἠθέλησαν· οὕτως καὶ ὁ υἱὸς τοῦ ἀνθρώπου μέλλει
    πάσχειν ὑπ' αὐτῶν. (Mt 17:12)

18. ὑμεῖς φίλοι μού ἐστε ἐὰν ποιῆτε ἃ ἐγὼ ἐντέλλομαι
    ὑμῖν. (Jn 15:14)

II. Translate into Greek:
1. There is a certain woman standing here who has suffered
   greatly. (Mt 16:28)
2. And having descended with him they stood on that place.
   (Lk 6:17)
3. They will set this sheep on their right hand. (Mt 25:33)

III. Mk 11:27 – 12:27.

ἵστημι, **Present Middle and Passive
Indicative, Imperfect Middle and Passive
Indicative, Present Middle and Passive
Imperative, Subjunctive, Participle, and
Infinitive. The Verbs** ἱστάνω **and** στήκω.
Difficult Verbs: χαίρω, ἁμαρτάνω,
κλαίω.

Lesson 60.

ἵστημι, Present Middle and Passive Indicative, Imperfect Middle and Passive Indicative, Present Middle and Passive Imperative, Subjunctive, Participle, and Infinitive.

The present middle and passive of ἵστημι is conjugated as follows (cf. V 11, 21; DV 134; VP 1-3, 7-8, 11; for the participle cf. also Adj 1):

Middle and Passive Voices, Indicative Mood, Present Tense

	Singular	Plural
1st Person	ἵστα–μαι	ἱστά–μεθα
2nd Person	ἵστα–σαι	ἵστα–σθε
3rd Person	ἵστα–ται	ἵστα–νται

Middle and Passive Voices, Indicative Mood, Imperfect Tense

	Singular	Plural
1st Person	ἱστά–μην	ἱστά–μεθα
2nd Person	ἵστα–σο	ἵστα–σθε
3rd Person	ἵστα–το	ἵστα–ντο

Middle and Passive Voices, Imperative Mood, Present Tense

	Singular	Plural
2nd Person	ἵστα–σο	ἵστα–σθε
3rd Person	ἱστά–σθω	ἱστά–σθωσαν

Middle and Passive Voices, Subjunctive Mood, Present Tense

	Singular	Plural
1st Person	ἱστῶμαι	ἱστώμεθα
2nd Person	ἱστῇ	ἱστῆσθε
3rd Person	ἱστῆται	ἱστῶνται

ἱστῇ < ἱστά–ησαι.

There is no present middle or passive optative in the New Testament.

Middle and Passive Voices, Participial Mood, Present Tense

Singular

	Masculine	Feminine	Neuter
n	ἱστά–μενος	ἱστα–μένη	ἱστά–μενον
v	ἱστά–μενε	ἱστα–μένη	ἱστά–μενον
g	ἱστα–μένου	ἱστα–μένης	ἱστα–μένου
d	ἱστα–μένῳ	ἱστα–μένῃ	ἱστα–μένῳ
a	ἱστα–μενον	ἱστα–μένην	ἱστά–μενον

Plural

	Masculine	Feminine	Neuter
n	ἱστά–μενοι	ἱστά–μεναι	ἱστά–μενα
v	ἱστά–μενοι	ἱστά–μεναι	ἱστά–μενα
g	ἱστα–μένων	ἱστα–μένων	ἱστα–μένων
d	ἱστα–μένοις	ἱστα–μέναις	ἱστα–μένοις
a	ἱστα–μένους	ἱστα–μένας	ἱστά–μενα

The present middle and passive infinitives have the same form: ἵστα–σθαι.

There is no strong aorist middle, nor is the weak aorist found in the middle voice.

The passive voice of ἵστημι is used at times in an intransitive sense (e.g., Mt 2:9 and 12:25).

The Verbs ἱστάνω and στήκω.

There are two verbs related to ἵστημι which call for special comment. The verb ἱστάνω, *I make stand, I establish*, is found in the present system. It is conjugated like λύω. The verb στήκω, *I stand* [intransitive], is based on the weak perfect stem of ἵστημι. It is used in the present tense and is also conjugated like λύω.

Difficult Verbs: χαίρω, ἁμαρτάνω, κλαίω.

χαίρω, *I rejoice* [V 6, DV 338, VP 1-3]

χαίρω	χαρήσομαι	—	—	—	ἐχάρην
Mt 5:12	Lk 1:14				Mt 2:10
	[passive deponent]				[passive deponent]

This verb is regular in the present system, and deponent in the future and aorist. It is a passive deponent in these tenses, and the aorist is strong. The fact that the aorist is strong and is deponent gives the future the appearance of being a middle form whereas it is in fact passive because it is formed on the basis of the aorist passive. Both deponent forms have the same active meaning as in the present system.

ἁμαρτάνω, *I sin* [V 7; DV 15; VP 1, 4]

ἁμαρτάνω	ἁμαρτήσω	ἥμαρτον	ἡμάρτηκα	—	—
1 Cor 6:18	Mt 18:21	Mt 27:4	1 Jn 1:10		
		ἡμάρτησα			
		Mt 18:15			

There are two aorists, one weak and one strong. There are no perfect middle or passive forms in the New Testament, nor aorist passive.

κλαίω, *I weep* [V 1, DV 155, VP 1]

κλαίω	κλαύσω	ἔκλαυσα	—	—	—
Mt 2:18	Lk 6:25	Mt 26:75			

Vocabulary for Lesson 60.

ἱστάνω [V 7, VP 1] transitive: *I make stand; I constitute*. This verb is found only in the present system.

στήκω [V 2, VP 1] intransitive: *I stand*. This verb is found only in the present system.

___

χαίρω [V 6, DV 338, VP 1-4] *I rejoice*.

___

ἁμαρτάνω [V 7; DV 15; VP 1, 4] *I sin*.

___

κλαίω [V 1, DV 155, VP 1] *I weep*.

___

ἀνέχομαι [ἀνά + ἔχω] [V 2, 22; DV 109; VP 2-3, 4] *I endure, I am patient* [with the genitive case].

γεύομαι [V 1, 22; VP 2-3] *I taste; I experience* [with the genitive case].

δέρω [V 6, DV 57, VP 1-3, 5] *I beat; I hit*.

διαμαρτύρομαι [διά + μαρτύρομαι] [V 6, 22; DV 187; VP 2-3] *I warn; I testify solemnly*.

ἐργάζομαι [V 5, 22, DV 94; VP 2-3] *I work; I trade*.

οἰκοδομέω [This is from two roots found in the words οἶκος and δόμος, *house*,. Although it is a compund it is treated as a single element for purpes of lengthening. Thus ᾠκοδόμησεν in Mk 12:1.] [V 8; DV 213; VP 1-3, 5-6] *I build; I encourage*.

ὀφείλω [V 6, DV 228, VP 1-3] *I owe; I ought*.

ὑστερέω [V 8, VP 1-3] *I lack; I am inferior* [governs accusative case].

χορτάζω (χορτάσω) [V 5, DV 1-3] *I feed; I satisfy*.

___

κἀκεῖ = καὶ ἐκεῖ [crasis] [Conj + Adv 1] *and there; also there*.

κἀκεῖθεν = καὶ ἐκεῖθεν [crasis] [Conj + Adv 1] *and from there* [time and place].

κἀκεῖνος = καὶ ἐκεῖνος [Conj + Adj 1Pro] *and that one; also that one.*

———

ὕστερον [Adv 2] *afterwards; finally.*

Exercises for Lesson 60.

I. Translate into English:
1. διαμαρτύρομαι ἐνώπιον τοῦ θεοῦ καὶ Χριστοῦ Ἰησοῦ, τοῦ μέλλοντος κρίνειν ζῶντας καὶ νεκρούς. . . . (2 Tim 4:1)
2. ὕστερον δὲ ἀπέστειλεν πρὸς αὐτοὺς τὸν υἱὸν αὐτοῦ. (Mt 21:37)
3. καὶ ἔρχεται ἡ μήτηρ αὐτοῦ καὶ οἱ ἀδελφοὶ αὐτοῦ καὶ ἔξω στήκοντες ἀπέστειλαν πρὸς αὐτὸν καλοῦντες αὐτόν. (Mk 3:31)
4. ὦ γενεὰ ἄπιστος, ἕως πότε μεθ᾽ ὑμῶν ἔσομαι; ἕως πότε ἀνέξομαι ὑμῶν; (Mt 17:17)
5. τί δὲ ὑμῖν δοκεῖ; ἄνθρωπος εἶχεν τέκνα δύο. καὶ προσελθὼν τῷ πρώτῳ εἶπεν, Τέκνον, ὕπαγε σήμερον ἐργάζου ἐν τῷ ἀμπελῶνι. (Mt 21:28)
6. μακάριοι οἱ πεινῶντες νῦν, ὅτι χορτασθήσεσθε. (Lk 6:21)
7. ὁ δὲ ἀκούσας καὶ μὴ ποιήσας ὅμοιός ἐστιν ἀνθρώπῳ οἰκοδομήσαντι οἰκίαν ἐπὶ τὴν γῆν χωρὶς θεμελίου. (Lk 6:49)
8. νόμον οὖν καταργοῦμεν διὰ τῆς πίστεως; μὴ γένοιτο, ἀλλὰ νόμον ἱστάνομεν. (Rom 3:31)
9. ὁ δὲ Ἰησοῦς ἐμβλέψας αὐτῷ ἠγάπησεν αὐτὸν καὶ εἶπεν αὐτῷ, Ἕν σε ὑστερεῖ· ὕπαγε ὅσα ἔχεις πώλησον καὶ δὸς τοῖς πτωχοῖς, καὶ ἕξεις θησαυρὸν ἐν οὐρανῷ, καὶ ἀκολούθει μοι. (Mk 10:21)
10. κἀκεῖ εὐαγγελιζόμενοι ἦσαν. (Acts 14:7)
11. οἱ δὲ ἀκούσαντες ἐχάρησαν καὶ ἐπηγγείλαντο αὐτῷ ἀργύριον δοῦναι. (Mk 14:11)
12. πόσον ὀφείλεις τῷ κυρίῳ μου; (Lk 16:5)
13. ὃ ὠφείλομεν ποιῆσαι πεποιήκαμεν. (Lk 17:10)
14. ἀλλὰ διὰ τῆς χάριτος τοῦ κυρίου Ἰησοῦ πιστεύομεν σωθῆναι κατὰ τὸν τρόπον καθ᾽ ὃν πιστεύομεν ὅτι κἀκεῖνοι σῴζονται. (Acts 15:11) [Cf. Lesson 66, Vocabulary, for the meaning of τρόπον.]
15. ἀναστὰς πορεύσομαι πρὸς τὸν πατέρα μου καὶ ἐρῶ αὐτῷ, Πάτερ, ἥμαρτον εἰς τὸν οὐρανὸν καὶ ἐνώπιον

σου, οὐκέτι εἰμὶ ἄξιος κληθῆναι υἱός σου. (Lk 15:18-19)

16. κἀκεῖθεν ᾐτήσαντο βασιλέα, καὶ ἔδωκεν αὐτοῖς ὁ θεὸς τὸν Σαούλ [*Saul*]. (Acts 13:21)

17. λέγω γὰρ ὑμῖν ὅτι οὐδεὶς τῶν ἀνδρῶν ἐκείνων τῶν κεκλημένων γεύσεταί μου τοῦ δείπνου. (Lk 14:24)

18. ἐκεῖνος δὲ ὁ δοῦλος ὁ γνοὺς τὸ θέλημα τοῦ κυρίου αὐτοῦ δαρήσεται πολλάς. (Lk 12:47] [πολλάς agrees with the word πληγάς which is understood from the context: *will be beaten many blows*. Verbs which in the active voice can govern a double accusative retain in the passive voice the accusative of thing. In Greek this is also possible when there is question of a dative case after the active verb instead of a second accusative. Cf. the English expression *I am given a book*.]

19. ἥδε γυνὴ εἱστήκει πρὸς τῷ μνημείῳ ἔξω κλαίουσα. (Jn 20:11)

II. Translate into Greek:
   1. And going out around the third hour they saw another man standing alongside the road. (Mt 20:3)
   2. Many things are lacking to you. (Mk 10:21)
   3. And we ought to wash each others' feet. (Jn 13:14)

III. Mk 12:28 – 13:13.

δείκνυμι, **Present Active Indicative,
Imperfect Active Indicative, Present Active
Imperative, Subjunctive, Participle, and
Infinitive. Difficult Verbs:** δείκνυμι,
στρέφω, φαίνω.

Lesson 61

δείκνυμι, **Present Active Indicative, Imperfect Active Indicative, Present Active Imperative, Subjunctive, Participle, and Infinitive.**

Another important verb in –μι is δείκνυμι, *I show*. It has distinctive endings only in the present system (V14; DV 55; VP 1-3, 9-10, 12; for the participle cf. also Adj 20):

Active Voice, Indicative Mood, Present Tense

	Singular	Plural
1st Person	δείκνυ–μι	δείκνυ–μεν
2nd Person	δείκνυ–ς	δείκνυ–τε
3rd Person	δείκνυ–σι(ν)	δεικνύ–ασι(ν)

Active Voice, Indicative Mood, Imperfect Tense

	Singular	Plural
1st Person	ἐ–δείκνυ–ν	ἐ–δείκνυ–μεν
2nd Person	ἐ–δείκνυ–ς	ἐ–δείκνυ–τε
3rd Person	ἐ–δείκνυ	ἐ–δείκνυ–σαν

Active Voice, Imperative Mood, Present Tense

	Singular	Plural
2nd Person	δείκνυ	δείκνυ–τε
3rd Person	δεικνύ–τω	δεικνύ–τωσαν

Active Voice, Subjunctive Mood, Present Tense

	Singular	Plural
1st Person	δεικνύ–ω	δεικνύ–ωμεν
2nd Person	δεικνύ–ῃς	δεικνύ–ητε
3rd Person	δεικνύ–ῃ	δεικνύ–ωσι(ν)

The accent does <u>not</u> fall on the last syllable of the subjunctive.

The present optative is not found in the New Testament.

Active Voice, Participial Mood, Present Tense

Singular

	Masculine	Feminine	Neuter
n	δεικνύ–ς	δεικνῦσα	δεικνύ–ν
v	δεικνύ–ς	δεικνῦσα	δεικνύ–ν
g	δεικνύ–ντος	δεικνύσης	δεικνύ–ντος
d	δεικνύ–ντι	δεικνύσῃ	δεικνύ–ντι
a	δεικνύ–ντα	δεικνῦσαν	δεικνύ–ν

Plural

	Masculine	Feminine	Neuter
n	δεικνύ–ντες	δεικνῦσαι	δεικνύ–ντα
v	δεικνύ–ντες	δεικνῦσαι	δεικνύ–ντα
g	δεικνύ–ντων	δεικνυσῶν	δεικνύ–ντων
d	δεικνῦσι(ν)	δεικνύσαις	δεικνῦσι(ν)
a	δεικνύ–ντας	δεικνύσας	δεικνύ–ντα

The present infinitive is δεικνύ–ναι.

The aorist endings are like the endings of λύω in all voices.

Difficult Verbs: δείκνυμι, στρέφω, φαίνω.

δείκνυμι, *I show* [V 14; DV 55; VP 1-3, 9-10, 12]

δείκνυμι	δείξω	ἔδειξα	—	δέδειγμαι	ἐδείχθην
Mt 4:8	Mk 14:15	Mt 8:4		Acts2:22	Heb 8:5

δεικνύω
Jn 2:18

στρέφω, *I turn* [transitive in the active voice] [V 4, DV 296, VP 1-4]

στρέφω	στρέψω	ἔστρεψα	—	ἔστραμμαι	ἐστράφην
Acts 13:46	Mt 12:44	Mt 5:39		Mt 17:17	Mt 7:6

The present active is used in a transitive sense (*I turn* [*someone* or *something else*]), *I return* [*someone* or *something else*]). The aorist passive is usually used in an intransitive sense (*I turned* [*myself*]) *I returned* [*myself*]).

φαίνω, *I shine, I appear* [V 7, DV 321, VP 1-4]

φαίνω	φανοῦμαι	ἔφανα —	—	ἐφάνην
Jn 1:5	1 Pt 4:18	Apoc 8:12		Mt 1:20

[φανήσομαι]
Mt 24:30

In the New Testament the present active is used intransitively. The middle is also used in this way. The future forms are deponent, one middle in form and the other passive. The aorist passive is strong.

Vocabulary for Lesson 61.

δείκνυμι / δεικνύω [V 14; DV 55; VP 1-3, 9-10, 12] *I show; I prove.*

ἐνδείκνυμαι [ἐν + δείκνυμαι] [V 14, 22; DV 55; VP 1-3, 9-10, 12] *I show; I prove.*

———

ἀναστρέφω [ἀνά + στρέφω] [V 4, DV 296, VP 1-4] intransitive: *I return, I stay*; passive forms: *I live, I conduct myself.*

ἐπιστρέφω [ἐπί + στρέφω] [V 4, DV 296, VP 1-4] transitive: *I cause to turn back; I change*; intransitive: *I turn (myself), I change (myself).*

στρέφω [V 4, DV 296, VP 1-4] transitive: *I turn (someone or something else), I give back; I change*; intransitive: *I turn (myself), I change (myself).*

ὑποστρέφω [ὑπό + στρέφω] [V 4, DV 296, VP 1-4] *I return* [intransitive sense]; *I go back*.

___

φαίνω [V 7, DV 321, VP 1-4] intransitive: *I shine; I appear*.

___

ἀναπαύω [ἀνά + παύω] [V 1, DV 233, VP 1-3] transitive: *I refresh*; intransitive: *I stop; I rest*.

κτίζω (κτίσω) [V 5, DV 169, VP 1-3] *I create*.

μοιχεύω [V 1, VP 1-3] *I commit adultery* [with the accusative or with the genitive].

νομίζω (νομίσω) [V 5, VP 1-3] *I think; I am accustomed to*.

παύομαι [V 1, 22; DV 233; VP 2-3] *I cease, I cease from* [used absolutely or with the participle; the active form is found at 1 Pt 3:10 with a transitive meaning: *I cause to cease*].

ποτίζω (ποτίσω) [V 5, VP 1-3] *I cause to drink; I water*.

σαλεύω [V 1, VP 1-3] *I shake*.

σφραγίζω (σφραγίσω) [V 5, DV 1-3] *I seal, I mark with a seal; I acknowledge*.

ὠφελέω [V 8; VP 1-3, 5-6] *I am useful; I benefit (someone else)* [with the accusative for the person benefitted].

___

ἀμφότεροι, –αι, –α [Adj 6] *both; all*.

Exercises for Lesson 61.

I. Translate into English:
1. ἐπείνασα καὶ ἐδώκατέ μοι ἐσθίειν, ἐδίψησα καὶ ἐποτίσατέ με, ξένος ἤμην καὶ συνηγάγετέ με. (Mt 25:35)
2. καὶ πῶς δεῖ ἐν οἴκῳ θεοῦ ἀναστρέφεσθαι; (1 Tim 3:15)
3. ἀπὸ τότε ἤρξατο ὁ Ἰησοῦς δεικνύειν τοῖς μαθηταῖς αὐτοῦ ὅτι δεῖ αὐτὸν εἰς τὴν ἁγίαν πόλιν ἀπελθεῖν καὶ πολλὰ παθεῖν ἀπὸ τῶν πρεσβυτέρων καὶ

ἀρχιερέων καὶ γραμματέων καὶ ἀποκτανθῆναι καὶ
τῇ τρίτῃ ἡμέρᾳ ἐγερθῆναι. (Mt 16:21)

4. ἡ σάρξ οὐκ ὠφελεῖ οὐδέν. (Jn 6:63)

5. δεῦτε πρός με πάντες οἱ κοπιῶντες, κἀγὼ ἀναπαύσω
   ὑμᾶς. (Mt 11:28)

6. καὶ οἱ ἀστέρες ἔσονται ἐκ τοῦ οὐρανοῦ πίπτοντες, καὶ
   αἱ δυνάμεις αἱ ἐν τοῖς οὐρανοῖς σαλευθήσονται. (Mk
   13:25)

7. ὁ λαβὼν αὐτοῦ τὴν μαρτυρίαν ἐσφράγισεν ὅτι ὁ θεὸς
   ἀληθής ἐστιν. (Jn 3:33)

8. ἐν αὐτῷ ἐκτίσθη τὰ πάντα ἐν τοῖς οὐρανοῖς καὶ ἐπὶ τῆς
   γῆς. (Col 1:16)

9. ἀλλὰ διὰ τοῦτο ἠλεήθην, ἵνα ἐν ἐμοὶ πρώτῳ ἐνδείξηται
   Χριστὸς Ἰησοῦς τὴν ἅπασαν μακροθυμίαν. (1 Tim
   1:16).

10. καὶ τὸ φῶς ἐν τῇ σκοτίᾳ φαίνει, καὶ ἡ σκοτία αὐτὸ
    οὐ κατέλαβεν. (Jn 1:5)

11. καὶ εἶπεν, Ἀμὴν λέγω ὑμῖν, ἐὰν μὴ στραφῆτε καὶ
    γένησθε ὡς τὰ παιδία, οὐκ εἰσελεύσεσθε εἰς τὴν
    βασιλείαν τῶν οὐρανῶν. (Mt 18:3)

12. ἦσαν δὲ δίκαιοι ἀμφότεροι ἐνώπιον τοῦ θεοῦ. (Lk 1:6)

13. καὶ ἐὰν μὲν ᾖ ἡ οἰκία ἀξία, ἐλθάτω ἡ εἰρήνη ὑμῶν ἐπ'
    αὐτήν· ἐὰν δὲ μὴ ᾖ ἀξία, ἡ εἰρήνη ὑμῶν πρὸς ὑμᾶς
    ἐπιστραφήτω. (Mt 10:13)

14. καὶ ἐλθόντες οἱ πρῶτοι ἐνόμισαν ὅτι πλεῖον
    λήμψονται. (Mt 20:10)

15. καὶ ἐγένετο ἐν τῷ εἶναι αὐτὸν ἐν τόπῳ τινὶ
    προσευχόμενον, ὡς ἐπαύσατο, εἶπέν τις τῶν μαθητῶν
    αὐτοῦ πρὸς αὐτόν, Κύριε, δίδαξον ἡμᾶς
    προσεύχεσθαι. (Lk 11:1)

II. Translate into Greek:
   1. On saying this the women turned around and they see the
      disciples of Jesus, and they did not know that they were
      the disciples of Jesus. (Jn 20:14)
   2. And then the signs of the son of man will appear in
      heaven. (Mt 24:30)
   3. He did not cease teaching and preaching the Good News of
      the Christ, Jesus. (Acts 5:42)

III. Mk 13:14-37.

δείκνυμι, **Present Middle and Passive Indicative, Imperfect Middle and Passive Indicative, Present Middle and Passive Imperative, Subjunctive, Participle, and Infinitive. Difficult Verbs:** φεύγω, ἥκω, μανθάνω.

Lesson 62

δείκνυμι, Present Middle and Passive Indicative, Imperfect Middle and Passive Indicative, Present Middle and Passive Imperative, Subjunctive, Participle, and Infinitive.

The middle and passive systems of δείκνυμι are conjugated as follows (V 14; DV 55; VP 1-3, 9-10, 12; for the participle cf. also Adj 1):

Middle and Passive Voices, Indicative Mood, Present Tense

	Singular	Plural
1st Person	δείκνυ–μαι	δεικνύ–μεθα
2nd Person	δείκνυ–σαι	δείκνυ–σθε
3rd Person	δείκνυ–ται	δείκνυ–νται

Middle and Passive Voices, Indicative Mood, Imperfect Tense

	Singular	Plural
1st Person	ἐ–δεικνύ–μην	ἐ–δεικνύ–μεθα
2nd Person	ἐ–δείκνυ–σο	ἐ–δείκνυ–σθε
3rd Person	ἐ–δείκνυ–το	ἐ–δείκνυ–ντο

Middle and Passive Voices, Imperative Mood, Present Tense

	Singular	Plural
2nd Person	δείκνυ–σο	δείκνυ–σθε
3rd Person	δεικνύ–σθω	δεικνύ–σθωσαν

Middle and Passive Voices, Subjunctive Mood, Present Tense

	Singular	Plural
1st Person	δεικνύ–ωμαι	δεικνυ–ώμεθα
2nd Person	δεικνύ–η	δεικνύ–ησθε
3rd Person	δεικνύ–ηται	δεικνύ–ωνται

δεικνύη < δεικνύ–ησαι.

Neither the present optative middle nor the present optative passive is found in the New Testament.

Middle and Passive Voices, Participial Mood, Present Tense

Singular

	Masculine	Feminine	Neuter
n	δεικνύ–μενος	δεικνυ–μένη	δεικνύ–μενον
v	δεικνύ–μενε	δεικνυ–μένη	δεικνύ–μενον
g	δεικνυ–μένου	δεικνυ–μένης	δεικνυ–μένου
d	δεικνυ–μένῳ	δεικνυ–μένη	δεικνυ–μένῳ
a	δεικνύ–μενον	δεικνυ–μένην	δεικνύ–μενον

Plural

	Masculine	Feminine	Neuter
n	δεικνύ–μενοι	δεικνύ–μεναι	δεικνύ–μενα
v	δεικνύ–μενοι	δεικνύ–μεναι	δεικνύ–μενα
g	δεικνυ–μένων	δεικνυ–μένων	δεικνυ–μένων
d	δεικνυ–μένοις	δεικνυ–μέναις	δεικνυ–μένοις
a	δεικνυ–μένους	δεικνυ–μένας	δεικνύ–μενα

The present infinitive form is δείκνυ–σθαι.

In the aorist middle the endings are like those of λύω.

Difficult Verbs: φεύγω, ἥκω, μανθάνω.

φεύγω, *I flee* [V 2; DV 326; VP 1-2, 4]

φεύγω	φεύξομαι	ἔφυγον	πέφευγα	—	—
Mt 2:13	Jn 10:5	Mt 8:33	Acts 16:27		

The future is a middle deponent. The aorist is strong.

ἥκω, *I have come* [V 2, DV116, VP 1]

ἥκω	ἥξω	ἦξα	ἦκα	—	—
Lk 15:27	Mt 8:11	Apoc 2:25	Mk 8:3		

This verb has perfect meanings even with non-perfect tenses.

μανθάνω, *I learn* [V 7; DV 185; VP 1, 4]

μανθάνω	—	ἔμαθον	μεμάθηκα	—	—
1 Cor 14:31		Mt 9:13	Jn 7:15		

There is a strong (second) aorist.

Vocabulary for Lesson 62.

φεύγω [V 2; DV 326; VP 1-2, 4] *I take flight; I disappear.*

―――

ἥκω [V 2, DV 116, VP 1] *I have come; I am present.*

―――

μανθάνω [V 7; DV 185; VP 1, 4] *I learn; I discover; I learn by experience.*

―――

ἀγνοέω [α privative + a root from γινώσκω. The augment is formed by lengthening the α: ἠγνόουν in Mk 9:32.] [V 8; VP 1-3, 5-6] *I do not know, I am ignorant.*

ἀναχωρέω [ἀνά + χωρέω] [V 8; VP 1-3] *I retire, I withdraw.*

ἀπειθέω [α privative + a root from πείθω. The augment is formed by lengthening the α: ἠπείθουν in Acts 19:9.] [V 8; VP 1-3, 5-6] *I disobey* [with the dative for the person or thing being disobeyed].

ἀτενίζω (ἀτενίσω) [V 5, VP 1-3] *I stare at* [with the dative case alone or with εἰς and the accusative].

εὐφραίνω [εὖ + a root from φρήν. The augment is formed by lengthening the ε: ηὐφράνθην.] [V 7, VP 1-3] *I make happy*; passive: *I am happy*.

κατανοέω [κατά + νοέω] [V 8; VP 1-3, 5-6] *I consider*; *I observe*.

μερίζω (μερίσω) [V 5, VP 1-3] *I divide*; *I distribute*.

νοέω [V 8; VP 1-3, 5-6] *I understand*; *I reflect*; *I think*.

———

μύρον, –ου, τό [N 7] *ointment, perfume*.

πετεινά, –ῶν, τά [N 7] *birds*.

σεισμός, –οῦ, ὁ [N 6m] *earthquake*.

σῖτος, –ου, ὁ [N 6m] *grain*; *wheat*.

———

μωρός, –ά, –όν [Adj 2] *foolish*.

Exercises for Lesson 62.

I. Translate into English:
1. πῶς οὐ νοεῖτε ὅτι οὐ περὶ ἄρτων εἶπον ὑμῖν; (Mt 16:11)
2. ὁ πιστεύων εἰς τὸν υἱὸν ἔχει ζωὴν αἰώνιον· ὁ δὲ ἀπειθῶν τῷ υἱῷ οὐκ ὄψεται ζωήν, ἀλλ᾽ ἡ ὀργὴ τοῦ θεοῦ μένει ἐπ᾽ αὐτόν. (Jn 3:36)
3. σὺ δέ, ὦ ἄνθρωπε θεοῦ, ταῦτα φεῦγε. (1 Tim 6:11)
4. καὶ συνάξω ἐκεῖ πάντα τὸν σῖτον καὶ τὰ ἀγαθά μου. (Lk 12:18)
5. ὅθεν, ἀδελφοὶ ἅγιοι, κατανοήσατε τὸν ἀπόστολον καὶ ἀρχιερέα ἡμῶν, Ἰησοῦν. (Heb 3:1)
6. πῶς οὗτος γράμματα οἶδεν μὴ μεμαθηκώς; (Jn 7:15)
7. καὶ πᾶς ὁ ἀκούων μου τοὺς λόγους τούτους καὶ μὴ ποιῶν αὐτοὺς ὁμοιωθήσεται ἀνδρὶ μωρῷ. (Mt 7:26)
8. ἔσονται σεισμοὶ κατὰ τόπους. (Mk 13:8)
9. καί τινες αὐτῶν ἀπὸ μακρόθεν ἥκασιν. (Mk 8:3)
10. ἐμβλέψατε εἰς τὰ πετεινὰ τοῦ οὐρανοῦ. (Mt 6:26)
11. οἱ δὲ ἠγνόουν τὸ ῥῆμα, καὶ ἐφοβοῦντο αὐτὸν ἐπερωτῆσαι. (Mk 9:32)
12. εἰς τί ἡ ἀπώλεια αὕτη τοῦ μύρου γέγονεν; (Mk 14:4)
13. ὁ δὲ Ἰησοῦς γνοὺς ἀνεχώρησεν ἐκεῖθεν. (Mt 12:15)

14. πᾶσα πόλις ἢ οἰκία μερισθεῖσα καθ᾽ ἑαυτῆς οὐ
    σταθήσεται. (Mt 12:25)
15. καὶ ἐρῶ τῇ ψυχῇ μου, Ψυχή, ἔχεις πολλὰ ἀγαθὰ
    κείμενα εἰς ἔτη πολλά· ἀναπαύου, φάγε, πίε,
    εὐφραίνου. (Lk 12:19)
16. καὶ πάντων οἱ ὀφθαλμοὶ ἐν τῇ συναγωγῇ ἦσαν
    ἀτενίζοντες αὐτῷ. (Lk 4:20)
17. ἠκούσατε ὅτι ἐρρέθη, Οὐ μοιχεύσεις. (Mt 5:27)
18. καὶ ὑπέστρεψαν οἱ ποιμένες δοξάζοντες καὶ
    αἰνοῦντες τὸν θεὸν ἐπὶ πᾶσιν ἃ ἤκουσαν καὶ
    εἶδον καθὼς ἐλαλήθη πρὸς αὐτούς. (Lk 2:20)

II. Translate into Greek:
    1. All those having heard the father and having learned will
       come to Jesus. (Jn 6:45)
    2. And one of them will come from afar. (Mk 8:3)
    3. And the woman, going out, fled from the tomb. (Mk
       16:8)

III. Mk 14:1-21.

ἵημι, **Present Active Indicative, Imperfect Active Indicative, Present Active Imperative, Subjunctive, Participle, and Infinitive.** ἵημι, **Aorist Active Indicative, Imperative, Subjunctive, Participle [Summary], and Infinitive.** ἵημι, **Middle and Passive Forms in the Present System [Summary]. Middle Forms in the Aorist System [Summary]. Difficult Verbs:** ἵημι / ἵω, αἱρέω, λείπω.

Lesson 63

ἵημι, **Present Active Indicative, Imperfect Active Indicative, Present Active Imperative, Subjunctive, Participle, and Infinitive.**

The simple verb ἵημι, *I send*, does not occur in the New Testament. But it is the basis for a compound verb of considerable importance: ἀφίημι, *I forgive*. The conjugation of the simple verb will be given here. The present active system is conjugated as follows (cf. V 12, 21; DV 131; VP 1-3, 9-10, 12; for the participle cf. also Adj 18):

Active Voice, Indicative Mood, Present Tense

	Singular	Plural
1st Person	ἵη–μι	ἵε–μεν
2nd Person	ἵη–ς	ἵε–τε
3rd Person	ἵη–σι(ν)	ἱᾶσι(ν)

The usual contrast between the long stem vowel in the singular and the short stem vowel in the plural should be noted.

Active Voice, Indicative Mood, Imperfect Tense

	Singular	Plural
1st Person	ἵον	ἵομεν
2nd Person	ἵες	ἵετε
3rd Person	ἵε(ν)	ἵον

These forms are not from ἵημι but from ἵω, which has the same meaning as ἵημι. It is the thematic form based on the ι of the non-thematic form which is the marker for the present system. The root of the verb is ἥ / ἕ.

Active Voice, Imperative Mood, Present Tense

	Singular	Plural
2nd Person	ἵει	ἵε–τε
3rd Person	ἱέ–τω	ἱέ–τωσαν

Active Voice, Subjunctive Mood, Present Tense

	Singular	Plural
1st Person	ἱῶ	ἱῶμεν
2nd Person	ἱῇς	ἱῆτε
3rd Person	ἱῇ	ἱῶσι(ν)

The present active optative does not exist in the New Testament.

Active Voice, Participial Mood, Present Tense

Singular

	Masculine	Feminine	Neuter
n	ἱείς	ἱεῖσα	ἱέ–ν
v	ἱείς	ἱεῖσα	ἱέ–ν
g	ἱέ–ντος	ἱείσης	ἱέ–ντος
d	ἱέ–ντι	ἱείσῃ	ἱέ–ντι
a	ἱέ–ντα	ἱεῖσαν	ἱέ–ν

Plural

	Masculine	Feminine	Neuter
n	ἱέ–ντες	ἱεῖσαι	ἱέ–ντα
v	ἱέ–ντες	ἱεῖσαι	ἱέ–ντα
g	ἱέ–ντων	ἱεισῶν	ἱέ–ντων
d	ἱεῖσι(ν)	ἱείσαις	ἱεῖσι(ν)
a	ἱέ–ντας	ἱείσας	ἱέ–ντα

The present active infinitive is ἱέ–ναι.

ἵημι, **Aorist Active Indicative, Imperative, Subjunctive, Participle [Summary], and Infinitive.**

The aorist active system is conjugated as follows (cf. V 12, 21; DV 131; VP 1-3; for the participle cf. also Adj 18):

Active Voice, Indicative Mood, Aorist Tense

	Singular	Plural
1st Person	ἧκ–α	ἧκ–αμεν
2nd Person	ἧκ–ας	ἧκ–ατε
3rd Person	ἧκ–ε(ν)	ἧκ–αν

Active Voice, Imperative Mood, Aorist Tense

	Singular	Plural
2nd Person	ἕ–ς	ἕ–τε
3rd Person	ἕ–τω	ἕ–τωσαν

Active Voice, Subjunctive Mood, Aorist Tense

	Singular	Plural
1st Person	ὧ	ὧμεν
2nd Person	ἧς	ἧτε
3rd Person	ἧ	ὧσι(ν)

There is no aorist active optative in the New Testament.

The aorist active participle is εἵς, εἷσα, ἕν (ἕντος, εἵσης, ἕντος) and is declined like the present participle of ἵημι.

The aorist active infinitive is εἷναι (< ἕ–εναι).

The presence of the reduplicating element ι in the present system, and its absence in the aorist, should be noted.

ἵημι, **Middle and Passive Forms in the Present System [Summary]. Middle Forms in the Aorist System [Summary].**

The use of the present system of ἵημι in the middle and passive voices is limited. The forms ἵεται (third person singular of the indicative mood) and ἵενται (third person plural of the indicative mood) are found in the present tense. The present middle and passive participle forms ἱέμενος, ἱεμένη, ἱέμενον are also found.

In the aorist middle system only the participle is found: ἕμενος, ἑμένη, ἕμενον. The presence and absence of the reduplicating element ι should be noted.

Difficult Verbs: ἵημι / ἵω, αἱρέω, λείπω.

ἵημι, *I send* [V 12, 21; DV 131; VP 1-3, 9-10, 12]

ἵημι	ἥσω	ἧκα	—	εἷμαι	ἕθην
Mt 3:15	Mt 6:14	Mt 6:12		Heb 12:12	Mt 24:2

ἵω				ἕωμαι	
Mk 1:34				Lk 5:20	

The simple verb ἵημι is not found in the New Testament. The principal compound verb based on it is ἀφίημι from which most of the above forms are taken.

αἱρέω, *I take, I grasp* [V 8, 22; DV 7; VP 2-3, 4]

·αἱρέω	ἑλῶ	εἷλον	—	ἥρημαι	ἡρέθην
Acts 16:27	2 Thes 2:8	Mt 2:16		2 Cor 9:7	Lk 23:32

[αἱρέομαι]	αἱρήσομαι	εἱλάμην			
	Phil 1:22	2 Thes 2:13			

The simple verb αἱρέω occurs only a few times in the New Testament, as a deponent (αἱρέομαι, *I choose*). The above forms are taken for the most part from compound verbs having αἱρέω as a base. The aorist stem is ἑλ-. The ε is lengthened in the perfect middle and passive, but not in the aorist passive. αἱρέω is easily confused with αἴρω in both form and meaning.

λείπω, *I lack* [V 4, DV 181, VP 1-3]

λείπω	λείψω	ἔλιπον	—	λέλειμμαι	ἐλείφθην
Lk 18:22	Eph 5:31	Mk 12:21		Acts 25:14	Jn 8:9

The use of the simple verb λείπω is relatively infrequent in the New Testament. The above forms are taken for the most part from its compounds. The aorist active is strong. Some of the forms of λείπω can be confused with some of the forms of the verb λαμβάνω.

Vocabulary for Lesson 63.

ἀφίημι / ἀφίω [ἀπό + ἵημι] [V 12, 21; DV 131; VP 1-3, 9-10, 12] *I dismiss; I forgive (sin); I send; I allow; I leave.*

συνίημι [σύν + ἵημι] [V 12, 21; DV 131; VP 1-3, 9-10, 12] *I understand.*

___

αἱρέομαι [V 8, 22; DV 131; VP 2-3, 4] *I prefer; I choose.*

ἀναιρέω [ἀνά + αἱρέω] [V 8; DV 7; VP 1-3, 4] *I take away; I abolish; I kill.*

ἀφαιρέω [ἀπό + αἱρέω] [V 8; DV 7; VP 1-3, 4] *I remove; I take away.*

___

ἐγκαταλείπω [ἐν + κατά + λείπω] [V 4, DV 181, VP 1-4] *I desert, I abandon.*

καταλείπω [κατά + λείπω] [V 4, DV 181, VP 1-4] *I leave* [a place or thing].

λείπω [V 4, DV 181, VP 1-4] transitive: *I leave, I abandon*; intransitive: *I lack.*

___

ἁρπάζω (ἁρπάσω) [V 3, 5; DV 27; VP 1-4] *I take by force.* This verb is usually found as a dental, but it also has palatal forms.

στηρίζω (στηρίσω and στηρίξω) [V 3, 5; DV 295; VP 1-3] *I establish; I strengthen.* The two future forms show that the root can be considered as a dental or as a palatal.

ταπεινόω [V 10; VP 1-3, 5-6] *I humble, I humiliate.*

___

ἀναστροφή, -ῆς, ἡ [N 1] *conduct.*

βουλή, -ῆς, ἡ [N 1] *firm purpose; plan.*

τάλαντον, –ου, τό [N 7] *talent*. This was a sizeable unit of money in the ancient world.

———

φρόνιμος, –ος, –ον [Adj 5] *intelligent; prudent*.

χωλός, –ή, –όν [Adj 1] *lame*.

Exercises for Lesson 63.

I. Translate into English:
1. καὶ φοβηθεὶς ἀπελθὼν ἔκρυψα τὸ τάλαντόν σου ἐν τῇ γῇ· ἴδε ἔχεις τὸ σόν. (Mt 25:25)
2. καὶ εἷς τις ἐξ αὐτῶν ἀφεῖλεν τὸ οὖς τοῦ δούλου τοῦ ἀρχιερέως τὸ δεξιόν. (Lk 22:50)
3. ὅστις οὖν ταπεινώσει ἑαυτὸν ὡς τὸ παιδίον τοῦτο, οὗτός ἐστιν ὁ μείζων ἐν τῇ βασιλείᾳ τῶν οὐρανῶν. (Mt 18:4)
4. τότε ὁ βασιλεὺς ἀποστείλας ἀνεῖλεν πάντας τοὺς παῖδας. (Mt 2:16)
5. ὅτι οἱ υἱοὶ τοῦ αἰῶνος τούτου φρονιμώτεροι ὑπὲρ τοὺς υἱοὺς τοῦ φωτὸς εἰς τὴν γενεὰν τὴν ἑαυτῶν εἰσιν. (Lk 16:8)
6. καὶ προσκαλεσάμενος πάλιν τὸν ὄχλον ἔλεγεν αὐτοῖς, Ἀκούσατέ μου πάντες καὶ σύνετε. (Mk 7:14)
7. καὶ προσῆλθον αὐτῷ τυφλοὶ καὶ χωλοὶ ἐν τῷ ἱερῷ, καὶ ἐθεράπευσεν αὐτούς. (Mt 21:14)
8. τέκνον, ἀφίενταί σου αἱ ἁμαρτίαι. (Mk 2:5)
9. καὶ σύ ποτε ἐπιστρέψας στήρισον τοὺς ἀδελφούς σου. (Lk 22:32)
10. ἀκούσας δὲ ὁ Ἰησοῦς εἶπεν αὐτῷ, Ἔτι ἕν σοι λείπει· πάντα ὅσα ἔχεις πώλησον καὶ δὸς πτωχοῖς, καὶ ἕξεις θησαυρὸν ἐν τοῖς οὐρανοῖς, καὶ ἀκολούθει μοι. (Lk 18:22)
11. καὶ νῦν λέγω ὑμῖν, ἀπόστητε ἀπὸ τῶν ἀνθρώπων τούτων καὶ ἄφετε αὐτούς· ὅτι ἐὰν ᾖ ἐξ ἀνθρώπων ἡ βουλὴ αὕτη ἢ τὸ ἔργον τοῦτο, καταλυθήσεται. (Acts 5:38)
12. ὁ θεός μου ὁ θεός μου, εἰς τί ἐγκατέλιπές με; (Mk 15:34)
13. Ἰησοῦς οὖν γνοὺς ὅτι μέλλουσιν ἔρχεσθαι καὶ ἁρπάζειν αὐτὸν ἵνα ποιήσωσιν βασιλέα ἀνεχώρησεν πάλιν εἰς τὸ ὄρος αὐτὸς μόνος. (Jn 6:15)

14. καὶ καταλιπὼν αὐτοὺς ἀπῆλθεν. (Mt 16:4)
15. ἠκούσατε γὰρ τὴν ἐμὴν ἀναστροφήν ποτε, ὅτι ἐδίωκον τὴν ἐκκλησίαν τοῦ θεοῦ. (Gal 1:13)

II. Translate into Greek:
1. All sins and blasphemies will be forgiven this man, but the blasphemies of the Spirit will not be forgiven. (Mt 12:31)
2. The soldiers were killed as well as the young men who obeyed them. (Acts 5:36)
3. And all died without leaving a descendant [literally, "not leaving seed"]. (Mk 12:21)

III. Mk 14:22-50.

> ἀπόλλυμι and ὄμνυμι [Summary]. φημί,
> Selected Forms. εἶμι, Selected Forms.
> Comparison of Adverbs. Difficult Verbs:
> ἀπόλλυμι / ἀπολλύω, ὄμνυμι / ὀμνύω,
> πίμπλημι.

Lesson 64

ἀπόλλυμι and ὄμνυμι [Summary].

The important verbs ἀπόλλυμι, *I destroy*, and ὄμνυμι, *I swear*, are conjugated like δείκνυμι. Cf. V 14.

φημί, Selected Forms.

φημί, *I say*, is conjugated like ἵστημι. Like δίδωμι, τίθημι, ἵστημι and ἵημι it shows vowel gradation: φη– and φα–. The forms used in the New Testament are as follows:

φημί: present active indicative, first person singular [enclitic];

φησί(ν): present active indicative, third person singular [enclitic];

φασί(ν): present active indicative, third person plural [enclitic];

ἔφη: imperfect active indicative, third person singular.

εἶμι, Selected Forms.

Because of its resemblance to the verb εἰμί, the verb εἶμι, *I come, I go* should be noted. (Despite the resemblance of the first person singular of the present indicative the roots are quite different: in εἰμί, *I am*, the root is εσ–, while in εἶμι, *I go*, the root is εἰ– or ἰ–.) It is found in the New Testament only as a part of compound verbs. The following forms are found:

ἴασι(ν): present indicative active, third person plural;

ᾔει: imperfect indicative active, third person singular;
ᾔεσαν: imperfect indicative active, third person plural;
ἰόντος: present participle active, masculine genitive
    singular;
ἰούσῃ: present participle active, feminine dative singular;
ἰόντων: present participle active, masculine genitive plural;
ἰέναι: present active infinitive.

Comparison of Adverbs.

Some adverbs are formed from adjectives, others are not. Those adverbs in the positive degree which are, are formed from the positive degree of adjectives in one of two ways: 1) through the use of the neuter accusative singular (e.g., μικρόν, *for a little (while)*; 2) through the use of the suffix –ως (e.g., κακῶς, *badly*).

The comparative and superlative degrees of adverbs are usually, but not always, formed from the comparative and superlative degrees of the corresponding adjectives. The comparative degree is often formed by taking the neuter accusative singular of the comparative degree of the adjective: σοφώτερον, *more wisely*. The superlative degree is often formed by taking the neuter accusative plural of the superlative degree of the adjective: σοφώτατα, *most wisely*. Some comparative and superlative degrees of the adverb are formed irregularly. A selection of these forms is given in Lesson 65.

The superlative degree of the adverb is rare in the New Testament. Its place is often taken by the comparative degree. The superlative degree can have either a relative or an absolute meaning (relative meaning: *most wisely* ; absolute meaning: *very wisely*).

The idiomatic use of ὡς with the superlative should be noted. In this usage the ὡς with the superlative means *as . . . as possible* (e.g., ὡς σοφώτατα, *as wisely as possible*).

Difficult Verbs: ἀπόλλυμι / ἀπολλύω, ὄμνυμι / ὀμνύω, πίμπλημι.

ἀπόλλυμι / ἀπολλύω, *I destroy, I perish* [V 14; DV 217; VP 1-2, 4, 9]

| ἀπόλλυμι | ἀπολέσω | ἀπώλεσα | ἀπόλωλα | — | — |
| Mt 9:17 | Mt 16:25 | Mt 2:13 | Mt 10:6 | | |

ἀπολλύω   ἀπολῶ   ἀπωλόμην
Jn 12:25   Acts 27:34   Mt 5:29

    The active voice is transitive (*I destroy*) except in the perfect, which is intransitive (*I have perished*). The middle voice is intransitive (*I perish*). There is an alternative form in the present system based on the the use of the root as a thematic verb: ἀπολλύω. The aorist active is weak (first), the aorist middle is strong (second).

ὄμνυμι / ὀμνύω, *I swear* [V 14; DV 219; VP 1, 9]

ὄμνυμι   —   ὤμοσα   —   —   —
Mk 14:71   Mt 23:16

ὀμνύω
Heb 6:16

    There is an alternate form for the present system based on a use of the root as a thematic verb: ὀμνύω.

πίμπλημι, *I fill* [V 11, 21; DV 244; VP 1-3, 7]

[πίμπλημι]   —   ἔπλησα   —   πέπλησμαι   ἐπλήσθην
                        Mt 27:48   Lk 6:25   Mt 22:10

    The present is not found in the New Testament, nor is the future or the perfect active.

Vocabulary for Lesson 64.

ἀπόλλυμι / ἀπολλύω [ἀπό + ὄλλυμι] [V 14; DV 217; VP 1-2, 4, 9]
    transitive: *I destroy*; *I lose*; intransitive: *I perish* [perfect active is intransitive].

ὄμνυμι / ὀμνύω [V 14; DV 219; VP 1, 9] *I swear.*

πίμπλημι [V 11, 21; DV 244; VP 1-3, 7] *I fill* [the thing which is being used to fill is expressed either by the simple genitive or by ἐκ with the genitive]; *I fulfill.*

ἄπειμι [ἀπό + εἰμι] [V 15, DV 77] *I go.*

εἴσειμι [εἰς + εἰμι] [V 15, DV 77] *I enter.*

ἔξειμι [ἐκ + εἰμι] [V 15, DV 77] *I depart.*

ἔπειμι [ἐπί+ εἰμι] [V 15, DV 77] *I am next.*

σύνειμι [σύν + εἰμι] [V 15, DV 77] *to gather together* [used of crowds].

φημί [V 11, DV 327, VP 7] *I say.* This verb is enclitic in the present tense. It is often used to introduce a direct quotation.

δαιμονίζομαι [V 5, 23; VP 3] *I am possessed by a demon.*

διαλέγομαι [διά + λέγομαι] [V 2, 22, 23; VP 2-3] *I converse with; I debate with; I address.* The simple dative is usually used with all meanings.

ἐκπλήσσομαι [ἐκ + πλήσσομαι] [V 3, 23; DV 254; VP 3-4] *I am amazed; I am stricken with fear.*

ἐμπαίζω [ἐν + παίζω] (ἐμπαίξω) [V 3, DV 229, VP 1-3] *I mock; I make fun of* [with dative].

ἐπιζητέω [ἐπί + ζητέω] [V 8, VP 1-3, 5-6] *I seek; I desire.*

καταισχύνω [κατά + αἰσχύνω] [V 7, DV 10, VP 1-3] *I shame; I disgrace.*

δράκων, −οντος, ὁ [N 22] *dragon; serpent* [the devil].

ἐλεημοσύνη, −ης, ἡ [N 1] *alms; gift.*

ζύμη, −ης, ἡ [N 1] *leaven.*

θερισμός, −οῦ, ὁ [N 6m] *harvest.*

καπνός, −οῦ, ὁ [N 6m] *smoke.*

ἕξ [Adj 21] *six*.

Exercises for Lesson 64.

I. Translate into English:
1. πάντα γὰρ ταῦτα τὰ ἔθνη ἐπιζητοῦσιν. (Mt 6:32)
2. καὶ ἀποκριθέντες τῷ Ἰησοῦ εἶπαν, Οὐκ οἴδαμεν. ἔφη
   αὐτοῖς καὶ αὐτός, Οὐδὲ ἐγὼ λέγω ὑμῖν ἐν ποίᾳ
   ἐξουσίᾳ ταῦτα ποιῶ. (Mt 21:27) [ἐν ποίᾳ ἐξουσίᾳ
   introduces an indirect question; cf. Lesson 69.]
3. ἄλλην παραβολὴν ἐλάλησεν αὐτοῖς· Ὁμοία ἐστὶν ἡ
   βασιλεία τῶν οὐρανῶν ζύμῃ. (Mt 13:33)
4. καὶ ἐπλήσθησαν πάντες θυμοῦ ἐν τῇ συναγωγῇ
   ἀκούοντες ταῦτα. (Lk 4:28)
5. τότε λέγει τοῖς μαθηταῖς αὐτοῦ, Ὁ μὲν θερισμὸς πολύς,
   οἱ δὲ ἐργάται ὀλίγοι. (Mt 9:37)
6. καί, Ὃς ἂν ὀμόσῃ ἐν τῷ θυσιαστηρίῳ, οὐδέν ἐστιν· ὃς
   δ᾽ ἂν ὀμόσῃ ἐν τῷ δώρῳ τῷ ἐπάνω αὐτοῦ ὀφείλει. (Mt
   23:18)
7. καὶ ἐκ τῶν στομάτων αὐτῶν ἐκπορεύεται πῦρ καὶ
   καπνός. (Apoc 9:17)
8. ὃς γὰρ ἐὰν θέλῃ τὴν ψυχὴν αὐτοῦ σῶσαι ἀπολέσει
   αὐτήν· ὃς δ᾽ ἂν ἀπολέσει τὴν ψυχὴν αὐτοῦ ἕνεκεν
   ἐμοῦ καὶ τοῦ εὐαγγελίου σώσει αὐτήν. (Mk 8:35)
9. ὁ πιστεύων ἐπ᾽ αὐτῷ οὐ καταισχυνθήσεται. (Rom 9:33)
10. καὶ προσελθόντες ἤγειραν αὐτὸν λέγοντες, Κύριε,
    σῶσον, ἀπολλύμεθα. (Mt 8:25)
11. τεσσεράκοντα καὶ ἓξ ἔτεσιν οἰκοδομήθη ὁ ναὸς οὗτος,
    καὶ σὺ ἐν τρίσιν ἡμέραις ἐγερεῖς αὐτόν· (Jn 2:20)
    [ἔτεσιν is simple dative to express time; cf. Lesson 79.
    οἰκοδομήθη: the text in John has no augment.]
12. οἱ δὲ ἀδελφοὶ παραγενόμενοι εἰς τὴν συναγωγὴν
    ἀπήεσαν. (Acts 17:10)
13. παραδοθήσεται γὰρ τοῖς ἔθνεσιν καὶ ἐμπαιχθήσεται.
    (Lk 18:32)
14. ὁ δὲ ἀνὴρ ὁ χωλὸς εἶδεν τοὺς ἀποστόλους μέλλοντας
    εἰσιέναι εἰς τὸ ἱερόν. (Acts 3:2-3)
15. πωλήσατε τὰ ὑπάρχοντα ὑμῶν καὶ δότε ἐλημοσύνην.
    (Lk 12:33)
16. ὁ ἀπόστολος, μέλλων ἐξιέναι τῇ ἐπαύριον, διελέγετο
    τοῖς μαθηταῖς. (Acts 20:7) [τῇ ἐπαύριον (ἡμέρᾳ):
    dative of time; cf. Lesson 79.]

17. καὶ ἀκούσαντες οἱ ὄχλοι ἐξεπλήσσοντο ἐπὶ τῇ διδαχῇ αὐτοῦ. (Mt 22:33)

18. τῇ τε ἐπιούσῃ ἡμέρᾳ ὤφθη αὐτοῖς. (Acts 7:26) [τῇ . . . ἐπιούσῃ ἡμέρᾳ: dative of time; cf. Lesson 79.]

19. καὶ ἐβλήθη ὁ δράκων ὁ μέγας, ὁ ὄφις ὁ ἀρχαῖος, ὁ καλούμενος Διάβολος, ὁ πλανῶν τὴν οἰκουμένην ὅλην. (Apoc 12:9)

20. πολὺς ὄχλος συνῄει πρὸς τὸν Ἰησοῦν. (Lk 8:4)

21. οἱ μαθηταὶ διελέχθησαν πρὸς ἀλλήλους ἐν τῇ ὁδῷ. (Mk 9:34)

22. ἔφερον πρὸς αὐτὸν πάντας τοὺς κακῶς ἔχοντας καὶ τοὺς δαιμονιζομένους. (Mk 1:32)

II. Translate into Greek:
1. And often they threw her into fire in order to kill her. (Mk 9:22)
2. God gave his Son so that all believing in him may not perish but have eternal life. (Jn 3:16)
3. The disciples went out of the synagogue and debated with him. (Acts 17:2)

III. Mk 14:51-72.

δύναμαι, **Present Deponent Indicative, Imperfect Deponent Indicative, Present Deponent Subjunctive, Optative, Participle [Summary], and Infinitive. ἐπίσταμαι [Summary]. Comparison of Irregular Adverbs. Difficult Verbs:** δύναμαι, μιμνῄσκομαι, τρέχω.

Lesson 65

δύναμαι, Present Deponent Indicative, Imperfect Deponent Indicative, Present Deponent Subjunctive, Optative, Participle [Summary], and Infinitive.

The important deponent verb δύναμαι, *I can, I am able*, is conjugated like the middle and passive forms of ἵστημι in the present system. In the other systems the endings do not demand special treatment (cf. V 11, 22, 23; DV 66; VP 2-3, 11; for the present participle cf. also Adj 1):

Deponent, Indicative Mood, Present Tense

	Singular	Plural
1st Person	δύνα–μαι	δυνά–μεθα
2nd Person	δύνα–σαι / δύνῃ	δύνα–σθε
3rd Person	δύνα–ται	δύνα–νται

Deponent, Indicative Mood, Imperfect Tense

	Singular	Plural
1st Person	ἐ–δυνά–μην	ἐ–δυνά–μεθα
2nd Person	ἐ–δύνα–σο	ἐ–δύνα–σθε
3rd Person	ἐ–δύνα–το	ἐ–δύνα–ντο

The augment ἠ– is also found.

The imperative is not found in the New Testament.

Deponent, Subjunctive Mood, Present Tense
	Singular	Plural
1st Person	δύνωμαι	δυνώμεθα
2nd Person	δύνῃ	δύνησθε
3rd Person	δύνηται	δύνωνται

δύνῃ < δύνησαι.

Deponent, Optative Mood, Present Tense
	Singular	Plural
1st Person	δυναίμην	δυναίμεθα
2nd Person	δύναιο	δύναισθε
3rd Person	δύναιτο	δύναιντο

The deponent present participle is δυνά–μενος, –η, –ον.

The deponent present infinitive is δύνα–σθαι.

ἐπίσταμαι [Summary].

The much less frequently used verb ἐπίσταμαι, *I know*, is found only in the indicative and participle of the present system. It is also conjugated like the middle and passive forms of ἵστημι.

Comparison of Irregular Adverbs.

Some of the more important adverbs which are irregularly compared are the following:

Positive Degree	Comparative Degree	Superlative
εὖ, *well*	κρεῖσσον	[βέλτιστα]
	κρεῖττον	
	βέλτιον	
κακῶς, *badly*	ἧσσον	
Cf. Lesson 47.	ἧττον	
καλῶς, *well*	κάλλιον	
Cf. Lesson 35.		

[μάλα], *very*   μᾶλλον   μάλιστα
                            Cf. Lesson 30.   Cf. Lesson
                                                        56.

μικρόν, *a little (while)*   ἔλασσον
  Cf. Lesson 26.   ἔλαττον

πολύ, *greatly*   πλεῖον
πολλοῦ   πλέον
πολλά
πολλῷ

ταχύ, *quickly*   τάχειον   τάχιστα
  Cf. Lesson 57.   τάχιον
ταχέως

Words in brackets [ ] are not found in the New Testament.

Difficult Verbs: δύναμαι, μιμνήσκομαι, τρέχω.

δύναμαι, *I can, I am able* [V 11, 22, 23; DV 66; VP 2-3, 11]

δύναμαι   δυνήσομαι   —   —   —   ἠδυνήθην
Mt 3:9   Mk 3:25   Mt 17:16

The future is a middle deponent; the aorist is a passive deponent. In the aorist the form ἠδυνάσθην is also found.

μιμνήσκομαι, *I remember* [V 2, 18, 22, 23; DV 200; VP 3]

μιμνήσκομαι   μνησθήσομαι   —   —   μέμνημαι   ἐμνήσθην
Heb 2:6   Heb 10:17   1 Cor 11:2 Mt 5:23

This is a passive deponent whose forms occasionally have a true passive meaning. The perfect has present force.

τρέχω, *I run* [V 2; DV 315; VP 1, 4]

τρέχω   —   ἔδραμον   —   —   —
Jn 20:2   Mt 27:48

Vocabulary for Lesson 65.

δύναμαι [V 11, 22, 23; DV 66; VP 2-3, 11] *I can; I am able; I have the right to; I have the power to.*

μιμνῇσκομαι [V 2, 18, 22, 23; DV 200; VP 3] *I remember* [with the genitive case for the person or thing remembered]. Although this verb is usually a passive deponent, in some texts the passive form has a truly passive meaning: *I am remembered.*

———
τρέχω [V 2; DV 315; VP 1, 4] *I run.*

———
ἐκλέγομαι [ἐκ + λέγομαι] [V 2, 22; DV 180; VP 2-3] *I choose; I select.*

ἐπίσταμαι [V 11, 23; DV 91; VP 11] *I know; I understand.*

παιδεύω [V 1, VP 1-3] *I educate; I chastise.*

———
βέλτιον [Adv 3] *better.*

ἔλασσον, ἔλαττον [Adv 3] *a short while.* less

ἧσσον, ἧττον [Adv 3] *worse.*

κάλλιον [Adv 3] *better.*

κρεῖσσον, κρεῖττον [Adv 3] *better.*

πλεῖον, πλέον [Adv 3] *more.*

πολύ, πολλοῦ, πολλά, πολλῷ [Adv 3] *greatly.*

τάχειον, τάχιον [Adv 2] *more quickly.*

ταχέως [Adv 2] *quickly.*

τάχιστα [Adv 2] *most quickly.*

———
παιδίσκη, -ης, ἡ [N 1] *maidservant.*

παράδοσις, -εως, ἡ [N 28f] *tradition.*

Exercises for Lesson 65.

I. Translate into English:
1. θέλω ἐλθεῖν ὡς τάχιστα πρὸς αὐτούς.
2. ὅτε οὖν ἠγέρθη ἐκ νεκρῶν, ἐμνήσθησαν οἱ μαθηταὶ αὐτοῦ ὅτι τοῦτο ἔλεγεν, καὶ ἐπίστευσαν τῇ γραφῇ καὶ τῷ λόγῳ ὃν εἶπεν ὁ ᾿Ιησοῦς. (Jn 2:22)
3. παιδεύσας οὖν αὐτὸν ἀπολύσω. (Lk 23:16)
4. ἄνδρες ἀδελφοί, ὑμεῖς ἐπίστασθε ὅτι ἀφ᾿ ἡμερῶν ἀρχαίων, ἐν ὑμῖν ἐξελέξατο ὁ θεὸς διὰ τοῦ στόματος μου, τὰ ἔθνη ἀκοῦσαι τὸν λόγον τοῦ εὐαγγελίου καὶ πιστεῦσαι. (Acts 15:7)
5. καὶ ἡ παιδίσκη ἰδοῦσα αὐτὸν ἤρξατο πάλιν λέγειν τοῖς παρεστῶσιν ὅτι, Οὗτος ἐξ αὐτῶν ἐστιν. (Mk 14:69)
6. καὶ προσήνεγκα αὐτὸν τοῖς μαθηταῖς σου, καὶ οὐκ ἠδυνήθησαν αὐτὸν θεραπεῦσαι. (Mt 17:16)
7. καὶ ἔλεγεν αὐτοῖς, Καλῶς ἀθετεῖτε τὴν ἐντολὴν τοῦ θεοῦ, ἵνα τὴν παράδοσιν ὑμῶν στήσητε. (Mk 7:9)
8. ἐὰν θέλῃς, δύνασαί με καθαρίσαι. (Mk 1:40)
9. ἐλεύσομαι δὲ ταχέως πρὸς ὑμᾶς, ἐὰν ὁ κύριος θελήσῃ. (1 Cor 4:19)
10. καὶ ἰδὼν τὸν ᾿Ιησοῦν ἀπὸ μακρόθεν ἔδραμεν καὶ προσεκύνησεν αὐτῷ. (Mk 5:6)
11. λέγει οὖν αὐτῷ ὁ ᾿Ιησοῦς, ῝Ο ποιεῖς ποίησον τάχιον. Jn 13:27)
12. καὶ ὅσα ἐν τῇ πόλει ἐκείνῃ ἐμοὶ διηκόνησεν, βέλτιον σὺ γινώσκεις. (2 Tim 1:18)
13. οὐκ ἔστιν θεὸς νεκρῶν ἀλλὰ ζώντων· πολὺ πλανᾶσθε. (Mk 12:27)
14. εἰ περισσοτέρως ὑμᾶς ἀγαπῶ, ἧσσον ἀγαπῶμαι; (2 Cor 12:15)
15. ἐὰν μὴ περισσεύσῃ ὑμῶν ἡ δικαιοσύνη πλεῖον τῶν γραμματέων, οὐκ εἰσελεύσεσθε εἰς τὴν βασιλείαν τῶν οὐρανῶν. (Mt 5:20)
16. προσεληλύθατε αἵματι κρεῖττον λαλοῦντι παρὰ τὸ τοῦ προφήτου. (Heb 12:24)
17. χήρα ὀνομαζέσθω μὴ ἔλαττον ἐτῶν ἐξήκοντα [sixty] γεγονυῖα. (1 Tim 5:9)

II. Translate into Greek:
1. Now the apostles stood up and ran to the tomb. (Lk 24:12)
2. If you (pl.) should place your gifts upon the altar and there remember that your brothers have something against

you, leave your gifts there and go to your brothers. (Mt 5:23-24)

3. His disciple was asking him, "Why was I unable to cast out the unclean spirit?" (Mk 9:28)

III. Mk 15:1-20.

κάθημαι, Present Deponent Indicative,
Imperfect Deponent Indicative, Present
Deponent Imperative [Summary],
Participle [Summary], and Infinitive.
Difficult Verbs: κάθημαι, ἐλέγχω,
τρέπω, τίκτω, κερδαίνω.

Lesson 66

κάθημαι, Present Deponent Indicative, Imperfect Deponent Indicative, Present Deponent Imperative [Summary], Participle [Summary], and Infinitive.

The deponent –μι verb κάθημι, *I sit*, is a compound verb, with the prefix κατά and the root possibly ἡς, but in practice the augment is placed before the prefix (cf. V 17, 22; DV 139; VP 2; for the participle, cf. also Adj 1):

	Deponent, Indicative Mood, Present Tense	
	Singular	Plural
1st Person	κάθ–η–μαι	καθ–ή–μεθα
2nd Person	κάθ–η	κάθ–η–σθε
3rd Person	κάθ–η–ται	κάθ–η–νται

κάθῃ < κάθηι< κάθηαι <κάθησαι.

	Deponent, Indicative Mood, Imperfect Tense	
	Singular	Plural
1st Person	ἐ–καθ–ή–μην	ἐ–καθ–ή–μεθα
2nd Person	ἐ–κάθ–η–σο	ἐ–κάθ–η–σθε
3rd Person	ἐ–κάθ–η–το	ἐ–κάθ–η–ντο

The present imperative is found in the second person singular: κάθου (from κάθησο).

The subjunctive and optative are not found in the New Testament.

The present participle is καθ–ή–μενος, –η, –ον.

The present infinitive is καθ–ῆ–σθαι.

Difficult Verbs: κάθημαι, ἐλέγχω, τρέπω, τίκτω, κερδαίνω.

κάθημαι, *I sit* [V 17, 22; DV 139; VP 2]

| κάθημαι | καθήσομαι | — | — | — | — |
| Mt 9:9 | Mt 19:28 | | | | |

This compound verb is treated as a non-compound—the augment is prefixed to the κ even though the stem begins with the η. The verb is a middle deponent in both present and future.

ἐλέγχω, *I convict, I convince, I reprove* [V 2, DV 80; VP 1-3]

| ἐλέγχω | ἐλέγξω | ἤλεγξα | — | — | ἠλέγχθην |
| Lk 3:19 | Jn 16:8 | Mt 18:15 | | | Jn 3:20 |

τρέπω, *I turn* [V 4, DV 313, VP 1-3]

| τρέπω | — | ἔτρεψα | — | — | ἐτράπην |
| Acts 26:1 | | Mt 8:21 | | | Acts 28:16 |

The aorist passive is strong. The simple verb τρέπω does not occur in the New Testament. The above forms are from the compound verb ἐπιτρέπω, *I permit*.

τίκτω, *I give birth to* [V 2, 21; DV 189; VP 1-4]

| τίκτω | τέξομαι | ἔτεκον | — | — | ἐτέχθην |
| Jn 16:21 | Mt 1:21 | Mt 1:25 | | | Mt 2:2 |

κερδαίνω, *I gain* [V 7, DV 152, VP 1-3]

| — | κερδήσω
Jas 4:13 | ἐκέρδησα
Mt 16:26 | — | — | ἐκερδήθην
1 Pt 3:1 |

ἐκέρδανα
1 Cor 9:21

The present system is not found in the New Testament. There are two aorist active forms.

Vocabulary for Lesson 66.

κάθημαι [V 17, 22; DV 139; VP 2] *I sit; I am seated; I stay.*
___

ἐλέγχω [V 2, DV 80, VP 1-3] *I convict, I convince, I reprove.*
___

ἐπιτρέπω [ἐπί + τρέπω] [V 4, DV 313, VP 1-3] *I permit; I allow.*
___

τίκτω [V 2, 21; DV 310; VP 1-4] *I give birth to*; passive: *I am born.*
___

κερδαίνω [V 7, DV 152, VP 1-3] *I gain.*
___

καταντάω [κατά + ἀντάω] [V 9; DV 1; VP 1-3, 5-6] *I come to* [takes εἰς with the accusative]

καταρτίζω [κατά + ἀρτίζω] (καταρτίσω) [V 5, VP 1-3] *I repair; I prepare.*

κλέπτω [V 4, 5; DV 158; VP 1-3] *I steal.*
___

Ἰουδαῖος, -α, -ον [Adj 2, N 6m] *Jewish*; as a substantive: *a Jew.*
                                        a Judean

τίμιος, -α, -ον [Adj 2] *precious; honored.*
___

συνεργός, -οῦ, ὁ [N 6m] *co-worker.*

τρόπος, -ου, ὁ [N 6m] *manner; way of life.*

χοῖρος, -ου, ὁ [N 6m] *pig, swine.*

Exercises for Lesson 66.

I. Translate into English:
1. ὁ οὖν διδάσκων ἕτερον σεαυτὸν οὐ διδάσκεις; ὁ κηρύσσων μὴ κλέπτειν κλέπτεις; (Rom 2:21)
2. τίς ἐξ ὑμῶν ἐλέγχει με περὶ ἁμαρτίας; (Jn 8:46)
3. θεοῦ γάρ ἐσμεν συνεργοί. (1 Cor 3:9)
4. καὶ ἰδοὺ συλλήμψῃ ἐν γαστρὶ καὶ τέξῃ υἱόν, καὶ καλέσεις τὸ ὄνομα αὐτοῦ Ἰησοῦν. (Lk 1:31)
5. τίμιος ἔστω ὁ γάμος ἐν πᾶσιν. (Heb 13:4)
6. καὶ παρεκάλεσαν αὐτὸν λέγοντες, Πέμψον ἡμᾶς εἰς τοὺς χοίρους, ἵνα εἰς αὐτοὺς εἰσέλθωμεν. καὶ ἐπέτρεψεν αὐτοῖς. (Mk 5:12-13)
7. οὗτος ὁ Ἰησοῦς ὁ ἀναλημφθεὶς ἀφ᾽ ὑμῶν εἰς τὸν οὐρανὸν οὕτως ἐλεύσεται κατὰ τὸν τρόπον καθ᾽ ὃν ἐθεάσασθε αὐτὸν πορευόμενον εἰς τὸν οὐρανόν. (Acts 1:11)
8. καὶ μεταβὰς ἐκεῖθεν ὁ Ἰησοῦς ἦλθεν παρὰ τὴν θάλασσαν, καὶ ἀναβὰς εἰς τὸ ὄρος ἐκάθητο ἐκεῖ. (Mt 15:29)
9. οὐκ ἔστιν μαθητὴς ὑπὲρ τὸν διδάσκαλον, κατηρτισμένος δὲ πᾶς ἔσται ὡς ὁ διδάσκαλος αὐτοῦ. (Lk 6:40)
10. τί γὰρ ὠφελεῖται ἄνθρωπος κερδήσας τὸν κόσμον ὅλον ἑαυτὸν δὲ ἀπολέσας; (Lk 9:25) [τί is an accusative of respect: *(in) what (respect) does it profit a man. . ?* .]
11. ἢ ἀφ᾽ ὑμῶν ὁ λόγος τοῦ θεοῦ ἐξῆλθεν, ἢ εἰς ὑμᾶς μόνους κατήντησεν; (1 Cor 14:36)
12. ποῦ ἐστιν ὁ τεχθεὶς βασιλεὺς τῶν Ἰουδαίων; (Mt 2:2)

II. Translate into Greek:
1. And the robbers came so that as a result all of the poor got into boats and sat far from the land. (Mt 13:2)
2. Women, when they give birth, have grief, because their hour has come. (Jn 16:21)
3. A vessel of anger is he, prepared for destruction. (Rom 9:22)

III. Mk 15:21-47.

A System of Transcription. Difficult Verbs:
χέω / χύννω, ἐσθίω, εὑρίσκω, ξηραίνω,
καίω, τυγχάνω, ἐάω.

Lesson 67

A System of Transcription.

It is useful to have knowledge of a system of transcription of Greek into characters proper to a different language. Such systems of transcription differ among themselves according to the possibilities of the receptor language and the typographical possibilities of reproduction.
    The following transcriptions have been chosen as a typical example of how such a system works:

α = a	ι = i	ρ = r	αυ = au
β = b	κ = k	σ, ς = s	ευ = eu
γ = g	λ = l	τ = t	ηυ = ēu
δ = d	μ = m	υ = u	ου = ou
ε = e	ν = n	φ = ph	υι = ui
ζ = z	ξ = x	χ = ch	ʽ = h
η = ē	ο = o	ψ = ps	ᾳ = a̦ or ai
θ = th	π = p	ω = ō	ῃ = e̦ or ēi
			ῳ = o̦ or ōi

    Thus Mk 1:1-5 can be expressed as follows:

1:1   Archē tou euaggeliou Iēsou Christou [huiou theou].

1:2   Kathōs gegraptai en tǭ Esaïą tǭ prophētę,
        Idou apostellō ton aggelon mou pro prosōpou sou,
        hos kataskeuasei tēn hodon sou·

1:3   phōnē boōntos en tę erēmǭ,
        Hetoimasate tēn hodon kyriou,
        eutheisas poieite tas tribous autou —

1:4   egeneto Iōannēs [ho] baptizōn en tę erēmǭ kai kēryssōn
        baptisma metanoias eis aphesin hamartiōn.

1:5   kai exeporeueto pros auton pasa hē Ioudaia chōra kai hoi
        Hierosolymitai pantes, kai ebaptizonto hyp᾽ autou en tǭ
        Iordanę potamǭ exomologoumenoi tas hamartias autōn.

Difficult Verbs: χέω / χύννω, ἐσθίω, εὑρίσκω, ξηραίνω, καίω,
τυγχάνω, ἐάω.

χέω / χύννω, *I pour* [V 7, 8; DV 341; VP 1-3, 5-6]

χέω	χεῶ	ἔχεα	—	—	—
Mt 9:17	Acts 2:17	Jn 2:15			

χύννω	—	—	—	κέχυμαι	ἐχύθην
Mt 23:35				Lk 11:50	Lk 5:37

        The simple verb χέω does not exist in the New Testament. All
the forms above have been taken from the compound verb
ἐκχέω/ἐκχύννω.

ἐσθίω, *I eat* [V 1, DV 101, VP 1-4]

| ἐσθίω | φάγομαι | ἔφαγον | — | — | — |
| Mt 9:11 | Lk 17:8 | Mt 12:4 | | | |

The variant ἔσθω is also found in the present system.

εὑρίσκω, *I find* [V 2, DV 106, VP 1-4]

| εὑρίσκω | εὑρήσω | εὗρον | εὕρηκα | — | εὑρέθην |
| Mt 7:8 | Mt 7:7 | Mt 2:8 | Jn 1:45 | | Mt 1:18 |

The contrast between the η of the future and the perfect active on the one hand and the ε of the aorist passive on the other should be noted.

ξηραίνω, *I dry up* [V 7, DV 210, VP 1-3]

| ξηραίνω | — | ἐξήρανα | — | ἐξήραμμαι | ἐξηράνθην |
| Mk 9:18 | | Jas 1:11 | | Mk 3:1 | Mt 13:6 |

This liquid can easily be confused in its augmented or reduplicated forms with a compound verb having the prefix ἐκ (ἐξ).

καίω, *I burn; I light* [V 1, DV 141, VP 1-4]

καίω	καύσω	ἔκαυσα	—	κέκαυμαι	ἐκαύθην
Mt 5:15	Lk 3:17	Mt 13:30		Heb 12:18	Rom 1:27
					ἐκάην
					Apoc 8:7

τυγχάνω, *I obtain; I happen* [V 7, DV 317, VP 1-4]

| τυγχάνω | — | ἔτυχον | τέτυχα | — | — |
| Acts 24:2 | | Lk 20:35 | Heb 8:6 | | |

The aorist and perfect are strong. This verb governs the genitive case.

ἐάω, *I permit, I allow* [V 9; DV 68; VP 1, 5]

ἐάω   ἐάσω   εἴασα   —   — —
Lk 22:51   1 Cor 10:13   Mt 24:43

εἴων [imperfect]
Lk 4:41

The augment is irregular in the imperfect and aorist.

Vocabulary for Lesson 67.

ἐκχέω [ἐκ + χέω] [V 7, 8; DV 341; VP 1-3, 5-6] *I pour out.*
___

ἐσθίω [V 1, DV 101, VP 1-4] *I eat.* Cf. Lesson 10.

κατεσθίω [κατά + ἐσθίω] [V 1, DV 101, VP 1-4] *I devour, I eat up.*
___

εὑρίσκω [V 2, DV 106, VP 1-4] *I find.* Cf. Lesson 10.
___

ξηραίνω [V 7, DV 210, VP 1-3] intransitive: *I dry up* [the passive is
    used intransitively].
___

καίω [V 1, DV 141, VP 1-4] *I burn; I light.*

κατακαίω [κατά + καίω] [V 1, DV 141, VP 1-4] *I burn up.*
___

τυγχάνω [V 7, DV 317, VP 1-4] *I obtain; I happen* [This verb governs
    the genitive case.].
___

ἐάω [V 9; DV 68; VP 1, 5] *I permit; I allow; I let go.*
___

τύπτω [V 4, 5; DV 319; VP 1-5] *I strike, I beat; I injure; I punish.*
    Forms based on τύπτω are found only in the present system.
    In the future active and aorist active the verb πατάσσω is used
    (i.e., πατάξω, ἐπάταξα). In the aorist passive the verb πλήσσω
    is used in its strong aorist form (i.e., ἐπλήγην). In the aorist
    active the verb παίω is also found (i.e., ἔπαισα).

χωρίζω (χωρίσω) [V 5, VP 1-3] *I separate.* In the passive it can have
    the meaning *I depart.*
___

ὕψιστος, –η, –ον [Adj 1] *highest*. ὁ ὕψιστος, *God* [N 6m].

———

φύσις, –εως, ἡ [N 28f] *nature*.

χρυσίον, –ου, τό [N 7] *gold*.

Exercises for Lesson 67.

I. Translate into English:
1. οὗτος ἔσται μέγας καὶ υἱὸς ὑψίστου κληθήσεται. (Lk 1:32)
2. ὁ εὑρὼν τὴν ψυχὴν αὐτοῦ ἀπολέσει αὐτήν, καὶ ὁ ἀπολέσας τὴν ψυχὴν αὐτοῦ ἕνεκεν ἐμοῦ εὑρήσει αὐτήν. (Mt 10:39)
3. ἡμεῖς φύσει Ἰουδαῖοι καὶ οὐκ ἐξ ἐθνῶν ἁμαρτωλοί, εἰδότες δὲ ὅτι οὐ δικαιοῦται ἄνθρωπος ἐξ ἔργων νόμου ἐὰν μὴ διὰ πίστεως Ἰησοῦ Χριστοῦ. . . (Gal 2:15-16) [φύσει is a dative of respect: *by nature*.]
4. ἐμνήσθησαν οἱ μαθηταὶ αὐτοῦ ὅτι γεγραμμένον ἐστίν, ὁ ζῆλος τοῦ οἴκου σου καταφάγεταί με. (Jn 2:17)
5. ἀργύριον καὶ χρυσίον οὐχ ὑπάρχει μοι, ὃ δὲ ἔχω τοῦτό σοι δίδωμι. (Acts 3:6)
6. καὶ ἔρχεται εἰς οἶκον· καὶ συνέρχεται πάλιν ὁ ὄχλος, ὥστε μὴ δύνασθαι αὐτοὺς μηδὲ ἄρτον φαγεῖν. (Mk 3:20)
7. τίς ἡμᾶς χωρίσει ἀπὸ τῆς ἀγάπης τοῦ Χριστοῦ; (Rom 8:35)
8. καί γε ἐπὶ τοὺς δούλους μου ἐν ταῖς ἡμέραις ἐκείναις ἐκχεῶ ἀπὸ τοῦ πνεύματός μου, καὶ προφητεύσουσιν. (Acts 2:18)
9. προφήτευσον ἡμῖν, Χριστέ, τίς ἐστιν ὁ παίσας σε; (Mt 26:68)
10. καὶ εἰσῆλθεν πάλιν εἰς τὴν συναγωγήν. καὶ ἦν ἐκεῖ ἄνθρωπος ἐξηραμμένην ἔχων τὴν χεῖρα. (Mk 3:1)
11. καὶ ἐπλήγη τὸ τρίτον τοῦ ἡλίου. (Apoc 8:12)
12. καὶ εἶπαν πρὸς ἀλλήλους, Οὐχὶ ἡ καρδία ἡμῶν καιομένη ἦν ἐν ἡμῖν ὡς ἐλάλει ἡμῖν ἐν τῇ ὁδῷ, ὡς διήνοιγεν ἡμῖν τὰς γραφάς; (Lk 24:32) [διήνοιγεν: for the meaning cf. Lesson 74, John 7:34.]
13. τότε λέγει αὐτοῖς ὁ Ἰησοῦς, Πάντες ὑμεῖς σκανδαλισθήσεσθε ἐν ἐμοὶ ἐν τῇ νυκτὶ ταύτῃ, γέγραπται γάρ, Πατάξω τὸν ποιμένα. (Mt 26:31)

14. καὶ τὸ τρίτον τῆς γῆς κατεκάη, καὶ τὸ τρίτον τῶν δένδρων κατεκάη, καὶ πᾶς χόρτος κατεκάη. (Apoc 8:7)
15. καὶ ἔτυπτον εἰς τὴν κεφαλὴν αὐτοῦ. (Mt 27:30)
16. διὰ τοῦτο πάντα ὑπομένω διὰ τοὺς ἐκλεκτούς, ἵνα καὶ αὐτοὶ σωτηρίας τύχωσιν τῆς ἐν Χριστῷ Ἰησοῦ μετὰ δόξης αἰωνίου. (2 Tim 2:10)
17. ἐξήρχετο δὲ καὶ δαιμόνια ἀπὸ πολλῶν, λέγοντα ὅτι Σὺ εἶ ὁ υἱὸς τοῦ θεοῦ. Καὶ ἐπιτιμῶν οὐκ εἴα αὐτὰ λαλεῖν, ὅτι ᾔδεισαν τὸν Χριστὸν αὐτὸν εἶναι. (Lk 4:41)

II. Translate into Greek:
   1. And at once the fig trees in that region dried up. (Mt 21:19)
   2. We found our sheep which were lost. (Lk 15:6)
   3. For he does not wash his hands when he eats bread. (Mt 15:2)

III. Mk 16:1-20.

Explanatory Note at the End of Lessons 1-67.

This lesson concludes the first section of this introduction to the morphology of the Greek of the New Testament. At this point the student has seen all the common words (as opposed to proper nouns) of the New Testament which occur more than twelve times. This includes all the more important difficult verbs. All the essential forms of words have been seen as well.

The remaining portion of this first part of *An Introduction to the Study of New Testament Greek* will be devoted to a reading of the Gospels of Mark and of John. Thus the material studied up until now can be used as it is intended to be used, in the reading of the New Testament. For a thorough introductory knowledge of these texts more vocabulary and syntax will be needed. The treatment of additional vocabulary and syntax will be added gradually as the reading of Mark progresses. Only the more fundamental points of syntax will be mentioned: a systematic presentation of syntax must await the second part of this grammar.

The Genitive Absolute. Mark 1:1-34.

Lesson 68.

The Genitive Absolute.

The "genitive absolute" is found frequently in the Greek text of the New Testament. It is a subordinate phrase composed of a noun or pronoun and a participle, the latter agreeing with the noun or pronoun in gender and number. Both the noun/pronoun and the participle are in the genitive case (hence the word "genitive"). The subordinate phrase is conceived of as being separated from the main clause syntactically (hence the word "absolute"). The genitive absolute can express various meanings with reference to the main clause: causality, opposition, time, condition, general circumstances. The meaning must be determined from the context. At Mk 1:32 the words Ὀψίας . . . γενομένης constitute a genitive absolute with the meaning *When it was evening*. The words and their context indicate that the genitive absolute here has a temporal connotation.

If a genitive absolute is to be truly "absolute", it must. strictly speaking, be grammatically independent of the rest of the sentence. In the Greek of the New Testament this independence is not always present. For example, at Mk 5:2 the text reads: . . . ἐξελθόντος αὐτοῦ ἐκ τοῦ πλοίου . . . , ὑπήντησεν αὐτῷ . . . ἄνθρωπος (*When he came from the boat, a man met him*). This idea could also have been expressed as follows, without the use of a genitive absolute: ἄνθρωπος ὑπήντησεν αὐτῷ ἐξελθόντι ἐκ τοῦ πλοίου (*A man met him coming from the boat*). In the latter sentence the word *he* (αὐτός) is not repeated as it is in the sentence with the genitive absolute. The fact that the word *he* occurs in both the genitive absolute and in the independent clause shows that the genitive absolute is not really "absolute", i.e., is not really syntactically cut off or independent from the main clause. Such a genitive absolute is termed an "illegitimate" genitive absolute. It occurs in the New Testament alongside of genitive absolutes which are "legitimate", i.e., in which the noun or pronoun of the genitive absolute does not occur in the main clause. In this "legitimate" type of genitive absolute, the genitive absolute is really "absolute", i.e., really syntactically cut off or independent from the main clause. For examples of "legitimate" genitive absolutes cf. Mk 4:17, 5:35, and 6:54. For examples of "illegitimate" genitive absolutes cf. Mk 6:22, 9:28, and 10:17. It is doubtful if the authors of the New Testament really adverted to the distinction between "legitimate" or "illegitimate" genitive absolutes or even cared. They simply chose the expression which would most effectively convey their meaning. But the distinction is emphasized here to help the student understand the nature of the construction.

Mark 1:1-34

The word lists which follow here and in subsequent lessons are designed to give all the words in the relevant portion of text which have not been seen in the first sixty-seven lessons. Once given, these words will not be repeated. All are listed in the index of Greek words at the end of volume II of this grammar. They include proper nouns. The references in brackets [ ] to New Testament texts indicate where another example of the word in question may be found.

1:2 - Ἡσαΐας, -ου, ὁ [N 5] *Isaiah* [Mt 3:3]; κατασκευάζω [κατά + σκευάζω] (κατασκευάσω) [V 5, VP 1-3] *I prepare* [Lk 1:17] // **1:3** - τρίβος, -ου, ἡ [N 6f] *path* [Mt 3:3] // **1:4** - Ἰωάν[ν]ης, -ου, ὁ [N 4] *John* [Mt 3:1] // **1:5** - Ἰουδαία, -ας, ἡ [N 2] *Judaea* [Mt 2:1]; Ἱεροσολυμίτης, -ου, ὁ [N 4] *inhabitant of Jerusalem* [Jn 7:25] // **1:6** - κάμηλος, -ου, ὁ/ἡ [N 6m, N6f] *camel* [Mt 3:4]; ζώνη, -ης, ἡ [N 1] *belt* [Mt 3:4]; δερμάτινος, -η, -ον [Adj 1] *made of leather* [Mt 3:4]; ἀκρίς, -ίδος, ἡ [N 14f] *locust* [Mt 3:4]; μέλι, -ιτος, τό [N 17] *honey* [Mt 3:4]; ἄγριος, -α, -ον [Adj 2] *wild* [Mt 3:4] // **1:7** - κύπτω [V 4, 5; DV 173; VP 1-3] *I stoop down* [Jn 8:6]; ἱμάς, -άντος, ὁ [N 13m] *strap* [Lk 3:16]; ὑπόδημα, -ατος, τό [N 16] *sandal* [Mt 10:10] // **1:9** - Ναζαρέτ (Ναζαρά, Ναζαρέθ) [N 32] *Nazareth* [Mt 2:23]; Γαλιλαία, -ας, ἡ [N 2] *Galilee* [Mt 2:22] // **1:10** - εὐθύς [Adv 2] *at once* [Mt 3:16]; σχίζω (σχίσω) [V 5, DV 301, VP 1-3] *I split* [Mt 27:51]; περιστερά, -ᾶς, ἡ [N 2] *dove* [Mt 3:16]

1:16 - Σίμων, -ωνος, ὁ [N 21m] *Simon* [Mt 4:18]; ἀμφιβάλλω [ἀμφί + βάλλω] [V 6, DV 32, VP 1-4] *I cast a net* [hapax legomenon]; ἁλιεύς, -έως, ὁ [also ἀλεεύς] [N 29] *fisherman* [Mt 4:18] // **1:18** - δίκτυον, -ου, τό [N 7] *fish net* [Mt 4:20] // **1:19** - προβαίνω [πρό + βαίνω] [V 7, DV 31, VP 1-2] *I go forward* [Mt 4:21]; 'Ιάκωβος, -ου, ὁ [N 6m] *James* [Mt 4:21]; Ζεβεδαῖος, -ου, ὁ [N 6m] *Zebedee* [Mt 4:21] // **1:20** - μισθωτός, -οῦ, ὁ [N 6m] *hired man* [Jn 10:12].

1:21 - Καφαρναούμ, ἡ [N 32] *Capernaum* [Mt 4:13] // **1:23** - ἀνακράζω [ἀνά + κράζω] [V 3, DV 163, VP 1-3] *I cry out* [Lk 4:33] // **1:24** - Ναζαρηνός, -οῦ, ὁ [N 6m] *Nazarene* [Lk 4:34] // **1:25** - φιμόω [V 10; VP 1-3, 5-6] *I muzzle*, i.e., *silence* [Mt 22:12] // **1:26** - σπαράσσω [V 3, VP 1-3] *I cause convulsions* [Mk 9:26] // **1:27** - θαμβέομαι [V 8, 23; VP 3, 6] *I am shocked* [Mk 10:24]; συζητέω [σύν + ζητέω] [V 8; VP 1-3, 5-6] *I question* [Lk 22:23]; ἐπιτάσσω [ἐπί + τάσσω] [V 3, DV 303, VP 1-3] *I command* [Lk 4:36] // **1:28** - πανταχοῦ [Adv 1] *everywhere* [Lk 9:6]; περίχωρος, -ου, ἡ [N 6f] *surrounding district* [Mt 3:5]

1:30 - πενθερά, -ᾶς, ἡ [N 2] *mother-in-law* [Mt 8:14]; πυρέσσω [V 3, VP 1-3] *I have a fever* [Mt 8:14] // **1:31** - πυρετός, -οῦ, ὁ [N 6m] *fever* [Mt 8:15] // **1:32** - δύ(ν)ω [V 1, DV 67, VP 1-3] *I set* [of sun] [Lk 4:40] // **1:33** - ἐπισυνάγω [ἐπί + σύν + ἄγω] [V 2, DV 5, VP 1-4] *I gather together* [of a group] [Mt 23:37] // **1:34** - ποικίλος, -η, -ον [Adj 1] *various* [Mt 4:24]

Once the passage has been worked through it should be read quietly at least three times to get the feel for the meaning of the new vocabulary, and then should be read at least three times out loud.

Exercise for Lesson 68.

Translate into Greek:

Now after Jesus had been heard, his disciples went to the surrounding districts preaching the good news of God and saying, "The times have been fulfilled and the judgment of God is approaching". (Mk 1:14-15)

Lesson 69

Indirect Questions.

Indirect questions are questions placed in dependence on a verb in an independent clause. The verb in the independent clause need not be a verb of asking—the word οἶδα is often used. Indirect questions are introduced by a word used to introduce a direct question (i.e., τίς, πῶς) or εἰ.

English		Greek	
a	*What are they saying?*	a'	τί λέγουσιν;
b	*I know what they are saying.*	b'	οἶδα τί λέγουσιν.
c	*I knew what they were saying.*	c'	ᾔδειν τί λέγουσιν.

When the direct question in English (a) becomes an indirect question (b) it keeps the same tense and mood as the direct question, if the main verb is present and is viewed as being contemporary with the time of the indirect question. But if the main verb is in past time and is viewed as being contemporary with the time of the indirect question, the tense of the indirect question is changed to the past (c). In Greek this change of tense does not take place, as is clear from the examples a', b', and c', because Greek prefers to retain the time of the direct question even when the question becomes indirect.

If the direct question is deliberative (i.e., if it uses a subjunctive to express doubt about a course of action—cf. below, Lesson 74), the indirect question also uses a subjunctive, i.e., it uses the exact form of the direct question, which is the basic rule for indirect questions: the indirect question uses the exact form of the direct question.

a	*What should he do?*	a'	τί ποιήσῃ;

b   *He does not know*   b'   οὐκ οἶδε τί ποιήσῃ.
     what he should do.

c   *He did not know*   c'   οὐκ ᾔδει τί ποιήσῃ.
     what he should do.

Here the English usage is the same as the Greek in that the
form of the direct question is conserved in the indirect questions both
in the present and in the past.
For examples of indirect questions cf. Mk 1:24, 2:25, and 9:6.

Mark 1:35 – 2:28

1:35 - ἔννυχα [Adv 2] *during the night* [hapax] // **1:36** - καταδιώκω
[κατά + διώκω] [V 2, DV 64, VP 1-3] *I look for* [hapax] // **1:38** -
ἀλλαχοῦ [Adv 1] *elsewhere* [hapax]; κωμόπολις, –εως, ἡ [N 28f]
market town [hapax]

1:40 - λεπρός, -οῦ, ὁ [N 6m] *leper* [Mt 8:2]; γονυπετέω [V 8; VP 1-3, 5-
6] *I kneel* [Mt 17:14] // **1:41** - σπλαγχνίζομαι (ἐσπλαγχνίσθην) [V 5,
23; VP 3] *I feel compassion* [Mt 9:36] // **1:42** - λέπρα, –ας, ἡ [N 2]
leprosy [Mt 8:3] // **1:43** - ἐμβριμάομαι [ἐν + βριμάομαι] [V 9, 22, 23;
VP 2-3, 6] *I speak harshly to* [Mt 9:30] // **1:44** - καθαρισμός, -οῦ, ὁ
[N 6m] *purification* [Lk 2:22]; προστάσσω [πρός + τάσσω] [V 3, DV
303, VP 1-3] *I prescribe* [Mt 1:24]; Μωϋσῆς, –έως, ὁ [N 29, 33] *Moses*
[Mt 8:4] // **1:45** - διαφημίζω [διά + φημίζω] (διαφημίσω) [V 5, VP 1-3]
I spread (news of) [Mt 9:31]; φανερῶς [Adv 3] *openly* [Jn 7:10];
πάντοθεν [Adv 1] *from all sides* [Lk 19:43]

2:2 - χωρέω [V 8; VP 1-3, 5-6] *to have room* [intransitive; transitive:
to make room [Mt 19:11] // **2:3** - παραλυτικός, –οῦ, ὁ [N 6m] *cripple*
[Mt 4:24] // **2:4** - ἀποστεγάζω [ἀπό + στεγάζω] (ἀποστεγάσω) [V 5,
VP 1-3] *I unroof* [hapax]; στέγη, –ης, ἡ [N 1] *roof* [Mt 8:8];
ἐξορύσσω [V 3, DV 141, VP 1-3] *I make an opening* [Gal 4:15];
χαλάω [V 9; VP 1-3, 5-6] *I lower* [Lk 5:4]; κράβαττος, –ου, ὁ [N 6m]
cot [Jn 5:8] // **2:9** - εὐκοπώτερος, –α, –ον [εὔκοπος, –η, –ον (Adj 1)]
easier [Mt 9:5]

2:14 - Λευί (Λευίς, Λευεί) [N 32] *Levi* [Lk 3:24]; Ἀλφαῖος, –ου, ὁ [N
6m] *Alphaeus* [Mt 10:3]; τελώνιον, –ου, τό [N 7] *tax house* [Mt 9:9]
// **2:15** - συνανάκειμαι [σύν + ἀνά + κεῖμαι] [V 17, DV 148, VP 2-3] *I*

recline at table with [Mt 9:10] // **2:16** - Φαρισαῖος, –ου, ὁ [N 6m]
Pharisee [Mt 3:7] // **2:17** - ἰατρός, –οῦ, ὁ [N 6m] *physician* [Mt 9:12]
2:19 - νυμφών, –ῶνος, ὁ [N 21m] *wedding hall* [Mt 9:15] // **2:20** -
ἀπαίρω [ἀπό + αἴρω] [V 6, DV 8, VP 1-3] *I take away* [Mt 9:15]

2:21 - ἐπίβλημα, –ατος, τό [N 16] *patch* [Mt 9:16]; ῥάκος, –ους, τό [N
31] *piece of cloth* [Mt 9:16]; ἄγναφος, –ος, –ον [Adj 5] *unshrunk* [Mt
9:16]; ἐπιράπτω [ἐπί + ῥάπτω] [V 4, 5; VP 1-3] *I sew on* [hapax];
σχίσμα, –ατος, τό [N 16] *tear* [Mt 9:16] // **2:22** - ἀσκός, –οῦ, ὁ [N 6m]
wineskin [Mt 9:17]; ῥήγνυμι [V 14; DV 272; VP 1-3, 9, 12] *I burst*
[Mt 9:17] [In the present system also found as ῥήσσω (V 3).]

2:23 - παραπορεύομαι [παρά + πορεύομαι] [V 1, 22, 23; DV 260; VP 3]
I go by [Mt 27:39]; σπόριμα, –ων, τά [N 7] *crops* [from σπόριμος, –ος,
–ον (Adj 5) *sown*] [Mt 12:1]; τίλλω [V 6, VP 1-3] *I pick* [Mt 12:1] //
2:25 - Δαυ(ε)ίδ [N 32] *David* [Mt 1:1] // **2:26** -᾽Αβιαθάρ [N 32]
Abiathar [hapax]; πρόθεσις, –εως, ἡ [N 28f] *laying out* [In other
contexts this word can have the meaning *purpose* (Mt 12:4).]

Once the passage has been worked through it should be read
quietly at least three times to get the feel for the meaning of the new
vocabulary, and then should be read at least three times out loud.

Exercise for Lesson 69.

Translate into Greek:

And they said to the lepers who had been healed, "See that you
say nothing to anyone, but go, show yourselves to the priests
and bring what Moses   commanded for the purification as a
witness for them". (Mk 1:44) [Cf. Prohibitions, Lesson 72.]

Lesson 70

Repetition of Negatives.

Repetition of negatives in Greek is a common practice and results in greater emphasis on the negation. For example, ὅρα μηδενὶ μηδὲν εἴπῃς (Mk 1:44—cf. Lesson 72 for the use of the aorist subjunctive in prohibitions) is stronger than ὅρα μηδέν τινι εἴπῃς. Current English does not permit this usage: repetition of a negative, where not a barbarism, results in an affirmation. The double negative in the Greek sentence must have the negation emphasized in a different way in English, perhaps, *See to it that you say not one word to anyone*. The unemphatic Greek sentence used for contrast could perhaps in English be rendered *See to it that you tell no one*.

For other examples of repetition in the use of negatives cf. Mk 2:2, 3:20, and 3:27.

Mark 3:1-35.

3:2 - παρατηρέω [παρά + τηρέω] [V 8; VP 1-3, 5-6] *I watch closely* [Lk 6:7] // **3:3** - ξηρός, -ά, -όν [Adj 2] *dry* [Mt 12:10] // **3:4** - κακοποιέω [κακο + ποιέω] [V 8; DV 258; VP 1-3, 5-6] *I do evil* [Lk 6:9]; σιωπάω [V 9; VP 1-3, 5-6] *I am silent* [Mt 20:31] // **3:5** - περιβλέπομαι [περί + βλέπομαι] [V 4, 22; DV 43; VP 2-3] *I look around* [Lk 6:10]; συλλυπέομαι [σύν + λυπέομαι] [V 8, 22; VP 2-3] *I feel sorry for* [hapax legomenon]; πώρωσις, -εως, ἡ [N 28f] *hardness* [Rom 11:25]; ἀποκαθίστημι [ἀπό + καθίστημι] [V 11, 21; DV 134; VP 1-3, 7-8, 11] *I restore* [Mt 12:13] // **3:6** - Ἡρῳδιανοί, -ῶν, οἱ [N 6m] *Herodians* [Mt 22:16]; συμβούλιον, -ου, τό [N 7] *plan* [Mt 12:14]

3:8 - Ἱεροσόλυμα, -ων, [τά] [N 7, 33] [also Ἱερουσαλήμ, ἡ (N 32)] *Jerusalem* [Mt 2:1]; Ἰδουμαία, -ας, ἡ [N 2] *Idumea* [hapax]; Τύρος, -ου, ἡ [N 6f] *Tyre* [Mt 11:21]; Σιδών, -ῶνος, ἡ [N 21f] *Sidon*

[Mt 15:21] // **3:9** - πλοιάριον, –ου, τό [N 7] *small boat* [Jn 6:22]; προσκαρτερέω [πρός + καρτερέω] [V 8; VP 1-3, 5-6] *I remain at hand* [Acts 1:14] // **3:10** - μάστιξ, –ιγος, ή [N 9f] *disease* [also: *scourge* (the basic meaning)] [Lk 7:21]

3:16 - Πέτρος, –ου, ὁ [N 6m] *Peter* [Mt 4:18] // **3:17** - Βοανηργές [N 32] *Boanerges* [hapax]; βροντή, –ῆς, ή [N 1] *thunder* [Jn 12:29] // **3:18** - Φίλιππος, –ου, ὁ [N 6m] *Philip* [Mt 10:3]; Βαρθολομαῖος, –ου, ὁ [N 6m] *Bartholomew* [Mt 10:3]; Μαθθαῖος, –ου, ὁ [N 6m] *Matthew* [Mt 9:9]; Θωμᾶς, ὁ [N 5, 33] *Thomas* [Lk 6:15]; Θαδδαῖος, –ου, ὁ [N 6m] *Thaddaeus* [Mt 10:3]; Καναναῖος, –ου, ὁ [N 6m] *Cananaean* [Mt 10:4] // **3:19** - Ἰούδας, ὁ [N 5, 33] *Judas* [Mt 10:4]; Ἰσκαριώθ, ὁ [N 32] *Iscariot* [Lk 6:16]

3:22 - Βεελζεβούλ [N 32] *Beelzebul* [Mt 10:25] // **3:27** - διαρπάζω [διά + ἀρπάζω] (διαρπάσω) [V 5, DV 27, VP 1-3] *I plunder* [Mt 12:29] // **3:28** - ἁμάρτημα, –ατος, τό [N 16] *sin* [Rom 3:25]

3:34 - κύκλῳ [Adv 1] *round about* [Lk 9:12] [also found as a preposition with the genitive: *round* (Prep 1)]

Once the passage has been worked through it should be read quietly three times to get the feel for the meaning of the new vocabulary, and then should be read at least three times out loud.

Exercise for Lesson 70.

Translate into Greek:

> And they come into the houses of the village; and the crowds gather again so that Jesus and his disciples are unable even to eat bread. (Mk 3:20)

Lesson 71

The Hortatory Subjunctive.

The "hortatory subjunctive" consists of a subjunctive in the main clause of a sentence to express an exhortation. The verb is always in the first person. (And thus, in a sense, this construction supplies the lacuna for the lack of the first person in the imperative mood.) Cf. Mk 1:38: ἄγωμεν ἀλλαχοῦ εἰς τὰς ἐχομένας κωμοπόλεις — *Let us go elsewhere into the nearby market towns.* Cf. also Mk 4:35, 9:5, and 14:42.

Mark 4:1-41.

4:5 - πετρῶδες, –ους, τό [from πετρώδης, -ης, -ες (Adj 15)] *rocky ground* [Mt 13:5]; ἐξανατέλλω [ἐκ + ἀνά + τέλλω] [V 6, DV 306, VP 1-3] *I spring up* [Mt 13:5]; βάθος, –ους, τό [N 31] *depth* [Mt 13:5] // **4:6** - ἀνατέλλω [ἀνά + τέλλω] [V 6, DV 306, VP 1-3] *I rise* [Mt 4:16]; καυματίζω (καυματίσω) [V 5, VP 1-3] *I scorch* [Mt 13:6] // **4:7** - συμπνίγω [σύν + πνίγω] [V 2, DV 257, VP 1-4] *I choke* [Mt 13:22] // **4:8** - τριάκοντα [Adj 21] *thirty* [Mt 13:8]; ἐξήκοντα [Adj 21] *sixty* [Mt 13:8]

4:17 - πρόσκαιρος, –ος, –ον [Adj 5] *temporary* [Mt 13:21]; διωγμός, –οῦ, ὁ [N 6m] *persecution* [Mt 13:21] // **4:19** - μέριμνα, –ης, ἡ [N 3] *anxiety* [Mt 13:22]; ἀπάτη, –ης, ἡ [N 1] *deception* [Mt 13:22] // **4:20** - παραδέχομαι [παρά + δέχομαι] [V 2, 22; DV 58; VP 2-3] *I accept* [Acts 15:4]; καρποφορέω [καρπός + φορέω] [V 8; VP 1-3, 5-6] *I bear fruit* [Mt 13:23]

4:21 - μόδιος, –ου, ὁ [N 6m] *basket* [Mt 5:15]; κλίνη, –ης, ἡ [N 1] *bed* [Mt 9:2]; λυχνία, –ας, ἡ [N 2] *lampstand* [Mt 5:15] // **4:22** - ἀπόκρυφος, –ος, –ον [Adj 5] *secret* [Lk 8:17]

4:24 - μετρέω [V 8; VP 1-3, 5-6] *I measure* [Mt 7:2]

4:26 - σπόρος, -ου, ὁ [N 6m] *seed* [Lk 8:5] // **4:27** - βλαστάω [V 9; DV 42; VP 1-3, 5-6] *I sprout* [This word is also found in the present system as βλαστάνω (V 7).] [Mt 13:26]; μηκύνω [V 7, VP 1-3] *I lengthen* [hapax] // **4:28** - αὐτόματος, -η, -ον [Adj 1] *by itself* [Acts 12:10] // **4:29** - δρέπανον, -ου, τό [N 7] *sickle* [Apoc 14:14]

4:31 - κόκκος, -ου, ὁ [N 6m] *grain (of seed)* [Mt 13:31]; σίναπι, -εως, τό [N 33] *mustard plant* [Mt 13:31] // **4:32** - λάχανον, -ου, τό [N 7} *vegetable* [Mt 13:32]; κλάδος, -ου, ὁ [N 6m] *branch* [Mt 13:32]; σκιά, -ᾶς. ἡ [N 2] *shade* [Mt 4:16]; κατασκηνόω [κατά + σκηνόω] [V 10; VP 1-3, 5-6] *I dwell in* [Mt 13:32]

4:37 - κῦμα, -ατος, τό [N 16] *wave* [Mt 8:24]; γεμίζω (γεμίσω) [V 5; VP 1-3] *I fill* [Lk 14:23] // **4:38** - πρύμνα, -ης, ἡ [N 3] *stern (of a ship).* [Acts 27:29]; προσκεφάλαιον, -ου, τό [N 7] *cushion* [hapax]; μέλει [V 6, 19; DV 193; VP 1] [used with dative case] *it concerns* [Mt 22:16] // **4:39** - διεγείρω [διά + ἐγείρω] [V 6, DV 70, VP 1-3] *I awake; I rise* [Lk 8:24]; κοπάζω (κοπάσω) [V 5, VP 1-3] *I cease* [Mt 14:32]; γαλήνη, -ης, ἡ [N 1] *calm* [used with regard to the sea] [Mt 8:26] // **4:40** - δειλός, -ή, -όν [Adj 1] *afraid* [Mt 8:26]

Exercise for Lesson 71.

Translate into Greek:

> To you (sg.) are given the mysteries of the kingdom of heaven; but to all outside every word happens in a parable. (Mk 4:11)

Prohibitions. Mark 5:1-43.

Lesson 72

Prohibitions.

<u>Positive</u> commands in the present tense of the imperative mood usually convey the idea of a general precept, i.e., a rule of conduct to be followed in more than one situation, i.e., the action is thought of as not terminated. (Cf. above, Lesson 12.) Positive commands in the aorist tense of the imperative mood usually convey the idea of a command for a specific case—a rule of conduct to be followed in one situation, i.e., the action is thought of as being terminated. (Cf. above, Lesson 19.)

Negative specific commands (i.e., specific prohibitions) are expressed by the <u>present imperative</u> if they mean that the person commanded is to stop doing an action which is underway, and by the <u>aorist subjunctive</u> if they mean that the person commanded is not to begin doing the action. The present imperative is used in order to indicate that the action is not terminated, i.e., is in the process of taking place; the negative shows that the process should stop. The aorist subjunctive is used to indicate that the action is being viewed as a whole, i.e., as terminated conceptually (hence the subjunctive), with the negative showing that the process should not be thought of as taking place at all, i.e., as beginning. Examples of both these prohibitions in regard to specific commands are found in the following texts: Mk 6:50 (μή φοβεῖσθε [present imperative negated]—"stop being afraid"); Mk 8:26 (μηδέ . . . εἰσέλθῃς [aorist subjunctive negated—"do not begin to enter").

If the prohibition is a <u>general precept</u>, the <u>present imperative</u> is used to express the customary nature of the prohibition, and the <u>aorist subjunctive</u> is used to intensify this command into an absolute "never". The negated present imperative would seem to be used to indicate that something should not become a practice, i.e., open to repetition. The negated aorist subjunctive would seem to be used again as a viewing of an action as conceptually terminated and negated to show that the entire act is not to occur. Examples of both these prohibitions in regard to general commands are found in the following texts: Mk 13:21 (μὴ πιστεύετε [present imperative]—"do not believe [it]"); Mk 10:19 (μὴ φονεύσῃς [aorist subjunctive]—"you shall not kill"). Mk 10:19 is a stronger general prohibition than Mk 13:21.

There are exceptions to the above generalizations. The student should accordingly not try to make all prohibitions fit into the generalizations.

Mark 5:1-43

5:1 - Γερασηνός, -ή, -όν [Adj 1] *of Gerasa* [Lk 8:26] // **5:2** - ὑπαντάω [ὑπό + ἀντάω] [V 9; VP 1-3, 5-6] *I go to meet; I meet* [with dative case] [Mt 8:28] // **5:3** - κατοίκησις, -εως, ἡ [N 28f] *dwelling* [hapax]; μνῆμα, -ατος, τό [N 16] *grave* [Lk 8:27]; ἅλυσις, -εως, ἡ [N 28f] *chain* [Lk 8:29] // **5:4** - πέδη, -ης, ἡ [N 1] *chain (for feet)* [Lk 8:29]; διασπάω [διά + σπάω] [V 9; DV 288; VP 1-3, 5-6] *I tear apart* [Acts 23:10]; συντρίβω [σύν + τρίβω] [V 4, DV 316, VP 1-4] *I shatter* [Mt 12:20]; δαμάζω (δαμάσω) [V 5, VP 1-3] *I subdue* [Jas 3:7] // **5:5** - κατακόπτω [κατά + κόπτω] [V 4, 5; DV 161; VP 1-3] *I cut* [hapax] // **5:7** - ὁρκίζω (ὁρκίσω) [V 5, VP 1-3] *I adjure* [Acts 19:13]; βασανίζω (βασανίσω) [V 5, VP 1-3] *I torment* [Mt 8:6] // **5:9** - λεγιών, -ῶνος, ἡ [N 21m] *legion* [i.e., a large number] [Mt 26:53]

5:11 - ἀγέλη, -ης, ἡ [N 1] *herd* [Mt 8:30]; βόσκω [V 2, VP 1-3] *I feed* [Mt 8:30] // **5:13** - ὁρμάω [V 9; VP 1-3, 5-6] *I rush* [Mt 8:32]; κρημνός, -οῦ, ὁ [N 6m] *precipice* [Mt 8:32]; δισχίλιοι, -αι, -α [Adj 6] *two thousand* [hapax]; πνίγω [V 2, DV 257, VP 1-4] *I choke* [Mt 13:7] // **5:15** - ἱματίζω (ἱματίσω) [V 5, VP 1-3] *I clothe* [Lk 8:35]; σωφρονέω [V 8; VP 1-3, 5-6] *I am in my right mind* [Lk 8:35] // **5:16** - διηγέομαι [διά + ἡγέομαι] [V 8, 22; DV 115; VP 2-3] *I recount* [Lk 8:39] // **5:17** - ὅριον, -ου, τό [N 7] *boundary* [Mt 2:16] // **5:20** - Δεκάπολις, -εως, ἡ [N 28f] *Decapolis* [Mt 4:25]

5:21 - διαπεράω [διά + περάω] [V 9; VP 1-3, 5-6] *I cross over* [Mt 9:1] // **5:22** - ἀρχισυνάγωγος, -ου, ὁ [N 6m] *head of a synagogue* [Lk 8:49]; Ἰάϊρος, -ου, ὁ [N 6m] *Jairus* [Lk 8:41] // **5:23** - θυγάτριον, -ου, τό [N 7] *little daughter* [Mk 7:25] // **5:24** - συνθλίβω [σύν + θλίβω] [V 4, DV 126, VP 1-3] *I press; I crowd* [Mk 5:31] // **5:26** - δαπανάω [V 9; VP 1-3, 5-6] *I spend* [Lk 15:14] // **5:29** - πηγή, -ῆς, ἡ [N 1] *spring* [Jn 4:6] // **5:33** - τρέμω [V 7, VP 1-3] *I tremble* [Lk 8:47]; προσπίπτω [πρός + πίπτω] [V 4, 5; DV 248; VP 1-4] *I fall down before* [with dative case] [Lk 5:8]

5:35 - σκύλλω [V 6, VP 1-3] *I trouble* [Mt 9:36] // **5:36** - παρακούω [παρά + ἀκούω] [V 1, DV 11, VP 1-3] *I take no heed of* [Mt 18:17]; μόνον [Adv 3] *only* [Mt 5:47] // **5:37** - συνακολουθέω [σύν + ἀκολουθέω] [V 8; VP 1-3, 5-6] *I accompany* [Lk 23:49] // **5:38** - θόρυβος, -ου, ὁ [N 6m] *uproar* [Mt 26:5]; ἀλαλάζω (ἀλαλάσω) [V 3, VP 1-3] *I wail* [1 Cor 13:1] // **5:39** - θορυβέω [V 8; VP 1-3, 5-6] *I set in an uproar* [Mt 9:23] // **5:40** - καταγελάω [κατά + γελάω] [V 9; DV 47; VP 1-3, 5-6] *I ridicule* [with the genitive case] [Mt 9:24] // **5:41** - ταλ(ε)ιθα [N 32] *little girl* [Aramaic] [hapax]; κουμ [V 20] *get up!* [Aramaic] [hapax]; μεθερμηνεύω [μετά + ἑρμηνεύω] [V 1, VP 1-3] *I translate* [Mt 1:23]; κοράσιον, -ου, τό [N 7] *little girl* [Mt 9:24] // **5:42** - ἔκστασις, -εως, ἡ [N 28f] *amazement* [Lk 5:26] // **5:43** - διαστέλλομαι [διά + στέλλομαι] [V 6, 22; DV 292; VP 2-3] *I command* [with dative case] [Mt 16:20]

Exercise for Lesson 72.

Translate into Greek:

And she came to Jesus and she sees the demoniacs—the ones who had had a legion—seated, clothed, and rational, and she was afraid. (Mk 5:15)

τί with the Meaning *Why?*   Mark 6:1-56.

Lesson 73

τί with the Meaning *Why?*

The interrogative pronoun τί has two meanings when used to introduce a question: 1) *what?*; 2) *why?* . The two meanings are distinguished by the context.

τί in the sense of *what?* is the ordinary use of the interrogative pronoun in the neuter gender. It is found with this meaning in both the nominative (τί ἐγένετο; *What happened?*) and accusative cases (τί βλέπεις; *What do you see?*). τί in the sense of *why?* is explained grammatically as an accusative of specification (*in regard to what?*), although the average person was probably not aware of this when speaking.

For τί in the sense of *what?* cf. Mk 2:9, 6:24, and 10:17.

For τί in the sense of *why?* cf. Mk 2:7, 2:8, and 5:35.

The expression διὰ τί is also used to express the meaning *why?*. Cf. Mk 2:18, 7:5, and 11:31.

Mark 6:1-56

6:3 - τέκτων, -ονος, ὁ [N 20m] *carpenter* [Mt 13:55]; Μαρία, -ας, ἡ [N 2] [also Μαριάμ, ἡ (N 32)] *Mary* [Mt 1:16]; Ἰωσῆς, -ῆτος, ὁ [N 33] *Joses* [Mk 15:40] // **6:4** - ἄτιμος, -ος, -ον [Adj 5] *dishonored* [Mt 13:57] // **6:5** - ἄρρωστος, -ος, -ον [Adj 5] *sick* [Mt 14:14] // **6:6** - ἀπιστία, -ας, ἡ [N 2] *unbelief* [Mt 13:58]; περιάγω [περί + ἄγω] [V 2, DV 5, VP 1-4] *I go around* [Mt 4:23] // **6:8** - πήρα, -ας, ἡ [N 2] *bag* [Mt 10:10]; χαλκός, -οῦ, ὁ [N 6m] *money* [literally, *copper*] [Mt 10:9] // **6:9** - ὑποδέομαι [ὑπό + δέομαι] [V 8, 22; DV 59; VP 2-3, 6] *I put on* [used for shoes, sandals] [Acts 12:8]; σανδάλιον, -ου, τό [N 7] *sandal* [Acts 12:8] // **6:11** - ἐκτινάσσω [ἐκ + τινάσσω] [V 3, VP 1-3] *I shake off* [Mt 10:14]; ὑποκάτω [Prep 1] *under* [with genitive case] [Mt 22:44] // **6:13** - ἀλείφω [V 4, DV 12, VP 1-3] *I anoint* [Mt 6:17]; ἔλαιον, -ου, τό [N 7] *olive oil* [Mt 25:3]

6:14 - Ἡρῴδης, –ου, ὁ [N 4] *Herod* [Mt 14:1] // **6:15** - Ἠλ(ε)ίας, –ου, ὁ [N 5] *Elijah* [Mt 11:14] // **6:16** - ἀποκεφαλίζω [ἀπό + κεφαλίζω] (ἀποκεφαλίσω) [V 5, VP 1-3] *I behead* [Mt 14:10] // **6:17** - Ἡρῳδιάς, –άδος, ἡ [N 14f] *Herodias* [Mt 14:6] // **6:20** - συντηρέω [σύν + τηρέω] [V 8; VP 1-3, 5-6] *I protect* [Mt 9:17]; ἀπορέω [α privative + a root from πόρος] [V 8; VP 1-3, 5-6] *I am puzzled* [Lk 24:4]; ἡδέως [Adv 3] *gladly* [Mk 12:37] // **6:21** - εὔκαιρος, –ος, –ον [Adj 5] *opportune* [Heb 4:16]; γενέσια, –ων, τά [N 7] *birthday* [Mt 14:6]; μεγιστάν, –ᾶνος, ὁ [N 33] *nobleman* [Apoc 6:15] / **6:22** - ὀρχέομαι [V 8, 22; VP 2-3] *I dance* [Mt 11:17] // **6:23** - ἥμισυς, –εια, –υ [Adj 14] *half* [as noun, N 32] [Lk 19:8] // **6:25** - σπουδή, –ῆς, ἡ [N 1] *haste* [Lk 1:39]; ἐξαυτῆς [Adv 3] *at once* [Acts 10:33]; πίναξ, –ακος, ἡ [N 8f] *dish* [Mt 14:8] // **6:26** - περίλυπος, –ος, –ον [Adj 5] *deeply distressed* [Mt 26:38]; ὅρκος, –ου, ὁ [N 6m] *oath* [Mt 5:33] // **6:27** - σπεκουλάτωρ, –ορος, ὁ [N 26] *executioner* [hapax] // **6:29** - πτῶμα, –ατος, τό [N 16] *corpse* [Mt 14:12]

6:31 - εὐκαιρέω [εὖ + a root from καιρός; but at Acts 17:21 the imperfect is ηὐκαίρουν.] [V 8; VP 1-3, 5-6] *I have an opportunity* [Acts 17:21] // **6:33** - πέζῃ [Adv 3] *on foot* [Mt 14:13]; συντρέχω [σύν + τρέχω] [V 2; DV 315; VP 1-4] *I run together with* [Acts 3:11] // **6:37** - διακόσιοι, , –αι, –α [Adj 6] *two hundred* [Jn 6:7] // **6:39** - ἀνακλίνω [ἀνά + κλίνω] [V 7, DV 159, VP 1-3] *I make one recline* [Mt 8:11]; συμπόσιον, –ου, τό [N 7] *group* [hapax]; χλωρός, –ά, –όν [Adj 2] *green* [Apoc 6:8] // **6:40** - πρασιά, –ᾶς, ἡ [N 2] *block (of persons)* [hapax]; πεντήκοντα [Adj 21] *fifty* [Lk 7:41] // **6:41** - κατακλάω [κατά + κλάω] [V 9; DV 156; VP 1-3, 5-6] *I break into pieces* [Lk 9:16] // **6:43** - κλάσμα, –ατος, τό [N 16] *fragment* [Mt 14:20]; κόφινος, –ου, ὁ [N 6m] *basket* [Mt 16:9] // **6:44** - πεντακισχίλιοι, –αι, –α [Adj 6] *five thousand* [Mt 16:9]

6:45 - ἀναγκάζω (ἀναγκάσω) [V 5, VP 1-3] *I compel* [Mt 14:22]; Βηθσαϊδά, –ᾶς, ἡ [N 2] *Bethsaida* [Mt 11:21] // **6:46** - ἀποτάσσομαι [ἀπό + τάσσομαι] [V 3, 22; DV 303; VP 1-3] *I leave; I say good-bye* [Lk 9:61] // **6:48** - ἐλαύνω [V 7, DV 79, VP 1-3] *I drive* [Lk 8:29]; ἐναντίος, –α, –ον [Adj 2] *contrary* [Mt 14:24]; τέταρτος, –η, –ον [Adj 1] *fourth* [Mt 14:25] // **6:49** - φάντασμα, –ατος, τό [N 16] *apparition* [Mt 14:26] // **6:50** - θαρσέω [V 8; VP 1-3, 5-6] *I have courage* [Mt 9:22] // **6:52** - πωρόω [V 10; VP 1-3, 5-6] *I harden* [Jn 12:40]

6:53 - Γεννησαρέτ, ἡ [N 32] *Gennasaret* [Mt 14:34]; προσορμίζομαι [πρός + ὁρμίζομαι] (προσορμίσομαι) [V 5, 23; VP 3] *I come into harbor* [hapax] // **6:55** - περιτρέχω [περί + τρέχω] [V 2; DV 315; VP

1-4] *I run about* [hapax]; περιφέρω [περί + φέρω] [V 6, DV 324, VP 1-4] *I bring around* [2 Cor 4:10] // **6:56** - κράσπεδον, –ου, τό [N 7] *edge* [Mt 9:20]

Exercise for Lesson 73.

Translate into Greek:

> And, coming out of the boat, they saw a large crowd, and they had pity on them, because they were like sheep not having a good shepherd, and they began to teach them many things. (Mk 6:34)

Deliberative Questions. Mark 7:1-37.

Lesson 74

Deliberative Questions.

A deliberative question is a question placed in doubt or wonder about a course of action. In Greek the deliberative question is expressed by the subjunctive mood: τί αἰτήσωμαι; *What am I to request?* (Cf. Mk 6:24.) The question can be addressed to another person, as in the example from Mark, or it can be an expression addressed to one's self, as if there were deliberation out loud.

When the subjunctive mood is found in an indirect question, it is usually a sign that the original question was deliberative: οὐκ οἶδα τί αἰτήσωμαι. *I do not know what I am to request.* The subjunctive is used here not because the question is indirect but because the question would take the subjunctive were it to be expressed directly, i.e., it is deliberative in nature: the speaker is in doubt about a course of action.

For examples of direct deliberative questions cf. Mk 10:17 and 12:14, and Lk 3:10. For examples of indirect deliberative questions cf. above, Lesson 69, and the discussion there of indirect questions.

Mark 7:1-37.

7:2 - ἄνιπτος, -ος, -ον [Adj 5] *unwashed* [Mt 15:20] // **7:3** - πυγμή, -ῆς, ἡ [N 1] *fist* [hapax] // **7:4** - ἀγορά, -ᾶς, ἡ [N 2] *market-place* [Mt 11:16]; ξέστης, -ου, ὁ [N 4] *jug* [hapax]; χαλκ(ε)ίον, -ου, τό [N 7] *copper utensil* [hapax] // **7:6** - χεῖλος, -ους, τό [N 31] *lip* [Mt 15:8]; πόρρω [Adv 1] *far* [Mt 15:8] // **7:7** - μάτην [Adv 3] *in vain* [Mt 15:9]; σέβομαι [V 4, 22; DV 279; VP 2] [used only in present system] *I reverence* [Mt 15:9]; ἔνταλμα, -ατος, τό [N 16] *commandment* [Mt 15:9] // **7:10** - κακολογέω [V 8; VP 1-3, 5-6] *I speak ill of* [Mt 15:4]; τελευτάω [V 9; VP 1-3, 5-6] *I die* [literally, *I complete*] [Mt 2:19] // **7:11** - κορβᾶν [N 32] [Aramaic word for *gift*] *korban* [hapax] // **7:13**

- ἀκυρόω [V 10; VP 1-3, 5-6] *I invalidate* [Mt 15:6]; παρόμοιος, –α, –ον [Adj 2] *like* [hapax]

7:18 - ἀσύνετος, –ος, –ον [Adj 5] *lacking in understanding* [Mt 15:16] // **7:19** - ἀφεδρών, –ῶνος, ὁ [N 21m] *latrine* [Mt 15:17] // **7:21** - κλοπή, –ῆς, ἡ [N 1] *theft* [Mt 15:19]; φόνος, –ου, ὁ [N 6m] *murder* [Mt 15:19] // **7:22** - μοιχεία, –ας, ἡ [N 2] *adultery* [Mt 15:19]; πλεονεξία, –ας, ἡ [N 2] *greed* [Lk 12:15]; πονηρία, –ας, ἡ [N 2] *malice* [Mt 22:18]; δόλος, –ου, ὁ [N 6m] *deceit* [Mt 26:4]; ἀσέλγεια, –ας, ἡ [N 2] *indecency* [Rom 13:13]; ὑπερηφανία, –ας, ἡ [N 2] *arrogance* [hapax]; ἀφροσύνη, –ης, ἡ [N 1] *foolishness* [2 Cor 11:1]

7:24 - λανθάνω [V 7; DV 178; VP 1-4] *I escape notice* [Lk 8:47] // **7:26** - Ἑλληνίς, –ίδος·, ἡ [N 14f] *Greek woman* [Acts 17:12]; Συροφοινίκισσα, –ης, ἡ [N 3] *Syrophoenician woman* [hapax] // **7:27** - κυνάριον, –ου, τό [N 7] *puppy* [Mt 15:26] // **7:28** - ψιχίον, –ου, τό [N 7] *crumb* [Mt 15:27]

7:32 - μογιλάλος, –ος, –ον [Adj 5] *speaking with difficulty* [hapax] // **7:33** - δάκτυλος, –ου, ὁ [N 6m] *finger* [Jn 8:6]; πτύω [V 1, DV 266, VP 1-3] *I spit* [Jn 9:6] // **7:34** - στενάζω (στενάξω) [V 3, DV 292, VP 1-3] *I groan* [Rom 8:23]; εφφαθα [V 20] [Aramaic word] *be opened!* [hapax]; διανοίγω [διά + ἀνοίγω] [V 2, DV 20, VP 1-4] *I open* [Lk 2:23] // **7:35** - ὀρθῶς [Adv 3] *properly* [Lk 7:43] // **7:37** - ὑπερπερισσῶς [Adv 3] *beyond all measure* [hapax]; ἄλαλος, –ος, –ον [Adj 5] *dumb* [Mk 9:17]

Exercise for Lesson 74.

Translate into Greek:

> And, summoning him again, they kept saying to him: "Listen to us and understand". (Mk 7:14)

The Complementary Infinitive. ἵνα
Introducing a Noun Clause. Mark 8:1 –
9:29.

Lesson 75

The Complementary Infinitive. ἵνα Introducing a Noun Clause.

The infinitive is used in New Testament Greek after a variety of
verbs to "complete" their meaning. Hence, the designation
"complementary infinitive". Among such verbs are θέλω (cf. Mk
6:19, 6:26, 6:48), δύναμαι (cf. Mk 1:40, 2:4, 2:7), ἄρχομαι (cf. Mk 1:45,
2:23, 4:1) and μέλλω (cf. Mk 10:32, Mk 13:4, Jn 4:47). Also to be noted
are the expressions ἱκανός εἰμι and ἄξιός εἰμι, each of which can
govern a complementary infinitive (cf. Mk 1:7, 1 Cor 15:9, Lk
15:19.21, Acts 13:25, Apoc 4:11).

In addition to its use to express purpose, a clause consisting of
ἵνα and the subjunctive can be used as a "noun clause" following
certain verbs. That is to say, it is a clause which takes the place of a
noun, just as does the complementary infinitive. (A ἵνα purpose
clause is an "adverbial clause" because it functions like an adverb.)
The ἵνα noun clause also shows a certain analogy to the
complementary infinitive inasmuch as it completes the meaning of
the verb on which it depends. These verbs which can take a ἵνα
noun clause must be learned from the text. For example, θέλω can
be followed by a ἵνα noun clause (cf. Mk 6:25, 9:30, 10:35), but
δύναμαι, ἄρχομαι, and μέλλω cannot. The expressions ἱκανός εἰμι
and ἄξιός εἰμι can also govern a ἵνα noun clause (cf. Mt 8:8 and Jn
1:27).

Mark 8:1 – 9:29.

8:2 - προσμένω [πρός + μένω] [V 7, DV 197, VP 1-3] *I stay with* [Mt
15:32] // **8:3** - νῆστις, –ιδος, ὁ/ἡ [Adj 22] *hungry; fasting* [Mt 15:32];
ἐκλύομαι [ἐκ + λύομαι] [V 1, 23; VP 3]] *I am weak* [Mt 15:32] // **8:4**
- ἐρημία, –ας, ἡ [N 2] *desert* [Mt 15:33] // **8:7** - ἰχθύδιον, –ου, τό [N 7]

small fish [Mt 15:34] // **8:8** - περίσσευμα, –ατος, τό [N 16] *surplus* [Mt 12:34]; σπυρίς, –ίδος, ἡ [N 14f] *basket* [Mt 15:37] // **8:9** - τετρακισχίλιοι, –αι, –α [Adj 6] *four thousand* [Mt 15:38] // **8:10** - Δαλμανουθά, ἡ [N 32] *Dalmanutha* [hapax]

8:12 - ἀναστενάζω [ἀνά + στενάζω] (ἀναστενάξω) [V 3, DV 293, VP 1-3] *I groan deeply* [hapax]

8:14 - ἐπιλανθάνομαι [ἐπί + λανθάνομαι] [V 7, 22; DV 178; VP 2-3] *I forget* [Mt 16:5]

8:23 - ἐκφέρω [ἐκ + φέρω] [V 6, DV 324, VP 1-4] *I take out* [Lk 15:22]; ὄμμα, –ατος, τό [N 16] *eye* [Mt 20:34] // **8:25** - διαβλέπω [διά + βλέπω] [V 4, DV 43, VP 1-3] *I see clearly* [Mt 7:5]; τηλαυγῶς [Adv 3] *distinctly* [hapax]

8:27 - Καισάρεια, –ας, ἡ [N 2] *Caesarea* [Mt 16:13]

8:31 - ἀποδοκιμάζω [ἀπό + δοκιμάζω] (ἀποδοκιμάσω) [V 5, VP 1-3] *I reject* [Mt 21:42] // **8:36** - ζημιόω [V 10; VP 1-3, 5-6] *I lose* [Mt 16:26] // **8:37** - ἀντάλλαγμα, –ατος, τό [N 16] *exchange* [Mt 16:26] // **8:38** - ἐπαισχύνομαι [ἐπί + αἰσχύνομαι] [V 7, 23; DV 10; VP 3] *I am ashamed* [Lk 9:26]; μοιχαλίς, –ίδος, ἡ [N 14f] *adulteress* [Mt 12:39]

9:2 - ὑψηλός, –ή, –όν [Adj 1] *high* [Mt 4:8]; μεταμορφόω [μετά + μορφόω] [V 10; VP 1-3, 5-6] *I transform* [Mt 17:2] // **9:3** - στίλβω [V 4, VP 1-3] *I glisten* [hapax]; γναφεύς, –έως, ὁ [N 29] *bleacher* [hapax]; λευκαίνω [V 7, VP 1-3] *I bleach* [Apoc 7:14] // **9:4** - συλλαλέω [σύν + λαλέω] [V 8; VP 1-3, 5-6] *I talk with* [Mt 17:3] // **9:6** - ἔκφοβος, –ος, –ον [Adj 5] *terrified* [Heb 12:21] // **9:7** - ἐπισκιάζω [ἐπί + σκιάζω] (ἐπισκιάσω) [V 5, VP 1-3] *I cast a shadow over* [Mt 17:5] // **9:8** - ἐξάπινα [Adv 3] *suddenly* [hapax]

9:12 - ἀποκαθιστάνω [ἀπό + κατά + ἱστάνω] [V 7, VP 1] *I restore* [Acts 1:6]; ἐξουδενέω [ἐκ + root connected with οὐδέν] [V 8; VP 1-3, 5-6] *I despise* [Lk 18:9]

9:15 - ἐκθαμβέομαι [ἐκ + θαμβέομαι] [V 8, 23; VP 3, 6] *I am utterly amazed* [Mk 14:33]; προστρέχω [πρός + τρέχω] [V 2, DV 315, VP 1-4] *I run up to* [Mk 10:17] // **9:18** - ἀφρίζω [verbal form of ἀφρός, *foam*] (ἀφρίσω) [V 5, VP 1-3] *I foam* [Mk 9:20]; ὀδούς, –οντος, ὁ [N 33] *tooth* [Mt 5:38]; τρίζω (τρίσω) [V 3, VP 1-3] *I grind* [hapax] // **9:20** - συσπαράσσω [σύν + σπαράσσω] [V 3, VP 1-3] *I convulse* [Lk 9:42];

κυλίω [V 1, VP 1-3] *I roll* [hapax] // **9:21** - παιδιόθεν [Adv 2] *from childhood* [hapax] // **9:22** - βοηθέω [V 8; VP 1-3, 5-6] [with dative case] *I help* [Mt 15:25] // **9:25** - ἐπισυντρέχω [ἐπί + σύν + τρέχω] [V 2, DV 315, VP 1-4] *I run together with* [hapax]

Exercise for Lesson 75.

Translate into Greek:

And, coming to the disciple, he saw a great crowd around him, and a scribe disputing with him. (Mk 9:14 and Acts 6:9)

The Infinitive as an Expression of Purpose.
Mark 9:30 – 10:34.

Lesson 76.

The Infinitive as an Expression of Purpose.

One of the uses of the infinitive in the New Testament is to express purpose. This parallels the English usage: *I came to see you.* In the New Testament this use of the infinitive to express purpose is frequently found with a verb expressing motion of some kind, especially the verb ἔρχομαι: οὐκ ἦλθον καταλῦσαι ἀλλὰ πληρῶσαι—*I came not to destroy but to fulfil* (Mt 5:17).

Cf. also Mk 2:17, 3:14, and 10:45.

Two other ways of expressing purpose have already been seen: 1) ἵνα or ὅπως with the subjunctive, in Lesson 5; 2) the future participle, in Lesson 17.

Mark 9:30 – 10:34.

9:36 - ἐναγκαλίζομαι [ἐν + ἀγκαλίζομαι] (ἐναγκαλίσομαι) [V 5, 22; VP 2-3] *I embrace* [Mk 10:16]

9:42 - περίκειμαι [περί + κεῖμαι] [V 17, DV 148] *I am placed around* [Lk 17:2], μύλος, –ου, ὁ [N 6m] *millstone* [Mt 18:6]; ὀνικός, –ή, –όν [Adj 1] *of a donkey* [Mt 18:6]; τράχηλος, –ου, ὁ [N 6m] *neck* [Mt 18:6] // **9:43** - ἀποκόπτω [ἀπό + κόπτω] [V 4, 5; DV 161; VP 1-3] *I cut away* [Jn 18:10]; κυλλός, –ή, –όν [Adj 1] *disabled* [Mt 15:30]; γέεννα, –ης, ἡ [N 3] *Gehenna* [Mt 5:22]; ἄσβεστος, –ος, –ον [Adj 5] *unquenchable* [Mt 3:12] // **9:47** - μονόφθαλμος, –ος, –ον [Adj 5] *with one eye* [Mt 18:9] // **9:48** - σκώληξ, –ηκος, ὁ [N 8m] *worm* [hapax]; σβέννυμι [V 14; DV 278; VP 1-3, 9, 12] *I quench* [Mt 12:20] // **9:49** - ἁλίζω (ἁλίσω) [V 5, VP 1-3] *I salt* [Mt 5:13] // **9:50** - ἄναλος, –ος, –ον [Adj 5] *insipid* [hapax]; ἀρτύω [V 1, VP 1-3] *I season* [Lk 14:34]; εἰρηνεύω [V 1, VP 1-3] *I live in peace* [Rom 12:18]

10:1 - συμπορεύομαι [σύν + πορεύομαι] [V 1, 22, 23; DV 260; VP 3] *I come together* [of a crowd] [Lk 7:11]; εἴωθα [V 18, DV 73] *I am accustomed* [Mt 27:15] // **10:4** - ἀποστάσιον, -ου, τό [N 7] *bill of divorce* [Mt 5:31] // **10:5** - σκληροκαρδία, -ας, ἡ [N 2] *hardness of heart* [Mt 19:8] // **10:6** - ἄρσην, -ην, -εν [Adj 16] *male* [Mt 19:4] // **10:7** - προσκολλάομαι [πρός + κολλάομαι] [V 9, 23; VP 3, 6] *I join to* [Eph 5:31] // **10:9** - συζεύγνυμι [σύν + ζεύγνυμι] [V 14; DV 111; VP 1-3, 9, 12] *I am united to* [Mt 19:6] // **10:11** - μοιχάομαι [V 9, 23; VP 3, 6] *I commit adultery* [Mt 5:32]

10:14 - ἀγανακτέω [V 8, VP 1-3, 5-6] *I am indignant* [Mt 20:24] // **10:16** - κατευλογέω [κατά + εὐ + a root connected with λόγος] [V 8, VP 1-3, 5-6] *I bless* [hapax]

10:19 - φονεύω [V 1, VP 1-3] *I murder* [Mt 5:21]; ψευδομαρτυρέω [ψευδο- + μαρτυρέω; the augment is before ψευδο-: ἐψευδομαρτύρουν, Mk 14:56] [V 8; VP 1-3, 5-6] *I give false witness* [Mt 19:18]; ἀποστερέω [ἀπό + στερέω] [V 8; VP 1-3, 5-6] *I defraud* [1 Cor 6:7] // **10:20** - νεότης, -ητος, ἡ [N 13f] *(time of) youth* [Lk 18:21] // **10:22** - στυγνάζω (στυγνάσω) [V 5, VP 1-3] *I am gloomy* [Mt 16:3]; κτῆμα, -ατος, τό [N 16] *possession* [Mt 19:22]

10:23 - δυσκόλως [Adv 3] *with difficulty* [Mt 19:23] // **10:24** - δύσκολος, -ος, -ον [Adj 5] *difficult* [hapax] // **10:25** - τρυμαλιά, -ᾶς, ἡ [N 2] *eye (of a needle)* [hapax]; ῥαφίς, -ίδος, ἡ [N 14m] *needle* [Mt 19:24] // **10:26** - περισσῶς [Adv 3] *exceedingly* [Mt 27:23] // **10:27** ἀδύνατος, -ος, -ον [Adj 5] *impossible* [Mt 19:26] // **10:30** - ἑκατονταπλασίων, -ων, -ον [Adj 11] *hundred-fold* [Mt 19:29]

10:32 - συμβαίνω [σύν + βαίνω] [V 7; DV 31; VP 1-3] *I happen* [Lk 24:14] // **10:34** - ἐμπτύω [ἐν + πτύω] [V 1; DV 266; VP 1-3] *I spit on* [Mt 26:67]; μαστιγόω [V 10; VP 1-3, 5-6] *I scourge* [Mt 10:17]

Exercise for Lesson 76.

Translate into Greek:

Now Jesus, looking at them, loved them and said to them, "One thing is lacking to you; go, sell all that you have and give to the poor, and you shall have treasure in heaven, and come follow me". (Mk 10:21)

Emphatic Negation. Mark 10:35 – 11:33.

Lesson 77.

Emphatic Negation.

Emphatic negation in the New Testament can be expressed through use of a repeated negative, as was explained above in Lesson 70. Another frequently used method for emphatic negation is the use of οὐ μή together as a unit, followed by the aorist subjunctive: ὅστις ἐκ τοῦ Χριστοῦ ἐστιν οὐ μὴ ἀποθάνῃ—*Whoever is of Christ will not die.* Cf. Mk 9:1, 9:41, 10:15, and 13:19. At times the future indicative is found in place of the aorist subjunctive. Cf. Mk 13:31, Mt 16:22, and Lk 21:33. This use of the future indicative instead of the aorist subjunctive is relatively infrequent.

Mark 10:35 – 11:33.

10:35 - προσπορεύομαι [πρός + πορεύομαι] [V 1, 22, 23; DV 260; VP 3] *I come to* [hapax] // **10:37** - ἀριστερός, -ά, -όν [Adj 2] *left* [as opposed to right] [Mt 6:3] // **10:40** - εὐώνυμος, -ος, -ον [Adj 5] *left* [as opposed to right] [Mt 20:21] // **10:42** - κατακυριεύω [κατά + κυριεύω] [V 1, VP 1-3] *I lord it over* [with the genitive case] [Mt 20;25]; κατεξουσιάζω [κατά + ἐξουσιάζω] (κατεξουσιάσω) [V 5, VP 1-3] *I exercise authority over* [with the genitive case] [Mt 20:25] // **10:45** - λύτρον, -ου, τό [N 7] *ransom* [Mt 20:28]

10:46 - Ἰερ(ε)ιχώ, ἡ [N 32] *Jericho* [Mt 20:29]; Τιμαῖος, -ου, ὁ [N 6m] *Timaeus* [hapax]; Βαρτιμαῖος, -ου, ὁ [N 6m] *Bartimaeus* [hapax]; προσαίτης, -ου, ὁ [N 4] *beggar* [Jn 9:8] // **10:50** - ἀποβάλλω [ἀπό + βάλλω] [V 6, DV 32, VP 1-4] *I throw off* [Heb 10:35]; ἀναπηδάω [ἀνά + πηδάω] V 9; VP 1-3, 5-6] *I spring up* [hapax] // **10:51** - ραββουν(ε)ι [N 32] *my master* [Aramaic word] [Jn 20:16]

11:1 - Βηθφαγή, ἡ [N 32] *Bethpage* [Mt 21:1]; Βηθανία, -ας, ἡ [N 2] [Mt 21:17] // **11:2** - κατέναντι [Prep 1] *opposite* [Mt 21:2]; πῶλος,

–ου, ὁ [N 6m] *colt* [Mt 21:2] // **11:4** - ἄμφοδον, –ου, τό [N 7] *street* [hapax] // **11:8** - στρώννυμι [V 14; DV 297; VP 1-2, 9, 12] *I spread* [Mt 21:8]; στιβάς, –άδος, ἡ [N 14f] *leafy branch* [hapax] // **11:9** - ὡσαννά [Inter] *hosanna* [Hebrew for *save now, we pray*] [Mt 21:9]

11:13 - φύλλον, –ου, τό [N 7] *leaf* [Mt 21:19]; σῦκον, –ου, τό [N 7] *fig* [Mt 7:16]

11:15 - κολλυβιστής, –οῦ, ὁ [N 4] *money changer* [Mt 21:12]; καθέδρα, –ας, ἡ [N 2] *chair* [Mt 21:12]; καταστρέφω [κατά + στρέφω] [V 4, DV 296, VP 1-4] *I overturn* [Mt 21:12] // **11:17** - σπήλαιον, –ου, τό [N 7] *cave* [Mt 21:13] // **11:19** - ὀψέ [Adv 2] *late* [Mt 28:1]

11:21 - ἀναμιμνήσκω [ἀνά + μιμνήσκω] [V 2, DV 200, VP 1-3] *I remind* [1 Cor 4:17]; καταράομαι [κατά + ἀράομαι] [V 9, 22; VP 2-3] *I curse* [Mt 25:41] // **11:32** - ὄντως [Adv 3] *truly, really* [Jn 8:36]

Exercise for Lesson 77.

Translate into Greek:

> And they entered Jerusalem and went into the temple, and after looking around at everything, when it was already late, they left for Bethania in order to sleep there and take their rest. (Mk 11:11 and 14:41)

Lesson 78

Attraction of the Relative.

A relative pronoun usually takes its gender and number from its antecedent, but its case from its use in its own clause: ἀκούσατε τοῦ λόγου ὃν λέγω—*Listen to the word which I speak*. The relative pronoun ὃν is masculine and singular because its antecedent, λόγος, is masculine and singular. It is accusative because it is used in its own clause as the direct object of λέγω, a verb which governs the accusative case when it has a direct object.

But, at times, the relative pronoun takes not only its gender and number but its case as well from its antecedent: ἀκούσατε τοῦ λόγου οὗ λέγω—*Listen to the word which I speak*. The relative pronoun οὗ is not only masculine and singular because λόγου is masculine and singular, but genitive as well, because λόγου is genitive, even though it is grammatically the direct object of λέγω. It has been "attracted" into the case of its antecedent. Cf. Mk 7:13 and Jn 15:20.

At times an antecedent is attracted into the case of a relative pronoun which follows it. Thus the word Λίθον in Mt 21:42 is accusative because the following relative pronoun, ὃν, is accusative.

Mark 12:1 – 13:13.

12:1 - φυτεύω [V 1, VP 1-3] *I plant* [Mt 15:13]; περιτίθημι [περί + τίθημι] [V 12, 21; DV 309; VP 1-3, 7-8, 11] *I put around* [Mt 21:33]; φραγμός, –οῦ, ὁ [N 6m] *fence* [Mt 21:33]; ὀρύσσω [V 3, DV 226, VP 1-3] *I dig* [Mt 21:33]; ὑπολήνιον, –ου, τό [N 7] [part of a] *wine press* [hapax]; πύργος, –ου, ὁ [N 6m] *tower* [Mt 21:33]; ἐκδίδωμι [ἐκ + δίδωμι] [V 13; DV 62; VP 1-3, 7-8, 11] *I lease* [Mt 21:33]; ἀποδημέω [ἀπό + a root from δῆμος, *people*] [V 8; VP 1-3, 5-6] *I am away on a journey* [Mt 21:33] // **12:4** - κεφαλιόω [V 10; VP 1-3, 5-6] *I hit over* *the head* [hapax]; ἀτιμάζω [α privative + a root connected with τιμή] (ἀτιμάσω) [V 5, VP 1-3] *I insult* [Lk 20:11] // **12:6** - ἐντρέπω [ἐν + τρέπω] [V 4, DV 313, VP 1-4] *I put to shame* [passive: *I am ashamed; I respect*] [Mt 21:37] // **12:10** - γωνία, –ας, ἡ [N 2] *corner* [Mt 6:5] // **12:11** - θαυμαστός, –ή, –όν [Adj 1] *wonderful* [Mt 21:42]

12:13 - ἀγρεύω [V 1, VP 1-3] *I catch* [hapax] // **12:14** - κῆνσος, –ου, ὁ [N 6m] *tax* [Mt 17:25] // **12:15** - ὑπόκρισις, –εως, ἡ [N 28f] *hypocrisy* [Mt 23:28] // **12:16** - ἐπιγραφή, –ῆς, ἡ [N 1] *inscription* [Mt 22:20]; Καῖσαρ, –αρος, ὁ [N 33] *Caesar, emperor* [Mt 22:17] // **12:17** - ἐκθαυμάζω [ἐκ + θαυμάζω] (ἐκθαυμάσω) [V 5, DV 120, VP 1-3] *I marvel* [hapax]

12:18 - Σαδδουκαῖος, –ου, ὁ [N 6m] *Sadducee* [Mt 3:7] // **12:19** - ἐξανίστημι [ἐκ + ἀνά + ἵστημι] [V 11, 21; DV 134; VP 1-3, 7-8, 11] *I raise up* [Lk 20:28] // **12:22** - ἔσχατον [Adv 2] *last* [1 Cor 15:8] // **12:25** - γαμίζω (γαμίσω) [V 5, VP 1-3] *I give in marriage* [Mt 22:30] // **12:26** - βάτος, –ου, ὁ/ἡ [N 6m, N 6f] *bush* [Lk 6:44]; Ἀβραάμ, ὁ [N 32] *Abraham* [Mt 1:1]; Ἰσαάκ, ὁ [N 32] *Isaac* [Mt 1:2]; Ἰακώβ, ὁ [N 32] *Jacob* [Mt 1:2]

12:29 - Ἰσραήλ, ὁ [N 32] *Israel* [Mt 2:6] // **12:30** - διάνοια, –ας, ἡ [N 2] *mind* [Mt 22:37] // **12:33** - σύνεσις, –εως, ἡ [N 28f] *understanding* [Lk 2:47]; ὁλοκαύτωμα, –ατος, τό [N 16] *whole-burnt offering* [Heb 10:6] // **12:34** - νουνεχῶς [Adv 3] *intelligently* [hapax]; μακράν [Adv 1] *far off* [Mt 8:30]

12:38 - στολή, –ῆς, ἡ [N 1] *long robe* [Lk 15:22]; ἀσπασμός, –οῦ, ὁ [N 6m] *greeting* [Mt 23:7] // **11:39** - πρωτοκαθεδρία, –ας, ἡ [N 2] *chief seat* [Mt 23:6]; πρωτοκλισία, –ας, ἡ [N 2] *place of honor* [Mt 23:6] // **12:40** - πρόφασις, –εως, ἡ [N 28f] *pretext* [Lk 20:47]; μακρά [Adv 2] *for a long time* [Lk 20:47]

12:41 - γαζοφυλάκιον, –ου, τό [N 7] *treasury* [Lk 21:1] // **12:42** - λεπτόν, –οῦ, τό [N 7] *lepton* [small coin] [Lk 12:59]; κοδράντης, –ου, ὁ [N 4] *quadrans* [coin] [Mt 5:26] // **12:44** - ὑστέρησις, –εως, ἡ [N 28f] *need* [Phil 4:11]; βίος, –ου, ὁ [N 6m] *livelihood* [Lk 8:14]

13:4 - συντελέω [σύν + τελέω] [V 8; DV 305; VP 1-3, 5-6] *I accomplish* [Lk 4:2] // **13:7** - θροέομαι [V 8, 23; VP 3, 6] *I am alarmed* [Mt 24:6] // **13:8** - λιμός, –οῦ, ὁ/ἡ [N 6m, N 6f] *famine* [Mt 24:7]; ὠδίν, –ῖνος, ἡ [N 33] *birth pang* [Mt 24:8] // **13:11** - προμεριμνάω [πρό + μεριμνάω] [V 9; VP 1-3, 5-6] *I am anxious* *beforehand* [hapax] // **13:12** - ἐπανίστημι [ἐπί + ἀνά + ἵστημι] [V 11, 21; DV 134; VP 1-3, 7-8, 11] *I rise against* [Mt 10:21]

Exercise for Lesson 78.

Translate into Greek:

> Why do you (sg.) tempt us? Bring us a denarius so that we may see it and ask you whose is the image and inscription. (Mk 12:15-16)

The Simple Genitive, Dative, and Accusative
as Indications of Time. Mark 13:14 – 14:31.

Lesson 79

The Simple Genitive, Dative, and Accusative as Indications of Time.

With regard to expressions of time, the simple genitive tends to be used to indicate "time within which"; the simple dative, "time when"; the simple accusative, "time how long". This usage is not rigid and much depends on the meaning of the words used and the context.

For the simple genitive indicating "time within which", cf. Mt 24:20: προσεύχεσθε δὲ ἵνα μὴ γένηται ἡ φυγὴ ὑμῶν χειμῶνος μηδὲ σαββάτῳ—*Pray that your flight not take place during the winter or on a Sabbath*. For similar uses of the genitive, cf. Mt 2:14, Lk 18:7, and Jn 8:2.

For the dative to express "time when", cf. Mt 24:42: γρηγορεῖτε οὖν, ὅτι οὐκ οἴδατε ποίᾳ ἡμέρᾳ ὁ κύριος ὑμῶν ἔρχεται—*Watch out, therefore, because you do not know on what day your Lord is coming*. Cf. also the expression σαββάτῳ, *on a sabbath*, in Mt 24:20. For similar uses of the dative, cf. Mt 28:1 and Mk 14:12.

For the accusative to express "time how long", cf. Jn 2:12: καὶ ἐκεῖ ἔμειναν οὐ πολλὰς ἡμέρας—*And they remained there not many days*. For similar uses of the accusative, cf. Mk 4:27, Lk 2:37, and Lk 21:37.

As was stated above, this usage is not rigid. For a genitive to express "time when" instead of a dative, cf. Acts 26:13. For a dative to express "time how long" instead of an accusative, cf. Lk 8:29. For an accusative to express "time when" instead of a dative, cf. Jn 4:52.

Mark 13:14 – 14:31.

13:14 - βδέλυγμα, –ατος, τό [N 16] *abomination* [Mt 24:15]; ἐρήμωσις, –εως, ἡ [N 28f] *desolation* [Mt 24:15] // 13:15 - δῶμα, –ατος, τό [N 16]

LESSON 79

roof [Mt 10:27] // **13:17** - θηλάζω (θηλάσω) [V 3, VP 1-3] *I suckle* [Mt 21:16] // **13:20** - κολοβόω [V 10; VP 1-3, 5-6] *I cut short* [Mt 24:22] **13:22** - ψευδόχριστος, -ου, ὁ [N 6m] *false Messiah* [Mt 24:24]; ψευδοπροφήτης, -ου, ὁ [N 4] *false prophet* [Mt 7:15]; ἀποπλανάω [ἀπό + πλανάω] [V 9; VP 1-3, 5-6] *I mislead* [1 Tim 6:10] // **13:23** - προλέγω [πρό + λέγω] [V 2, DV 179, VP 1-4] *I tell beforehand* [2 Cor 13:2] // **13:24** - σκοτίζω (σκοτίσω) [V 5, VP 1-3] *I darken* [Mt 24:29]; σελήνη, -ης, ἡ [N 1] *moon* [Mt 24:29]; φέγγος, -ους, τό [N 31] *light* [Mt 24:29] // **13:27** - ἄκρον, -ου, τό [N 7] *extremity* [Mt 24:31]

13:28 - ἀπαλός, -ή, -όν [Adj 1] *tender* [Mt 24:32]; ἐκφύω [ἐκ + φύω] [V 1, DV 336, VP 1-4] *I produce* [Mt 24:32]; θέρος, -ους, τό [N 31] *summer* [Mt 24:32]

13:33 - ἀγρυπνέω [V 8; VP 1-3, 5-6] *I am alert* [Lk 21:36] // **13:34** - ἀπόδημος, -ος, -ον [Adj 5] *away from home* [hapax]; θυρωρός, -οῦ, ὁ [N 6m] *porter* [Jn 10:3] // **13:35** - μεσονύκτιον, -ου, τό [N 7] *midnight* [Lk 11:5]; ἀλεκτοροφωνία, -ας, ἡ [N 2] *cockcrow* [hapax] // **13:36** - ἐξαίφνης [Adv 2] *suddenly* [Lk 2:13]

14:1 - ἄζυμος, -ος, -ον [Adj 5] *unleavened* [τὰ ἄζυμα (N 7), *Feast of Unleavened Bread* (Mt 26:17)]

14:3 - ἀλάβαστρον, -ου, τό [N 7] *alabaster (flask)* [Mt 26:7]; νάρδος, -ου, ἡ [N 6f] *oil of nard* [Jn 12:3]; πιστικός, -ή, -όν [Adj 1] *genuine* [This seems to be the most likely of various interpretations.] [Jn 12:3]; πολυτελής, -ής, -ές [Adj 15] *expensive* [1 Tim 2:9]; καταχέω [κατά + χέω] [V 8; DV 341; VP 1-3, 5-6] *I pour down over* [with genitive case] [Mt 26:7] // **14:5** - πιπράσκω [V 2, 21; DV 247; VP 1-3] *I sell* [Mt 13:46]; τριακόσιοι, -αι, -α [Adj 6] *three hundred* [Jn 12:5] // **14:7** - εὖ [Adv 3] *well* [Mt 25:21] // **14:8** - προλαμβάνω [πρό + λαμβάνω] [V 7, DV 176, VP 1-3] *I anticipate* [1 Cor 11:21]; μυρίζω (μυρίσω) [V 5, VP 1-3] *I anoint* [hapax]; ἐνταφιασμός, -οῦ, ὁ [N 6m] *burial* [Jn 12:7] // **14:9** - μνημόσυνον, -ου, τό [N 7] *memorial* [Mt 26:13]

14:11 - εὐκαίρως [Adv 2] *opportunely* [2 Tim 4:2]

14:13 - ἀπαντάω [ἀπό + ἀντάω] [V 9, VP 1-3] *I meet* [with dative case] [Lk 17:12]; κεράμιον, -ου, τό [N 7] *clay jar* [Lk 22:10] // **14:14** - οἰκοδεσπότης, -ου, ὁ [N 4] *master of the house* [Mt 10:25]; κατάλυμα, -ατος, τό [N 16] *guest room* [Lk 2:7] // **14:15** - ἀνάγαιον, -ου, τό [N 7] *upstairs room* [Lk 22:12] // **14:20** - ἐμβάπτω [ἐν +

βάπτω] [V 4, 5; DV 34; VP 1-3] *I dip* [Mt 26:23]; τρύβλιον, –ου, τό [N
7] *dish* [Mt 26:23] // **14:24** - ἐκχύννω [ἐκ + χύννω] [V 7, DV 341, VP 1-
3] *I pour out* [Mt 23:35] // **14:25** - γένημα, –ατος, τό [N 16] *crop* [Mt
26:29] // **14:26** - ὑμνέω [V 8; VP 1-3, 5-6] *I sing a hymn* [Mt 26:30]
14:27 - πατάσσω [V 3, DV 232, VP 1-3] *I strike* [Mt 26:31];
διασκορπίζω [διά + σκορπίζω] (διασκορπίσω) [V 5, VP 1-3] *I
scatter* [Mt 25:24] // **14:30** - δίς [Adv 2] *twice* [Lk 18:12] // **14:31** -
ἐκπερισσῶς [Adv 3] *with insistence* [hapax]; συναποθνῄσκω [σύν +
ἀπό + θνῄσκω] [V 2, DV 127, VP 1-4] *I die with* [with dative case] [2
Cor 7:3]

Exercise for Lesson 79.

Translate into Greek:

> In truth I say to you that when these things are preached,
> what she has done will be spoken in memory of her. (Mk 14:9)

The "Redundant Pronoun" in a Relative
Clause. Mark 14:32 – 15:15.

Lesson 80

The "Redundant Pronoun" in a Relative Clause.

In the Greek of the New Testament there is sometimes found a
pronoun in a relative clause which, to a speaker of English, seems
to be redundant. The following is a simplified example: αὐτός
ἐστιν ᾧ δίδωμι τὸν ἄρτον αὐτῷ—*He is the one to whom I give the
bread.* The pronoun αὐτῷ seems superfluous to a speaker of
English, and there is no need to try to include it in a translation.

This phenomenon may be related in the New Testament to the
fact that in Hebrew and Aramaic the relative pronoun is
indeclinable and thus requires a pronoun or pronomial suffix in the
relative clause to specify the antecedent to which the relative
pronoun refers.

Cf. Mk 1:7, Mk 7:25, and Jn 13:26.

Mark 14:32 – 15:15.

14:32 - χωρίον, –ου, τό [N 7] *piece of land* [Mt 26:36]; Γεθσημαν(ε)ί [N
32] *Gethsemane* [Mt 26:36] // **14:33** - ἀδημονέω [V 8; VP 1-3, 5-6] *I
am much distressed* [Mt 26:37] // **14:36** - αββα, ὁ [N 32] [Aramaic
word] *father* [Rom 8:15]; παραφέρω [παρά + φέρω] [V 6, DV 324, VP
1-4] *I take away* [Lk 22:42] // **14:38** - πρόθυμος, –ος, –ον [Adj 1] *eager*
[Mt 26:41] // **14:40** - καταβαρύνω [κατά + βαρύνω] [V 7, VP 1-3] *I
weigh down* [hapax]

14:44 - σύσσημον, –ου, τό [N 7] *signal* [hapax]; ἀσφαλῶς [Adv 3]
securely [Acts 2:36] // **14:45** - καταφιλέω [κατά + φιλέω] [V 8; VP 1-
3, 5-6] *I kiss affectionately* [Mt 26:49] // **14:47** - σπάω [V 9; DV 175;
VP 1-3, 5-6] *I draw (a sword)* [Acts 16:27]; παίω [V 1, DV 230, VP 1-3]
I strike [Mt 26:68]; ὠτάριον, –ου, τό [N 7] *ear* [Jn 18:10]

14:51 - νεανίσκος, -ου, ὁ [N 6m] *young man* [Mt 19:20]; σινδών, -όνος, ἡ [N 20f] *linen cloth* [Mt 27:59]

14:54 - ἔσω [Adv 1] *inside* [Mt 26:58]; αὐλή, -ῆς, ἡ [N 1] *courtyard* [Mt 26:3]; συγκάθημαι [σύν + κάθημαι] [V 17, 22; DV 89; VP 2-3] *I sit with* [Acts 26:30]; θερμαίνω [V 7, VP 1-3] *I warm* [Jn 18:18] // **14:56** - ἴσος, -η, -ον [Adj 1] *equal* [i.e., standing in agreement] [Mt 20:12] // **14:58** - χειροποίητος, -ος, -ον [Adj 5] *made by human hands* [Acts 7:48]; ἀχειροποίητος, -ος, -ον [Adj 5] *not made by human hands* [2 Cor 5:1] // **14:60** - καταμαρτυρέω [κατά + μαρτυρέω] [V 8; VP 1-3, 5-6] *I testify against* [with the genitive case] [Mt 26:62] // **14:61** - εὐλογητός, -ή, -όν [Adj 1] *blessed* [as substantive: *The Blessed One*, i.e., God] [Lk 1:68] // **14:63** - διαρρήγνυμι [διά + ῥήγνυμι] [V 14; DV 272; VP 1-3, 9, 12] *I tear* [Mt 26:65] [also found in the present as διαρ(ρ)ήσσω] // **14:65** - περικαλύπτω [περί + καλύπτω] [V 4, 5; DV 143; VP 1-3] *I cover up* [Lk 22:64]; κολαφίζω (κολαφίσω) [V 5, VP 1-3] *I strike* [Mt 26:67]; ῥάπισμα, -ατος, τό [N 16] *slap* [Jn 18:22] // **14:68** - προαύλιον, -ου, τό [N 7] *forecourt* [hapax] // **14:70** - Γαλιλαῖος, -α, -ον [Adj 2] *Galilean* [Mt 26:69] // **14:71** - ἀναθεματίζω [ἀνά + θεματίζω] (ἀναθεματίσω) [V 5, VP 1-3] *I curse* [Acts 23:12]

15:1 - ἀποφέρω [ἀπό + φέρω] [V 6, DV 324, VP 1-4] *I lead away* [Lk 16:22]; Π(ε)ιλᾶτος, -ου, ὁ [N 6m] *Pilate* [Mt 27:2]

15:7 - Βαραββᾶς, -ᾶ, ὁ [N 33] *Barabbas* [Mt 27:16]; στασιαστής, -οῦ, ὁ [N 4] *revolutionary* [hapax] // **15:10** - φθόνος, -ου, ὁ [N 6m] *envy* [Mt 27:18] // **15:11** - ἀνασείω [ἀνά + σείω] [V 1, DV 280, VP 1-3] *I stir up* [Lk 23:5] // **15:15** - φραγελλόω [V 10; VP 1-3, 5-6] *I flog* [Mt 27:26]

Exercise for Lesson 80.

Translate into Greek:

And while the disciples were down below in the courtyard, some maidservants of the high priests enter and, seeing them warm themselves, look at them and say, "You also were with him". (Mk 14:66-67)

Lesson 81

Adversative καί.

The word καί has a variety of possible nuances. One common interpretation is that καί can have the nuance of *however, but,* or some other adversative expression. Such an interpretation often seems appropriate when the καί is found at the beginning of a clause which contains a negative, or which continues discourse which arises from a negative. For example, Jn 1:10: ἐν τῷ κόσμῳ ἦν, καὶ ὁ κόσμος δι᾽ αὐτοῦ ἐγένετο, καὶ ὁ κόσμος αὐτὸν οὐκ ἔγνω—*He was in the world, and the world came into being through him, but the world did not know him.* Such an interpretation of Jn 1:10, while plausible, is not the only interpretation possible. For example, the author may be using καί in the additive sense of *and* to achieve solemnity through repetition and cumulation of detail. Cf. Mk 6:19, 7:24, and 9:18.

Mark 15:16 – 16:20.

15:16 - πραιτώριον, –ου, τό [N 7] *praetorium* [Mt 27:27]; συγκαλέω [σύν + καλέω] [V 8; DV 142; VP 12-3, 5-6] *I call together* [Lk 9:1]; σπεῖρα, ης, ἡ [N 3] *cohort* [Mt 27:27] // **15:17** - ἐνδιδύσκω [ἐν + δύω] [V 2, VP 1-3] *I clothe* [Lk 16:19]; πορφύρα, –ας, ἡ [N 2] *purple cloth* [Lk 16:19]; πλέκω [V 2, DV 251, VP 1-3] *I twist together* [Mt 27:29]; ἀκάνθινος, –η, –ον [Adj 1] *thorny* [Jn 19:5] // **15:19** - κάλαμος, –ου, ὁ [N 6m] *reed* [Mt 27:29]; γόνυ, –ατος, τό [N 33] *knee* [Lk 5:8] // **15:20** - ἐκδύω [ἐκ + δύω] [V 1, DV 67, VP 1-3] *I take off* (*clothes*) [Mt 27:28]

15:21 - ἀγγαρεύω [V 1, VP 1-3] *I press into service* [Mt 5:41]; Κυρηναῖος, –α, –ον [Adj 2] *of Cyrene* [Mt 27:32]; Ἀλέξανδρος, –ου, ὁ [N 6m] *Alexander* [Acts 4:6]; Ῥοῦφος, –ου, ὁ [N 6m] *Rufus* [Rom 16:13] // **15:22** - Γολγοθᾶ, ἡ [N 2] *Golgotha* [Mt 27:33]; κρανίον, –ου, τό [N 7] *skull* [Mt 27:33] // **15:23** - σμυρνίζω (σμυρνίσω) [V 5, VP 1-

3] *I spice with myrrh*, i.e., *I drug* [hapax] // **15:24** - διαμερίζω [διά + μερίζω] (διαμερίσω) [V 5, VP 1-3] *I divide among* [Mt 27:35]; κλῆρος, -ου, ὁ [N 6m] *lot* [in the sense of something used to decide a disputed matter by chance, e.g., dice] [Mt 27:35] // **15:26** - ἐπιγράφω [ἐπί + γράφω] [V 4, DV 53,VP 1-4] *I inscribe* [Acts 17:23] // **15:29** - κινέω [V 8; DV 153; VP 1-3, 5-6] *I move* [Mt 23:4]; οὐά [Inter] *ha!* [hapax] // **15:32** - συσταυρόω [σύν + σταυρόω] [V 10; VP 1-3, 5-6] *I crucify together with* [Mt 27:44]; ὀνειδίζω (ὀνειδίσω) [V 5, VP 1-3] *I taunt* [Mt 5:11]

15:33 - ἔνατος, -η, -ον [Adj 1] *ninth* [Mt 20:5]; ελωι [N 32] *my God* [Aramaic] [Mt 27:46]; λεμα [Adv 1] *why?* [Aramaic] [Mt 27:46]; σαβαχθανι [V 20] *you have forsaken me* [Aramaic] [Mt 27:46] // **15:36** - σπόγγος, -ου, ὁ [N 6m] *sponge* [Mt 27:48]; ὄξος, -ους, τό [N 31] *sour wine* [Mt 27:48]; καθαιρέω [κατά + αἱρέω] [V 8, DV 7, VP 1-3, 5-6] *I take down* [Lk 1:52] // **15:37** - ἐκπνέω [ἐκ + πνέω] [V 8; DV 256; VP 1-3, 5-6] *I expire* [Lk 23:46] // **15:38** - καταπέτασμα, -ατος, τό [N 16] *curtain* [Mt 27:51] // **15:39** - κεντυρίων, -ωνος, ὁ [N 21m] *centurion* [Mk 15:44] // **15:40** - Μαγδαληνή, -ῆς, ἡ [N 1] *woman of Magdala* [Mt 27:56]; Σαλώμη, -ης, ἡ [N 1] *Salome* [Mk 16:1] // **15:41** - συναναβαίνω [σύν + ἀνά + βαίνω] [V 7, DV 31, VP 1-3] *I go up with* [Acts 13:31]

15:42 - παρασκευή, -ῆς, ἡ [N 1] *day of preparation* [Mt 27:62]; προσάββατον, -ου, τό [N 7] *the day before the Sabbath* [hapax] // **15:43** - Ἰωσήφ, ὁ [N 32] *Joseph* [Mt 27:57]; Ἀριμαθαία, -ας, ἡ [N 2] *Arimathea* [Mt 27:57]; εὐσχήμων, -ων, -ον [Adj 11] *influential* [Acts 13:50]; βουλευτής, -οῦ, ὁ [N 4] *councilor* [Lk 23:50] // **15:44** - πάλαι [Adv 2] *some time ago* [Mt 11:21] // **15:45** - δωρέομαι [V 8, 22; VP 2-3] *I grant* [2 Pet 1:3] // **15:46** - ἐνειλέω [ἐν + εἰλέω] [V 8; DV 76; VP 1-3, 5-6] *I wrap in* [hapax]; λατομέω [V 8; VP 1-3, 5-6] *I hew* [Mt 27:60]; προσκυλίω [πρός + κυλίω] [V 1, DV 171, VP 1-3] *I roll up to* [Mt 27:60]

16:1 - διαγίνομαι [διά + γίνομαι] [V 7, 21, 22, 23; DV 49; VP 1-3] *I pass* [temporal] [Acts 25:13]; ἄρωμα, -ατος, τό [N 16] *spice* [Lk 23:56] // **16:3** - ἀποκυλίω [ἀπό + κυλίω] [V 1, DV 171, VP 1-3] *I roll away* [Mt 28:2] // **16:8** - τρόμος, -ου, ὁ [N 6m] *trembling* [1 Cor 2:3]

THE LONGER ENDING OF MARK: **16:10** - πενθέω [V 8; VP 1-3, 5-6] *I mourn* [Mt 5:4] // **16:12** - μορφή, -ῆς, ἡ [N 1] *form* [Phil 2:6] // **16:17** - παρακολουθέω [παρά + ἀκολουθέω] [V 8; VP 1-3, 5-6] *I follow upon* [with dative case] [Lk 1:3] // **16:18** - θανάσιμος, -η, -ον [Adj 1] *deadly*

[hapax]; βλάπτω [V 4, 5; DV 41; VP 1-3] *I harm* [Lk 4:35] // **16:20** -
συνεργέω [σύν + root from ἔργον] [V 8; VP 1-3, 5-6] *I cooperate* [Rom
8:28]; βεβαιόω [V 10; VP 1-3, 5-6] *I confirm* [Rom 15:8];
ἐπακολουθέω [ἐπί + ἀκολουθέω] [V 8; VP 1-3, 5-6] *I follow upon*
[with dative case] [1 Tim 5:10]

THE SHORTER ENDING OF MARK: συντόμως [Adv 2] *briefly* [Acts
24:4]; ἐξαγγέλλω [ἐκ + ἀγγέλλω] [V 6, DV 2, VP 1-4] *I tell* [1 Pet 2:9];
ἀνατολή, -ῆς, ἡ [N 1] *rising (of the sun)*) [Mt 2:1]; δύσις, -εως, ἡ [N
28f] *west* [hapax]; ἱερός, -ά, -όν [Adj 2] *holy* [1 Cor 9:13]; ἄφθαρτος,
-ος, -ον [Adj 5] *imperishable* [Rom 1:23]

Exercise for Lesson 81.

Translate into Greek:

> And on entering the tomb he saw young men, some seated on
> the right and some on the left, clothed in white garments, and
> he was amazed. (Mk 16:5 and 15:27)

John 1:1-34

Lesson 82

John 1:1-34

1:9 - φωτίζω (φωτίσω) [V 5, VP 1-3] *I shed light on* [Lk 11:36]

1:14 - σκηνόω [V 10; VP 1-3, 5-6] *I dwell* [Apoc 7:15] // **1:18** - πώποτε [Adv 2] *ever* [Lk 19:30]; κόλπος, –ου, ὁ [N 6m] *bosom* [Lk 6:38]; ἐξηγέομαι [ἐκ + ἡγέομαι] [V 8, 22; DV 115; VP 2-3] *I explain* [Lk 24:35]

1:19 - Λευ(ε)ίτης, –ου, ὁ [N 4] *Levite* [Lk 10:32] // **1:22** - ἀπόκρισις, –εως, ἡ [N 28f] *answer* [Lk 2:47] // **1:23** - εὐθύνω [V 7, VP 1-3] *I straighten* [Jas 3:4]

1:29 - ἀμνός, –οῦ, ὁ [N 6m] *lamb* [Acts 8:32]

Exercise for Lesson 82.

Translate into Greek:

> On whom you (pl.) see the angels descending and remaining, these are the ones baptizing. (Jn 1:33)

John 1:35 – 2:12.

Lesson 83

John 1:35 – 2:12.

1:42 - Κηφᾶς, –ᾶ, ὁ [N 33] *Cephas* [1 Cor 1:12]; ἑρμηνεύω [V 1, VP 1-3] *I interpret* [Heb 7:2]

1:45 - Ναθαναήλ, ὁ [N 32] *Nathanael* [Jn 21:2] // **1:47** - ᾽Ισραηλ-(ε)ίτης, –ου, ὁ [N 4] *Israelite* [Acts 2:22]

2:1 - Κανά, ἡ [N 32] *Cana* [Jn 21:2] // **2:6** - λίθινος, –η, –ον [Adj 1] *made of stone* [2 Cor 3:3]; ὑδρία, –ας, ἡ [N 2] *water jar* [Jn 4:28]; μετρητής, –οῦ, ὁ [N 4] *measure* [hapax] // **2:7** - ἄνω [Adv 1] *up* [Acts 2:19] // **2:8** - ἀντλέω [V 8; VP 1-3, 5-6] *I draw (water)* [Jn 4:7]; ἀρχιτρίκλινος, –ου, ὁ [N 6m] *head waiter* [Jn 2:9] // **2:10** - μεθύσκω [V 2, VP 1-3] *I make drunk* [Lk 12:45] [The word μεθύω (V 1, VP 1-3), *I am drunk*, is also found (Mt 24:49).]

Exercise for Lesson 83.

Translate into Greek:

> On the next day, again the disciples of John and a hundred of their friends were standing there, and, gazing at the crowd following, they say, "Look at the people without a shepherd". (Jn 1:35-36)

John 2:13 – 3:21.

Lesson 84

John 2:13 – 3:21.

2:14 - κερματιστής, –οῦ, ὁ [N 4] *money changer* [hapax] // **2:15** - φραγέλλιον, –ου, τό [N 7] *whip* [hapax]; σχοινίον, –ου, τό [N 7] *cord* [Acts 27:32]; κέρμα, –ατος, τό [N 16] *coin* [hapax]; ἀνατρέπω [ἀνά + τρέπω] [V 4, DV 313, VP 1-4] *I overturn* [2 Tim 2:18] // **2:16** - ἐντεῦθεν [Adv 1] *from here* [Lk 4:9]; ἐμπόριον, –ου, τό [N 7] *market* [hapax]

3:1 - Νικόδημος, –ου, ὁ [N 6m] *Nicodemus* [Jn 7:50] // **3:4** - γέρων, –οντος, ὁ [N 22] *old man* [hapax] // **3:12** - ἐπίγειος, –ος. –ον [Adj 5] *earthly* [1 Cor 15:40] // **3:20** - φαῦλος, –η, –ον [Adj 1] *worthless* [Rom 9:11]

Exercise for Lesson 84.

Translate into Greek:

> Now the disciples themselves were not entrusting themselves to him on account of their knowing everyone, and because they did not have need that anyone should witness to man. (Jn 2:24-25)

John 3:22 – 4:42.

Lesson 85

John 3:22 – 4:42.

3:22 - διατρίβω [διά + τρίβω] [V 4, DV 316, VP 1-3] *I stay* [intransitive] [Acts 12:19] // **3:23** - Αἰνών, ἡ [N 32] *Aenon* [hapax]; Σαλείμ, τό [N 32] *Salim* [hapax] // **3:25** - ζήτησις, –εως, ἡ [N 28f] *discussion* [Acts 15:2] // **3:29** - νύμφη, –ης, ἡ [N 1] *bride* [Mt 10:35] // **3:30** - ἐλαττόω [V 10; VP 1-3, 5-6] *I make smaller* [Heb 2:7]

4:2 - καίτοιγε [Conj] *and yet* [hapax] // **4:4** - Σαμάρ(ε)ια, –ας, ἡ [N 2] *Samaria* [Lk 17:11] // **4:5** - Συχάρ, ἡ [N 32] *Sychar* [hapax] // **4:6** - ὁδοιπορία, –ας, ἡ [N 2] *journey* [2 Cor 11:26]

4:9 - Σαμαρῖτις, –ιδος, ἡ [N 14f] *Samaritan woman* [hapax]; συγχράομαι [σύν + χράομαι] [V 9, 22; DV 342; VP 2-3, 6] *I associate with* [hapax]; Σαμαρ(ε)ίτης, –ου, ὁ [N 4] *Samaritan man* [Mt 10:5] // **4:10** - δωρεά, –ᾶς, ἡ [N 2] *gift* [Acts 2:38] // **4:11** - ἄντλημα, –ατος, τό [N 16] *bucket* [hapax]; φρέαρ, –ατος, τό [N 16] *well* [Lk 14:5]; βαθύς, –εῖα, –ύ [Adj 14] *deep* [Lk 24:1] // **4:12** - θρέμμα, –ατος, τό [N 16] *domesticated animals* [hapax] // **4:14** - ἅλλομαι [V 6, 22; DV 14; VP 2-4] *I spring up* [Acts 3:8] // **4:15** - ἐνθάδε [Adv 2] *to this place* [Lk 24:41]

4:23 - προσκυνητής, –οῦ, ὁ [N 4] *worshipper* [hapax]

4:27 - μέντοι [Conj] *however* [2 Tim 2:19]

4:31 - μεταξύ [Adv 2] *meanwhile* [Acts 13:42] [This word is also a preposition with the genitive (Prep 1), *between* (Mt 18:15).] // **4:32** - βρῶσις, –εως, ἡ [N 28f] *food* [Mt 6:19] // **4:35** - τετράμηνος, –ου, ὁ [N 6f] *period of four months* [hapax]

4:42 - λαλιά, –ᾶς, ἡ [N 2] *speech* [Mt 26:73]

Exercise for Lesson 85.

Translate into Greek:

If you (pl.) knew the gifts of God and who are the ones saying
to you, "Give us to drink", you would have asked them and
they would have given you living water. (Jn 4:10)

John 4:43 – 5:30.

Lesson 86

John 4:43 – 5:30.

4:46 - βασιλικός, -ή, όν [Adj 1] *royal* [Acts 12:20] // **4:52** -
πυνθάνομαι [V 7, 22; DV 267; VP 1-4] *I inquire* [Mt 2:4]; κομψότερον
[Adv 3] *better* [hapax]; ἕβδομος, -η, -ον [Adj 1] *seventh* [Heb 4:4]

5:2 - κολυμβήθρα, -ας, ἡ [N 2] *pool* [Jn 5:7]; ἐπιλέγω [ἐπί + λέγω] [V
2, DV 179, VP 1-4] *I call* [hapax]; Ἑβραϊστί [Adv 3] *in
Hebrew / Aramaic*, i.e., in the language of the Jews [Apoc 9:11];
Βηθζαθά, ἡ [N 32] *Bethzatha* [Mt 11:21]; στοά, -ᾶς, ἡ [N 2]
colonnade [cf. Acts 3:11] // [**5:4** - ταραχή, -ῆς, ἡ [N 1] *disturbance*
[hapax]; δήποτε [Adv 2] *at any time* [hapax]; νόσημα, -ατος, τό [N
16] *disease* [hapax]] // **5:5** - ὀκτώ [Adj 21] *eight* [Lk 2:21]

5:13 - ἐκνεύω [ἐκ + νεύω] [V 1, VP 1-3] *I move off* [hapax]

5:21 - ζῳοποιέω [V 8; DV 258; VP 1-3, 5-6] *I make alive* [Rom 4:17]

Exercise for Lesson 86.

Translate into Greek:

> The weak answered them, "Sirs, we have no one so that,
> when the waters have been stirred, they may put us into the
> pool; for while we are going there, others go down before us".
> (Jn 5:7)

John 5:31 – 6:21.

Lesson 87

John 5:31 – 6:21.

5:35 - ἀγαλλιάω [V 9; DV 1; VP 1-3, 5-6] [also found as a middle and passive deponent, ἀγαλλιάομαι [V 22, 23] *I am glad* [Mt 5:12; Lk 1:47; Lk 10:21] // **5:37** - εἶδος, –ους, τό [N 31] *appearance; shape* [Lk 3:22] // **5:39** - ἐραυνάω [V 9; DV 93; VP 1-3, 5-6] *I search, I examine* [Rom 8:27]

6:1 - Τιβεριάς, –άδος, ἡ [N 14f] *Tiberias* [Jn 21:1] // **6:3** - ἀνέρχομαι [ἀνά + ἔρχομαι] [V 2, 22; DV 99; VP 2-3] *I go up* [Gal 1:17] // **6:7** - ἀρκέω [V 8; DV 25; VP 1-3, 5-6] *I suffice* [Mt 25:9] // **6:9** - παιδάριον, –ου, τό [N 7] *youth* [hapax]; κρίθινος, –η, –ον [Adj 1] *made of barley* [Jn 6:13]; ὀψάριον, –ου, τό [N 7] *fish* [Jn 21:9] // **6:12** - ἐμπί(μ)πλημι [ἐν + πί(μ)πλημι] [V 11; DV 244; VP 1-3, 7-8, 11] [also ἐμπιπλάω (V 9; DV 242; VP 1-3, 5-6)] *I fill* [Lk 1:53] // **6:13** - βιβρώσκω [V 2, 21; DV 39; VP 1-3] *I eat* [hapax]

6:19 - εἴκοσι [Adj 21] *twenty* [Lk 14:31]

Exercise for Lesson 87.

Translate into Greek;

> Then the disciples, lifting their eyes and seeing that many people were coming to them, say to their friends, "Where are we to purchase bread so that these people may eat?" (Jn 6:5)

John 6:22 – 7:9.

Lesson 88

John 6:22 – 7:9.

6:22 - συνεισέρχομαι [σύν + εἰς + ἔρχομαι] [V 2, 22; DV 99; VP 1-4] *I go in with* [Jn 18:15] // **6:31** - μάννα, τό [N 32] *manna* [Heb 9:4]

6:41 - γογγύζω (γογγύσω) [V 5, DV 52, VP 1-3] *I grumble* [Mt 20:11] // **6:44** - ἕλκω [V 2, DV 84, VP 1-3] *I drag* [Acts 16:19] // **6:45** - διδακτός, -ή, -όν [Adj 1] *taught* [1 Cor 2:13]

6:52 - μάχομαι [V 2, 22; VP 2-3] *I fight* [Acts 7:26] // **6:54** - τρώγω [V 2, VP 1-3] *I eat* [Mt 24:38] // **6:55** - πόσις, -εως, ἡ [N 28f] *drinking; a drink* [Rom 14:17]

6:60 - σκληρός, -ά, -όν [Adj 2] *hard* [Mt 25:24] // **6:62** - πρότερος, -α, -ον [Adj 2] *earlier; past* [Eph 4:22] [(τό) πρότερον (Adv 2) *earlier; before* (Jn 9:8)]

7:2 - σκηνοπηγία, -ας, ἡ [N 2] *Feast of Tabernacles* [hapax]

Exercise for Lesson 88.

Translate into Greek:

> After this, one of his disciples went away and was walking with him no more. (Jn 6:66)

John 7:10 – 8:11.

Lesson 89

John 7:10 – 8:11.

7:12 - γογγυσμός, -οῦ, ὁ [N 6m] *murmuring* [Acts 6:1]

7:14 - μεσόω [V 10; VP 1-3, 5-6] *I am in the middle* [hapax] // **7:17** - πότερον [Adv 3] *whether* [hapax] // **7:22** - περιτέμνω [περί + τέμνω] [V 7; DV 307; VP 1-3] *I circumcise* [Lk 1:59] // **7:23** - χολάω [V 9] *I am angry with* [with the dative case] [hapax] // **7:24** - ὄψις, -εως, ἡ [N 28f] *external appearance; face* [Jn 11:44]

7:30 - πιάζω (πιάσω) [V 5, DV 241] *I seize* [Acts 3:7] // **7:35** - διασπορά, -ᾶς, ἡ [N 2] *diaspora* [Jas 1:1]

7:38 - ῥέω [V 8; DV 271; VP 1-3, 5-6] *I flow* [hapax]

7:42 - Βηθλέεμ, ἡ [N 32] *Bethlehem* [Mt 2:1]

7:49 - ἐπάρατος, -η, -ον [Adj 1] *accursed* [hapax]

8:2 - ὄρθρος, -ου, ὁ [N 6m] *early morning* [Lk 24:1] // **8:4** - αὐτόφωρος, -ος, -ον [Adj 5] *in the act* [hapax] // **8:5** - λιθάζω (λιθάσω) [V 5, VP 1-3] *I stone; I kill by stoning* [Jn 10:31] // **8:6** - καταγράφω [κατά + γράφω] [V 4, DV 53,VP 1-4] *I write* [hapax] // **8:7** - ἀνακύπτω [ἀνά + κύπτω] [V 4, 5; DV 173; VP 1-3] *I straighten up* (in the sense of "unbend") [Lk 13:11]; ἀναμάρτητος, -ος, -ον [Adj 5] *without sin* [hapax] // **8:8** - κατακύπτω [κατά + κύπτω] [V 4, 5; DV 173; VP 1-3] *I bend down* [hapax]

Exercise for Lesson 89.

Translate into Greek:

Now when the month was already half over, the disciples went up into the temple and were teaching. The Jews thereupon were amazed, saying, "How do these men know Scripture when they have never studied?" (Jn 7:14-15)

John 8:12 – 9:12.

Lesson 90

John 8:12 – 9:12

8:29 - ἀρεστός, –ή, –όν [Adj 1] *pleasing* [Acts 6:2]

8:32 - ἐλευθερόω [V 10, VP 1-3, 5-6] *I set free* [Rom 6:18]

8:44 - ἀνθρωποκτόνος, –ος, –ον [Adj 5] *murderer* [1 Jn 3:15]

9:1 - γενετή, –ῆς, ἡ [N 1] *birth* [hapax] // **9:6** - χαμαί [Adv 1] *on the ground* [Jn 18:6]; πηλός, –οῦ, ὁ [N 6m] *mud* [Rom 9:21]; πτύσμα, –ατος, τό [N 16] *spittle* [hapax]; ἐπιχρίω [ἐπί + χρίω] [V 1, DV 344, VP 1-3] *I spread on, I smear* [Jn 9:11] // **9:7** - Σιλωάμ, ὁ [N 32] *Siloam* [Lk 13:4] // **9:8** - προσαιτέω [πρός + αἰτέω] [V 8; VP 1-3, 5-6] *I beg* [hapax]

Exercise for Lesson 90.

Translate into Greek;

> If God were your (sg.) father, you would love me. (Jn 8:42)

Lesson 91

John 9:13 – 10:21.

9:21 - ἡλικία, –ας, ἡ [N 2] *age* [Mt 6:27] // **9:22** - συντίθημι [σύν + τίθημι] [V 12, 21; DV 309; VP 1-3, 7-8, 11] active: *I put together*; middle: *I make an agreement* [Lk 22:5]; ἀποσυνάγωγος, –ος, –ον [Adj 5] *expelled from the synagogue* [Jn 12:42]

9:28 - λοιδορέω [V 8; VP 1-3, 5-6] *I insult* [Acts 23:4] // **9:31** - θεοσεβής, –ής, –ές [Adj 15] *God-fearing* [hapax]

10:1 - ἀλλαχόθεν [Adv 1] *from elsewhere* [hapax] // **10:6** - παροιμία, –ας, ἡ [N 2] *simile* [2 Pet 2:22]

10:9 - νομή, –ῆς, ἡ [N 1] *pasture* [2 Tim 2:17] // **10:12** - λύκος, –ου, ὁ [N 6m] *wolf* [Mt 7:15]; σκορπίζω (σκορπίσω) [V 5, VP 1-3] *I scatter* [Mt 12:30] // **10:16** - ποίμνη, –ης, ἡ [N 1] *flock* [Mt 26:31]

10:20 - μαίνομαι [V 7, 22, 23; VP 2-3] *I rave* [Acts 12:15]

Exercise for Lesson 91.

Translate into Greek:

> The men answered and said to him, "In this there is certainly something remarkable, that you (sg.) do not know where they are from, and they opened our eyes". (Jn 9:30)

John 10:22 – 11:44.

Lesson 92

John 10:22 – 11:44.

10:22 - ἐγκαίνια, –ων, τά [N 7] *Feast of the Dedication* [hapax] //
10:23 - Σολομών, –ῶνος, ὁ [N 21m] *Solomon* [Mt 1:6] // **10:24** -
κυκλόω [V 10; VP 1-3, 5-6] *I surround* [Lk 21:20]

11:1 - Λάζαρος, –ου, ὁ [N 6m] *Lazarus* [Lk 16:20]; Μάρθα, –ας, ἡ [N
2] *Martha* [Lk 10:38] // **11:2** - ἐκμάσσω [ἐκ + μάσσω] [V 3, DV 188] *I
wipe* [Lk 7:38] // **11:9** - προσκόπτω [πρός + κόπτω] [V 4, 5; DV 161;
VP 1-3] intransitive: *I stumble* [Mt 4:6] // **11:11** - ἐξυπνίζω [ἐκ +
ὑπνίζω] (ἐξυπνίσω) [V 5, VP 1-3] *I wake (someone) from sleep*
[hapax] // **11:13** - κοίμησις, –εως, ἡ [N 28f] *sleep* [hapax]; ὕπνος, –ου,
ὁ [N 6m] *sleep* [Mt 1:24] // **11:16** - Δίδυμος, –ου, ὁ [N 6m] *Twin* [Jn
20:24]; συμμαθητής, –οῦ, ὁ [N 4] *fellow-disciple* [hapax]

11:18 - δεκαπέντε [Adj 21] *fifteen* [Acts 27:28] // **11:19** -
παραμυθέομαι [παρά + μυθέομαι] [V 8, 23; VP 3] *I console* [1 Th
2:12] // **11:20** - καθέζομαι [The etymology is κατά + ἕζομαι, but the
augment is placed before the κατά in the New Testament : Mt 26:55,
ἐκατεζόμην.] (καθεσθήσομαι) [V 5, 23; DV 137; VP 3] *I remain*
[literally: *I sit*] [Mt 26:55]

11:28 - λάθρᾳ [Adv 3] *secretly* [Mt 1:19] // **11:35** - δακρύω [V 1, VP
1-3] *I weep* [hapax]

11:38 - ἐπίκειμαι [ἐπί + κεῖμαι] [V 17, DV 148] *I am placed at* [Lk
5:1] // **11:39** - ὄζω (ὄσω) [V 5, VP 1-3] *I stink* [hapax]; τεταρταῖος, –
α, –ον [Adj 2] *of the fourth day* [hapax] // **11:42** - περιίστημι [περί +
ἵστημι [V 11; DV 134; VP 1-3, 7-8, 11] transitive: *I place around*;
intransitive: *I stand around* [Acts 25:7] // **11:43** - κραυγάζω
(κραυγάσω) [V 5, VP 1-3] *I shout; I cry out* [Mt 12:19] // **11:44** -
κειρία, –ας, ἡ [N 2] *strip of cloth* [hapax]; σουδάριον, –ου, τό [N 7]

face-cloth [Lk 19:20]; περιδέω [περί + δέω] [V 8; DV 59; VP 1-3, 5-6] *I wrap around* [hapax]

Exercise for Lesson 92.

Translate into Greek:

> When, then, the disciples heard that their friends were ill, they waited in the places where they were for three days. (Jn 11:6)

John 11:45 – 12:43.

Lesson 93

John 11:45 – 12:43.

11:48 - ' Ρωμαῖος, –α, –ον [Adj 2] *Roman* [Acts 2:10] // **11:49** - Καϊάφας, –α, ὁ [N 33] *Caiaphas* [Mt 26:3]

11:54 - 'Εφραίμ, ὁ [N 32] *Ephraim* [hapax]

11:55 - ἁγνίζω (ἁγνίσω) [V 5, VP 1-3] *I sanctify* [Acts 21:24] // **11:57** - μηνύω [V 1, VP 1-3] *I make known* [Lk 20:37]

12:3 - λίτρα, –ας, ἡ [N 2] *(Roman) pound* [Jn 19:39]; πολύτιμος, –ος, –ον [Adj 5] *expensive* [Mt 13:46]; ὀσμή, –ῆς, ἡ [N 1] *smell* [2 Cor 2:14] // **12:6** - γλωσσόκομον, –ου, τό [N 7] *money-box* [Jn 13:29]

12:13 - βαΐον, –ου, τό [N 7] *palm branch* [hapax]; φοῖνιξ, –ικος, ὁ [N 8m] [also φοίνιξ] *palm tree, palm branch* [Apoc 7:9] // **12:14** - ὀνάριον, –ου, τό [N 7] *young donkey* [hapax] // **12:15** - ὄνος, –ου, ὁ/ἡ [N 6m, 6f] *donkey* [Mt 21:2]

12:33 - σημαίνω [V 7, DV 281, VP 1-3] *I give a sign; I make known* [Apoc 1:1]

12:40 - τυφλόω [V 10; VP 1-3, 5-6] *I blind* [2 Cor 4:4]

12:42 - ὅμως [Adv 3] *nevertheless* [1 Cor 14:7] // **12:43** - ἤπερ [Conj] *than* [strengthened form of ἤ] [hapax]

Exercise for Lesson 93.

Translate into Greek:

The ones loving themselves lose themselves, and the ones hating themselves in this world will guard themselves for everlasting life. (Jn 12:25)

John 12:44 – 13:38.

Lesson 94

John 12:44 – 13:38.

13:4 - λέντιον, –ου, τό [N 7] *towel* [Jn 13:5]; διαζώννυμι [διά + ζώννυμι] [V 14; DV 114; VP 1-3, 9, 12] *I gird* [Jn 21:7] // **13:10** - λούω [V 1, DV 183, VP 1-3] *I wash* [Acts 9:37]

13:18 - πτέρνα, –ης, ἡ [N 3] *heel* [hapax]

13:24 - νεύω [V 1, VP 1-3] *I nod* [with the dative case] [Acts 24:10] // **13:25** - στῆθος, –ους, τό [N 31] *breast* [Lk 18:13] // **13:26** - βάπτω [V 4, 5; DV 34; VP 1-3] *I dip* [Lk 16:24]; ψωμίον, –ου, τό [N 7] *piece of bread* [Jn 13:27]

13:33 - τεκνίον, –ου, τό [N 7] *little child* [1 Jn 2:1]

Exercise for Lesson 94.

Translate into Greek:

> Amen, amen I say to you (pl.), slaves are not greater than their masters, nor apostles greater than those sending them. (Jn 13:16)

John 14:1 – 15:27.

Lesson 95

John 14:1 – 15:27.

14:2 - μονή, –ῆς, ἡ [N 1] *room* [Jn 14:23]

14:18 - ὀρφανός, –ή, –όν [Adj 1] *alone; orphaned* [Jas 1:27] // **14:21** - ἐμφανίζω [ἐν + φανίζω] (ἐμφανίσω) [V 5, VP 1-3] *I make known* [Mt 27:53]

14:26 - ὑπομιμνήσκω [ὑπό + μιμνήσκω] [V 2, 21; DV 200; VP 1-3] *I remind* [Lk 22:61] // **14:27** - δειλιάω [V 9; VP 1-3, 5-6] *I am cowardly* [hapax]

15:2 - κλῆμα, –ατος, τό [N 16] *branch* [Jn 15:4]

15:25 - δωρεάν [Adv 3] *gratuitously* [Mt 10:8]

15:26 - παράκλητος, –ου, ὁ [N 6m] *intercessor* [1 Jn 2:1]

Exercise for Lesson 95.

Translate into Greek:

> If you (sg.) remain in me and my word remains in you, whatever you wish, ask for it, and it will happen for you. (Jn 15:7)

John 16:1 – 17:26.

Lesson 96

John 16:1 – 17:26.

16:2 - λατρεία, –ας, ἡ [N 2] *worship* [Rom 9:4]

16:13 - ὁδηγέω [V 8; VP 1-3, 5-6] *I guide* [Mt 15:14]

16:20 - θρηνέω [V 8; VP 1-3, 5-6] *I lament* [Mt 11:17]

Exercise for Lesson 96.

Translate into Greek:

> And you (sg.), then, it is true, now have grief; but then I shall
> see you again, and your heart will be glad, and no one will
> take your joy from you. (John 16:22)

John 18:1-40.

Lesson 97

John 18:1-40.

18:1 - χείμαρρος, –α, –ον [Adj 2] [also found as χειμάρρους, –α, –ουν (Adj 4)] *flowing (stream)*, as substantive, the place of a flowing stream or *wadi* [N 6m] [hapax]; Κεδρών, ὁ [N 32] *Kidron* [hapax]; κῆπος, –ου, ὁ [N 6m] *garden* [Lk 13:19] // **18:3** - φανός, –οῦ, ὁ [N 6m] *lantern* [hapax]; ὅπλον, –ου, τό [N 7] *weapon* [Rom 6:13] // **18:5** - Ναζωραῖος, –ου, ὁ [N 6m] *Nazarene* [Mt 2:23] // **18:10** - Μάλχος, – ου, ὁ [N 6m] *Malchus* [hapax] // **18:11** - θήκη, –ης, ἡ [N 1] *sheath (of a sword)* [hapax]

18:13 - Ἄννας, –α, ὁ [also found as Ἄννας] [N 33] *Annas* [Lk 3:2]; πενθερός, –οῦ, ὁ [N 6m] *father-in-law* [hapax] // **18:14** - συμβουλεύω [σύν + βουλεύω] [V 1, VP 1-3] *I advise* [with dative case] [Mt 26:4]

18:18 - ἀνθρακιά, –ᾶς, ἡ [N 2] *charcoal fire* [Jn 21:9]; ψῦχος, –ους, τό [N 31] *cold* [Acts 28:2]

18:28 - μιαίνω [V 7, VP 1-3] *I defile* [Tit 1:15] // **18:29** - κατηγορία, –ας, ἡ [N 2] *accusation* [1 Tim 5:19] // **18:36** - ἀγωνίζομαι (ἀγωνίσομαι) [V 5, 22; VP 2-3] *I struggle* [Lk 13:24] // **18:37** - οὐκοῦν [Adv 3] *so; then* [hapax]

18:39 - συνήθεια, –ας, ἡ [N 2] *custom* [1 Cor 8:7]

Exercise for Lesson 97.

Translate into Greek:

We have spoken openly to the world: we taught at all times in the synagogue and in the temple, where our enemies gather, and in secret we said nothing. (Jn 18:20)

John 19:1-42.

Lesson 98

John 19:1-42.

19:5 - φορέω [V 8; DV 332; VP 1-3, 5-6] *I wear* [Mt 11:8]

19:12 - ἀντιλέγω [ἀντί + λέγω] [V 2, DV 179, VP 1-4] *I contradict* [with dative case] [Lk 2:34]

19:13 - βῆμα, -ατος, τό [N 16] *tribunal* [Mt 27:19]; Λιθόστρωτον, -ου, τό [N 7] *Stone Pavement* [hapax]; Γαββαθα [Aramaic word] [N 32] *Gabbatha* [hapax]

19:19 - τίτλος, -ου, ὁ [N 6m] *notice* [Jn 19:20] // **19:20** - Ῥωμαϊστί [Adv 3] *in Latin* [hapax]; Ἑλληνιστί [Adv 3] *in Greek* [Acts 21:37]

19:23 - ἄραφος, -ος, -ον [Adj 5] *seamless* [hapax]; ὑφαντός, -ή, -όν [Adj 1] *woven* [hapax] // **19:24** - λαγχάνω [V 7, DV 174, VP 1-4] *I cast lots* [Lk 1:9]; ἱματισμός, -οῦ, ὁ [N 6m] *clothing* [Lk 7:25] // **19:25** - Κλωπᾶς, -ᾶ, ὁ [N 33] *Clopas* [hapax]

19:29 - μεστός, -ή, -όν [Adj 1] *full* [Mt 23:28]; ὕσσωπος, -ου, ὁ/ἡ [N 6m, N 6f] [also found as ὕσσωπον, -ου, τό (N 7)] *hyssop* [Heb 9:19] // **19:30** - κλίνω [V 7, DV 103, VP 1-3] *I bow* [Mt 8:20]

19:31 - κατάγνυμι [κατά + ἄγνυμι] [V 14; DV 3 (The augment has become part of the stem.); VP 1-4, 9, 12] *I break* [Mt 12:20]; σκέλος, -ους, τό [N 31] *leg* [Jn 19:32] // **19:34** - λόγχη, -ης, ἡ [N 1] *spear* [hapax]; πλευρά, -ᾶς, ἡ [N 2] *side* [Acts 12:7]; νύσσω [V 3, DV 208, VP 1-4] *I stab* [hapax] // **19:36** - ὀστοῦν, -οῦ, τό [N 33] [also found as ὀστέον, -ου, τό (N 7)] *bone* [Mt 23:27] // **19:37** - ἐκκεντέω [ἐκ + κεντέω] [V 8; VP 1-3, 5-6] *I pierce* [Apoc 1:7]

19:39 - μίγμα, –ατος, τό [N 16] *mixture* [hapax]; σμύρνα, –ης, ἡ [N 3] *myrrh* [Mt 2:11]; ἀλόη, –ης, ἡ [N 1] *aloes* [hapax] // **19:40** - ὀθόνιον, –ου, τό [N 7] *linen cloth* [Lk 24:12]

Exercise for Lesson 98.

Translate into Greek:

> Therefore the Jew, since it was preparation day, lest the body remain on the cross on the Sabbath (for the day of that Sabbath was great), asked Pilate that its legs might be broken and that it be taken away. (Jn 19:31)

John 20:1-31.

Lesson 99

John 20:1-31.

20:4 - προτρέχω [πρό + τρέχω] [V 2, DV 315, VP 1-4] *I run ahead* [Lk 19:4] // **20:5** - παρακύπτω [παρά + κύπτω] [V 4, 5; DV 173; VP 1-3] *I stoop* [Lk 24:12] // **20:7** - ἐντυλίσσω [ἐν + τυλίσσω] [V 3, DV 318] *I roll up* [Mt 27:59]

20:15 - κηπουρός, -οῦ, ὁ [N 6m] *gardener* [hapax]

20:22 - ἐμφυσάω [ἐν + φυσάω] [V 9; VP 1-3, 5-6] *I breathe on* [hapax]

20:25 - ἧλος, -ου, ὁ [N 6m] *nail* [Jn 20:25]

Exercise for Lesson 99.

Translate into Greek:

> And the angels say to them, "Women, why are you weeping?" And they say to them, "They have taken away our Lord, and we do not know where they have placed him". (Jn 20:13)

John 21:1-25.

Lesson 100

John 21:1-25.

21:3 - ἀλιεύω [V 1, VP 1-3] *I fish* [hapax] // **21:4** - πρωΐα, –ας, ἡ [N 2] *morning* [Mt 27:1]; αἰγιαλός, –οῦ, ὁ [N 6m] *shore* [Mt 13:2] // **21:5** - προσφάγιον, –ου, τό [N 7] *something to eat* [hapax] // **21:7** - ἐπενδύτης, –ου, ὁ [N 4] *outer garment* [hapax] // **21:8** - πῆχυς, –εως, ὁ [N 33] *cubit* [Mt 6:27]; σύρω [V 6, VP 1-3] *I drag* [Acts 8:3] // **21:9** - ἀποβαίνω [ἀπό + βαίνω] [V 7, DV 31, VP 1-3] *I disembark* [Lk 5:2] // **21:12** - ἀριστάω [V 9; VP 1-3, 5-6] *I breakfast* [Lk 11:37]; ἐξετάζω [ἐκ + ἐτάζω] (ἐξετάσω) [V 5, VP 1-5] *I question* [Mt 2:8]

21:16 - ποιμαίνω [V 7, DV 259VP 1-3] *I shepherd* [Mt 2:6] // **21:18** - ζώννυμι [V 14; DV 71; VP 1-3, 9, 12] [also found as ζωννύω (V 1, DV 114, VP 1-3)] *I gird* [Acts 12:8]; γηράσκω [V 2, DV 48, VP 1-3] *I grow old* [Heb 8:13]

21:25 - οἶμαι [shortened form of οἴομαι] [V 1, 22; DV 134; VP 2-3] *I think* [Phil 1:17]

Exercise for Lesson 100.

Translate into Greek:

> Amen, amen I say to you (pl.), when you were younger you girded yourselves and you were walking wherever you wished; but when you grow old, you will stretch out your hands, and another will gird you, and will bring you where you do not wish. (Jn 21:18)

Appendix

Aspect in the Greek Verbal System.

Introduction

In order to achieve even an introductory knowledge of the complex problem of "aspect" in the verbal system of New Testament Greek, it is appropriate to situation the topic in its morphogical and semantic context of root, stem, voice and tense.

I. The Root

The root of a verb is constituted by the letters which give the verb its semantic identity. For example, λυ– is the root of the verb λύω, and gives to any verbal form in which it is found the basic semantic identity or meaning of *to loose*. (The infinitive form is chosen in English to communicate this meaning because the infinitive is the most abstract of the verbal forms in both Greek and English.) So also, for example, γραφ– is the root for γράφω and gives to all the verbal forms of that verb the basic semantic meaning *to write*, and πιστευ– is the root for πιστεύω and gives to all the verbal forms of that verb the basic semantic meaning of *to believe*. The root does not exist by itself, of course, but always in some specific verbal form having voice, mood, and tense. If it is an infinitive, these are all the attributes it has. If the verbal form is a participle, i.e., a verbal adjective, it has voice, mood, and tense, plus gender, number, and case. And if the verbal form is one of the other moods—indicative, subjunctive, imperative, optative—it has voice, mood, and tense, plus person and number.

It is important to know that not all verbs are as regular as λύω, γράφω, and πιστεύω. Some verbs are irregular in the sense that the basic root is changed in different tense systems. The verb λέγω, for example, has the root λέγ– in the present tense system of the active voice, the root ἐρ– in the future tense system of the active voice, and the root εἰπ– in the aorist tense system of the active voice. Hence it is necessary to learn that these three quite different roots have the same basic semantic value according to the different tense-voice systems. Such "irregular" verbs are found in this grammar listed under the category "difficult verbs".

II. The Stem

The stem of a verb is the modification of the root to indicate aspect and voice. Thus the verb λύω, with its root λυ–, has the present active stem λυ–, the future active stem λυσ–, the aorist active stem λυσ(α)–, and the perfect active stem λελυκ–. (Ambiguity, as in the future active and aorist active stems of λύω, is resolved by the endings, and by other aspects of the context.) In the middle voice the present stem is λυ–, the future stem is λυσ–, the aorist stem is λυσ(α)–, and the perfect stem is λελυ–. In the passive voice the present stem is λυ–, the future stem is λυθησ–, the aorist stem is λυθη–, and the perfect stem is λελυ–. Ambiguities with regard to the middle and passive voices—which are identical in form—are thus possible for forms in the present and perfect tense systems, but are usually resolved by elements in the context.

III. Voice

Voice is the grammatical category which indicates the relation of the subject of a verb to the action which the verb expresses. In Greek there are three voices: 1) Active voice indicates that the real subject of the action expressed by a verb is the same as the grammatical subject of that action. Thus, *I hold the book* is an example of a verb, *to hold*, in the active voice because *I* is the real subject of the action (*I* am the one acting) and is also the grammatical subject of the sentence. 2) Passive voice indicates that the real subject of the action expressed by the verb is not the same as the grammatical subject of that action. The sentence *The book is held by me* is an example of a verb, *to hold*, in the passive voice because the real subject of the action, *I*, is not the grammatical subject of the sentence. 3) Middle voice indicates that the real subject and grammatical subject coincide, as in the active voice, but in addition that the subject has a special relation to the action expressed by the verb. Such a relation may be, for example, reflexive, as in the English sentence *I wash* [sc., *myself*] as opposed to *I wash the child*. Or the middle voice may express an idiomatic convention, such as the use of the Greek verb *I am first* (ἄρχω), which, when used in the middle voice, means *I begin*. In New Testament Greek the use of the middle voice is limited.

IV. Aspect

A. The Present and Aorist Aspects

Aspect is a term which is the subject of much difference of opinion in contemporary discussions about New Testament Greek. The beginning student should be aware of such differences and should accept in a particularly critical way much of what is stated about aspect, including much of what is stated in this grammar. In addition, in this grammar an approach to the problem will be adopted which does not attempt to convey to the student the historical background of the Greek verbal system, a background which was probably unknown to the authors of the New Testament and which did not serve them as a guide in their writing. The approach adopted will be based on an attempt to view the much-discussed problem of aspect as the authors themselves seemed to view it.

In this grammar aspect will be defined as that grammatical category which expresses the viewpoint of the speaker about the intrinsic action of the verb, i.e., the action of the verb conveyed directly by the stem with no further indications.

The present aspect is conveyed by the present stem, and indicates that the action of the verb is being viewed as not terminated. That is to say, the action is viewed from within, as it were, and as continuing. The aorist aspect is conveyed by the aorist stem, and indicates that the action of the verb is being viewed as terminated. That is to say, action which is viewed from without, as it were, and as not continuing. These are the two principal aspects of the Greek verb in the New Testament. Most verbal forms are either present or aorist, and the subtle interplay of non-terminated (i.e., present) and terminated (i.e., aorist) aspects is one of the basis frameworks of all New Testament texts.

Thus, for example, in the sentence ἀπόλυε τοὺς δούλους, *Free the slaves*, ἀπόλυε, a present imperative, is translated as *free* with the implication that the the present stem is conveying the idea of an action being viewed as not terminated, i.e., it is to continue. In the sentence ἀπόλυσον τοὺς δούλους, *Free the slaves*, ἀπόλυσον, an aorist imperative, is translated *Free* with the implication that the aorist stem is conveying the idea of an action being viewed as terminated, i.e., it is not to continue. In this example the English language does not express the categories of termination or non-termination by the verbal form itself, and must use other means to convey them if this is desired by the speaker.

B. The Perfect Aspect

The perfect aspect is conveyed by the perfect stem and indicates that the action of the verb is viewed as prior in some way and has resulted in a completion which endures. Thus, for example, in the sentence ἔρχομαι ἀπολελυκὼς τοὺς δούλους, *I come having freed the slaves*, the perfect participle ἀπολελυκώς indicates that the action of the freeing was prior to the act of coming and that the act of freeing is viewed as continuing in its result so that I am a person being enduringly regarded as one who has committed this action of freeing. Ordinarily, in most treatments of the perfect, the resulting completion is emphasized rather than the prior action on which it is based. In this grammar the priority of the action will be emphasized rather than the resulting state which endures. The perfect aspect is much less used than is either the present or aorist, and hence is not involved, at least to the same extent, in a constant interplay of contrasts as are these two aspects.

C. The Future Aspect

In many treatments of the Greek verbal system the future stem is not regarded as expressing an aspect in the same way as the other three stems do. The future stem is usually regarded as not expressing an aspect at all, but simply as indicating a time value involving the future in some way. Certainly the future stem is more obviously temporal than the other stems. But it is doubtful if the New Testament authors made a distinction between aspect in the true sense (present, aorist, perfect) and non-aspect (future), given that distinct stems were used to express each of the four with no further elaboration. Hence, in this grammar, the future aspect will be regarded as being on a par with the other three aspects.

The future aspect indicates subsequent action in some way. Thus, in the sentence ἔρχομαι ἀπολύσων τοὺς δούλους, *I come in order to free the slaves*, ἀπολύσων, the future participle, is used to indicate that the action of freeing is subsequent to the action of coming and, by implication, as an indication of intent or purpose. (Not all uses of the future indicate purpose, of course. In fact, very few do. But this usage does underline the fact that the New Testament authors regarded the future stem as indicating what was subsequent in some way.) Like the perfect aspect, the future aspect is relatively infrequent as compared with the present and the aorist.

V. Tense

The word "tense" is another term used in connection with Greek verbs. Care must be used in understanding what is meant by this term for it is fundamentlly ambiguous and is used in two distinct but related senses.

A. Tense in the Indicative Mood

In the indicative mood and only in the indicative mood the word "tense" indicates the time of speaking, either past, present, or future. This time is indicated by the aspect, i.e., the stem, plus the augment for the past. In the present indicative the time is considered to be contemporary with the act of speaking of the speaker: ἀπολύω τοὺς δούλους—I free the slaves as I speak. The present stem is conveying the idea of an action being viewed as not terminated, i.e., as continuing. In the aorist indicative the time is considered to be completely past as regards the act of speaking of the speaker: ἀπέλυσα τοὺς δούλους—I freed the slaves at some point in the past: the aorist stem indicates action being viewed as terminated, i.e., viewed as not continuing. The augment indicates that this terminated action is viewed as having taken place in the past with relation to the time in which the speaker is speaking.
    In the perfect indicative the time is considered to be prior as regards the act of speaking: ἀπολέλυκα τοὺς δούλους—I have freed the slaves at some point prior to my speaking and, the implication is, they remained free up to the time of my speaking. (This implication of the present result of a prior action ordinarily distinguishes the perfect from the aorist; in the aorist there is no implication in the verb itself that the slaves remain free up to the time of speaking, although this is sometimes indicated by some word or words in the context.) In the future indicative the time is considered to be subsequent as regards the act of speaking of the speaker: the future stem indicates subsequent action: ἀπολύσω τοὺς δούλους—I shall free the slaves at some point subsequent to my speaking.
    The present stem may also be used with an augment to indicate a non-terminated action in the past: ἀπέλυον τοὺς δούλους, I was freeing the slaves—at some time in the past I was engaged in the act of freeing the slaves and this act is viewed as non-terminated. Perhaps it was eventually terminated, perhaps not; the

verbal form itself (the present stem used with an augment, i.e., the imperfect) is noncommittal in the matter.

The historical origin of the future tense is different from the present, aorist, and perfect tenses and as such is often given special treatment. But, as was said above, in a grammar for beginners it seems best to regard the future tense as the authors of the New Testament seemed to regard it, as a tool for expressing subsequent action on a par with the other tools needed to express other kinds of verbal categories involving tense.

Further, the subsequent action of the verb indicated by the future stem seems normally to be unspecified as to continuing, non-continuing, or perfect action. This non-specificity is often taken to indicate relation to the aorist tense, which shows striking similarities to the future in its morphology. In this view the aorist, like the future, is non-specific with regard to the type of action of the verb; both future and aorist simply indicate the happening of the verb with no additional nuance: both future and aorist are "undefined" (ἀόριστος, *undefined*). To the author of this grammar the authors of the New Testament do seem to regard the future tense as being unspecified as to continuing, non-continuing, or perfect action. But the authors of the New Testament seem to regard the aorist as expressing action viewed as terminated, i.e., non-continuing, as was explained above, notwithstanding the designation "aorist".

past time	imperfect tense (present stem—non-terminated action in the past)
	aorist tense (aorist stem—terminated action in the past)
perfect time	perfect tense (perfect stem—prior action, the effect of which usually continues to the present as an enduring result)
present time	present tense (present stem)
future time	future tense (future stem)

Note that in the outline given above the aspect of the verb is always conveyed by the stem and as such is an essential determining factor for the tense. The endings (and, in the case of past tenses, the augment) show that the mood is indicative. Thus the reader knows that the aspect involved indicates a true tense, i.e., explicitly indicates time in relation to the time of speaking. Hence, in the indicative mood, aspect and tense are distinct, though not separable.

B. "Tense" in the Non-Indicative Moods

1. "Tense" in the Imperative, Subjunctive, and Optative Moods

In the other moods besides the indicative, that is, in the imperative, subjunctive, optative, infinitive, and participle, the word "tense" does not indicate time in relation to the time of speaking. Rather, it is a synonym for aspect. Thus in the imperative mood the present tense indicates simply that the action referred to is being viewed as non-terminated: ἀπόλυε τοὺς δούλους, *Keep freeing the slaves,* i.e., a continuing process is commanded. But the aorist tense of the imperative mood indicates that the action referred to is being viewed as terminated: ἀπόλυσον τοὺς δούλους—*Free the slaves,* i.e., a limited, determined action is commanded. This same distinction applies to the subjunctive: ἔρχομαι ἵνα ἀπολύω τοὺς δούλους—*I come in order to keep freeing the slaves.* Contrast this use of the present subjunctive with the use of the aorist subjunctive: ἔρχομαι ἵνα ἀπολύσω τοὺς δούλους—*I come in order to free the slaves* (a limited, determined action). And the optative: ἀπολύοιμι τοὺς δούλους—*May I keep freeing the slaves*; ἀπολύσαιμι τοὺς δούλους—*May I free the slaves* (a limited, determined). In each of these moods "tense" means aspect, either present or aorist.

The imperative, subjunctive, and optative moods do not have a future "tense". The perfect "tense" is found—rarely—in the imperative and subjunctive moods. There it normally indicates a prior action with a lasting result..

The imperative mood normally refers to future time, but indirectly, inasmuch as a command has to be fulfilled in the future. The same is true when the subjunctive and optative moods are used as principal verbs in a clause. An exhortation (subjunctive) and wish (optative) normally refer to the future, following the same principle as the imperative. But this indication of time in relation to the speaker is conveyed implicitly, not explicitly as in the use of the indicative mood..

2. "Tense" in the Infinitive Mood

In the infinitive mood the context of the "tenses" must be noted. The infinitive mood has all four "tenses". But an important distinction must be kept in mind: i) when the infinitive represents a subordinate clause indicating a fact in temporal relation to a main verb, and ii) when the infinitive does not represent a subordinate clause indicating a fact in temporal relation to a main verb.

a. The Infinitive Used to Represent a Subordinate Clause Indicating a Fact in Temporal Relation to a Main Verb

When the infinitive is used to represent a subordinate clause indicating a fact in relation to a main verb, its "tense" indicates relative time with regard to this verb on which it depends. λέγω αὐτὸν ἀπολύειν τοὺς δούλους—*I say that he is freeing the slaves.* The use of the present stem in the accusative with the infinitive construction indicating a fact means that the present "tense" expresses non-terminated action and hence, by implication, action which is contemporary with the action of the verb on which it depends, λέγω. λέγω αὐτὸν ἀπολῦσαι τοὺς δούλους—*I say that he freed the slaves.* The use of the aorist stem in the accusative with the infinitive construction indicating a fact means that the aorist "tense" expresses terminated action and hence, by implication, action which takes place before the action of the verb on which it depends, λέγω. λέγω αὐτὸν ἀπολύσειν τοὺς δούλους—*I say that he will free the slaves.* The use of the future stem in the accusative with the infinitive construction indicating a fact means that the future "tense" expresses subsequent action and hence action which takes place after the action of the verb on which it depends, λέγω. λέγω αὐτὸν ἀπολελυκέναι τοὺς δούλους—*I say that he has freed the slaves.* The use of the perfect stem in the accusative with the infinitive construction indicating a fact means that the perfect "tense" expresses action which takes place prior to the action of the main verb so that the result of that action remains up to the time of the main verb.

Relative time, of course, can be expressed also after main verbs in past, future, and perfect tenses, i.e., εἶπον (*I said*), ἐρῶ (*I* shall say), and εἴρηκα (*I have said*) and after main verbs in other moods as well.

b. The Infinitive Used to Represent a Subordinate Clause Not Indicating a Fact in Temporal Relation to a Main Verb

The infinitive mood can be used to represent a subordinate clause which does not indicate a fact in temporal relation to a main verb. For example, in the sentence θέλω ἀπολύειν τοὺς δούλους—*I wish to free the slaves*—the infinitive ἀπολύειν is not designed to give a temporal relationship to the verb θέλω. Rather it is designed to complement the meaning of the verb so that the object of the wishing is known. If the present infinitive—ἀπολύειν—is used to express the idea "free", the implication is only that the act is not viewed as terminated and so the sense is that I want to keep freeing the slaves. If the aorist infinitive—ἀπολύσαι—is used to express the idea "free", the implication is only that the act is viewed as terminated and so the sense is that I want to free the slaves in a limited, determined action. Ordinarily only the present and the aorist infinitives are used in situations where there is no intention to indicate a temporal relation to the main verb.

3. "Tense" in the Participial Mood

In the participial mood there is no major distinction such as in the infinitive mood regarding the indication or non-indication of a temporal relation to another verb. Participles are usually used to represent a temporal relation to another verb. Thus ἔρχομαι ἀπολύων τοὺς δούλους, *I come freeing the slaves*, uses the present stem of the participle to indicate that the action of freeing is viewed as non-terminated, i.e., by inference, taking place as I come or contemporary with my coming. ἔρχομαι ἀπολύσας τοὺς δούλους, *I come having freed the slaves*, uses the aorist stem of the participle to indicate that the action of freeing is viewed as terminated, i.e., by inference, as having taken place previous to my coming (with no implication as to the continued result of the action of freeing). ἔρχομαι ἀπολελυκὼς τοὺς δούλους, *I come having freed the slaves*, uses the perfect stem of the participle to indicate that the action of freeing is viewed as prior, i.e., by inference, as having taken place previous to my coming (with the implication that the result of the action of freeing continues from the time of the action to the present time). ἔρχομαι ἀπολύσων τοὺς δούλους, *I come about to free the slaves*, uses the future stem of the participle to indicate that the action of freeing is viewed as subsequent, i.e., as still to take place as I come. But in this latter instance, when the future participle is used, there is also the possibility that the idea intended is one of purpose: *I come in order to free the slaves*.

VI. Conclusions

The above presentation is rudimentary. It is designed to give a student an introductory view of a complicated phenomenon. The student should always be ready to examine the Greek verb in its individual context and note how it fits in or does not fit into the phenomena cited above. The same is true for other theories of the function of aspect. Further, all of the above interpretations of aspect must be qualified by the realization of the fact that at the time of the New Testament the Greek language had a long history of change and development. The interpretation which searches for general patterns should always be ready to take into account the factor of unique phenomena. Finally, there is no guarantee that the New Testament authors all used the Greek verbal system in exactly the same way.

But as regards tense the following can be categorically stated: tense explicitly indicates time in relation to the time of speaking only in the indicative mood of the Greek verb. In the other moods tense is better written "tense", for it is not explicitly temporal in the sense that it directly indicates time in relation to the speaker. In these other moods "tense" is equivalent to aspect. Thus there are really two meanings of tense: 1) tense, which has an explicitly temporal meaning with regard to time in relation to the speaker, and 2) "tense", which does not have an explicitly temporal meaning with regard to time in relation to the speaker.

Two further cautions are in place:

1) Even in the indicative mood aspect exists for the simple reason that the stem exists. But the fact that the indicative mood is in question shows that aspect is being viewed as explicitly temporally relevant with regard to absolute time. (In the past tenses of the indicative mood augments are used to supplement the role of the stem.)

2) Only in the aorist tense of the indicative mood does the aorist directly indicate a past action. In the other moods the

aorist does not directly indicate a past action; it is there a "tense" and not a tense, and directly indicates only terminated action.

Finito di stampare il 30 giugno 1998

Tipografia " Giovanni Olivieri "
Via dell'Archetto, 10 - 00187 Roma